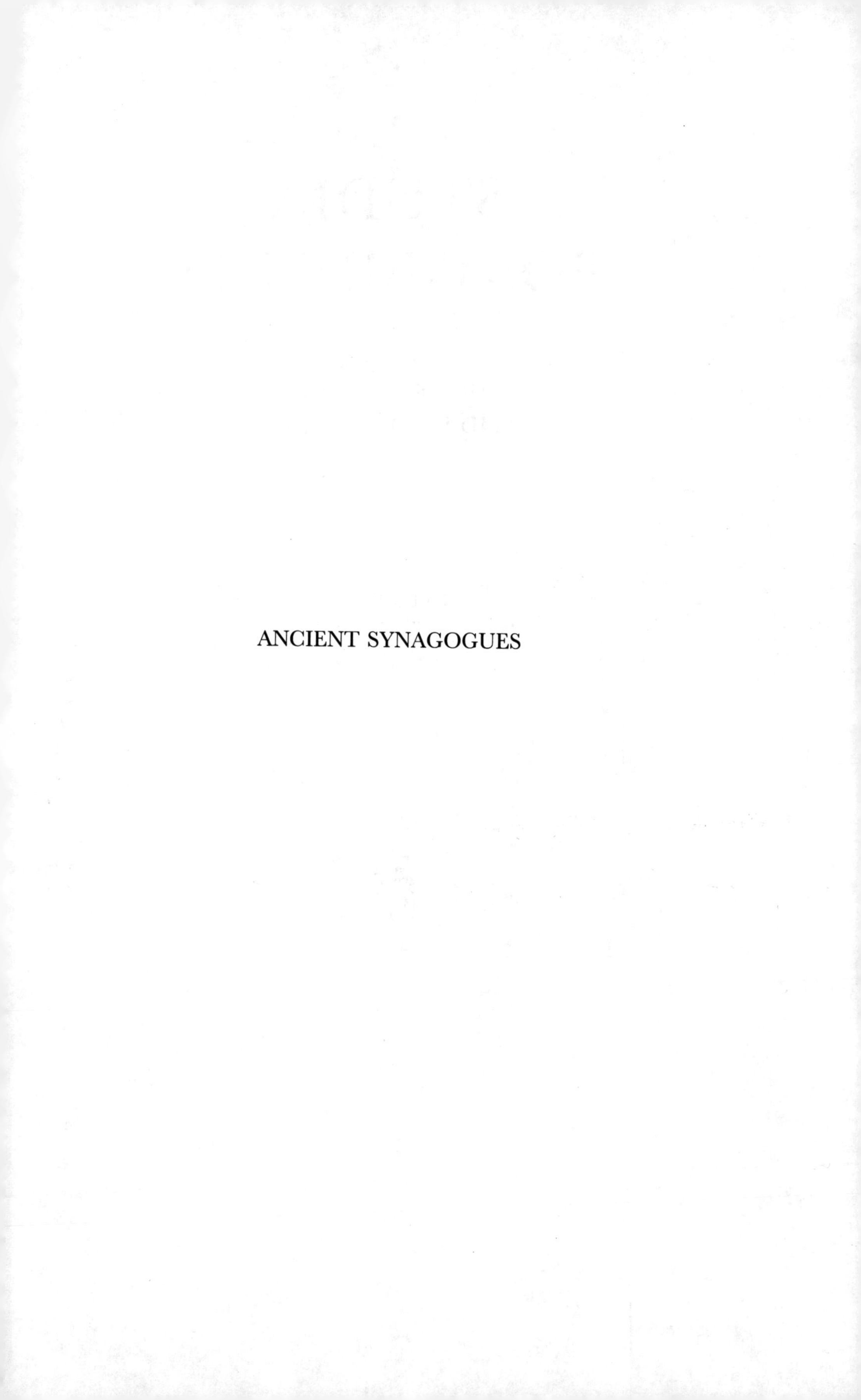

ANCIENT SYNAGOGUES

STUDIA POST-BIBLICA

GENERAL EDITOR
DAVID S. KATZ (Tel Aviv)

VOLUME 47, 1

ANCIENT SYNAGOGUES

Historical Analysis and Archaeological Discovery

EDITED BY

DAN URMAN

AND

PAUL V.M. FLESHER

VOLUME ONE

E.J. BRILL
LEIDEN · NEW YORK · KÖLN
1995

The paper in this book meets the guidelines for permanence and durability of the Committee on Production Guidelines for Book Longevity of the Council on Library Resources.

Library of Congress Cataloging-in-Publication Data

Ancient synagogues : historical analysis and archaeological discovery, vol. 1 / edited by Dan Urman and Paul V.M. Flesher
p. cm. — (Studia post-Biblica, ISSN 0169-9717 ; v. 47, 1)
[Vol. 2 includes bibliographical references and indexes.]
ISBN 9004102426 (vol. 1)
ISBN 9004102434 (vol. 2)
ISBN 9004099042 (set)
1. Synagogues—Palestine—History. 2. Synagogues—Middle East—History. 3. Synagogue architecture—Palestine. 4. Synagogue architecture—Middle East. 5. Palestine—Antiquities. 6. Middle East—Antiquities. I. Urman, Dan. II. Flesher, Paul Virgil McCracken. III. Series.
BM653.A495 1994
296.6'5'09015—dc20 94-36799
CIP

Die Deutsche Bibliothek – CIP-Einheitsaufnahme

Ancient synagogues : historical analysis and archaeological discovery / ed. by Dan Urman and Paul V.M. Flesher. - Leiden ; New York ; Köln : Brill, 1994
(Studia post-Biblica ; Vol. 47, 1)
ISBN 90-04-10242-6
NE: Urman, Dan [Hrsg.]; GT

ISSN 0169-9717
ISBN 90 04 10242 6 (*vol. 1*)
ISBN 90 04 10243 4 (*vol. 2*)
ISBN 90 04 09904 2 (*set*)

PRINTED IN THE NETHERLANDS

For

Mety

and

Caroline

מָצָא אִשָּׁה מָצָא טוֹב
וַיָּפֶק רָצוֹן מֵיהוה

He who finds a wife finds excellence
and obtains favor from the Lord.
Proverbs 18:22

TABLE OF CONTENTS

VOLUME ONE

III. SYNAGOGUES AND SETTLEMENTS: REPORTS AND ANALYSIS

IV. THE SYNAGOGUE'S NATURE AND THE JEWISH COMMUNITY

VOLUME TWO

V. THE SYNAGOGUE'S INTERNAL AESTHETICS

PREFACE

The destruction of the Jerusalem Temple in 70 C.E. was a major turning point in the development of Judaism. Without the Temple or the ability to replace it, Judaism could no longer function as the religion of sacrifice and sanctification God had detailed to Moses on Mt. Sinai. Over the following centuries, one institution arose to take the Temple's place in the life of the Jewish community, namely, the synagogue. It provided for a life of holiness without animal or vegetable sacrifice—for becoming sacred without performing the biblically sanctioned means of sanctification.

The means by which the synagogue became the dominant Jewish institution forms an arena of active scholarly analysis. The issue begins with the question of the synagogue's origins, but does not stop there. The ultimate question lies in how the synagogue became an accepted replacement for the Temple. Looking back from our perspective in the twentieth century, the transformation of a Temple-based Judaism into a synagogue-centered religion seems a natural development. But looking forward from 70 C.E.—just after the Temple's destruction—the picture must have seemed quite different. How could Jews worship God without a Temple? Even the Hebrew Bible—the reading of which became a central rite in synagogue worship—said that God should be worshipped by sacrifice in the Temple. It contained no comment about the synagogue at all, let alone a positive endorsement.

But the synagogue succeeded. When Islam conquered much of the Middle East in the early seventh century, synagogues had long been the dominant Jewish institution. Indeed, archaeological and literary records reveal that synagogues had been built not only in Palestine and surrounding areas, but also across the Mediterranean world and into the Tigris-Euphrates region. The literary record also shows that the synagogue was understood as a native Jewish institution, without which Jewish life and worship was impossible to envision. The rabbinic sages even imagined that during Temple times a synagogue had stood on the Temple Mount. They believed that worship in that synagogue had actually been more important than altar sacrifices.

Although published in two volumes, this collection of essays has a single focus—the synagogue during the centuries between the Temple's destruction and the rise of Islam, for it is at this time that the synagogue gained its central place in Judaism. The exploration of how this achievement occurred is divided into six different areas. In Section I, the essays examine how the synagogue began and try to delineate the evidence for the synagogue's existence and development prior to the Temple's destruction in 70. Section II centers on the development of the synagogue from 70 to the seventh century. It establishes the architectural development of the synagogue as an important indicator of how the synagogue linked itself to the Temple. The essays of Section III pick up on this issue of synagogue architecture as they analyze specific synagogue sites. Section IV's essays take a different approach to the question of the synagogue's success, focusing on the question of the synagogue's function in the Jewish community. Some of these articles explore the roles the synagogue played in the community and the religion, while others attempt to distinguish it from other institutions, such as the study house. Section V's articles look at how the synagogues used artistic and architectural forms to express aspects of Jewish myths and beliefs. Much of this artwork linked the early synagogue to the Temple. Finally, Section VI sets out the range of synagogues and other public structures in the Golan, the full extent of which has never been delineated in a published form.

Yet this collection of essays should be seen not only from a topical perspective but also from the perspective of the field of synagogue studies. The collection's emphasis is on recent studies, because in the 1970's the study of ancient synagogues entered a period of significant debate. At the start of that decade, archaeologists and other scholars still tried to fit their findings into paradigms several decades old. By its end, those paradigms had come under serious question. Since then, scholars have been striving to develop new ways of analyzing and understanding the origins, development, and nature of the earliest synagogues.

The goal of these two volumes is to communicate scholarly advances to those not immediately involved in the debates. Even though the study of ancient synagogues has important ramifications for many fields—early Christianity, hellenistic Judaism, and rabbinic Judaism, to name the most obvious—many of the above-mentioned changes in synagogue studies have gone largely unnoticed, especially in the English-speaking world. Although there are many reasons for this, two stand out. First, the most active part of the debate has taken place in Israel. There, early synagogues have been debated in journals and *festschriften* as well as in several collections of essays devoted exclusively to early synagogues. Little of this discussion has reached beyond Israel's borders. Second, while new analyses of synagogues have taken place among western scholars, some of the most incisive articles were published outside the mainstream journals. This has rendered access to these studies difficult.

This book brings together original, translated, and reprinted essays on ancient synagogues from an international spectrum of scholars. Together the articles provide a broad portrait of the current scholarly understanding and debate of the early development of the synagogue. The editors have chosen articles that work together to present a balanced view of the current scholarly knowledge about the ancient synagogue and the questions they are asking. This means that the authors do not always agree with each other, nor do the editors always agree with them. Indeed, the editors of this volume often disagree with each other. But through the disagreements and the debates, we think that this collection of essays provides a comprehensive portrayal of the early synagogue.

The editors have furthermore designed this collection of essays for scholars who do not specialize in the study of ancient synagogues, but who need to understand the synagogue and its communal role: scholars of New Testament, early Christianity, Second-Temple Judaism, and rabbinic Judaism, to mention just a few. The volume is thus more than just a collection of articles; it provides its readers with a solid grounding in the scholarship of the ancient synagogue. Any scholar who studies the essays in this collection—beginning with "A Reader's Guide"—will gain a comprehensive understanding of the origins of the synagogue and the changes it underwent, and will understand the synagogue's place in the Jewish community's religious life.

The editors have standardized the spelling of names of archaeological sites throughout most of the volume. When possible, we have used the spelling of the *New Encyclopedia of Archaeological Excavations in the Holy Land* (E. Stern, ed., 4 vols. [New York: Simon & Schuster, 1993]). Those articles reprinted from English, however, we have kept as close to their original form as possible. In doing so, we have kept their original spellings. In addition, in his section on the Golan, D. Urman has set out the alternate spellings and names for each site.

This book was prepared for camera-ready copy on an Apple Macintosh Centris 650 and was printed on a Hewlett-Packard LaserJet 4M. The English language font is Intellifont CG Times, with Linguist's Software supplying the foreign language fonts: Hebraica, Graeca, and IPA.

There are many people we would like to thank for helping make this book a reality. First and foremost we want to thank the contributors for allowing us to publish their work, for without them there would have been no book at all. Dr. Nathan H. Reisner, Ms. Bati Leviteh, Dr. Nathaniel Stampfer, and Dr. Fiona Ritchie translated articles with flowing expertise. They are credited in each of their articles. We would also like to thank the many institutions and individuals who gave their permission for us to reproduce essays, pictures, maps, and drawings. They are credited in the relevant articles, the List of Figures, and the List of Plates.

Dan Urman would like to thank the Ben-Gurion University of the Negev for allowing him to take a leave of absence, the Department of Religious

Studies at the University of North Carolina at Charlotte for appointing him the Swift Distinguished Professor of Judaic Studies for the year 1993-1994, and the Humanities Research Centre of the Australian National University for appointing him as a Visiting Fellow for 1994. The generosity of these institutions made it possible for Dan to complete his contributions to this collection. The latter two provided excellent facilities, congenial hospitality, and extensive support during his labors.

Paul Flesher would like to thank the University of Wyoming for all its help and support. It gives him particular pleasure to thank Dean Oliver Walter of the College of Arts and Sciences, the Department of English and its successive chairs Mark Booth and Janet Constantinides, and the Religious Studies Program. He would also like to acknowledge the Elie Wiesel Fund of the Judaic Studies Program at Northwestern University. Robert Torry and Caroline McCracken-Flesher proofread the entire manuscript before final printing, and Carolyn Anderson read the opening material; all helped improve the quality of the volume. Carol Ryzak, Keith Kanbe, and Chris Shearer accurately typed many pages of this collection.

Any volume of this size and variety can be a nightmare of crossed wires, especially since the project was carried out across four continents, with the editors only occasionally on the same one. To all who have helped this book instead become a dream of collaboration—both those mentioned by name and those unmentioned—we thank you.

In closing this Preface, we dedicate this book to our wives, Mety Urman and Caroline McCracken-Flesher, who watched their husbands disappear under the burden of this project. Whenever we lifted our heads they were there to provide support, comfort, and sage advice. When we were buried under the tasks of editing, coordinating, and writing, they provided the spark that reminded us of the joy in life.

Paul V. M. Flesher
Dan Urman

LIST OF FIGURES

ANCIENT SYNAGOGUES—A READER'S GUIDE

It has become a commonplace to describe a scholarly field undergoing changes as experiencing a 'paradigm shift.' For the study of ancient synagogues that would be an understatement; in this field, many paradigms are shifting. Indeed, the standard explanations of some of the most important aspects of the field—so old and accepted they have almost had the status of facts—have come into question and have even been discarded by many scholars. These paradigms are decades—in some cases, centuries—old. This reorientation in the study of ancient synagogues began some twenty-five years ago and has been nothing less than exhilarating for the field. The debate among archaeologists, epigraphers, historians of Judaism, and literary critics has been fervent. It has brought forth clarification of issues, formulation of new questions, reconceptualization of old questions, methodological innovation, and, of course, ongoing excavation, analysis and reinterpretation of archaeological and literary data.

The rapidity of developments in the study of ancient synagogues, accompanied by the constant shifts and changes in the details of the debates, has unfortunately made it difficult for scholars in cognate fields—such as New Testament, early Christianity, Second-Temple Judaism, and Rabbinic Judaism—to keep track of where matters stand. Not only do the ongoing debates require constant attention, but they are often carried on in hard-to-get publications and in languages uncommon on the scholarly circuit. Indeed, most of the Israeli protagonists in the debate write primarily in modern Hebrew, a language outside the mastery of too many North American and European scholars. Since sides are often drawn along national or linguistic boundaries, this phenomenon leaves many scholars hearing only half the debate.

The editors envision these two volumes of essays as a guide to understanding the current state of scholarly analysis of the ancient synagogue as well as a collection that points toward future directions. We have brought together groups of essays on central issues of the field—issues which constitute the key areas of scholarly knowledge of the ancient synagogue. The essays come from three languages: English, Hebrew, and French. Some are original pieces commissioned specifically for this collection, others have been translated into English, and a few were originally composed in English and are reprinted here. By bringing together the work of scholars from three continents, this collection is able to present the most complete picture of the international state of ancient synagogue scholarship to date.

The six sections of articles in these volumes focus on what the editors consider to be the main areas of knowledge and debate in the study of ancient synagogues. The first section, "The Origins of the Ancient Synagogues," looks at how scholars understand the evidence about the earliest synagogues. The second section, "The Development of Ancient Synagogues," focuses on the series of changes, improvements, and evolution that the synagogues underwent in the initial centuries of its existence. Section three, "Synagogues and Settlements: Reports and Analysis," provides a look at important synagogues, groups of synagogues, and new evidence of synagogues, throughout the land of Israel. Section four, "The Synagogue's Nature and the Jewish Community," is in many ways the most important subject, for it discusses the nature of the synagogue as a community institution. It is the Jewish community and its religious practices that make the synagogue into an important building. Starting the second volume, section five, "The Synagogue's Internal Aesthetics," looks at the art found in the ancient synagogues and at the internal design of the synagogue itself. The issue here is whether these have meaning and if so, what is that meaning and how is it conveyed? Finally, section six, "Public Structures and Jewish Communities in the Golan Heights," reveals new evidence of extensive Jewish settlement and building in that region.

Each section can be read in two ways. To begin with, each article can be seen by itself, standing alone and arguing its position without reference to the other articles of the section or the collection. Just as important, however, each section's articles complement each other, and when taken together portray the issue in a way that goes beyond any single article. This does not mean that the writers agree with each other, or that they are even on the same side of the debate. Instead, we have tried to present a selection of articles that not only reveal the current status of the issue but also form a trajectory indicating the direction of the debate's movement. This trajectory may in turn suggest the future of the debate.

So that readers will not have to guess about how the groups of essays interact, this Readers' Guide will set out how the editors envisioned each group of essays. It will provide the necessary background for understanding the central issues debated by the articles. For each section, it will point beyond the individual articles to indicate how they represent an aspect of the current understanding of ancient synagogues and thus contribute to a larger picture. It is ultimately the larger picture that the editors hope this collection of essays will provide.

The first task such a Guide should accomplish is to define the term 'synagogue.' As used in modern scholarly terminology, the term 'synagogue' has two meanings. First, 'synagogue' refers to an architectural structure. Sometimes this structure is simply a public building, and sometimes it comprises a complex—with rooms, courtyards and other architectural features associated with it. Second, 'synagogue' can also refer to the community of people that built and used the building. This is by far the more important usage, for if we do not know the building's importance to the community—how they used it and what they did in it—the building becomes little more than an interesting footnote in the history of public architecture. If we understand how ancient Jews used a synagogue building in the practice of their religion, however, the discovery of a synagogue building then reveals important information about the community that lived near it and used it.

Now that we have defined the modern scholarly meaning of the term synagogue, let us move to the ancient world and identify what ancient designations this modern term encompasses. The oldest term comes from the hellenistic world of third century B.C.E. Egypt, *proseuche* (pl. *proseuchai*) (προσευχή). It means 'prayer house' or 'prayer hall.' By the first century C.E., the New Testament and Josephus use the term *sunagoge* (συναγωγή) to refer to the building where the Jewish community meets. *Sunagoge* literally means 'a gathering place.'[1] The term appears earlier in the Septuagint, but there it translates the Hebrew *qahal* ('assembly') and is used to reference the people Israel (e.g., Num. 22:4). Finally, a synagogue is sometime referred to as a 'holy place,' a *hagios topos* (ἅγιος τόπος). This term is often found in inscriptions referring to the particular synagogue in which the inscription is found. It does not designate synagogues exclusively, however, for it can also refer to temples.

The Hebrew terms for synagogue stem from the rabbinic literature of the second through sixth centuries C.E. The two main Greek terms have corresponding Hebrew terms. The most commonly used term for synagogue is the *bet kneset* or *bet ha-kneset* (pl. *batei kneset*) (Hebrew: בית כנסת); like *sunagoge*, this term literally means, 'the house of gathering.' It is used to designate the place of public prayer and worship. On a rare occasion, rabbinic literature occasionally uses a term corresponding to proseuche, namely, *bet tefilah*, or *bet ha-tefilah* (Hebrew: בית תפלה). There are two terms sometimes associated with the synagogue. First, the study house or school is the *bet midrash* or *bet ha-midrash* (pl. *batei midrash*) (Hebrew: בית מדרש); this can be literally translated as 'the house of interpretation.' Second, the court is the *bet din* or *bet ha-din* (pl. *batei din*) (Hebrew: בית דין); this term literally means 'the house of judgment.' The court is run by the

[1] Not surprisingly, the terms for identifying synagogues form one of the most confusing aspects of synagogue study. There is ongoing scholarly discussion about whether the different terms refer to the same institution or to separate institutions.

rabbis and is where they apply the law to those who come before them, while the study house is where the rabbis train their disciples. One of the ongoing scholarly debates over these terms is whether each of these is a physically separate site, perhaps housed in different buildings, or whether they take place in the same building—namely, the synagogue building—and are just differentiated by their central activity. Other terms are occasionally used to refer to the synagogue, but these are the most frequent. So, with these preliminaries in hand, let us turn our attention to the essays in this collection.

I. THE ORIGINS OF THE SYNAGOGUE

If we ask when and where the Israelite Temple was first established, we get a clear straightforward answer. It was built by Solomon during his 39-year reign (961-922 B.C.E.) in Jerusalem. The book of 1 Kings describes the Temple's construction, and other sources which mention the early Temple essentially corroborate that account. To be sure, Solomon's Temple was related an earlier institution, the tabernacle, but the Temple itself has a clearly identifiable beginning.

Not so with the other important Jewish religious institution, the synagogue. If we ask when and where the synagogue was first established, we receive no decisive response. The scholarship of the last half-century supplies a multiplicity of answers which leaves the non-specialist lost in a maze of contradictory proposals. Even within the past 15 years, one can find published claims that the synagogue began in Babylonia during the Exile of the sixth-century B.C.E., that it started in Egypt in the third century B.C.E., or that was developed in Palestine itself. And readers will find no help in sorting out the possibilities from L. I. Levine's introductory article "Synagogues" in *The New Encyclopedia of Archaeological Excavations in the Holy Land*. He simply lists five different theories of the synagogue's beginnings, without providing any guidance concerning the acceptance or reliability of any of them.[2] Whereas little over a decade ago, Levine could confidently assert that the "general consensus" was that the synagogue originated with Babylonian Exiles from the destruction of the First Temple, he now will not choose among the competing proposals;[3] the present debate is too hot and heavy. The reason for this debate is that the scholarly consensus of the past few centuries has fallen into disrepute. To help the reader understand how the present situation developed, let us provide a brief history of scholarship on this question.

---

[2] *NEAEHL*, vol. 4, p. 1421.

[3] Levine, "Ancient Synagogues," p. 3.

The earliest claims about the synagogue's origins appear in the first century C.E. In the New Testament, the Acts of the Apostles implies that Moses founded the synagogue. Acts 15:21 reads, "For from early generations Moses has had in every city those who preach him, for he is read every sabbath in the synagogues." Similarly, Josephus attributes the weekly reading of Scripture to Moses (*Against Apion* 2:17 [175]). Philo directly credits Moses for daily and weekly meetings for learning moral principles that are held in prayer houses (*proseuchai*).[4] Even Targum Pseudo-Jonathan (from later in the rabbinic period) attributes the early synagogue to the time of Moses. Its rendering of Exodus 18:20 gives Moses the role of establishing the prayer for the *bet ha-kneset*. The theory of the Mosaic origins of the synagogue was adopted by the thinkers and writers of the Christian Church and was strongly defended "as late as the seventeenth century by the Dutch Christian scholar and theologian, Hugo Grotius."[5]

Grotius' work may have been the final foray for the Mosaic origins of the synagogue, however, for the position was superseded by the theory put forth by Carlo Sigonio in the late sixteenth century.[6] He attributed the synagogue's origins to the time of the Israelites' exile in Babylonia and their return in the sixth century B.C.E. This understanding of the synagogue's origins became the dominant scholarly paradigm and reigned without serious challenge until the 1970's.[7] It did not begin with Sigonio, however, but appeared initially in rabbinic writings.[8] The Bavli indicates that the *shekinah* accompanied the people Israel into exile in Babylonia and inhabited two synagogues they built there, one in Nehardea and the other in Hutsal (B. Meg. 29a). Later, in the tenth century C.E., Rav Sherira Gaon claimed in his *Iggeret* (letter) that the Exiles founded these two synagogues upon building stones brought from the Jerusalem Temple.[9]

Although Sigonio's proposal established a new paradigm for the synagogue's origins, the paradigm was not immune from scholarly alteration.

---

[4] Philo, *Vita Moses* II, § 39 (215-216). See also *Special Laws* II, § 15 (62) and *Praep. Ev.* viii § 7 (12-13).

[5] Gutmann, "Origins," p. 1. Gutmann cites I. Sonne, "Synagogue," in *IDB*, vol. 4 (1962), p. 479 for the reference to Grotius.

[6] "Prolegomenon," in Gutmann, *Synagogue*, p. X. For Sigonio's comment, see Gutmann's footnote #1, citing C. Sigonio, *De republica Hebraeorum*, Libri VII (Francofurti, 1583), p. 86.

[7] To be sure, this consensus had its share of counterproposals. In the 1930's, a quiet but persistent series of scholars began to propose alternate modes for the start of synagogues. Solomon Zeitlin suggested that the synagogue began with the *maamad*. See Zeitlin, "Origin." E. Rivkin followed that idea up with a similar suggestion. See Rivkin, "Nonexistence."

[8] Indeed, while the idea of the Mosaic origins of the synagogue came out of early Jewish literature in the hands of the church (Josephus, New Testament, and Philo), the Babylonian origins' idea was founded largely upon statements in rabbinic texts.

[9] Levin edition, pp. 72-73, quoted by Oppenheimer below. See the discussion of this question in Oppenheimer's article later in this volume.

Some scholars claimed that the synagogue formed part of Josiah's reforms and was then exported to Babylonia during the Exile.[10] Others have argued that it began with Ezra upon the return from Exile.[11] But the basic identification of the synagogue with the Exile has remained the dominant explanation of its origins up to the closing decades of the twentieth century.

Starting in the 1970's, the theory that the synagogue originated in Babylonia began to undergo serious questioning. By the mid-1980's, a full-scale debate raged over the issue of the synagogue's beginnings, with established and younger scholars on both sides.

The main impetus for calling into question the synagogue's Babylonian origins lay in the way most of its proponents used supporting evidence. When evidence was used—which was not always the case—it was interpreted anachronistically or made to bear conclusions that it simply could not support. An example of this can be found in the opening section of the article "Synagogue" in the *Encyclopedia Judaica*, written by L. I. Rabinowitz.[12]

> Although there is no mention of the synagogue in Ezra and Nehemiah and the post-Exilic prophets, it can be assumed that the returned Exiles brought with them the rudiments of that institution to which they had given birth during their exile. In this connection it is germane to draw attention to the fact that the establishment of the synagogue implies the evolution of standard forms of service, and the Talmud ascribes the formulation of the earliest prayers (the *Amidah*, *Kiddush*, and the *Havdalah*) to Ezra and his successors, the Men of the Great Synagogue (Ber. 33a).[13]

There are several representative problems with the use of evidence here. First, Rabinowitz begins by admitting that the post-Exilic works do not mention the synagogue at all. That is to say, they provide no evidence for it. Second, he then assumes (without any basis at all) that the exiles started synagogues in Babylonia, and then brought them back to Israel. Third, Rabinowitz then uses the Babylonian Talmud as primary evidence for events some eight or nine centuries earlier, namely, "the formulation of the earliest prayers." The Bavli's composition is too far removed from the supposed events to lend them any credibility. Finally, Rabinowitz misrepresents the evidence he cites. The passage from the Bavli (Ber. 33a) does not claim that Ezra had anything to do with the start of the prayers, only the supposed

---

[10] J. Morgenstern, for instance, in *Studi Orientalistici in onore Giorgio Levi Della Vida*, vol. 2 (1956), cited by Gutmann, "Origin." See also the citations by Finkelstein on p. 3 of Finkelstein, "Origin."

[11] For further bibliographic information, see Gutmann, "Origin."

[12] Not R. Meier as cited by H. C. Kee, in Kee, "Transformation."

[13] *EJ* vol. 15, p. 582.

"Men of the Great Synagogue."[14] So not a single aspect of Rabinowitz's statement finds support.

Another typical violation of rules of evidence lies in the anachronistic interpretation of terminology. Again, let us cite Rabinowitz:

> More definite, however, is the reference to the "little sanctuary" in [Ezekiel] 11:16, and it may have been a true instinct which made the Talmud (Meg. 29a) apply it to the synagogue.[15]

Here we find Rabinowitz interpreting Ezekiel's "little sanctuary" (*miqdash me'at*) as a synagogue. A reading of the biblical text makes it clear that Ezekiel refers not to a social institution, but to God himself.[16] Rabinowitz attempts to lend support to his argument by citing the Bavli's later use of the term (a millennium later) to designate the synagogue. The anachronism here is simply stunning.[17]

We have singled out Rabinowitz's essay for criticism because as an encyclopedia entry, it represents a scholarly consensus rather than an idiosyncratic view. Our critique of him thus extends beyond his work to the scholarship represented by his essay. It should be clear, then, that the idea of the Babylonian origins of the synagogue has very little support in solid evidence. It has been based more on "eisegesis" and wishful thinking than on solid reasoning and firm data.[18]

The way forward now is to found a theory of the synagogue's origins on a solid interpretation of available evidence. It should not stem from imagined ideas of how it 'must have been' or from wild speculation beyond the

---

[14] The "Men of the Great Synagogue" is a category without any historical validation. Scholars have tried for years to identify this group, but without any single formulation gaining acceptance. The main problem is again the lack of contemporaneous evidence.

[15] *EJ* vol. 15, p. 581 (brackets supplied by editors).

[16] Indeed, commentaries on Ezekiel written by scholars unfamiliar with rabbinic literature focus on the interpretation of God as a "little sanctuary." They do not even consider the synagogue as a possible interpretation. See, for example, *Ezekiel 1: A Commentary on the Book of the Prophet Ezekiel, Chapters 1-24*, W. Zimmerli (Philadelphia: Fortress, 1979) p. 262. Eichrodt mentions the interpretation, but sees no basis for it, see W. Eichrodt, *Ezekiel: A Commentary* (Philadelphia: Westminster, 1970), pp. 144-146.

[17] *Miqdash me'at* is not the only biblical term that scholars have interpreted anachronistically. The meanings of *bet ha-am* (e.g., Jer. 39:8), *miqra* (e.g., Is. 4:5), and *mo'adei-el* (e.g., Ps. 74:8) have been likewise distorted. For further discussion, see Gutmann, "Origin," p. 74; Gutmann, "Origins," p. 1; Finkelstein, "Origin," pp. 3-4.

[18] The observation concerning using data from an appropriate time period also applies to geography (with the appropriate alterations); evidence concerning one geographical region should not be used for another. This is a usually a matter of common sense. Philo, a Jew from Egyptian Alexandria, obviously should be knowledgeable about the situation in Egypt. It would be inappropriate to apply his comments to first-century Babylonia, about which he neither claims knowledge nor even speaks about. E. R. Goodenough did this, and that application is one of the major criticisms against his work. Similarly, the Palestinian Talmud should be used as evidence of Palestine, while the Babylonian Talmud should be applied to circumstances in Babylonia and not in Palestine.

support of presently available data. By linking the scholarly understanding firmly to the data, a reliable picture of the present state of our knowledge will emerge. It may not be complete, it may require revision if significant new evidence comes to light, but it will at least describe what current scholarship can demonstrate, rather than what it can speculate.

The four essays of the first section conform admirably to this dictum. Each one takes seriously the available evidence and tries to build solid conclusions about the synagogue's origins on that evidence.

The article by J. G. Griffiths, "Egypt and the Rise of the Synagogue," begins with the earliest reliable evidence for the synagogue. Griffiths focuses on the inscriptions found at different sites in Egypt which refer to Jewish prayer houses. These stem largely from the third and second centuries B.C.E. Although widely known by the scholarly world, the inscriptions have been largely ignored as evidence for the start of the synagogue.[19] Griffiths decided to treat this evidence as that of the earliest synagogues. Thus rather than treating these as a brief stepping-stone from the Babylonian period into the first century, Griffiths sees these *proseuchai* as the start of synagogues. From that position, Griffiths then explores whether any specifically Egyptian influences can be found in the earliest synagogues. He finds possible influences in specific architectural features and in the emphasis found in Egyptian Jewry upon study. Certainly Egypt provides a better sources for these aspects, Griffiths concludes, than the hellenistic world.

L. L. Grabbe's article, "Synagogues in Pre-70 Palestine: A Re-assessment," nicely complements Griffiths'. Where Griffiths started with the earliest known evidence of synagogues anywhere, Grabbe searches for the earliest evidence for synagogues in Palestine. Grabbe makes five points, three of which are quite important. First, as does Griffiths, Grabbe argues that the synagogue begins in the diaspora. Second, after an examination of Josephus, the books of the Maccabees, and other apocryphal works, as well as archaeological evidence, he concludes that the synagogue does not appear in Palestine until sometime after the Hasmonaean era. Third, Grabbe argues that the synagogue, especially in Palestine, shows no specifically Pharisaic features, nor do the Pharisees appear to be particularly identified with the synagogue.

The essay by P. V. M. Flesher, "Palestinian Synagogues before 70 C.E.: A Review of the Evidence," begins by taking seriously Griffiths' work and building on that of Grabbe. Starting with the position that the synagogue was developed in third-century B.C.E. Egypt, he asks, when and where does this foreign institution enter Palestine? He shows that the synagogue first appears in Galilee, away from the Temple in Jerusalem. This happens most

[19] See the discussion and bibliography in Schürer, vol. 2, pp. 423-454, esp. pp. 425-426. Although see Hengel, "Proseuche."

assuredly by the first century C.E. and possibly at the end of the first century B.C.E. Flesher also shows that there is no indication that the synagogue becomes an important religious institution in Judea until long after the Temple's destruction. None of the so-called first-century synagogues found in Judea have any real support for either their identification as synagogues in some cases or their dating to the first century in others. The archaeological evidence for such synagogues is inconclusive and has been the object of conclusions which it simply cannot support. The literary evidence for first-century synagogues in Judea is either late (from the second century or later), or it refers to institutions created by foreign residents for their own needs. The sources speak of no synagogue as an indigenous, Palestinian institution.

A. Oppenheimer discusses the literary evidence for two Babylonian synagogues which, had their claims been true, would have been the earliest known synagogues—first built during the Babylonian exile of the sixth century B.C.E. But the ultimate conclusion of "Babylonian Synagogues with Historical Associations" is that they are not. Oppenheimer examines the synagogues of *Shaf ve-yatib* at Nehardea and one at Hutsal that were considered quite ancient during the rabbinic and the gaonic periods (fifth to tenth century). He instead shows how their illustrious past was created by the rabbis themselves.

II. THE DEVELOPMENT OF ANCIENT SYNAGOGUES

Of the four essays in this section, the first three—those of Groh, Tsafrir, and Foerster—continue chronologically from those of Grabbe and Flesher. Grabbe and Flesher discuss synagogues in first-century Palestine, while Groh and the others start with the next period of synagogues and continue on. But two important factors differentiate the two sets of articles. On the one hand, the first century reveals a paucity of evidence about synagogues; scholars struggle hard to interpret the little information we possess. Later centuries, by contrast, have provided a wealth of evidence about synagogues. So much evidence, in fact, that the scholarly focus shifts from "Were there synagogues?" to "What accounts for the differences among the synagogues?" Second, the Palestinian chronology of synagogues is discontinuous; the archaeological record reveals a gap between the so-called synagogues of the first century and those of the third century.[20] The size of this gap is debatable (the whole century? just the last fifty years? the first thirty years?),

[20] The Mishnah, by contrast, reveals no such gap. It presumably reflects the situation in Galilee in the late second century (if not earlier) and it assumes that the synagogue is one of the main institutions of the Jewish community.

but it is clear that no continuity exists between synagogues of the first century and those of the third century.[21]

The architectural development of Palestinian synagogues in the early centuries has, since the 1930's, been divided into a three-part scheme. Leaving out the so-called first-century synagogues, the scheme began with synagogues that more or less conformed to the design of a Graeco-Roman basilica. These have been called 'basilical' synagogues, as well as 'Galilean' synagogues—because most were found in the Galilee. These synagogues had a large, ornamental facade with three doors. This side faced Jerusalem; in the Galilee, it was the southern wall. Worshippers would enter through the doors and then, after finding their places, turn and pray towards the doors, since this was the direction of the (former) Jerusalem Temple. The roof was supported by two parallel rows of columns, crossed by a third row. This synagogue had neither a built-in Torah ark nor any internal artwork. The outside of the synagogue—usually the facade—contained a few carved reliefs.

The second design was termed the 'broadhouse.' In these rectangular buildings, the wall nearest Jerusalem was a long wall. In it was built a permanently fixed Torah niche. Near this niche was constructed a *bemah* (a platform) for speaking or reading the Torah. The entrance to this building was through doors in one of the short sides. It used no columns for roof support. Some of these synagogues had mosaic pavements. Initially, this was considered a transitional form between the earlier basilica design and the third design.

The third design could be called a 'basilica with an apse,' or an apsidal synagogue. Like the broadhouse type, the important wall was closest to Jerusalem. Only instead of a simple Torah niche, it now had a larger apse, often with a *bemah*. Whereas in the broadhouse where the Jerusalem wall was the long side of the rectangle, the apsidal synagogue placed the short side towards Jerusalem. The doors were now moved to the side opposite the apse, the side furthest from Jerusalem. The rows of columns were also reinstated, as in a basilica. Most of these synagogue contained mosaic floors.

For several decades, archaeologists used this typological scheme for dating. The basilica synagogues were considered to be from the second or third centuries (i.e., 'early'), the broadhouse was fourth century (i.e., 'transitional'), and the apsidal synagogues were fifth through sixth centuries (i.e., 'late'). This tie to dating has proved to be this scheme's downfall, however. For discoveries and conclusions by both American and Italian ar-

[21] The synagogue at Nabratein may be the only synagogue for which stratigraphic analysis demonstrates a second-century date. See the discussion and bibliography in D. Groh's essay in this volume.

chaeologists have occasioned the complete re-evaluation of the links between the different types and these dates.

The first major disruption came from the finds at Capernaum published by Corbo and Loffreda.[22] These discoveries required them to revise the dating of the Capernaum synagogue by about 200 years. Throughout most of the twentieth century, scholars had viewed the Capernaum synagogue as a basilica and therefore from the third century. But when Corbo and Loffreda excavated underneath the synagogue in a controlled stratigraphic manner, they discovered coins in a sealed locus that required them to redate the synagogue to the fifth century. This interpretation of the new evidence was so controversial that when it was published in the *Israel Exploration Journal*, the editor, M. Avi-Yonah, published a three-page rebuttal immediately following![23]

Corbo and Loffreda were not the only archaeologists to excavate synagogues that violated the three-part typology of Palestinian synagogues. A team of American archaeologists, lead by E. Meyers, excavated a synagogue a Khirbet Shema'.[24] It turned out to be the first broadhouse synagogue found in Galilee, but the dating was unexpected. The stratigraphic analysis required the date of the synagogue's foundation to be placed in the third century—a full century earlier than the typological scheme suggested. More recently, another team lead by Meyers found that the earliest stratum of the synagogue at Nabratein—another broadhouse—may be as old as the mid-second century.[25]

At this point in time, the debate still rages. Most American archaeologists have given up the notion of tying the typological scheme to a datable or developmental scheme. A few Israeli scholars have continued to defend it, but most have attempted to modify the scheme to make it more flexible. Only the apsidal synagogue still retains its earlier chronological link; it was probably in use from the fifth century up to the eighth century.[26]

Of the three articles on the development of Palestinian synagogues, the essay by D. Groh, "The Stratigraphic Chronology of the Galilean Synagogue from the Early Roman Period Through the Early Byzantine Period (ca. 420 C.E.)," presents an American approach to the question. He

---

22 V. Corbo, S. Loffreda and A. Spijkerman, *La Sinagoga di Cafarnao dopo gli scavi del 1969* (Jerusalem, 1970).

23 Loffreda, "Capernaum"; M. Avi-Yonah, "Editor's Note," *IEJ* 23 (1973): 43-45. For further bibliographical information, see Loffreda, "Capernaum" and Avi-Yonah, "Comments" in the bibliography.

24 See Meyers, *Khirbet Shema'*. Meyers' team included J. Strange, A. T. Kraabel, and D. Groh, among others.

25 See D. Groh's essay in this volume for further discussion and bibliography.

26 See G. Foerster's essay in this volume. See also E. Meyers and J. Strange, *Archaeology, the Rabbis, and Early Christianity* (Nashville: Abingdon, 1981), pp. 150-1.

eschews entirely the three-part scheme of synagogue development. In its place, he proposes a new pattern of development, based on fully published synagogues with clear stratigraphic analysis.[27] He begins with a brief mention of the first-century synagogues and continues through to the early fifth century, looking primarily at synagogues in the regions of the Galilee and the Golan.

Y. Tsafrir works largely within the framework of the three-part scheme of synagogue development. After defending the importance and value of the scheme for dating, his essay, "On the Source of the Architectural Design of the Ancient Synagogues in the Galilee: A New Appraisal," goes on to examine the development of the third-century synagogues. He shows that the Galilean synagogues constitute a break from any of the supposed first-century synagogues, and indeed are an original development of the third century. Tsafrir then explores possible architectural sources of inspiration for their design.

G. Foerster's essay, "Dating Synagogues with a 'Basilical' Plan and an Apse," focuses on the later apsidal synagogues. He carefully shows that they form an identifiable and datable group from the later period of early synagogue development.

The final article of this section shifts its geographical focus from the Land of Israel to the Diaspora. This shift reveals important differences between the two regions. The most obvious difference is that only a dozen or so synagogues are known in the whole Mediterranean and Middle Eastern region, as opposed to the hundreds of synagogues known in Israel. These synagogues reveal a different time range as well. The earliest archaeological excavations of a synagogue date to the second century B.C.E. (Delos), about a century earlier than any evidence for synagogues in Israel. The latest known diaspora synagogues of late antiquity are from the fourth century

[27] As Groh and other writers in this volume correctly observe, archaeology requires publication of finds, perhaps even more than analysis. Archaeology claims to be a scientific endeavor. In science, an experiment must be publicly explained so that it can be repeated and evaluated by other scientists. Since archaeology destroys a site through the process of excavation, nothing can be repeated. Publication of carefully gathered information, then, is the only control by which other archaeologists can evaluate the validity of conclusions. Thus, before any conclusions can be treated as reliable, the excavation's finds must have received more than just an announcement. The most reliable archaeological data for a site is that which has been fully published in a final report. Sites with ongoing excavations should receive regular publication in preliminary reports. Without this kind of publication, any statements by the excavators remain untested—and indeed untestable—by their peers; without debate and verification, interpretation of a site remains preliminary rather than proven. Unfortunately, archaeologists are notorious for failing to publish their material in a timely fashion. The synagogue at Masada—the most famous so-called first-century synagogue—received its publication nearly thirty years after its discovery was announced to the world. (See *Masada III*.)

(Stobi and Ostia), much earlier than the late boom in Palestinian synagogue building in the fifth and sixth centuries.

Kraabel's classic article from the late 1970's, "The Diaspora Synagogue: Archaeological and Epigraphic Evidence since Sukenik," ignores the inscriptional evidence for earlier diaspora synagogues and instead concentrates on excavated sites of the ancient synagogues. He describes the seven sites that had been excavated when he wrote and describes them. Kraabel's conclusion shows that these sites were shaped more by local influences than by any identifiable elements shared across the synagogues. Indeed, there seems to be no connections among them that would indicate a common thread of development either among themselves or in relationship to Palestinian synagogues.

III. SYNAGOGUES AND SETTLEMENTS: REPORTS AND ANALYSIS

The third section of these collected essays focuses on new archaeological data and its interpretation. Some essays focus strictly on the presentation of new material, while others take new discoveries and interpret them in light of previously analyzed material.

D. Amit is known for his involvement in the synagogues of southern Judea, having excavated both Maon and Anim with Z. Ilan. His essay, "Architectural Plans of Synagogues in the Southern Judean Hills and the Halakah," brings his expertise to the study of four synagogues of this region: Eshtemoa and Susiya as well as the two just mentioned. According to Amit, these synagogues reveal important variations within the typological scheme of synagogue design that stem from local concerns to adhere to particular halakic requirements. He argues that these four should be taken as an architectural group, because they share two important features that distinct them from most other Palestinian synagogues. Their entrances face due east, and they are long and narrow, with no columns to support the roof. Using an investigation of the halakah, Amit shows that the synagogue entrances face east because they are based on the model of the biblical Tabernacle, which was oriented towards the east. This decision, according to Amit, raises a problem; the axis of entrance is east-west, but the axis of prayer (towards Jerusalem) is south-north. So in what direction should one put the rows of columns to support the roof? If they go south-north, they interfere in the axis of entrance, but if they go east-west, they interfere with the axis of prayer. So the architect decided to eliminate the problem by not using the columns. This solved the problems of the columns interfering with either axis, but it also resulted in a long, narrow building.

The article by S. Dar and Y. Mintzker, "The Synagogue of Ḥorvat Sumaqa, 1983-1993," comprises a preliminary report on the excavations of this synagogue on Mt. Carmel. The Sumaqa synagogue provides an interesting comparison to both the Judean synagogues just discussed by Amit and the typological scheme of synagogue development. Like most basilical synagogues of the Galilee, this synagogue has two rows of columns in the main hall. However, its orientation is due east, with the entrance facade on the eastern wall. Thus it is like the Judean synagogues in following the halakic rule of eastern orientation, while it is like the Galilean synagogues in its interior design. Apparently, the problem of having columns cross the axis of entrance did not bother the builder. This synagogue should also be seen in the context of the two nearby synagogues of Husifah and Japhia, both of which face east, rather than south.

Z. Gal's article, "Ancient Synagogues in the Eastern Lower Galilee," like Amit's, provides an illustration of how the typological scheme of synagogue development requires modification to incorporate local differences brought about by social and geographical-ecological situations. Gal begins with a brief description of a survey of synagogue remains on the Issachar plateaus (in southeastern Galilee), none of which have been excavated. He then shows that the plateaus were marginal areas dependent upon the Bet-Shean and Harod valleys just below them to the east. When the valleys were active centers of Jewish population, that increased the settlement on the plateau, and vice versa. The synagogue remains in the valleys show that the major period of settlement was in the fourth and fifth centuries. Gal then argues that the synagogue finds from the survey on the plateau must also be from this time period, even though they share features with so-called 'early' synagogues of Galilee.

Finally, in the last essay in this section, "Early Photographs of Galilean Synagogues," D. Urman introduces a series of photographs of synagogue remains taken by C. W. Wilson and H. H. Kitchener during their surveys in Galilee in second half of the nineteenth century. Most have never before been published. These include early pictures of Meiron, Chorazin, and of the small synagogue at Bar'am, which has since "disappeared." The pictures constitute a historical record of archaeological remains over a century ago. Although these pictures are no substitute for excavations, they provide a perspective no longer available. The photographs of Capernaum, for example, reveal how little remained of the synagogue even before the arrival of Kohl and Watzinger at the turn of the century. While it is known that their widely reproduced drawing of a "reconstruction" of the synagogue was based on only two courses of stones, the pictures of fields of rubble at Capernaum visually bring home the extent to which the building's roof, second story, and even the design of the upper half of the first floor was speculation.

IV. THE SYNAGOGUE'S NATURE AND THE JEWISH COMMUNITY

The previous sections of this book have been concerned largely with the synagogue as a building. We have discussed questions such as: When did it start? What were its architectural designs? Where do we know they were built? But this is only the beginning of the story. For the ultimate question focuses not on the building itself, but on the community that built and used it. We could phrase it like this: If a Jewish community built a synagogue, what else do we know about them? That is to say, what do we learn about a Jewish settlement—village, town, or city—if we discover that they had a synagogue? For the presence and the nature of the synagogue are irretrievably linked to its community.

The answer to that question leads us to investigate the nature of the synagogue and to attempt to understand what functions a synagogue served. If it was a place of worship, what kind of worship? If the synagogue served as a location for other activities, what were those activities? Where such activities always religious in character, or did civil activities also take place there?

"The Communal Functions of the Synagogue in the Land of Israel in the Rabbinic Period" by Z. Safrai sets the stage for the articles in this section. He presents a maximalist view of the different activities that take place in a synagogue. Drawing from material as diverse as first-century inscriptions and medieval midrashim (such as Midrash HaGadol) from both Palestine and Babylonia, he argues that Palestinian synagogues not only served as prayer houses, but they were also important centers of study, housed the local court, served as hostels and inns, organized local charity, and provided the location for community meetings. It also served as the 'office' for local community officials and functioned as a gathering place for religious and community meals.

The strength of Safrai's presentation is unfortunately also its weakness. By providing the fullest possible view of what the synagogue could have been used for, his picture can be challenged by scholars who argue that a particular synagogue did not serve a certain function. Safrai is certainly correct in identifying the different functions a synagogue could serve, but it remains unclear whether, on the one hand, any single synagogue ever served all these functions, and on the other hand, whether all synagogues in Palestine during the "Hasmonaean and Rabbinic periods" fulfilled even most of these functions. This has left the door open for other scholars to discuss and debate the historical development of different synagogue functions and to attempt the identification of geographical differences. The remaining essays in this section do just that—for both Palestinian and diaspora synagogues.

A. Kasher's essay, "Synagogues as 'Houses of Prayer' and 'Holy Places' in the Jewish Communities of Hellenistic and Roman Egypt," discusses some of Safrai's themes, while adding the important issue of status to that of function. After emphasizing what the evidence presents as the two primary functions of synagogues in Egypt—namely, prayer and Torah study—Kasher identifies a third function. Synagogues in Egypt apparently serve as places of asylum. This reveals an important aspect of the synagogue's status not present elsewhere; the synagogue has become a 'holy place,' not in just a Jewish sense, but in a sense defined by its Egyptian context. In other words, the synagogue was legally designated by Egyptian authorities as equivalent to an Egyptian temple. This in turn led to the synagogue becoming the central organization of the Jewish community. By the first century, this brought on unfortunate events. When non-Jewish residents of Egyptian cities persecuted the Jews, for instance, they focused their wrath on the synagogues, destroying a large number of them.

With I. Gafni's essay, "Synagogues in Babylonia in the Talmudic Period," we turn from the Egyptian diaspora to the Babylonian. He shows that Babylonian synagogues had a distinctly different status from their Egyptian counterparts and explicitly shows that they had a less varied role than Safrai's portrayal of Palestinian synagogues. According to Gafni, Babylonian synagogues served only two functions, prayer and sometimes Torah study. Most other functions attributed to Palestinian synagogues, are taken care of elsewhere in a Babylonian Jewish community. Surprisingly, this emphasis on the specifically religious activities of prayer and Torah study makes the synagogue less holy rather than more holy. It also means that the synagogues do not serve the same role as community center. Thus when the Zoroastrians stirred up trouble against the Jews, for example, the synagogues did not bear the brunt of the attacks.

The essays now move from general examination of synagogal community functions to the analysis of a single specific issue. D. Urman's article, "The House of Assembly and the House of Study: Are they One and the Same?" examines the connection between the synagogue (the *bet kneset*) and the study house (the *bet midrash*). Reacting to the picture—drawn by Safrai, Hüttenmeister, and others—of the *bet midrash* as subsumed into the *bet kneset*, Urman shows through literary and archaeological analysis that this is too simple. Hüttenmeister, in particular, has answered the question of why so many synagogues have been found in Palestine and so very few study houses by arguing that the *bet midrash* was the name for an activity, which took place in a synagogue building. Urman shows that Hüttenmeister's criteria for identifying synagogues is so inexact that they could even identify a wine press as a synagogue. He goes on to suggest that many of the so-called synagogues that have been identified may actually be study houses. Indeed, he adduces both archaeological and literary evidence to show that at least from the third century in Palestine, the two institutions are considered to be in physically separate locations.

Following on the heels of Urman's study, Z. Ilan's "The Synagogue and Study House at Meroth" provides further hard evidence of the separation of the *bet kneset* and the *bet midrash*. Through analysis of the synagogue complex at Meroth which he excavated, Ilan shows that there were separate rooms and entrances for the synagogue and the study house. His essay also explicates evidence for other community and personal uses of the synagogue, including one individual's placement under the entryway of an amulet to give him the power to rule over the community.

R. Reich's essay, "The Synagogue and the *miqweh* in Eretz-Israel in the Second-Temple, Mishnaic, and Talmudic Periods," looks at another possible function of the synagogue, that of its association with cultic purity through the installation of immersion pools, that is, *miqwaot*. Reich shows that the archaeological evidence reveals that the *miqweh* and the synagogue are associated only in the so-called first-century synagogues. The synagogues in the rabbinic period show few links to such water installations. In fact, only one synagogue dated after the first century has a *miqweh* associated with it. So the conclusion of Reich's study is that the synagogues and the *miqwaot* are not linked and thus the synagogue does not serve as a locus for cultic purity.

VOLUME TWO

V. THE SYNAGOGUE'S INTERNAL AESTHETICS

Even though art in synagogues has been known for many decades, the very notion of synagogues having extensive representational art—particularly mosaic floors—remains a surprisingly touchy subject. It still seems, somehow, 'idolatrous.' But the present unease is nothing compared to the energy that archaeologists and other scholars of Judaism in late antiquity have expended trying to ignore and avoid the connection of art and Judaism in the synagogue. The problem is that rabbinic literature had for centuries led scholars to believe that ancient Jews had no representational art, that they were aniconic. According to this view, any figurative representation would have violated the second commandment against making images.

So in the early twentieth century, when some pictorial mosaic pavements were found with Hebrew inscriptions, scholars assigned them "to a hypothetical Judaeo-Christian community."[28] By the mid-1930's, with the discovery of extensive mosaic floors at Na'aran and Beth Alpha, and of

---

28 Avi-Yonah, "Synagogues," p. 271.

course the painted walls of the synagogue at Dura Europos, the scholarly world could no longer ignore the Jewish character of this art. So many denied its importance. Scholars from Albright to Watzinger argued that the synagogue art was merely decorative or that the images—even ones of pagan gods—had been emptied of any meaning.[29] Even though somebody had paid a lot of money to produce the art and others had gone to a lot of trouble to create it, according to these scholars, it went essentially unnoticed by those who worshipped at the synagogue. Surely, they argue, a 'good Jew' could not have prayed in front of the zodiac floor of Beth Alpha or before the full frontal nudity of Pharaoh's daughter at Dura if the art had meant something to them.[30]

The most extensive counter-attack came from by E. R. Goodenough. His massive twelve-volume *Jewish Symbols in the Greco-Roman Period* constructed an enormous case arguing that practically any Jewish image that could be identified had symbolic value.[31] Goodenough did an excellent job showing how Jewish images had symbolic meaning. Unfortunately he went too far when trying to assign meanings to specific images. Rather than admit that, for some symbols, modern scholarship simply lacked sufficient information to determine their meaning, he developed an overarching theory that enabled him to overcome this lack. Goodenough took the writings of the Neo-Platonist Philo of Alexandria and developed a mystical Judaism from them. Adding the notion of a universal psychological theory common to all Jews (surprisingly similar to C. G. Jung's notion of archetypes), Goodenough then argued that this could be applied to all Jewish symbols of the ancient world. This theory was met with derision almost as soon as it was published. Unfortunately, the negative reaction resulted in the ignoring of Goodenough's analyses of symbols that did not rely on the theory.

The upshot of Goodenough's spectacular demise is that any attempt to interpret the artwork as symbolic has become suspect. Scholars who want to pursue this promising avenue have been saddled with Goodenough's legacy. This has left the scholars who wish to deny the symbolic meaning of synagogue art and argue that it is merely decorative free to continue on their way. But more recently, the debate over the meaning and importance of synagogue art has begun to heat up again, and indeed, several volleys are taken in the essays which begin the second volume.

---

[29] See Albright in his *Archaeology and the Religion of Israel* (1942), p. 67; and Watzinger as cited in Goodenough, vol. 4, pp. 5-6. Goodenough provides an extensive discussion of scholars on this question in Goodenough, vol. 4, pp. 3-24.

[30] Dothan carries forward this explanation—that the symbols are empty of meaning—in the final report on his excavations of the synagogue at Hammath-Tiberias. He argues that the image of Helios in the mosaic floor there had lost all associations with pagan religion by the time of its creation in the fourth century. See Dothan, *Hammath Tiberias*, pp. 68-70.

[31] See Goodenough, esp. vols. 4 and 12.

A. Ovadiah's survey article "Art of the Ancient Synagogues in Israel" does an excellent job of bringing together the types of art archaeologists have discovered in synagogues across the land of Israel. He divides the art into two phases. The first phase belongs to the earlier type of synagogue, the Galilean basilica, which primarily displayed relief art on the outside of the synagogue, but had no artwork inside the building. The second phase occurs in the later synagogues and primarily consists of mosaic pavements. Ovadiah discusses the different types of mosaics and analyzes the subject matter of their representations.

The continual subtext of Ovadiah's discussion, however, is that none of these images have any symbolic meaning; they serve as decoration only. Once or twice Ovadiah suggests that a single image in a particular synagogue probably is an important symbol, but he closes his essay by making it clear that "The Jewish creative spirit in ancient times can be seen in religious law...but not in plastic arts or in aesthetic form."[32]

J. R. Branham's essay, "Vicarious Sacrality: Temple Space in Ancient Synagogues," looks at the ambiguous relationship between the Palestinian synagogues and the destroyed Jerusalem Temple. Drawing theories of sacred space from M. Eliade and J. Z. Smith, as well as theories of relationships from R. Girard, J. Neusner, and J. Derrida, Branham brings a nuanced approach to the analysis of the synagogue's link to the Temple. Branham brings in issues of orientation (especially east-facing orientation discussed by D. Amit earlier), *soragim* (barriers) in both the Temple and in synagogues, and artistic representations of the Torah ark/Temple sanctuary found in synagogue mosaic floors. In doing so, she shows how the synagogue attempts to imitate the Temple, even as it tries to establish it own identity. This identity is one in which the synagogue is far less sacred than the Temple, but in the latter's absence becomes the most sacred area remaining to Judaism.

One area of symbolic interpretation of synagogue art that has survived the past decades is that of the reredos at the Dura Europos synagogue. The reredos—the synagogue's central painting—acquired a messianic interpretation quite early in the history of its scholarship and has retained champions of that interpretation throughout all succeeding decades. P. V. M. Flesher's essay, "Rereading the Reredos: David, Orpheus, and Messianism in the Dura Europos Synagogue," launches a full-scale assault on that interpretation. He starts by reporting the results of a computer-assisted analysis of the David image and surrounding figures. The analysis reveals that David is depicted as a shepherd king and not as Orpheus. Flesher then questions the link between Orpheus, Orphism, and messianism, ultimately showing that Orpheus and

[32] Ovadiah, p. 316.

Orphism have no messianic beliefs. He concludes by arguing that none of the other Dura paintings require a messianic interpretation, thus putting the lie to the notion that Dura Judaism was infused with messianism.

At first hearing, this sounds as if Flesher sides with Ovadiah in denying that art has symbolic value. Actually, the opposite is the case. Flesher shows that the particular symbolic meaning of messiah and messianism does not appear in these images. But in fact he uses other interpretations of the symbolism to help establish that. Flesher's point is that symbolic interpretations attached to images must be supported by those images, not forced onto them.

This group of essays ends with a second by A. Ovadiah, "The Mosaic Workshop of Gaza in Christian Antiquity." Here Ovadiah takes up the question of how did the mosaic pavements of the synagogues get made? He answers it, at least for a couple of synagogues, by showing that at one time the city of Gaza had a workshop of mosaic artists. These were artists for hire and worked for anyone who paid them. Thus, Ovadiah can show that the same team constructed mosaics in two synagogues and in two churches in the Gaza area.

VI. PUBLIC STRUCTURES AND JEWISH COMMUNITIES IN THE GOLAN HEIGHTS

The final section of this collection on the early synagogue consists of a single essay on the evidence for Jewish communities in Late Antiquity on the Golan Heights. Long considered by most archaeologists as of secondary importance next to the Galilee, the Golan actually contains extensive remains of Jewish settlement from the centuries prior to Islam. Dan Urman, the author, draws upon the surveys and excavations of his years of involvement in Golan archaeology, as well as studies by other archaeologists, to provide the fullest picture to date of Jews in the Golan. The body of the article contains descriptions of sixty-five sites, with attention to the history of scholarly investigation, the evidence for Jewish occupation, and the conclusions that can be drawn. Urman shows that most of the evidence has yet to receive anything but the most superficial analysis. In fact, most of the Golan Jewish settlements of Late Antiquity still lack even preliminary excavations. Whereas other scholars have counted less than two dozen Jewish public structures, Urman brings previously unpublished evidence of over twice that many. In consequence, he argues, any sweeping conclusions about the chronology of Jewish habitation in the Golan or about the typology of their public structures relies more on imagination than on hard data.

In a sense, Urman's article on the Golan presents a microcosm of this collection as a whole. It reaches back to evidence about ancient synagogues and Jewish public structures that has been known to us for a century while engaging in the current debate about the interpretation of all the evidence concerning Jewish settlement. In the same way, the essays throughout these two volumes look at both old and newly discovered data concerning the origins, history, and nature of the early synagogue, as well as for interpreting its artistic and architectural character. By fresh analysis, inclusion of new material, and reevaluation of information long known to the scholarly community, the essays in this collection work towards an interpretation of the early centuries of the synagogue's existence. Through careful selection and juxtaposition of articles, the editors have aimed to provide scholars with both an understanding of the present debates concerning the ancient synagogue and a sense of the direction towards which the scholarly analysis of the ancient synagogue is heading.

SECTION I

THE ORIGINS OF ANCIENT SYNAGOGUES

EGYPT AND THE RISE OF THE SYNAGOGUE

J. GWYN GRIFFITHS*

While several historians regard the origins of the synagogue as a matter shrouded in obscurity and uncertainty, preference has often been given to the Babylonian hypothesis. In the predicament of exile, worship at the Temple in Jerusalem was no longer possible—indeed the First Temple was destroyed in 586 BC—and it has been surmised that the exiled Jews in Babylon made up for this grave loss by holding local gatherings of the people in which prayers were offered and psalms were sung.

S. W. Baron in his great *Social and Religious History of the Jews* (vol. 1, p. 126) is hesitant about the nature of these public gatherings, saying that "all statements about these public gatherings are made here with considerable diffidence, since little is known about what went on." Yet his next sentence has a note of certainty: "But it seems certain that they soon gave rise to the institution which became the foundation of Jewish life in the Diaspora—the synagogue." The prophets of the exile certainly bore witness to spiritual vitality; and Ezekiel (11:16) mentions a divine claim relating to the Jews of the Diaspora: *I have been for a while a sanctuary to them in the countries where they have gone.*[1] Whereas the Talmud applies these words to the existence of the synagogue in Babylonia, there is no precise reference here to an institution, only an assurance of divine solace. Still less convincing are the allusions by Ezekiel (8:1; 14:1; 20:1) to the elders who are sitting with him.[2] These allusions imply a practice of consultation followed by the prophet, but there is no suggestion of an institution. If the *Novelle* called the Book of Tobit is a product of the Babylonian Diaspora in the early second century BC, it is noteworthy that Tobit, although a deeply religious man, is never said to go to a synagogue.[3]

In the Book of Isaiah, on the other hand, it is maintained (19:19) that *in that day there shall be an altar to the Lord in the midst of the land of Egypt.* This comes at the end of a long doom oracle against Egypt. We are told that there will be five cities in Egypt where people will speak Hebrew and

* This essay was originally published in *Journal of Theological Studies* 38, no. 1 (1987): 1-15. It is reprinted by the permission of Oxford University Press.

[1] Cf. the versions of RSV and NEB.

[2] Cf. L. Rabinowitz in *EJ*, vol. 15, p. 580.

[3] Nor does the book mention the Sabbath. Cf. R. H. Pfeiffer, *History of New Testament Times* (New York, 1949), 281.

profess loyalty to Yahweh. We are thus reminded that the Jewish Diaspora concerned not only Babylonia, but also Egypt, as well as other areas. In Egypt the Diaspora dates from at least the sixth century BC. The words we have quoted probably derive from the post-exilic era. According to Josephus they were invoked by the Jewish priest Onias IV in support of his project, in about 160 BC, to build a temple at Leontopolis (Tell el-Yahudiya) in the Delta.[4] The word 'altar' (מִזְבֵּחַ) certainly implies sacrifices, and also, therefore, a temple. Since sacrifices were forbidden outside Israel (Deut. 12:13-14; cf. Tobit 1:4, *Jerusalem...the one place of sacrifice*), Onias was challenging the sacred law on this point in his erection of a Jewish temple in Egypt. Unlike the temple, the synagogue did not offer sacrifices, and to us its code of ritual seems so much simpler and more attractive in this matter. I recall one of my teachers, Theodore H. Robinson, once remarking that if we were enabled to be transported back in time to visit the temple in Jerusalem, our first reaction would be one of shock at finding that it appeared to us more like a slaughterhouse or abattoir than a temple. To a great extent the same was true of Egyptian temples, as the massive altars in the open courts testify. As for the Jewish presence in Egypt, it was of course the colony in Elephantine that was the important fact in the early part of the first millennium BC. There is firm evidence that they built a temple (אגורא) of Yahweh (in the form Yah or Yaho). This was again in defiance or ignorance of the Deuteronomic rule. It was a temple used for sacrifices, and was not therefore a form of synagogue.[5] At the same time, it is relevant to our purpose to note that a measure of syncretism was practiced there. Deities other than Yahweh were recognized, and there are some clear signs of the influence of Egyptian religion.[6]

THE EARLIEST SYNAGOGUES

It is in the third century BC that the synagogue emerges in Egypt with full and clear evidence in the archaeological and epigraphic record which includes details of date. A limestone slab now in the Alexandrian Museum bears an inscription which must have been displayed in the synagogue whose foundation it mentions. It opens with the words IN HONOUR OF KING PTOLEMY

---

[4] Hengel, *Hellenism*, vol. 1, p. 16, thinks that 'Thmuis in the South' was perhaps the location of the temple mentioned in Isa. 19:19. There was one town of this name in the Eastern Delta, and another in Upper Egypt near Edfu.

[5] Emil G. Kraeling, *The Brooklyn Museum Aramaic Papyri* (New Haven, 1953), p. 100; cf. B. Porten, *Archives from Elephantine* (Berkeley, 1968), pp. 105-186, esp. 109-113, and in *Cambridge History of Judaism*, vol. 1 (1984), pp. 385-93.

[6] Cf. Morton Smith in *Cambridge History of Judaism*, vol. 1 (1984), pp. 226-7 and p. 224 on the girl named Isiwer ('Great is Isis'); Ronald Williams in *The Legacy of Egypt*, J. R. Harris, ed., 2nd. ed. (Oxford, 1971), p. 261.

AND OF QUEEN BERENICÊ, HIS SISTER AND WIFE, AND THEIR CHILDREN, an allusion that pinpoints the reign of Ptolemy III Euergetes (246-221 BC). The inscription ends with the brief statement that the Jews founded this synagogue (the verb here must be understood), for which the term προσευχή is used. The word means 'prayer' and is used in the Septuagint (Isa. 56: 7) of the Temple as a 'House of Prayer' (οἶκος τῆς προσευχῆς). But now in this occurrence and in many others it means 'Place of Prayer,' of a sanctuary or chapel in which prayer was offered. This 'Place of Prayer' was built at Schedia, near the modern Kôm el-Gize, some 20 miles from Alexandria. Schedia had some commercial importance, and Jews were there supervisors of dues relating to the Nile and canals. What strikes us about the opening phrase of the inscription is the honour paid by the Jews of the synagogue to the reigning Ptolemy and his wife. Was it in any sense an honour that implied recognition of the divinity which the Ptolemies claimed and therefore challenged the essence of Jewish religion? The preposition ὑπέρ is used in the opening phrase—'for' or 'on behalf of.' Perhaps 'in honour of' is too strong a translation. It is fair to note, at any rate, that expressions plainly denoting divinity, such as θεοὶ ἀδελφοί, 'Brother-and-Sister Deities,' are conspicuous by their absence, and here I am including the many other inscriptions relating to synagogues in Egypt. Certainly there is deference to the reigning Ptolemies, but it does not amount to worship.[7] In the case of Schedia the deference may be a measure of gratitude for advantages enjoyed by the Jewish community there.

From the same reign in the third century comes the dedication of a synagogue in Arsinoë-Crocodilopolis, a city of some importance in the Fayûm. The opening formula is exactly the same as in the inscription from Schedia, which D. M. Lewis published as No. 1440 in his "Appendix on Inscriptions" in the third volume of the *Corpus Papyrorum Judaicarum* [=*CPJ*] edited by V. A. Tcherikover and A. Fuks (1964); the dedication from Arsinoë-Crocodilopolis (No. 1532A in the same volume) is naturally linked by Lewis with that from Schedia: "the text joins 1440 as the earliest known synagogue inscriptions." Both inscriptions used the term προσευχή for 'synagogue.' That there was a synagogue at Arsinoë-Crocodilopolis is also confirmed by a land-survey made there in the second century (*CPJ* i. 134 = P. Tebt. 86), although we cannot be sure that the reference there is to the same synagogue; indeed two synagogues (one a προσευχή, the other an εὐχεῖον) are located in the town in a papyrus of AD 113 (*CPJ* ii. 432). What is significant about the inscription from the third century BC is that it estab-

[7] Fraser, *Alexandria*, vol. 1, p. 116, speaks of "a diluted form of devotion" and on p. 283 of "limited recognition." The cult-title 'Benefactors' (Εὐεργέται) does occur in two inscriptions but without the normal concomitant 'Gods' (θεοί).

lishes the existence of a synagogue in the Fayûm at an early date, and this in a community far removed from Alexandria.

Inscriptions referring to synagogues in Egypt multiply in the second century BC and in the following century. The second century included the erection of the temple of Onias IV, to which we have already referred. Since this was planned on the lines of the Jerusalem Temple, it stands severely outside the orbit of the synagogues in Egypt. At the same time it is a mark of the vitality of Jewish religious activity in Lower Egypt; and the many synagogues attested in the country by the end of the first century AD are in localities of Lower Egypt and the Fayûm.[8] In the second century BC these institutions began to appear in other countries, notably in Syria at Antioch[9] and in the Aegean at Delos.[10] It was not until the first century AD or perhaps a little before it that the first synagogue is attested in Palestine.[11]

Literary evidence supplements the picture for Egypt. In an account of the desecration of synagogues in Alexandria in AD 38 Philo (*Legat.* 20.132) states that they were numerous in each section of the city. The official sections were five in number, so that a large total is suggested.

At this point we need to look at some puzzling features of the terminology in use. The word synagogue is in origin a Greek word, and the first meaning of συναγωγή is a gathering of persons, whether of individuals or of a public assembly. In this wide sense it appears first in Egypt in the second century BC, but with a non-Jewish reference (of Idumaeans at Memphis, *OGIS* 737.1). In the Septuagint (Exod. 12:3) it is used of the whole congregation of Israel. Clearly it has a fairly wide scope of meaning, and the term προσευχή, 'place of prayer,' is much more specific; it is the term preferred by Philo, although he uses also both συναγωγή and συναγώγιον (see Leisegang's Index). Προσευχή is certainly the normal term used in the inscriptions and papyri; only in one papyrus is the word εὐχεῖον used, and that also means 'place of prayer.'[12] In Emil Schürer's *History*, as revised by Vermes, Millar, and Black (Schürer, vol. 2, pp. 439-40), it is stated that "in the older linguistic usage of the Diaspora, συναγωγή does not yet have this meaning (of the building). Where it appears at all, it signifies 'the congregation,' while the regular expression for the meeting-house is προσευχή." By the first century AD, of course, the New Testament often uses συναγωγή of the meeting-house (Schürer, vol. 2, p. 439 n. 60). The question arises as to

---

[8] *CPJ*, vol. 1, p. 8. Schürer, vol. 2, p. 425, note 5.

[9] Krauss, p. 63.

[10] Sukenik, *ASPG*, pp. 1 & 40; A. Plassart in *Mélanges Holleaux* (Paris, 1913), pp. 201-15; Georges Daux in *BCH* 87 (1963): 689-878, esp. 873-4.

[11] Sukenik, *ASPG*, pp. 69ff. on that at the Ophel in eastern Jerusalem. Cf. Y. Yadin, *Masada* (London, 1966), p. 185 on the synagogue there, and the doubts of J. Gutmann in *Arch. Anz.* lxxxvii (1972), p. 40 n. 18.

[12] *CPJ*, vol. 2, no. 432 (Arsinoë); cf. vol. 1, no. 8.

what terms were used in Hebrew. The Septuagint used the word συναγωγή to translate the Hebrew עֵדָה, of the community assembled, but many of these allusions may naturally long antedate the emergence of the synagogue. A phrase בֵּית הָעָם, 'house of the people,' occurs in Jeremiah's account (39:8) of the fall of Jerusalem, but Rudolph's emendation to a plural is widely accepted,[13] so that the reference is not to any institutional building, but simply to the houses of the people. כְּנֶסֶת (Aram. כְּנִשְׁתָּא) or בֵּית כְּנֶסֶת is the word eventually used in Hebrew for 'synagogue,' with the sense of 'House of Assembly,' while the meaning 'House of Prayer' is conveyed by בֵּית תְּפִלָּה, a phrase adapted from Isa. 56:7. A term used in the wisdom of Ben Sira has been not unnaturally invoked. The author makes an appeal to the unlearned:

> Draw near to me, you who need instruction,
> And lodge in my house of learning.
>
> Ben Sira 51:23

For the last phrase the Greek has ἐν οἴκῳ παιδείας the original Hebrew בְּבֵית מִדְרָשִׁי. This book was probably written in Palestine in the early part of the second century BC, and rendered into Greek at Alexandria later in the century; and it is not surprising that an allusion to the teaching activity of the synagogue has been seen here.[14]

While the educational role of the synagogue was of basic importance, the Jews evolved a system of education independently of it. The truth is that the early synagogue fulfilled many various roles, though not of equal significance. In addition to being a home of prayer and study, it could serve social and political aims, acting as a public assembly-room, a judicial tribunal, a lodging-place, an advisory legal office or information centre, and a place of asylum.[15] Yet the two paramount purposes were worship and study, as allusions in both Philo and Josephus make clear. Philo asks in his *Life of Moses* (2.216):

> What are our houses of prayer (προσευκτήρια) throughout the cities but schools (διδασκαλεῖα) of prudence and courage...?

Josephus tells us that the weekly assembly is devoted to "the learning of our customs and Law" (*Antiq.* 16.43). He also says that Moses established the Law to be the most excellent and essential form of study (*Contra Apionem*, 3.175; cf. *Antiq.* 4.12). His emphasis is thus on the Torah as a παίδευμα, and on the educational function of the synagogue.

---

[13] Nötscher, *Jeremias*, p. 277; J. Bright, *Jeremiah* (New York: Doubleday, 1965), p. 240.
[14] Hengel, *Hellenism*, vol. 1, p. 132 and vol. 2, p. 54, n. 165; Schürer, vol. 2, p. 419, n. 31.
[15] *CPJ*, vol. 1, no. 8.

By today a minority of scholars have recognized the evident likelihood that the synagogue had its origin in Egypt. Thus Bo Reicke, a New Testament scholar, has stated that "essentially, then, the Jewish synagogue system can be derived from Ptolemaic Egypt, where the Hel lenistic associations with their meeting places influenced its development."[16] A Semitic scholar, B. J. Roberts, has similarly maintained that "it is no accident, to my mind, that it is in Egypt, and in a Hellenistic background, that we find the remains of the oldest synagogue among the Jews, for in its essence, the synagogue is a school, and an institution that belongs more to the Greek ideal than the Jewish."[17] It will be observed that both these scholars, while accepting an origin in Egypt, assume that the only impetus derived from Egypt was the Greek culture of its Ptolemaic rulers. The possibility of an Egyptian influence is not even considered.

Let us take an instance where the ignoring of the Egyptian dimension (perhaps indeed the ignorance of it) seems quite startling. Bo Reicke refers specifically, in the statement quoted above, to the influence of the 'Hellenistic associations.'[18] These were undoubtedly influential; and the Essene community in Jewish Palestine provides an example on the Hellenistic model, with the הַיַּחַד corresponding to the Greek τὸ κοινόν.[19] But in Graeco-Roman Egypt associations of worshippers were extremely popular, and they have been abundantly documented for Egyptian religious contexts.[20] If religion was the initial bond, there were many social implications in the manner of friendly societies, and allusions are made to occasions of convivial hilarity, especially under the auspices of Isis and Sarapis. With the spread of the Egyptian cults outside Egypt, these religious clubs remained an attractive feature of the privileges extended to believers.[21] Within Egypt the Greek and Egyptian traditions doubtless made some impact on each other, and both can be assumed to have influenced Jewish practices in this matter in the evolution of the synagogue. Some antecedents in the

---

[16] Reicke, *New Testament*, pp. 119-20.

[17] Bleddyn J. Roberts, in an essay on "Hellenism and Judaism" in *Cefndir y Testament Newydd*, ed. J. Gwyn Griffiths (Llandysul, 1966), pp. 31-2 (here translated from the Welsh).

[18] He does note (Reicke, *New Testament*, p. 120) that meetings of associations sometimes occurred in temples in Egypt.

[19] Hengel, *Hellenism*, vol. 1, p. 244. For the general rights of association accorded to Jews under Roman law see Jean Juster, *Les Juifs dans l'Empire Romain* (New York, 1914), vol. 1, pp. 413ff.

[20] Mariano San Nicolò, *Ägyptisches Vereinswesen zur Zeit der Ptolemäer und Römer*, 2 vols. (Munich, 1913-15); A. E. R. Boak, in *TAPA* 68 (1937): 212-22; W. Erichsen, *Die Satzungen einer ägyptischen Kultgenossenschaft aus der Ptolemäer-zeit* (Copenhagen, 1959); A. F. Shore, in *B. M. Quarterly* 36 (1971): 16-19; Cenival, *Associations*.

[21] J. Leclant, in *BIFAO* 55 (1955): 178; K. Parlasca, *Die römischen Mosaiken in Deutschalnd* (Berlin, 1959), pp. 56-7; J. Gwyn Griffiths, "The Isiac Jug from Southwark," *JEA* 59 (1973): 233-6.

Pharaonic era have been adduced by Bruyère[22] and Lüddeckens,[23] both relying mainly on evidence from Deir el-Medinah, where the latter (p. 197) finds something rather more expansive in the form of a 'Dorfgemeinschaft.'

Any suggestion that the Jewish communities may have been influenced by Egyptian practices must face up to the linguistic situation and also the question of psychological attitudes. At first sight the linguistic evidence suggests strongly that any non-Jewish influence on the development of the synagogue must have come from the development of Greek culture in Egypt. The Greek nomenclature of the synagogue suggests this, whether in the term προσευχή or εὐχεῖον, or in συναγωγή itself. It is likely that Josephus[24] (*Antiq.* 16.6.2 [164], Loeb, 8 (1963), p. 272) once quotes the term σαββατεῖον to mean 'synagogue,' and that is of course of Hebrew origin. The Egyptians used a wealth of words to denote temples and parts of temples, as well as sanctuaries and chapels. Indeed the *Wörterbuch* (vi. 154) lists twenty-three Egyptian expressions under 'Tempel,' and now we have an admirably detailed analysis of them.[25] Perhaps the most striking of these expressions is *Horizon of Eternity*, *ꜣḫt (nt) nḥḥ* (*Wb.* i. 17. 19); and perhaps the closest to προσευχή is *pr dwꜣt*, the *House of the Morning*, possibly the *House of Morning Worship* in view of the likely etymological connection between the words *dwꜣ* for 'morning' and 'adoration.'[26] Ritually it was a place of purification, and Faulkner (*Dict* 90) renders it simply as 'robing-room.' We are told in the Piankhi Stela that the King, after taking over every important cult-centre, first enacted rites of purification in the *per-dwat* and then made offerings in the *ḥwt-nṯr*, *the House of the God*, a very common word for 'temple.'[27] In the Ptolemaic era the *per-dwat* was a small room placed either in the forecourt of the temple, as in Philae, or in the vestibule of the main hall, as at Edfu.[28] This room, however, was but a minor adjunct of the temple and not important enough to be considered as a centre of religious influence. Much more important was another temple ad-

---

22 *Mert Seger* (MIFAO 58, Cairo, 1930), pp. 57, 85-6. Cf. Cenival, *Associations*, p. 141, who sees a college of priests acting there; see also the reservations of Michel Muszynski in *Or. Lov. Per.* 8 (1977): 159 n. 60.

23 In *Z. für Religions- und Geistesgeschichte* 20 (1968): 193-211. More narrowly defined was the 'gang' of workmen, on which see J. F. Borghouts in *Gleanings from Deir el-Medina*, ed. R. J. Demarée and Jac J. Janssen (Leiden, 1982), pp. 71ff.

24 Quoting a decree of Augustus. For the use of συναγωγή of Greek cultic societies, see Schürer, vol. 2, pp. 429-30.

25 Spencer, *Temple*.

26 *Wb.* v. 426; Blackman, in *JEA* 5 (1918):153-4.

27 *Urk.* iii. 35.6-9; cf. Spencer, *Temple*, p. 20.

28 Bonnet, *RÄRG*, p. 634, citing Kees; Fairman, *Worship and Festivals* (1954), plan opp. p. 168; Sylvie Cauville, *Edfou* (1984), plan 2; cf. also Kees, *Götterglaube*, pp. 100-1. For the frequent use of *pr* in the names of local temples see *Lexikon der Ägyptologie* (=*LÄ*), iv (1982), 929-35.

junct, the Per Ankh, the 'House of Life,' and although its name has no parallel in the expressions used for the synagogue, its spiritual significance, as we shall see, provides a parallel of basic importance.

It seems likely that the Jewish communities in Egypt in the Ptolemaic era used Greek for the most part both in private conversation and in public affairs, unlike the earlier settlement in Elephantine, where Aramaic was spoken and written. One has to be cautious, admittedly, about the fact that the synagogal inscriptions are almost all in Greek. This was, after all, the official language of the ruling authorities and dedications in synagogues show a desire, as we have seen, to maintain an attitude of respect to them. The language of official inscriptions can, however, be misleading. In Roman Britain nearly all the inscriptions are in Latin, but it would be foolish to assume that most of the people spoke Latin; the great majority must have spoken a Celtic language. One might compare the use of Latin on tombstones in several countries long after Latin had ceased to be spoken.[29] Nevertheless it was in Alexandria that the Old Testament was translated into the Greek of the Septuagint, and by the late third century BC the Pentateuch had already been translated.[30] While some papyri of uncertain date have preserved fragments of Hebrew prayers, and that language may have been used for parts of the synagogue service in the early Ptolemaic period, the translation of the scriptures into Greek was probably in response to an urgent need.[31] As for the Jewish attitude to the Egyptian language, it is not easy to invoke evidence of either interest or antipathy in terms of daily contact. Sometimes Egyptian names were taken by Jews, but it has been maintained that there is little evidence of their learning Egyptian in its Demotic form.[32] In literary terms this judgment is certainly not acceptable. There are aspects of the work of Ben Sira and of the Wisdom of Solomon that betray a clear impress of Egyptian influence from the direction both of the Wisdom Literature and of the Isis-cult. Nor should it be forgotten, as far as public recognition was concerned, that the Egyptian language was accorded a degree of official status, as in the trilingual decrees of Canopus (238 BC) and Memphis (196 BC), where Egyptian is represented in two of the three forms. If Greek was dominant in Alexandria, Egyptian prevailed in the *chôra* and was probably spoken there even by the Jewish population, since it was the "general language of the entire country around them."[33]

---

[29] Smallwood, p. 133.

[30] Fraser, *Alexandria*, vol. 1, p. 690.

[31] Fraser, *Alexandria*, vol. 1, p. 284; vol. 2, p. 443 n. 777.

[32] M. Hengel, *Juden, Griechen und Barbaren* (Stuttgart, 1976), p. 127.

[33] *CPJ*, vol. 1, no. 44.

STRUCTURE AND FUNCTIONS

The inscriptions from Egypt tell us very little about the structure and material content of the synagogue buildings. A dedication from Athribis (Benha) states that a man named Hermias and his wife Philotera and their children gave "this ἐξέδρα for the προσευχή." D. M. Lewis (in *CPJ*, No. 1444, p. 143) translates ἐξέδρα as "this place for sitting" without further specifics. He rejects the view of Krauss (Krauss, p. 349) that it means a row of columns outside the principal building; but this view would be perfectly feasible if it is taken to include seating facilities near the columns.[34] Goodenough made the attractive suggestion that the reference was to the bench which eventually became a prominent feature of synagogues; or to the special seat called the 'Seat of Moses,' the throne of the chief man in the group.[35] A possible objection is that ἐξέδρα often means 'an outside seat' ('siège extérieur,' D.-S.); but an allusion to the 'benches' is suitable in that these, at any rate at a later stage, were located on the sides of the synagogue and not in the centre. as is clear in the remains of the synagogue at Capernaum (Kefar Nahum; cf. Mark 1:21), a building erected in the late second century AD.[36] Here the main hall is in the form of a basilica with colonnades; the base of the triangular front gable is arched in Syrian style, and the general plan shows Roman influence, as do the colonnades.[37] It is not surprising that synagogues in different areas show the influence of local traditions. The architectural evidence for the early phases in Egypt is very sparse, but there is one pointed reference to the building of a pylon. It is in an inscription from Xenephyris (Kôm el-Akhdar), 20 km. south-west of Damanhur, and states that *in honour of Ptolemy and Queen Cleopatra, his sister and wife, the Jews from Xenephyris* (have dedicated) *the pylon of the synagogue, the leaders being Theodorus and Achillion.*[38] The date is in the reign of Ptolemy VII Euergetes II (145-117 BC) and the leaders (προστάται) are those of the synagogue. There is no mistaking the distinctively Egyptian reference of the pylon,[39] the massive entrance to a temple with its two flanking towers, a system developed in the New Kingdom. 'Pylon' is in

---

[34] Cf. Daremberg-Saglio, *Dict.*, vol. 2 (1892), p. 881, quoting Vitruvius on the *exedra amplissima cum sedibus* which he advocated for the *palaestra*.

[35] Goodenough, vol. 2, p. 85.

[36] Sukenik, *ASPG*, pl. IVa.; Schürer, vol. 2, p. 442, n. 67. S. Loffreda, *A Visit to Capharnaum*, 7th ed. (Jerusalem, 1980), p. 49 (a date in the fourth of fifth century AD).

[37] Cf. M. Avi-Yonah, "Capernaum," *EJ*, vol. 5, pp. 136-9; Sukenik, *ASPG*, Pl. 1b (north colonnade).

[38] Frey, vol. 2, p. 367, no. 1441; D. M. Lewis, in *CPJ*, no. 1441.

[39] Fraser, *Alexandria*, vol. 2, p. 443 n. 773 (ad fin.). In the Ptolemaic era pylons did not always have the double flanking tower; cf. the pylon of Ptolemy III Euergetes I at Karnak in Bevan, *Egypt*, p. 215, fig. 35. See further Brigitte Jaroš-Deckert, in *LÄ* vol. 4 (1982), pp. 1202-5, esp. 1202.

origin a Greek word meaning 'gate way'; the Egyptian term was *Bekhent* (*Wb.* i.471.9). It would be a mistake, at the same time, to imagine the synagogue at Xenephyris in the Western Delta as a grandiose edifice. Probably the whole building, including the pylon, was of modest proportions; and the pylon may well have been a single tower. The great synagogue at Alexandria, as portrayed in the Jerusalem Talmud,[40] is not credited with a pylon, but it had a double colonnade within a basilica-type hall, and it is possible that this type was developed first in Egypt.[41]

If we turn from architecture to functions, we find that one of these derives directly from the tradition of the Egyptian temple. It was the right of asylum, bestowed in particular cases and perhaps transferred from local native temples.[42] The concept of asylum in a sacred place was well known to the religious traditions of Israel, Greece, and Egypt, and when we are dealing with religion in Egypt it is legitimate to assume that Egyptian customs are influential. In Egyptian belief the god was deemed to be supreme in his own temple, so that refuge to transgressors was warranted in the temple and its surroundings.[43] Without deleting the idea *in toto,* the Ptolemies insisted on restricting it to temples which received specific authority,[44] and they did this with some synagogues.[45]

Whatever the variety of functions, "their real purpose...was to serve as places where the people could meet for instruction and prayer."[46] Much has been written about the impact of Greek culture on Judaism, and not least in Egypt; yet it is remarkable that this dual basic purpose, combining worship and instruction, was not fully practised by any Greek institution. Hellenization was conveyed most vigorously through the media of the school and the gymnasium.[47] While both these institutions were much devoted to instruction, neither was regarded primarily as a place of worship.

---

[40] Goodenough, vol. 2, pp. 85-6; for its form as a basilica see Schürer, vol. 2, p. 443.

[41] Goodenough, vol. 2, p. 85.

[42] *CPJ*, vol. 1, no. 8; Fraser, *Alexandria*, vol. 1, p. 283, of Euergetes II; also vol. 2, p. 441 n. 766 (viii) and p. 442 n. 772 on *CIJ* 1449=Wilcken, *Chrest.* 54=*SB* 880, from an unknown site in Lower Egypt, an inscr. which "contains a renewal of an old grant of asylum," the king being probably Euergetes II, with the formula ending in the words τὴν προσευχὴν ἄσυλον. See also D. M. Lewis, in *CPJ* 144, No. 1449, who tends to accept Wilcken's view that the Latin renewal of the right relates to AD 270 and to Zenobia of Palmyra and her son.

[43] Erman, *Religion der Ägypter* (Berlin, 1934), pp. 359-60.

[44] E.g. the temple of Isis in Ptolemäis in 75 BC: see Bevan, *Egypt* p. 106; cf. H. I. Bell, *Cults and Creeds in Graeco-Roman Egypt* (Liverpool, 1953), pp. 52 and 54.

[45] Fraser, *Alexandria*, vol. 1, p. 283: "at least one, and probably more." He adds: "it may be chance that we know of no other foreign cult similarly respected." Cf. *CPJ* vol. 1, no. 8: "Ptolemaic kings granted to some synagogues the same right of asylum as was commonly granted to Egyptian temples."

[46] Schürer, vol. 2, p. 447.

[47] Hengel, *Hellenism*, vol. 1, pp. 65-83 (concerned mainly with Palestine). On "School and Synagogue" in Jewish tradition, see Schürer, vol. 2, pp. 415-63.

The Greek elementary school catered for children between seven and fourteen; then followed the ephebate and training in the gymnasium; and the latter was "dominated above all by physical exercise and also a degree of military training."[48] In all this the religious element was secondary. Literary training of course included the study of Homer, especially of the *Iliad,* but this did not have much to do with contemporary religion in any vital sense. Hermes and Heracles figure as the protective gods of the gymnasium, and there are allusions to sacrifices offered and to religious dedications. Essentially the gymnasium was a sports ground with a running track and also, quite often, a παλαίστρα, a site for wrestling. Literary and philosophical discussions took place, but they were peripheral to the main business, which was the pursuit of athletics.

Yet in Egypt the Jews also encountered a tradition which differed basically from that of the Greeks. In Alexandria and in the *chôra* the Egyptians associated education with the temples, and this was a long-standing tradition, although scribal schools had been attached also to the royal court and its administrative departments.[49] Instruction and worship were especially combined in the institution called the Per Ankh, 'the House of Life,' an adjunct of the temple which functioned both as a library and as a centre of special rites. It seems that the library was devoted to religious knowledge, but its scope included wider fields as well.[50] Questions of cult and ritual were dealt with, so that a spiritual ministry in a comprehensive sense was conducted by the priestly leaders. Copies of the Book of the Dead were probably produced there, and an Osirian ritual which bestowed life in the afterworld was enacted in the Per Ankh.[51] Of basic import in such rites was the reading of sacred texts, an activity prominent too in the Mystery cult attached to Isis; even in Cenchreae, the harbour of Corinth, in the second century AD the Isiac priest was obliged to read from a sacred Egyptian text

---

[48] Hengel, *Hellenism*, vol. 1, p. 66.

[49] A. Erman and H. Ranke, tr. C. Mathieu, *La Civilisation Égyptienne* (Paris, 1963), pp. 420ff.; H. Kees, *Kulturgeschichte: Ägypten* (Munich, 1933), p. 282. Hengel, *Hellenism*, vol. 1, p. 78, rightly points to the cultural and national importance of the Egyptian temples in the Hellenistic period.

[50] Theology, hymnology, magic, medicine, astronomy, and oneiromancy were among the subjects represented. See H. Brunner, *Altägyptische Erziehung* (Wiesbaden, 1957), p. 28; also Bunner in *LÄ* vol. 2 (1977), pp. 22-7; J.-C. Goyon, *Confirmation du pouvoir royal au nouvel an* (Cairo, 1972), pp. 38-41.

[51] Ph. Derchain, *Le Papyrus Salt 825* (Brussels, 1965), vol. 1, pp. 48ff. This papyrus is probably of early Ptolemaic date. Gardiner, in *JEA* 24 (1938): 157-79, had not been able to trace this activity; after a massive *Materialsammlung* he gave it the much too narrow meaning of 'scriptorium.' See further Serge Sauneron, tr. A. Morrissett, *The Priests of Ancient Egypt* (London, 1960), pp. 135-9; V. Wessetzky, "Die ägyptische Tempelbibliothek," in *Ausgewälte Schriften* (Budapest, 1981), pp. 147-52. In Isiac temples crypts were probably used to store books; see my *Apuleius of Madauros, The Isis-Book* (Leiden, 1975), pp. 284-5.

written in hieroglyphs or in hieratic.[52] Readings from scripture became a regular part of the synagogue service also; and in a more general sense the combination of worship and instruction points to an evident affinity between Egyptian and Jewish practice in these institutions. It is an affinity which the Greek school and gymnasium does not provide.

To demonstrate an Egyptian influence in this respect is naturally not an easy task. We cannot be sure what went on in the early synagogues. We have seen that both Philo and Josephus lay emphasis on the element of instruction relating to the Torah. Philo must have been an ardent member of a synagogue in Alexandria, and it is not surprising that the suggestion has been made that the type of sophisticated discussion found in his works, especially his allegorizing mode of interpreting the Old Testament, characterized the synagogues of his day in Egypt.[53] Goodenough's ambitious study, *Jewish Symbols in the Greco-Roman Period,* could be adduced in support of the suggestion, but several other scholars demur to the idea that Philo's approach was in any way typical of 'normative Judaism.'[54] It is true that be was a prominent leader of Alexandrian Jews, and his ideas must have made some impact on them. His method of allegorizing was drawn, in the main, from Platonism but he sometimes dealt with Egyptian themes.[55] Allegoristic was a common feature of Egyptian religious thought, its principal tool being etymology.[56] That is true also of Philo's approach, but he doubtless followed Greek practice in the matter. Indeed he cheerfully uses Greek etymologies to explain names such as Moses (=Νοῦς Τέλειος, Perfect Mind) and Pharaoh (=Νοῦς Ὑπέραυχος, Arrogant Mind).[57] His allegorical interpretation of the High Priest's Vestments may echo a tradition about Isis and Osiris (Goodenough, vol. 4, p. 208). It has been suggested that ideas found in Philo and Josephus may reflect a catechism used in the synagogue reception of proselytes; it is at any rate clear that an ethical tradition was evolved which may well have been the result of synagogue worship and study, since some of the offences mentioned, notably abortion and the exposing of children at birth, are not explicitly condemned in the Old

52 Apuleius, *Metam.* II. 22; cf. my remarks ad loc., p. 285.

53 Roberts, "Hellenism," pp. 31-32.

54 Nock, *Essays*, vol. 1, p. 464 (on a 'Philonic group'), though in vol. 2, p. 878 he accepts that there was no rigid norm under Rabbinic control. Cf. P. M. Fraser, in *JEA* 43 (1957): 103-4; Morton Smith, in *JBL* 86 (1967): 53-68, esp. 59; W. D. Davies, *Jewish and Pauline Studies* (Philadelphia, 1984), pp. 268 and 313.

55 Stein, *Philo*; Irmgard Christiansen, *Die Technik der allegorischen Auslegungwissenschaft bei Philon von Alexandrien* (Tübingen, 1969).

56 See my remarks on "Allegory in Greece and Egypt," *JEA* 53 (1967): 79-102, where I seek to show that a text like chap. 17 of the Book of the Dead is replete with 'Midrash.'

57 Stein, *Philo*, p. 61 with refs. Stein believes that these suggestions may be Philo's own, whereas the Hebrew etymologies used elsewhere were probably borrowed by him from other sources, since he is not likely to have known Hebrew.

Testament.[58] Some ritual practices were very probably borrowed from the Egyptian tradition. One of these was the placing of sacred scrolls in Jewish tombs, a custom attested in Palestine and in Roman catacombs, also in the synagogue of Priene.[59] Goodenough very properly invokes the Egyptian use of the Book of the Dead. In this connection the Jewish emphasis on immortality also points to Egypt, since neither Greece nor Israel provided such a strongly positive vision.[60] Again, Philo's account of the Therapeutae, a secluded religious Jewish community near Alexandria, gives indications of likely Egyptian influence, as the late lamented François Daumas has shown.[61] There are literary pointers in the same direction. Among them are the concept of Fate in Qoheleth (Ecclesiastes),[62] the ideology which suggests a link between Isis, the Logos, and Sophia in Philo and the Wisdom of Solomon,[63] and the influence of Demotic Wisdom on Ben Sira, a matter recently highlighted by an American scholar with particular reference to the Papyrus Insinger.[64] Egyptian impact in these respects may have been exercised through the medium of Greek writings by bilingual authors. That the Hermetic literature owes a considerable debt to Egyptian religion has been ably propounded of late in a study by Erik Iversen.[65]

---

[58] John. J. Collins, *Between Athens and Jerusalem. Jewish Identity in the Hellenistic Diaspora* (New York, 1983), p. 144, citing G. Klein for the idea of a catechism.

[59] Goodenough, vol. 4, p. 142. Scrolls in the synagogues may have been in the rooms called *adyta* by Goodenough, according to Nock, *Essays*, vol. 2, p. 887, and they included books other than scripture (Jerome, *Ep.* 36). But scrolls for current use were kept in the 'Ark,' and a *genizah* was used for storing. Larger annexes were used as "class-rooms for children and guest-rooms for strangers": see Sukenik, *ASPG*, pp. 48-9. On modern synagogue libraries and the forming of study-groups, see Samuel C. Heilman, *Synagogue Life* (Chicago, 1976), pp. 224-5. The Egyptian custom of incubation may have also been followed sometimes. Saul Lieberman, *Hellenism in Jewish Palestine* (New York, 1962), p. 121 n. 33 (ad fin.) refers to "the later Jewish belief in the efficacy of incubation in pagan temples." Cf. D. M. Lewis in *JSS* 2 (1957): 264-6 and A. Momigliano, *Alien Wisdom* (Cambridge, 1975), p. 87, on the Jewish slave Moschos (c. 250 BC) having incubation in the Temple of Amphiaraus in Boeotia in order to get light on his future. On this aspect of the cult there see A. Schachter, *Cults of Boiotia*, vol. 1 (London, 1981), p. 23.

[60] A. D. Nock, *Essays*, vol. 2, p. 904.

[61] Edn of Philo, *De vita contemplativa* (Paris, 1963). Cf. M. Whittaker, in *JTS*, n.s. 17 (1966): 127-8.

[62] Hengel, *Hellenism*, vol. 1, p. 125 and vol. 2, p. 85 n. 148, citing S. Morenz and D. Müller.

[63] Wilfred L. Knox, *Some Hellenistic Elements in Primitive Christianity* (London, 1944), p. 51 (on "mystical contemplation and the concept of the cosmic Wisdom"), p. 78 n. 2 (on "Egyptian religion in a Greek dress"), and p. 79 f. Cf. Nock, *Essays*, vol. 1, p. 460 and vol. 2, p. 882.

[64] Jack T. Sanders, *Ben Sira and Demotic Wisdom* (Chicago, 1983), cf. Miriam Lichtheim, *Late Egyptian Wisdom Literature in the International Context* (Freiburg, 1983), p. x.

[65] Erik Iversen, *Egyptian and Hermetic Doctrine* (Copenhagen, 1984), which deals for the most part with beliefs about cosmogony.

The Hellenistic era was marked by cultural and religious interpenetration, most of all in Alexandria. We must therefore eschew any idea of one-way traffic. Our remarks have shown that it is very likely that the earliest Jewish synagogues arose in Ptolemaic Egypt, and that in two respects—the pylon and the basilica—their architecture was sometimes influenced by the tradition of their environment. Their main purpose, which combined worship and instruction, may well reflect a double emphasis found in Egyptian religious institutions, especially in the Per Ankh.

Whatever influences are detected, however, the synagogue remains a Jewish creation. Institutionally it is the greatest communal creation of the Jewish genius.[66]

66 The above remarks were presented in a paper contributed to the Fourth International Congress of Egyptology held at Munich, 26 August-1 September 1985. Cf. also a section of a chapter on "The legacy of Egypt in Judaism" which I have contributed to a forthcoming volume of *The Cambridge History of Judaism*.

SYNAGOGUES IN PRE-70 PALESTINE: A RE-ASSESSMENT

LESTER L. GRABBE*

For 2,000 years the synagogue has been the centre of Jewish religious life, nor would one want to present any different picture for the time from the Mishnah to the present. There seems no question that the synagogue plays the role assumed for it both inside and outside Palestine at least by Amoraic times. It is when we move back to the time of the Second Temple that the standard assumptions about synagogues, as about so many things in Judaism, can no longer be taken for granted.

Unfortunately, the assumptions are so strong that questions of data and matters of historical evidence often seem to make little headway against the tide of tradition. They are confounded by that most persistent and hardy of species—the impregnable defence of 'what everyone knows,' the incontrovertible argument of 'what must have been.' This results in the use of the flimsiest of evidence to support sweeping conclusions, not to mention standard reconstructions which go on paragraph after paragraph without reference to a piece of primary data. Alternatively, discussions mix data from various periods and geographical areas without any discussion of the methodological problems for doing so. Thus, even the recent definitive treatment in the revised Schürer throws together material from the New Testament, very late rabbinic sources, inscriptions, archaeology, and Josephus without attempting to differentiate between them, though it is interesting to see that the notes sometimes contradict the text![1]

The purpose of this essay is to challenge some of the standard views about the development of the institution of the synagogue. In doing so, I do not want to quibble over definitions but am willing to cast my net as widely as possible in trying to find evidence of the institution, whatever terminology is used.[2] For convenience, the arguments are organized around five specific theses which challenge a number of the common assumptions:

---

* This essay was originally published in *Journal of Theological Studies* 39, no. 2 (1989): 401-410. It is reprinted by the permission of Oxford University Press.

[1] Schürer, vol. 2, pp. 423-54. On p. 450 the text states, "The Torah reading was so ordered that the whole of the Pentateuch was read consecutively in a three-yearly cycle," whereas n. 118 reads, "As the existence of the triennial cycle is nowhere attested in Tannaitic literature, its currency in the age of Jesus is merely conjectural."

[2] However, it is not enough to point to instances of public prayer and then immediately make the leap to the institution of the synagogue. Examples of public fasting and prayer are of course found in the Old Testament and other Jewish literature, but to speak of the

1. Synagogues originated in the Diaspora, probably in the Greek period

The earliest evidence which can in any reasonable way be related to the existence of synagogues comes from Ptolemaic Egypt.[3] Several inscriptions from the reign of Ptolemy III speak of the *proseuchē* place of prayer.'[4] This would place the earliest evidence about 250 BCE, well into the Hellenistic period. Subsequent to this, a variety of inscriptions from over the eastern Mediterranean world attest to dozens of these *proseuchai.* It is generally taken for granted that these inscriptions are to be connected with Jewish places of worship and, as already stated, I would not wish to quarrel with such a view. It seems to me that Philo's references to the *proseuchē* at various points is very much in keeping with the Standard interpretation.[5] However, it should be noted that not everyone agrees that the inscriptional references to the *proseuchē* should be related to the synagogue as such or always even to Jewish institutions of any sort.

Why should the synagogue have originated in the Diaspora? The standard answer is reasonable enough—that it was in the Jewish communities distant from Palestine that the need for a place of community worship was first acutely felt. But a further emphasis needs to be given to this point, which

---

institution of the synagogue presupposes the minimum of a regular (preferably weekly) public meeting for prayer and/or reading of the law. Some scholars attempt to distinguish between the terms *sunagōgē* and *proseuchē* or to make other distinctions. For example, J. Gutmann in Gutmann, "Origins," argues that the institution called a *proseuchē* was not really a synagogue. On the other hand, E. Rivkin tries to show that Philo uses *proseuchē* to refer to two separate institutions; see Rivkin, "Nonexistence," esp. pp. 350-4. S. B. Hoenig seems to exclude from his definition of synagogue those institutions in which the law was read but without the accompaniment of prayer; see Hoenig, "City-Square," esp. pp. 451-2. There may be truth in some of these arguments, though I remain skeptical, but for my purposes it seems better to be more rather than less encompassing.

[3] As is well known, various theories about the origin of the synagogue have been advanced, and they divide roughly into those which suppose an origin in Palestine and those which argue for the Diaspora; for a survey of earlier opinions, see H. H. Rowley, *Worship in Ancient Israel: Its Forms and Meaning* (London, 1967). However, I am looking for *evidence*, not speculation, and the earliest actual evidence is found in Egypt from about the middle of the third century BCE.

[4] See Hengel, "Proseuche." Most recently, J. G. Griffiths has argued that the earliest Jewish synagogues arose in Ptolemaic Egypt; see "Egypt and the Rise of the Synagogue," *JTS*, n.s. 38 (1987): 1-15. [It is reprinted in the present volume—Eds.]

[5] *Vita Mos.* 2.211-16; *In Flaccum*, 41, 45-9, 53; *Leg. ad Gaium*, 132-7, 156-7. By saying that Philo's references are consistent with the inscriptions, I do not mean to imply that there was no development in the two centuries or so preceding his writings. All one can say is that the interpretation of the *proseuchē* as some form of Diaspora synagogue is not an unreasonable one. Critics of this interpretation, such as Gutmann and Rivkin (n. 2 above) may have a point; however, I do not understand Gutmann's comment, "Whatever the *proseuchē* was cannot be definitely ascertained. That it was not a synagogue, however, appears evident" (p. 3). Why the 'house of prayer' could not be a synagogue, he does not make clear. Perhaps he should define what he means by 'synagogue' since he seems to differ from what others understand.

would also explain why it is only in the Greek period that we first meet indications of the existence of synagogues. This is the significant implication of being a temple-centred religion. It has been insufficiently appreciated what it means to have a religion which focuses on a central temple cult. Most discussions of post-exilic Judaism still seem to be heavily influenced by the Torah-centred Judaism of post-70 times. Even though the law was important to Judaism at least from the time of Ezra, nevertheless the social and psychological dynamics of a temple religion are quite different from those without a focal holy place. Of course, later Judaism evolved a variety of symbols and substitutes which continued to incorporate elements of temple worship, such as mythical views about Jerusalem, the various elements of the synagogue layout and architecture evoking the temple, and a liturgy which fulfilled the same spiritual and psychological needs as the original sacrificial cult. Nevertheless, Torah-centred Judaism with the synagogue as its community centre is quite different in important aspects from the worship which had the temple as its domain.[6]

Various factors are likely to have hindered any development of meeting places in the local communities. Even though the synagogue was only meant to complement temple worship, overtones of the old pre-exilic high places could not have been overlooked. There was also the known fact of rival temples such as those at Garizim and Elephantine. With such considerations, as well as other forces of religious conservatism, it would hardly be surprising that it took several centuries for the Diaspora to fill a religious need which may have been felt fairly early. Thus, the silence of our sources before about 250 BCE should not be thought accidental or peculiar: there is no reason to think that the Jews would have felt an urgent need for something like the synagogue, contrary to the assumptions of some who wish to argue for the early development of the institution.

2. The synagogue in Palestine is a post-Maccabean phenomenon

Jewish Literary Sources. We look in vain for any mention of synagogues before or during the Maccabean revolt. The Hebrew books of the old Testament make no reference to the *bêt kĕneset* which is the characteristic term for the synagogue in later Jewish writings, while attempts to connect passages such as Ezek. 11:16, Jer. 39:8, and Ps. 74:8 with the synagogue have generally been abandoned.[7] In the LXX the characteristic Greek terms

[6] See, e.g., R. Patai, *Man and Temple in Ancient Myth and Ritual* (1947; reprinted New York, 1967).

[7] Gutmann, "Origin." However, A. Gelston has recently argued that Ps. 74:8 refers to "non-sacrificial Yahwistic cultic centres" in his article, "A Note on Psalm LXXIV 8," *VT* 34 (1984): 82-7, although he does consider several other possibilities for interpreting the passage.

sunagōgē and *proseuchē* are also not found with reference to anything like the later institutions. One passage often adduced as a forerunner of the synagogue or even evidence for it is Neh. 8 in which the law is read publicly to the people. But the context is clearly about a unique occurrence, not a weekly event, nor does the format correspond to any synagogue service known from available evidence.[8]

The book of Tobit, which is usually taken to be pre-Maccabean, pictures a pious Jew, but what form does his piety take?[9] Regular attendance in the synagogue? No, he is rather said to go to the Jerusalem temple each year, taking his tithes with him. After his exile from Palestine, his piety is expressed either by his individual actions or in his home. Of course, Tobit is pictured as an exile from the captivity of Northern Israel, but this fiction hardly keeps the author from describing the beliefs and practices of his own time. If the synagogue was a regular part of Jewish life, it seems unlikely that it would have been ignored in such a writing.

The same applies to other writings which may be pre-Maccabean or at least not later than the Hasmonaean period: Judith, Ben Sira, letter of (pseudo-)Aristeas, Dan. 1-6, the so-called apocryphal sections of Daniel, Jubilees. None of these so much as hint at a place of regular community worship. Daniel, for example, prays three times a day in private. Pseudo-Aristeas describes Jerusalem and the temple but says nothing about the existence of synagogues. Neither the extant Hebrew text nor the Greek text of Ben Sira mention synagogue worship, though the temple and its cult are not passed over (50:1-21). Further, one may note that the description of Judaea and the Jewish state by Hecataeus of Abdera refers only to the temple and its cult.[10] This silence could of course be accidental for some of the writings since they may not necessarily have had occasion to refer to synagogues, but complete silence is at least unusual and becomes significant when it includes Tobit and especially Ben Sira, both of which would likely have mentioned the institution if it existed.

More important yet are the books of 1 and 2 Maccabees themselves. We have two independent descriptions of the crisis precipitated by the pollution of the temple under Antiochus Epiphanes. The troubles which befell faithful Jews at that time were horrendous (1 Macc. 1-2; 2 Macc. 5-7). Torture and

---

[8] For references to such arguments and a refutation of them, see H. G. M. Williamson, *Ezra, Nehemiah*, Word Biblical Commentary, vol. 16 (Waco, TX, 1985), pp. 281-2; Williamson's comments apply equally to the more recent similar suggestion by M. Fishbane, *Biblical Interpretation in Ancient Israel* (Oxford, 1985), p. 113.

[9] For a recent discussion of Tobit with bibliography, see G. W. E. Nickelsburg in M. Stone, ed., *Jewish Writings of the Second Temple Period*, Compendia Rerum ludaicarum ad Novum Testamentum, Sect. 2, vol. 3 (Assen/Philadelphia, 1984), pp. 40-46.

[10] *Apud* Diodorus Siculus 40.3.1-8. For a recent translation and commentary, see M. Stern, *Greek and Latin Authors on Jews and Judaism*, vol. 1 (Jerusalem, 1974), pp. 20-44.

death were the penalty for practising circumcision or keeping the Sabbath. Any scrolls of Holy Writ were destroyed and the owners executed. Pagan altars were set up in many different places, with Jews forced to participate in the worship. But where in all this was the desecration of synagogues or disruption of synagogue worship? Not a word in either 1 or 2 Maccabees, nor even in Josephus for that matter (*BJ* 1.1.2 §§ 34-5; *Antiq.* 12.5.4 §§ 248-56). As already noted, the odd reference to prayer and fasting or reading the law before battle can in no way be related to the institution of the synagogue (1 Macc. 3:47-8; 2 Macc. 8:23).

New Testament. The earliest literary references to synagogues in pre-70 Palestine are the New Testament Gospels and Acts. From this evidence, there seems to me no question that there were synagogues in Galilee already by the time of Jesus (though whether the detailed description found in such passages as Luke 4:16-30 has historical value for the early first century is another matter).[11] Josephus also attests the existence of a *sunagōgē* in Dora and Caesaraea (*BJ* 2.14.4-5 §§ 285-9; *Antiq.* 19.6.3 §§ 300-5), the one in Caesaraea being important for the beginning of the Jewish revolt in 66. He also speaks of *a proseuchē* in Tiberias (*Vita* 54 §§ 277-80).

Archaeological Data. Until a couple of decades ago there were still no known remains of a pre-70 synagogue (apart from the Theodotus inscription). This picture appears to have changed, though not everyone agrees. The first find was at Masada, followed by that of Herodium.[12] Although it is widely accepted that there are indeed pre-70 synagogues, even this identification has not gone unquestioned.[13] But accepting the standard identification, one should still note that both were built during the First Revolt. Yadin has argued that the pre-Revolt building remodeled by the Sicarii was also a synagogue but this is pure supposition. The only certainty is that it had been a stable, for which there is a considerable quantity of tangible evidence!

More significant because earlier is the building identified as a synagogue at Gamla.[14] Although the original excavator dated it to the time of Hyrcanus II (63-40 BCE), a more recent assessment has argued for the Herodian period,

---

[11] I remain agnostic about the position of S. Zeitlin, in Zeitlin, "Origin," that the synagogue arose from the "secular" house of assembly, as well as that of S. B. Hoenig, (Hoenig, "City-Square"), that it took its origin from religious activities in the city square. While both ideas are possible, I cannot agree with Zeitlin's theory of its origin under the Pharisees. See my thesis no. 3 below.

[12] See Yadin, *Masada*, pp. 181-7; Y. Yadin, "The Excavation of Masada," *IEJ* 15 (1965): 76-9; Foerster, "Masada."

[13] See especially the comments of M. J. S. Chiat about the difficulties of interpretation in Chiat, "First Century," as well as comments on the specific 'first century' synagogues in Chiat, *Handbook*, pp. 116-18, 204-7, 248-51, 282-4. Cf. also S. B. Hoenig, review of Yadin, *Masada* in *Jewish Bookland* (Apr. 1973): 8 (as cited by Gutmann but not available to me).

[14] S. Gutman, "Gamla." Chiat has also questioned this identification (see previous note).

23 BCE to 41 CE.[15] A recent report in a semi-popular journal has also claimed that remains of a pre-70 synagogue underlie the second-third- (or fifth-!) century building at Capernaum.[16] Although a more official report is not yet available, it seems clear that a first-century building does indeed lie below the later synagogue there, and it may be that this building is the Capernaum synagogue of the Gospels; however, firm evidence of identification has not become available. But assuming such evidence materializes, the real question is whether this synagogue is any older than the one at Gamla.

About the time of the First World War the Theodotus inscription was found on Mt. Ophel.[17] The original studies showed that it was from about the turn of the common era but palaeography could be no more precise than that. The *terminus ante quem* is usually given as 70: because the synagogue stood for several generations, it is unlikely that such was built between 70 and 135; after 135, Jews were prohibited from even entering the site of Jerusalem. If this dating is correct, it is evidence for a synagogue in Jerusalem which stood for a considerable period of time before the destruction under Titus. It has even been suggested that the Theodotus inscription came from the synagogue of 'freedman' mentioned in Acts 6:9, but this has now generally been discounted.[18]

Rabbinic Passages. Of a different character are such rabbinic statements as the one in Palestinian Talmud *Megillah* 3:1, 73d, that there were 480 synagogues destroyed in Jerusalem by Titus. This is often quoted though usually stated to be an 'exaggeration.'[19] How is it an exaggeration? Were there really only the 394 of the Babylonian Talmud *Ketubot* 105a? But perhaps even that figure is an exaggeration and the real number is 200. Or 100?, 50?, 20?, 10? The point is that such late rabbinical statements should be evaluated for what they are—worthless as historical information.[20]

---

[15] Z. Ma'oz, "Gamla."

[16] J. F. Strange and H. Shanks, "Synagogue Where Jesus Preached Found at Capernaum," *Biblical Archaeology Review* 9, no. 6 (Nov./Dec. 1983): 24-31. The dating of the later synagogue is hotly disputed; see the debate between the excavator S. Loffreda and the Israeli archaeologists G. Foerster and M. Avi-Yonah in Levine, *ASR*, pp. 52-62.

[17] For an extensive list of earlier studies, see Hüttenmeister and Reeg, vol. 1, pp. 192-94. Particularly valuable is the article by L. H. Vincent, "Decouverte de la 'Synagogue des Affranchis' a Jérusalem," *RB* 30 (1921): 247-77.

[18] E.g. Goodenough, vol. 1, p. 179, following Sukenik, *ASPG*, p. 70.

[19] E.g. S. Safrai, "The Synagogue and its Worship," in *Society and Religion in the Second Temple Period*, The World History of the Jewish People, First Series, vol. 8 (London, 1977), p. 67

[20] Potentially of more significance is the institution of the *ma'ămādôt*, lay groups corresponding to the twenty-four priestly courses (*mišmārôt*). According to such passages as the Mishnah Taa. 4:2-4, these groups met fasting and praying while their corresponding priestly court was in Jerusalem. If so, this might be evidence of synagogues while the temple was still standing. There are several points one can make about this. First, the passages which speak of the *ma'ămādôt* do not occur in the pre-70 stratum of tradition according to the analysis of Neusner, *Appointed Times*, vol. 5, pp. 171-2 and 231. Secondly, Josephus does not

To sum up this section, literary evidence indicates that the synagogue as an institution had reached Galilee and even Jerusalem by the first century CE. If the identification of buildings at Gamla and perhaps elsewhere is correct (a point disputed by some specialists), this lends credence to the literary evidence, as does the Theodotus inscription. Nevertheless, the available evidence is still in harmony with other literary evidence (especially Ben Sira, 1 and 2 Maccabees, and Tobit) that the synagogue in Palestine was a post-Maccabean phenomenon.

3. There is nothing particularly Pharisaic about the institution of the synagogue

A truism which one constantly reads about the Pharisees is that the synagogue was their *métier*. The synagogue is seen to have been an institution taken over and dominated by the Pharisees, even if not founded by them. But when the evidence is scrutinized, it is found to be non-existent—another case of 'what must have been.' Based on an assumption of the place and development of Pharisaism in Palestine, a hypothesis is then advanced about the synagogue as being under the control of Pharisees; unfortunately, it is not usually advanced as a hypothesis but as a fact or self-evident conclusion.[21]

The early sources on the Pharisees mention nothing in particular about them in relationship to synagogues. Josephus makes no mention of synagogues in his description of Pharisees (*BJ* 2.8.14 §§ 162 and 166; *Antiq.* 18.1.3 §§ 12-15). Only one New Testament passage suggests any particular connection: John 12:42 which states that many of the authorities (*archontes*) believed in Jesus but "for fear of the Pharisees they did not confess it, lest they should be put out of the synagogue." Readers will hardly need to be reminded that John is the latest of the Gospels, written long after 70. The

---

mention such an institution. Thirdly, the postulation of a lay organization parallel to the priestly is precisely the type of propaganda that one might expect from the Pharisees or their heirs in the post-70 period. The later traditions often attempt to give the picture that the pre-70 Priestly institutions such as the temple were governed by rabbis and other lay individuals rather than the priests. The ease with which the postulated *ma'ămād* fits the mode of such propaganda is very suspicious. Fourthly, even if such institutions are historical for the pre-70 period there is nothing in the tradition which suggests that they preceded the Maccabean revolt. Interestingly, S. Hoenig, who takes the institution of the *ma'ămādôt* at face value, still argues that the synagogue in Judaea is a post-70 phenomenon (Hoenig, "City-Square," pp. 448-53).

[21] Gutmann, "Origins," pp. 3-4; Zeitlin, "Origin," pp. 76-78; R. T. Herford, *The Pharisees* (London, 1924), pp. 88-103; cf . L. Finkelstein, *The Pharisees: The Sociological Background of their Faith* (Philadelphia, 1938), pp. 568-9.

early rabbinic traditions about the Pharisees also suggest no unusual connection between them and the *bêt kĕneset.*[22]

4. Considering the lateness of the synagogue in Palestine, the immense superstructure of scholarly hypothesis which has been erected on this basis should be treated with considerable caution

A variety of theories assume the synagogue as the *Sitz im Leben* of their central proposal, for example, those which presuppose a certain cycle of liturgical readings in the pre-70 synagogue. Several such theories have flourished in New Testament scholarship.[23] They have already been criticized on various grounds, but it seems to me that such theories must also presuppose a long liturgical history in the synagogue in Palestine, a further difficulty if the synagogue in Palestine is as late as I suggest.[24]

Similarly, much has been made of a supposed pre-70 'Palestinian Targum.' Without going into the long debate on the question, I think one can safely say that the origin of this Targum in the oral Aramaic translation of the synagogue service is almost universally taken for granted. And perhaps there was an Aramaic paraphrase of the Hebrew readings in the pre-70 Palestinian service, but I think we can no longer assume so. The regulations on the translation of scriptural readings in Mishnah *Megillah*, for example, seem all to date from the Ushan period.[25] Was translation into Aramaic a regular feature of pre-70 synagogue worship? Even if so, did our extant Targums originate in an oral setting as is normally taken for granted? Our earliest targumic evidence (from Qumran) almost certainly arises from a literary milieu.[26] Is the use of Aramaic translation in synagogue liturgy perhaps a para-Targumic or even a post-Targumic phenomenon rather than the origin of our extant Targums?[27] Some of these questions are probably

[22] See in particular J. Neusner, *Rabbinic Traditions about the Pharisees before 70*, 3 vols. (Leiden: Brill, 1971).

[23] E.g. A. Guiding, *The Fourth Gospel and Jewish Worship* (Oxford, 1960).

[24] See L. Morris, *The New Testament and the Jewish Lectionaries* (London, 1964); L. Crockett, "Luke 4.16-30 and the Jewish Lectionary Cycle," *JJS* 18 (1966): 13-46; I. Heinemann, "The 'Triennial' Cycle and the Calendar," *Tarbiz* 33 (1963-4): 362-8 (Eng. summary, III-IV); "The Triennial Lectionary Cycle," *JJS* 19 (1968): 41-8; J. R. Porter, "The Pentateuch and the Triennial Lectionary cycle," in F. F. Bruce, ed., *Promise and Fulfilment*, Essays presented to S. H. Hooke (Edinburgh, 1963), pp. 63-74.

[25] See Neusner, *Appointed Times*, vol. 5, pp. 174-8. A useful summary is found in Neusner, *Evidence*, pp. 82-8.

[26] The published Qumran targums are 4QtgLev, 4QtgJob, and 11QtgJob, the *editio princeps* being J. T. Milik, *Qumran Grotte 4, II*, DJD, vol. 6 (Oxford, 1977), pp. 86-90, and J. P. M. van der Ploeg and A. S. van der Woude, *Le Targum de Job de la Grotte XI de Qumran*, Koninklijke Nederlandse Ahdemie van Wetenschappen (Leiden: Brill, 1971).

[27] This is a question which I already asked in "The Jannes/Jambres Tradition in Targum Pseudo-Jonathan and Its Date," *JBL* 98 (1979): 394 n. 6. Did the extant Targums really arise in a scholarly context such as the academy rather than the liturgy? For an important recent

unaffected by the question of a late origin for the synagogue in Palestine, but for others the matter would seem to be crucial.

5. The rise of the synagogue was a fortuitous but vital development which paved the way for a post-temple Judaism which became necessary after 70

Although certain forms of Judaism functioned on a day-to-day basis without a temple before 70, it is very difficult to find a form which envisaged no temple.[28] This was one of the revolutionary developments in Christianity in that it rejected the need for a physical temple at a fairly early stage in its development. But the loss of the temple was a major trauma for Judaism as a whole, as evidenced by such works as 2 Baruch and 4 Ezra. Synagogues were not planned as a substitute for the temple but they were a useful vehicle to make the transition.[29]

CONCLUSIONS

To sum up, evidence for institutions generally accepted as synagogues is known for the Diaspora as early as Ptolemaic times. But when we look at Palestine itself, evidence for the existence of synagogues is lacking before the first century BCE and perhaps even until the first CE. The earliest literary references (the New Testament) put the synagogues as a flourishing institution in Galilee by about 30 CE as well as the existence of them in Jerusalem by about this time. Archaeological evidence has also been interpreted to show the existence of synagogues possibly as early as the first century BCE, though it should be noted that this interpretation has been disputed and the identification of these buildings as synagogues questioned. But the Theodotus inscription would appear to give evidence for a synagogue which stood for several generations before the fall of the temple in 70. All this strongly suggests that the synagogue as an institution came into Palestine only very late, well into post-Maccabean times, a conclusion not surprising

---

article discussing some of the problems about our knowledge of Targumic origins, see P. S. Alexander, "The Targumim and the Rabbinic Rules for the Delivery of the Targum," *Congress Volume: Salamanca* 1983 (VTSup 36; Leiden), pp. 14-28.

[28] The origin of the anti-temple sentiments in Acts 7-8 has been much debated. Although certain forms of Judaism, such as the Qumran community, may have functioned without a temple, they do not appear to have rejected it as such. The one anti-temple document is the 4th Sibylline oracle; on this see J. J. Collins, "The Place of the Fourth Sibyl in the Development of the Jewish Sibyllina," *JJS* 25 (1974): 365-80.

[29] See the concise but very useful discussion of M. Goodman, *State and Society in Roman Galilee, A.D. 132-232*, Oxford Centre for Postgraduate Hebrew Studies (Totowa, NJ, 1983), pp. 84-7.

when one considers the importance of the temple cult to Palestinian Judaism in pre-70 times.

By way of conclusion, I will say that I fully recognize the dangers of some of the proposals here. The data are meagre, and an archaeological find tomorrow could falsify some or all of what I have argued. Nevertheless, the correct scientific approach is one which proceeds from the extant evidence, even when there is not very much and even when the argument must sometimes be one from silence. This may have its hazards, but it is much preferable to the approach which proceeds on the basis of 'what everyone knows' or 'what must have been.'

PALESTINIAN SYNAGOGUES BEFORE 70 C.E. A REVIEW OF THE EVIDENCE *

PAUL VIRGIL MCCRACKEN FLESHER**

The origins of the synagogue have in recent years become a matter of debate. Although most scholars have believed for centuries that the synagogue orginated in Babylonia during the exile after 587 B.C.E. and was then brought into Palestine during the return from exile, there has been a distinct lack of evidence to support this belief.[1] Two recent articles, when seen together, have set the stage for a new direction on the question of early synagogues. The first article, by J. Gwyn Griffiths, argues a convincing case for tracing the synagogue's origins to Egypt.[2] Griffiths shows that the synagogue is first evidenced in the third century B.C.E. by pointing to the well-known dedication of a synagogue ('prayer house,' *proseuche*) to Ptolemy III Euergetes, who reigned from 246-221 B.C.E., as well as to the contemporary dedication of a synagogue at Arsinoë-Crocodilopolis. He further points to several inscriptions dated from the second and first centuries revealing the

* This article is a revised version of a paper given at the Midwest SBL meeting, Jan. 31, 1989. It grew out of a series of lectures I gave to the NEH Summer Seminar for College Teachers at Brown University in the summer of 1988. I am grateful to A. J. Levine of Swarthmore College for encouraging me to pursue these studies further. For reading and commenting on this paper in different drafts, I want to thank A. J. Levine, Roger Brooks, Dennis Groh, William R. Stegner and Walter Aufrecht. Their efforts have helped me improve the work. Needless to say, the responsibility for any shortcomings should be laid at my door. The essay has been updated for inclusion in this volume.

** This article was originally published in J. Neusner and E. S. Frerichs, eds., *Approaches to Ancient Judaism*, vol. 6 (Atlanta, GA: Scholars Press for Brown Judaic Studies, 1989), pp. 67-81. It is reprinted by the permission of the Editor, Brown Judaic Studies.

[1] For the standard position, see Schürer, vol. 2, pp. 423-463; Bright, John, *A History of Israel*, 3rd. ed. (Philadelphia: Westminster, 1981); Finkelstein, "Origin"; L. I. Levine, "The Second Temple Synagogue: The Formative Years," pp. 7-32 in Levine, *SLA*; and Levine, "Ancient Synagogues." For critiques and reassessment of that position, see Rivkin, "Nonexistence"; Chiat, "First-Century"; Hoenig, "City-Square." See also Gutmann, "Origins"; and S. Hoenig, "The Supposititious Temple-Synagogue," pp. 55-71 in Gutmann, *Synagogue*.

[2] Griffiths, J. Gwyn, "Egypt and the Rise of the Synagogue," *JThS*, 38 (1987) 1, pp. 1-15. [Eds.—It has been republished in the present volume.] Much of the inscriptional evidence Griffiths cites is well-known and has been discussed by other scholars. See, for example, Schürer, vol. 2, p. 425, n. 5; and *Theological Dictionary of the New Testament*, (Grand Rapids, MI: Eerdmans, 1964-76), vol. 7, pp. 811-812. The importance of Griffiths' article is that he uses this evidence to articulate a well-argued claim that the synagogue began in Egypt. See also Dion, Paul-Eugène, "Synagogues et Temples dans l'Égypte Hellénistique," *Science et Esprit*, 29 (1977): 45-75.

existence of synagogues in both Lower Egypt and the Fayûm. During the second century B.C.E. inscriptions concerning synagogues begin to appear in other places around the Mediterranean, most notably at Delos and Antioch, revealing the spread of synagogues beyond Egypt.[3] The startling contrast between the Diaspora and Palestine is mentioned by Griffiths, but is brought out most prominently in a article by Lester L. Grabbe.[4] Grabbe shows that evidence concerning Palestine does not indicate the existence of synagogues prior to the "Post-Maccabean" period. Indeed, Grabbe indicates, "when we look at Palestine itself, evidence for the existence of synagogues is lacking before the first century B.C.E. and perhaps even until the first C.E."[5]

Taken together, these two articles suggest that the synagogue in Palestine has been imported from the larger Mediterranean world. Indeed, we can document its existence in Egypt nearly two centuries before any evidence of its penetration into Palestine appears. While this conclusion may finally resolve the scholarly debate on origins, it opens up a new set of questions. Not least of these is, how was the synagogue—this foreign import—received in Palestine? The question is particularly acute because the synagogue and the activities that take place in it constitute an inherently different form of Judaism from that of the Jerusalem Temple, the cultic center of Israelite religion. This difference must be emphasized.

The Temple cult was a system of holiness and purity mediated through sacrifices offered by a holy caste of people, the priests. The ability of the common Israelite to participate was limited in general to two types of activity: (1) supporting the Temple cult by giving taxes, tithes and animals for sacrifice, and (2) watching the priests offer them. The priests were the only class of people who were permitted to conduct the rites within the heightened holiness of the Temple and its inner Court. In fact, they alone could safely enter that space. There were a few exceptions to this division of worship, most notably with regard to the Passover sacrifice and the Nazirite oath, but the distinction between priest and common Israelite remained; the priest carried out the activities of the Temple cult, the Israelite had few responsibilities with regard to the actual performance of worship.

The synagogue, by contrast, arose in a region without access to the Temple cult (i.e., in Egypt) and in a sense comprised a substitute for it. It served as a gathering place for all Israelites—priests and commoners—where they took part in worship. That worship seems to have consisted of prayers and Scripture reading, as far as the limited evidence indicates. There were no

---

[3] See Griffiths, p. 4, notes 9-10.

[4] Grabbe, Lester L., "Synagogues in Pre-70 Palestine: A Re-Assessment," *JThS* 39 (1988) 2, pp. 401-410. [Eds.—It has been republished in the present volume.]

[5] Grabbe, p. 410. In this collection, the quote appears on p. 25.

sacrifices and hence there existed no need to distinguish among the Israelite castes. Indeed, the only synagogue activity related to the Temple cult at Jerusalem seems to have been the collection of the annual Temple tax.[6] So the synagogue lacked the high levels of holiness that infused the Temple cult. From the perspective of the common Israelite, the non-priest, there were thus really two different Judaisms: the Temple cult from which he was generally excluded from meaningful participation, and the Judaism of the synagogue in which he was a full participant.

With these essential differences between the synagogue and the Temple cult in hand, we return to this essay's central question, what was the synagogue's reception when it entered Palestine? Since the synagogue originated in a region where there was no access to the Jerusalem Temple, an easy introduction of the synagogue into an area where such access was available should not be taken for granted. The Temple priests may have viewed the synagogue as an unholy competitor—after all, the Hebrew Scriptures provide no support for it.[7] It is also possible that such a stance was unnecessary; the proximity of the Temple cult may have made the synagogue seem inappropriate and unappealing to Jews native to Jerusalem. Conversely, the synagogue and the Temple cult may have cooperated and filled distinct but compatible roles in Palestinian society. Unfortunately, we lack the evidence to answer any of these in-depth questions. But we can investigate our question in a general manner by taking a demographic perspective and in essence doing a survey. By asking, "where and when, in pre-70 Palestine, do we find evidence concerning the establishment of the synagogue?" we can discover the distribution of synagogues in pre-70 Palestine. The pattern of distribution will reveal, to the limits of the data, the relationship between the synagogue and the Temple cult. We shall focus our analysis first on evidence from literary sources, then move to investigate the archeological evidence.[8] At each stage, we shall probe the reliability of the evidence so that the strength of the conclusions we ultimately draw will be clear.

---

[6] Josephus, in *Antiquities* xvi 164-173, indicates that Ceasar Augustus and other Roman officials decreed that, among other things, the Jews be permitted to store money for the Temple tax in their synagogues and to transport that money to the Jerusalem Temple without hindrance. It should also be noted that at one time there was a Jewish Temple on the island of Elephantine in the Nile near Aswan. A discussion of that temple is beyond the scope of this paper.

[7] Rabbinic eisegesis of Ps. 74:8, Neh. 8, and Is. 19:19 notwithstanding.

[8] This article will not include the rabbinic literature in its investigations; to be properly understood, rabbinic information concerning synagogues requires an extensive study of its own. I will point out, however, that none of the rabbinic texts published prior to about 250 C.E. refer to synagogues prior to 70. The tannaitic midrashim—the Mekhiltas, Sifra, the two Sifrés—rarely mention synagogues at all and never in a pre-70 context. The Mishnah, while it discusses synagogues in a number of places, never depicts them prior to 70 either. The prayers and activities that the Mishnah's framers portray as happening in the post-70 synagogue are depicted as part of the pre-70 Temple cult. It is not until the later texts, such as

In general terms what we shall discover is this: Palestine itself can be divided into two areas with regard to the success of establishing the synagogue as an institution. In the region around Jerusalem, which for the sake of this paper is roughly coextensive with the political boundaries of Judea, we find no evidence that the synagogue established itself as an important institution. The Temple cult apparently held sway in this area and maintained a religious environment that prevented the synagogue from gaining a foothold in the area. Conversely, the region north of Judea (Samaria, Galilee, Golan, Decapolis, Trachonitis, and so on) provided fertile ground for the establishment of the synagogue. This area, lying beyond the immediate religious influence of the Temple cult, evidences the naturalization and development of the synagogue by the early first century C.E. To work out the extent of these conclusions and their implications, we now turn to the analysis.

We begin by defining the object of our investigation—the synagogue. A synagogue forms the ongoing and central community institution in a Jewish town or village. On the one hand, its primary function is religious, for it constitutes a meeting place for prayer, worship, and scripture study. On the other hand, it may also serve less sacred activities by providing a bank for community or charity funds, a hostel, an office for community leaders, or it may simply function as a meeting place—since it usually is the largest public building in a town. In fact, although archaeology tends to focus on the architectural aspects of the synagogue, the building should be understood primarily as a place for the community—the people Israel. It is thus a mainstream institution, drawing its support and participants from the entire community of Jews, not just a small sector of society.

When we investigate the numerous Jewish documents written prior to 70 C.E., we discover this striking point: they contain little information concerning synagogues. In fact, only three sets of texts even mention synagogues in Palestine—the New Testament, Josephus and Philo. All other documents are silent. Nowhere in the Hebrew Bible can we find anything about synagogues.[9] Furthermore, the whole corpus of apocalyptic, pseudepigraphic. and other pre-70 Jewish literature is silent. No mention of any Palestinian synagogues appears in First or Second Maccabees, the Qumran

---

the Tosefta and the Talmuds, that synagogues are mentioned that supposedly existed prior to 70. The lateness of these texts, particularly in light of the silence of the earlier texts, renders the information from the later sources extremely suspect. Also note that Grabbe, in his article, makes a few preliminary observations.

[9] Several passages have been identified as possibly indicating synagogues, but upon further analysis it is clear that they do not. Among these are Ezek. 11:16, Neh. 8, Is. 19:19, Psalms 74:8 and Jer. 39:8.

texts, Jubilees, any of the Enoch texts, Aristeas or any of the testaments, to mention just a few documents.[10]

By contrast, the texts that point to the existence of Palestinian synagogues during Temple times reveal an interesting phenomenon. The synagogues they mention are primarily in places beyond the control of the Jerusalem Temple—in northern Palestine. This is certainly true for the synagogues found in Josephus. Although most of the synagogues Josephus mentions are in the diaspora, he describes three synagogues in Palestine. All lie in areas north of the Temple's immediate control—Tiberius in Galilee, Dor and Caesaria on the coast in northwestern Samaria.[11] Unfortunately, Philo's evidence is less substantial. He mentions Palestinian synagogues only in the context of the Essenes of Palestine-Syria, not with regard to Palestinian Jews in general or in Judea in particular.[12]

As for the New Testament—the gospels and the book of Acts, to be specific—it follows Josephus in providing a clear picture of synagogues in Galilee and northern Palestine, but reveals little solid evidence of them in Judea. The synoptic gospels almost unanimously place the synagogues with which Jesus interacts in Galilee. They mention, for example, specific instances in which Jesus teaches in synagogues at Nazareth and Capernaum, and frequently state that Jesus went to synagogues throughout Galilee.[13] The only possible exception appears at Luke 4:44, which states that Jesus taught in the synagogues of Judea. Joseph Fitzmyer, however, makes clear that the term "Judea" here has a general reference implying areas where Jews live (i.e., northern Palestine), rather than the territory of Judea proper.[14] This point is supported by the parallel passages (Mt 4:23, Mk 1:39) which clearly state that Jesus taught in the synagogues in Galilee. Furthermore, in the following section, to which this remark is a transition, Luke goes on to describe Jesus' activity in Galilee (Luke 5:1-11). Thus, Luke in particular, and the synoptic gospels in general, evidence synagogues only in Northern Palestine.[15]

The gospel of John echoes this emphasis on Galilee (Jn 6:59), but also repeatedly mentions, in the context of Jerusalem, that the Pharisees have

[10] Of course, in many of these texts we would not expect to find synagogues mentioned. But the question of this study is whether there *is* evidence, not whether we should expect evidence.

[11] For Tiberius, see *Life* 277, 280, 293. For Dor, see *Antiquities* xix 300 and for Ceasaria, see *War* ii 285-9. Josephus also mentions a synagogue in diasporan Antioch, *War* vii 44.

[12] *Quod omis prober liber sit*, 81. See also the mention of synagogues in Alexandria (in Eqypt) in *Flaccus* 45-8 and *Spec. Legat.* 20, 132.

[13] Mt. 4:23, 9:35, 13:54; Mark 1:21-29, 1:39, 3:1, 6:2; Luke 4:15-44, 7:5, 8:41; John 6:59.

[14] J. A. Fitzmyer, *The Gospel according to Luke (I-IX)*, (Garden City, NY: Doubleday, 1981), pp. 530-4.

[15] Again, the question before us is not whether we expect to find data in the synoptic gospels concerning synagogues in Judea, but whether there is such data.

threatened people who believe in Jesus with excommunication from the synagogue (Jn 9:22, 12:42, 16:2). But these passages provide no evidence of synagogues in Jerusalem either, for scholars have shown that these descriptions reflect the poor state of relations between Jews and Christians during the period in which John is writing—probably sometime after 80—and the location in which he writes—somewhere in the diaspora—rather than the state of affairs during Jesus' lifetime.[16] John therefore provides evidence for synagogues in Galilee and perhaps for some in the Mediterranean diaspora, but none for synagogues in Jerusalem.

Acts provides a different picture; it focuses primarily on synagogues in the diaspora: Antioch, Corinth, Athens and so on. Still it includes two sets of passages that mention synagogues in Jerusalem. First, Paul states that he persecuted Christians in Jerusalem synagogues in the three major speeches of his final captivity (Acts 22:19, 24:12, 26:11). But, unfortunately for the "Jerusalem Synagogue," Conzelmann, Haenchen and Cadbury all agree that these speeches are literary constructions composed by Luke and thus reflect a post-70 diaspora situation.[17]

Second, Acts 6:9 mentions "the synagogue which is called that of the Libertini, both Cyrenians and and Alexandrians."[18] While there are problems both with the interpretation of Acts six as a whole and with the phrase referring to synagogues in particular, scholars do not find any basis for doubting the existence of this particular synagogue.[19] So here we finally locate literary evidence for a pre-70 synagogue in Jerusalem. On the face of it, this passage shows that the distinction between Judea and Galilee intimated by the evidence above is incorrect. But if we study the passage more closely, we discover that it does not speak of a synagogue attended by Jerusalemites in general. Instead, this is the synagogue is of the "Cyrenians and Alexandrians"; it is a synagogue for foreigners, one group of which—the Alexandrians—even come from the country that has the oldest evidence concerning the establishment of synagogues. This implies, then, that the

---

[16] For discussion of this question, see R. E. Brown, *The Gospel according to John (i-xii)*, (Garden City, NY: Doubleday, 1966), pp. LXX-LXXIII, 374, 379-82, 487-8; J. L. Martyn, *History & Theology in the Fourth Gospel*, 2nd ed. (Nashville: Abingdon, 1979), pp. 37-63; R. Kimelman, "*Birkat Ha-Minim* and the Lack of Evidence for an Anti-Christian Jewish Prayer in Late Antiquity," in E. P. Sanders et al., eds., *Jewish and Christian Self-Definition*, vol. 2 (Philadelphia: Fortress, 1981), pp. 226-243; L. H. Schiffman, *Who Was a Jew?* (Hoboken, NJ: KTAV, 1985), pp. 53-61. I think that in general this judgement is correct, even though several of these authors do not properly use the rabbinic literature.

[17] H. Conzelmann, *Acts of the Apostles* (Philadelphia: Fortress, 1987), pp. xliii-xlv, 187; E. Haenchen, *The Acts of the Apostles* (Philadelphia: Westminster, 1971), pp. 103-10; H. J. Cadbury, "The Speeches in Acts," in F. J. Foakes Jackson and K. Lake, eds., *The Beginnings of Christianity*, vol. 5 (London: Macmillan, 1933), pp. 402-26.

[18] The translation is from F. J. Foakes Jackson and K. Lake, eds., *The Beginnings of Christianity*, vol. 4 (London: Macmillan, 1933), pp. 66-8.

[19] See the discussion in the previous citation.

institution is for Jews from foreign lands, not for native Jerusalemites. The passage does not indicate that the synagogue as an institution has successfully moved into Jerusalem and established itself as a religious force counter to the Temple cult.

We can shed more light on the position of synagogues in Jerusalem if we turn briefly to the Theodotus inscription.[20] This inscription was found at the bottom of a well—obviously not in its original placement—in what is presently called the Old City of Jerusalem. Some scholars have dated it to the pre-70 period, although there is no clear evidence to support this date. The plaque states that one Theodotus, a synagogue head and the grandson of a synagogue head, built a particular synagogue. If the dating is correct, scholars have suggested, then the grandfather may have headed a synagogue in Jerusalem in the early first century C.E. or even the late first century B.C.E. Unfortunately, this pushes the evidence too far.[21]

> Theodotus, son of Vettenos the priest and *archisynagogos*, son of a *archisynagogos* and grandson of a *archisynagogos*, who built the synagogue for purposes of reciting the Law and studying the commandments, and the hostel, chambers and water installations to provide for the needs of itinerants from abroad, and whose father, with the elders and Simonidus, founded the synagogue.[22]

The important point for our purposes is that the inscription reveals that the synagogue to which it refers has a nature similar to the one mentioned in Acts chapter six. One of the primary purposes of Theodotus' synagogue was to provide "hostel, chambers and water installations to provide for the needs of itinerants from abroad...." That is, the synagogue served as a inn where Jews from outside Palestine could come and stay during their visit in Jerusalem—the inscription refers to a religious boarding house. Like the passage in Acts, the inscription does not provide evidence to indicate that the synagogue had gained acceptance in Jerusalem as a religious institution

---

[20] See R. Weill, *La Cité de David* (Paris: Librairie Paul Geuthner, 1920), esp., pp. 186-90; L. H. Vincent, *RB* (1921): 247-277; T. Reinach, *REJ* (Jul/Sept. 1920,): 46-56; and A. Deissman, *Light from the Ancient East*, trans. by L. R. M. Strachan (New York: George H. Doran, 1927), pp. 439-441.

[21] Unfortunately, the date of this inscription is uncertain. The French scholars who initially studied it could not agree on the date. Some argued for a pre-70 dating, others for a Hadrianic or even Trajianic date. Furthermore, the archeologists who found the inscription did not use the modern methods of stratigraphic analysis. Indeed, it is not even known whether the inscription was below, in, or above the destruction layer of 70. Thus, the sure dating of this stone seems to be impossible. It could even be from the late third or early fourth century.

With regard to the grandfather, the inscription itself makes it clear that Theodotus himself built the synagogue in question, not his ancestors. Thus whatever synagogue his grandfather served, it was not this one; it could even have been one in another country. So the evidence reveals less certain information than we wish.

[22] Translation is from Kloner, "Synagogues," p. 11.

alongside the Temple cult. There is no hint that this synagogue is for natives of Jerusalem. The only evidence of synagogues in Judea is for foreigners, therefore, whether they be permanent residents or visitors. Neither the Theodotus inscription nor Acts reveals the synagogue as the Temple cult's co-institution.

The evidence from literary sources, then, points to the conclusion that the synagogue as an imported institution did not gain equal acceptance in all areas of Palestine. In Galilee—whose residents, like those in the diaspora, had no immediate access to the Temple—the synagogue seemed to have become broadly established by the early first century C.E. In Judea, by contrast, where the Temple cult was the main focus of religious activity, we find no evidence of the synagogue gaining acceptance as a major religious institution. The only evidence of synagogues in Jerusalem is linked to the needs of foreigners. Perhaps, if I may speculate momentarily, foreign visitors needed them to assist pilgimages, or, perhaps the synagogue served as a familiar religious and social center—a 'home away from home'—for those who were more permanent residents in the city.

The evidence from documentary sources has provided an intriguing hypothesis. We can test it further if we turn to the data derived from archaeological investigations.[23] The question now before us is whether archaeological remains confirm or contradict the distinction we have drawn between Galilee and Judea. To begin with, archaeologists have identified six potential pre-70, Palestinian synagogues. Two of these lie in Judea: Masada and Herodium; the other four in Galilee: Migdal, Chorazin, Capernaum, and Gamala.[24] Upon close inspection, not all of these buildings live up to their tentative identification as synagogues. This is true for Migdal. Here a later structure has obliterated most of the remains of the suggested synagogue. This precludes establishing the character of the original building, and thus prevents confirming that it is a synagogue.[25] Similarly, if there ever was a first-century synagogue at Chorazin, it was lost before archaeologists were able to study it thoroughly.[26] Finally, the Capernaum 'synagogue' at this

[23] I have provided a select bibliography for each of the sites under discussion. For a more extensive list of citations, see the entry and the bibliography for each site found in *NEAEHL*.

[24] The best statement of this position is Foerster, "Masada and Herodium." A shortened version was published as Foester, "Masada & Herodion." The claim concerning the remains of a possible first century synagogue at Capernaum was made in an article by J. F. Strange and H. Shanks, "Synagogue Where Jesus Preached Found at Capernaum," *Biblical Archeology Review* 9, no. 6 (Nov/Dec, 1983): 24-31.

[25] See "Migdal," pp. 116-118, in Chiat, *Handbook*; Chiat, "First-Century"; Corbo, V, "La Citta' Romana de Magdala," pp. 355-378 in *Studia Hierosolymitana*, (Jerusalem: 1976), esp. pp. 364-372; Foerster, "Masada & Herodium"; Foerster, "Masada"; and Hüttenmeister and Reeg, vol. 1, pp. 316-318.

stage remains pure speculation, based only on the discovery of a first-century structure. Thus there are only three structures for which sufficient evidence exists to discuss their possible identification as pre-70 Palestinian synagogues: two in Judea—Masada and Herodium, and one in Galilee—Gamala.

Even these buildings do not provide overwhelming amounts of information confirming their identity, however. First, none of these structures have any features that would identify them as specifically Jewish, let alone as synagogues. Their Jewish character is evident only from their location within an area identified with Jews. In fact, the architectural features that have been used to identify them as synagogues—the benches around the walls and the columns—appear also in structures not identified as synagogues, and only some of these are Jewish.[27] While it appears certain that the buildings were built and used by Jews, their lack of specifically Jewish features indicates the difficulty facing investigators who wish to ascertain their function. Second, the discipline of archaeology prides itself on the development of scientific methods that carefully record the site and permit later study and reconstruction. Part of this process comprises the publication of excavation reports that enable all scholars to study and interpret the site. However, the publications of the so-called pre-70 synagogues has generally been poor. The final reports for the synagogues at both Masada and Herodium took nearly three decades to appear. Thus most discussion of their identification and character has been on the basis of brief preliminary remarks, rather than on complete presentation of the data.

The so-called synagogue at Masada is the best known of the three structures.[28] Yigael Yadin identified a building built into the casemate wall as a synagogue. This structure was originally erected under Herod and later taken over by the rebels during the first revolt against Rome (68-73 C.E.). The rebels, Yadin claims, converted it into a synagogue.[29] They accomplished this by removing a wall, adding a floor, constructing a storage room and

---

[26] See "Chorozin," pp. 97-102 in Chiat, *Handbook*; Chiat, "First-Century"; Foerster, "Masada & Herodium"; Foerster, "Masada"; and Hüttenmeister and Reeg, vol. 1, pp. 275-81. Yeivin, Z., "Ancient Chorazin Comes back to Life, " *BAR* 13, no. 5 (1987): 22-39.

[27] See the discussion of *ecclesiasteria* and *bouleteria* by Zvi Ma'oz on p. 41 of Ma'oz, "Gamla." See also Foerster's discussion of the *pronaos*, pp. 26-28, in Foerster, "Masada" pp. 24-29. See also Yadin, *Preliminary Report*, p. 79.

[28] See Chen, "Design"; "Masada," pp. 248-251 in Chiat, *Handbook*; Chiat, "First-Century"; Foerster, "Masada & Herodium"; Foerster, "Masada"; Hüttenmeister and Reeg, vol. 1, pp. 314-315; Ma'oz, "Gamla"; Norman Mirsky, *Unorthodox Judaism* (Columbus: Ohio State, 1978), pp. 151-171; Ovadiah and Michaeli; Yadin, *Masada*, pp. 181-192; Yadin, *Preliminary Report*, pp. 76-79; and Yadin, "Synagogue." The final report is *Masada III*, pp. 402-413.

[29] Yadin, *Preliminary Report*, pp. 76-9.

adding four levels of stone benches around the inside walls. Why does Yadin identify this structure as a synagogue? (1) It is an assembly hall; (2) the "entrance faced east, and it was wholly oriented towards Jerusalem," as is expected of some later synagogues; (3) fragments of Deuteronomy and Ezekiel were found buried in the storage room.[30]

Although the building clearly is an assembly hall, the step from that identification to one of a synagogue is problematic. First of all, the orientation of the building derives not from the rebels but from the original Herodian structure. Second, Yadin's claim regarding orientation is actually a combination of two, mutally exclusive, theories regarding orientation. And when examined closely, neither theory is fulfilled. On the one hand, a building's orientation—at least as it has been applied in the study of synagogue remains—refers to the direction faced by the worshippers; the synagogue should be oriented so the worshippers can easily face the Temple in Jerusalem. But the modifications the rebels made to the room indicate that orientation towards the Temple was unimportant to them, for they built a storeroom *halfway* across the wall facing Jerusalem. Thus the wall towards which the worship would have been directed was irregular—hardly a suitable focus of worship. On the other hand, the second theory, found in Tosefta Megillah 3:22, requires the synagogue to be oriented in the same direction as the Jerusalem Temple, namely, with the front entrance directly facing the east.[31] The Masada synagogue is not, since it is aligned on a northwest-southeast axis. So neither aspect of Yadin's confused claim concerning orientation points to identification of this structure as a synagogue.

Furthermore, according to Yadin's preliminary report, the original (Herodian) floor of the building was covered with a deep layer of animal dung, indicating that it had been a barn. The dung was not removed before the new floor was laid down.[32] Given the sanctity and respect accorded a synagogue, it seems incongruent—if not sacrilegious—to build one over a dung heap. Finally, the buried scrolls by themselves hardly prove that this was a synagogue. For example, the literary and archeological evidence at

---

[30] Yadin, *Masada*, pp. 184 & 187-8. The final report, written by E. Netzer, explicity drops the criterium of orientation. Netzer apparently recognized its problems and decided it did not strengthen the argument for identifying the structure as a synagogue. See *Masada III*, vol. 3, p. 410. G. Foerster had also emphasized the matter of orientation in Foerster, "Masada & Herodium" and Foerster, "Masada," but the orientation of the synagogues at both Masada and Herodium derived from "the topography of the site" according to Ma'oz. See Ma'oz, "Gamla," p. 40.

[31] Note that the Tosefta's ruling is promulgated some 200 or so years after the destruction of Masada's synagogue.

[32] Yadin, *Preliminary Report*, p. 77. He seems to have ignored this when he suggests in *Masada*, p. 185, that Herod may have used the building as a synagogue also. See also the discussion in *Masada III*, pp. 410-413. Netzer conclusively shows that Herod built a synagogue neither at Masada nor at any other of his palaces or fortresses.

Qumran show that there was no synagogue there. Since Qumran's scrolls are nowhere associated with a synagogue, Masada's fragments cannot on their own indicate such a structure.[33] It is clear, therefore, that the identification of this structure as a synagogue is highly uncertain. Indeed, it could have been a place for the rebels to meet and plan strategy, a need common to most armies. Certainly, it is well situated for that purpose, overlooking the area where the Romans built their siege ramp.

The structure at Herodium has the same uncertainties as the Masada building.[34] First, although the building clearly is an assembly hall, we have no indication that it was used for religious purposes. Second, its orientation is a matter of the original structure and cannot be attributed to the remodelers.[35] Third, the site was again the location of a rebel army who, like the rebels at Masada, would have needed a place of conference and assembly for military reasons.

In addition to these identification problems, there is also a problem in dating the synagogue at Herodium. The primary proponent of a pre-70 date for the synagogue has been G. Foerster, who supervised the restoration of the site after the primary excavations had been completed. He argues that the synagogue dates to rebels who used the site as a fortress during the First Jewish Revolt (starting about 68 C.E.?).[36] By contrast, V. C. Corbo—the site's excavator—initially held that the stratigraphy at the site did not permit any distinction between the First and Second Jewish Wars. His description of the synagogue in his preliminary report always refers to "*le guerre giudaiche*" ("the jewish wars"), and does not link the 'synagogue' to one war or the other.[37] In the final report, however, Corbo states that the synagogue belongs to the Second Jewish Revolt ("*seconda rivolta gli zeloti*").[38] It is clear, therefore, that the structure at Herodium provides no sure evidence of a

---

[33] Indeed, fragments were found in other rooms at Masada without those rooms being designated as synagogues by the excavators.

[34] See Chen, "Design"; "Herodium," pp. 204-7 in Chiat, *Handbook*; Chiat, "First-Century"; Foerster, "Masada & Herodium"; Foerster, "Masada"; Corbo, "L'Herodion—quarta campagna"; V. Corbo, "The Excavation at Herodium," *Qad.* 1:4 (1968): 132-36; Hüttenmeister and Reeg, vol. 1, pp. 173-4; Ma'oz, "Gamla"; and Ovadiah and Michaeli. See Corbo's final report in Corbo, *Herodion*.

[35] Unlike the Masada synagogue which faces southeast, the Herodium synagogue faces due east. This at least is in agreement with the Tosefta regulation.

[36] See Foerster, "Masada & Herodium" and Foerster, "Masada." Nowhere in these writings does Foerster make a case for assigning to Herodium a date around 70. To my knowledge, no scholar has presented an archaeologically sound argument for dating the 'synagogue' at Herodium to the first century.

[37] See V. Corbo, "L'Herodion—quarta campagna," pp. 72, 101f. Cf. J. Patrich, "Corbo's Excavations at Herodium: A Review Article," *IEJ* 42 (1992): 241-245. Focster has had an advantage in this debate by publishing in English; all Corbo's reports have been in Italian.

[38] Corbo, *Herodion*, p. 107. I want to thank Jane Reverand and Philip Holt for assisting me with their expertise in Italian.

synagogue in the first century; if it is a synagogue, it most likely stems from the early second century.

Even if the structures Masada and Herodium could be shown to be synagogues, they would not provide information that could counter the distinction between Galilee and Judea evidenced by the literary data. Neither appears in a village, town, or city and thus they provide no evidence about the typical religious organization of Jewish society. Furthermore, they come late in the pre-70 period—it would be difficult to date the so-called 'synagogue' stage of their existences to a point much before 68 C.E.

The final building that has been suggested as a pre-70 synagogue, and the only viable possibility in Galilee, stands in Gamala.[39] It is not a remodeled building, like Masada and Herodium, but one designed and constructed for a specific purpose from the beginning. It has no later buildings constructed on it, as at Migdal, because the site was abandoned after its destruction. So here we have a clear example of a building that was built for the function it served. The question is whether this function was that of a synagogue.

The building was erected sometime between 20 B.C.E. and 40 C.E., and was used until the Romans destroyed Gamala in the war. Taken as a whole, its design differs significantly from that of the other two buildings. Like the others, it was a rectangular building with tiers of benches going around all four sides. Unlike them, however, it had four rows of columns arranged as a rectangle around the inside of the benches. It was large enough to hold a great number of people, being almost three times the size of the Masada structure. Furthermore, it seems to be an official structure in a community setting; the length of its use indicates that the people at Gamala endorsed its construction and used the building.

Two items indicate that the Gamala structure was probably a synagogue. First, on the lintel over the doorway, the builders carved a six-petalled rosette, a Jewish ornament commonly associated with religious contexts during this period. This suggests that the structure was not simply a civic meeting house, but that it had a religious purposes, namely, those of a synagogue. Second, the center of the meeting room was unpaved. As Zvi Ma'oz has pointed out, this area was probably one where people did not freely walk (otherwise it would have been paved), and it presumably was covered with

[39] B. Bar-Kochva,"Gamla and Gaulanitis," *ZDPV*, 92 (1976) 54-71; Anonymous, "Gamla: the Masada of the North," p*BAR* 5 (1979): 12-19; "Gamla," pp. 282-4 in Chiat, *Handbook*; Chiat, "First-Century"; V. Corbo, "La Citta' Romana de Magdala," pp. 355-378 in *Studia Hierosolymitana*, (Jerusalem: 1976), esp. pp. 364-372; Foerster, "Masada & Herodium"; Foerster, "Masada"; S. Gutman, "The Synagogue at Gamla," pp. 30-34 in Levine, *ASR*; S. Gutmann,"Gamla—1983," pp. 26-7 in *Excavations and Surveys in Israel* 3 (1984); S. Gutmann, "Gamla—1984/1985/1986," pp. 38-41 in *Excavations and Surveys in Israel*, 5 (1986): 88-89; Hüttenmeister and Reeg, vol. 1, pp. 524; Ma'oz, "Gamla"; and Ovadiah and Michaeli.

carpets.[40] In other words, this was an important focus of attention, but not casually accessed. In addition, a foundation stone was carefully placed within the unpaved area. Its location is well-suited for the placement of a *bemah* (for which it would have served as a support), the table from which the Torah scroll is read. Although none of this data provides total certainty, it seems probable that this building was a synagogue.

The archaeological evidence thus provides conclusions similar to those we derived from the literary evidence. That is to say, the data points to the existence of synagogues in Galilee prior to 70, but provides no firm evidence concerning Judea. While we would be overstating the case to claim that the archeological data demonstrates that there were no synagogues in Judea prior to the Temple's destruction, it is not incorrect to state that, apart from the evidence of synagogues for foreigners, there is no indication that synagogues became part of Jewish worship in Judea or in Jerusalem.

When we attempt to take seriously the data currently available to modern scholarship, therefore, we discover an important phenomenon. Within the limits of the evidence, it appears that an incompatibility existed between the synagogue and the Temple cult. The synagogue, which orginated in regions where there was no practical access to the Jerusalem Temple, did best in places that also lacked this access. In Galilee and other areas in northern Palestine, the synagogue established itself and became an important community institution. By contrast, in regions where the Temple cult exercised some control and where people lived close enough to attend sacrifices, bring tithes and so on without major expenditures of time, the synagogue is not evidenced as being broadly accepted by the populace. Thus Jerusalem and Judea provide no data to indicate that the synagogue was an important institution alongside the Temple.

The evidence, little as it is, also suggests that the synagogues known to have stood in Jerusalem belonged to or provided services for Jews from outside Palestine. This reinforces the hypothesis that the synagogue originated outside the Palestine—according to Griffiths, in Egypt. When Jews from abroad permanently resided in Jerusalem, they brought their foreign institution—the synagogue—with them. They apparently established it in their own sub-community, but there is no evidence to indicate that it spread throughout the native Jerusalem population. Although the synagogue became naturalized in Galilee after its introduction, that does not seem to have happened in Jerusalem.

---

[40] Ma'oz, "Gamla," pp. 38-9.

BABYLONIAN SYNAGOGUES WITH HISTORICAL ASSOCIATIONS

AHARON OPPENHEIMER*

In the Babylonian Jewish diaspora, especially after 200 C.E., several synagogues developed a reputation as 'historic' because of a tradition which linked them with the beginning of the Babylonian Diaspora. This reputation gave them a particularly holy and revered status. No evidence assigns similar importance to any synagogue in the Land of Israel or in any other land of the Jewish dispersion. Occasionally, some sources identify synagogues in the Land of Israel according to selected criteria—such as the origin of arrivals from various lands of the diaspora or the occupations of the worshippers—but no synagogue receives a reputation as historical or particularly revered in comparison to other synagogues.

The best known synagogue of the historically important synagogues is the "Synagogue of *Shaf ve-yateb* at Nehardea." Nehardea was an important Jewish center at least from the early first century C.E.[1] Flavius Josephus describes Nehardea as the center of Jewish sovereignty, under the leadership of the brothers Hasinai and Hanilai, who exercised authority around the years 20-35 C.E.[2] He also mentions Nehardea and nearby Nisibis as places where Babylonian Jewry used to deposit the half-shekel funds prior to delivering them to the Jerusalem Temple.[3] This evidence sheds light on the strength of the Jewish settlement in Nehardea, on its excellent defenses, and on the special relationship which it had with the Parthian rulers as early as the days of the Second Temple.[4]

---

* This essay was originally published in A. Kasher, A. Oppenheimer, and U. Rappaport, eds., *Synagogues in Antiquity* (Jerusalem, 1987), pp. 147-154. It has been translated with the permission of the author and of Yad Izhak Ben Zvi. It was translated by Dr. Nathaniel Stampfer.

1 Regarding the location of Nehardea, see Oppenheimer, Isaac & Lecker, pp. 286-287.

2 Josephus, *JA*, 18, 310-399.

3 *JA*, 18, 311-313. Regarding Nisibis near Nehardea, see A. Oppenheimer, "The Center at Nisibis in the Mishnaic Period," in M. Stern, ed., *Nation and History*, vol. 1 (Jerusalem, 1983), pp. 141-150 (in Hebrew).

4 Nehardea continues to maintain its prominence in the tannaitic period as well. Rabbi Aqiba journeyed there to establish an intercalated leap year, an episode which is itself astonishing, and highlights the status of Nehardea (M. Yeb. 16:7). Nehardea served as the first place of residence of the Exilarch (e.g., Y. Megillah 1, 71a), and there the first great academy stood (*Iggeret of Rab Sherira Gaon*, Levin edition, pp. 78-80).

It appears that one of the suburbs of Nehardea was called '*Shaf-yateb*,' in whose confines was a synagogue called by its name, 'the Synagogue of *Shaf ve-yateb*.'[5] This synagogue was so well liked by the amoraic sages of Babylonia that they used to worship there despite the presence of a statue within it:

> But that synagogue of *Shaf ve-yateb*, in Nehardea, which had a statue in it, Rav and Samuel and the father of Samuel and Levi used to go to pray there.[6]

This source is assigned to the beginning of the amoraic period, when the main rabbinic academy existed in Nehardea and the Exilarch lived there. The entire matter about the erection of a statue in a synagogue is inexplicable, for despite the biblical prohibition against graven images and likenesses, the *amoraim* mentioned preferred to worship in the Synagogue of *Shaf ve-yateb*.[7]

The important and venerable origins of the Synagogue of *Shaf ve-yateb* are revealed in the following source:

> It has been taught that Rabbi Simeon ben Yohai said: Come and see how beloved are Israel of the Holy One, blessed be He, that to every place to which they were exiled, there too did the *shekinah* accompany them. They went into exile in Egypt, the *shekinah* went with them...to Babylonia, the *shekinah* accompanied them. Where does the *shekinah* abide in Babylonia? Said Abbaye, In the synagogue at Hutsal and in the Synagogue of *Shaf ve-yateb* in Nehardea, and do not say [how can it be both] here and there, for sometimes it is here and sometimes there. Said Abbaye, May I be rewarded, from a parasang away I come to pray there.[8]

Abbaye reveals that he takes pains to walk a *parasang* (about four-and-a-half kilometers) in order to pray at the *Shaf ve-yateb* Synagogue in Nehardea or at the one in Hutsal. The reason for this is because the *shekinah*, which accompanies Israel into exile, is present in these synagogues. It is interesting to note that in Abbaye's time Nehardea was already far past its peak of splendor. From the viewpoint of its strength, Nehardea was already in decline at the beginning of the amoraic period. The well-known fortifications

---

[5] Epstein rejects on linguistic grounds the interpretation of the Geonim of '*shaf ve-yateb*' as meaning 'journeyed and settled' (see the quotation of Rab Sherira below) and demonstrates that the meaning of the two words is actually the same. In Syriac '*shaf*' means dwelling and staying in one place, and '*shaufa*'—a place of dwelling. The meaning '*shaf-yateb*' is, therefore, 'Dwelling Place,' as a place name. See Y. N. Epstein, "Zur Babylonisch. Aramäischen Lexikographie," in S. Krauss, ed., *Festschrift A. Schwarz* (Berlin, 1917), pp. 326-327.

[6] B. RH 24b. All the manuscripts and parallel versions in B. AZ 43b, Rab and Samuel are not mentioned.

[7] To that same period belongs the source in B. Niddah 13a, also "Rab Judah and Samuel once stood on the roof of the *Shaf ve-yateb* synagogue in Neharda...."

[8] B. Megillah 29a.

of Nehardea were in a dilapidated and neglected state; indeed, it was impossible to close the gates of the city because their lower half had sunk into the ground.[9] The Palmyrans destroyed Nehardea in the year 259 C.E., so the academy moved to Pumbeditha, and Abbaye was later appointed to head it. Some sages eventually returned to Nehardea, although a major academy no longer existed there.[10] One of these was Rav Dimi of Nehardea, a contemporary of Abbaye. Despite all this, Abbaye, who flourished in the middle of the fourth century, attaches importance to prayer in the Synagogue of *Shaf ve-yateb.* The tradition about the antiquity and importance of this synagogue was maintained even after Nehardea itself declined in its greatness and its academy had departed.

Rav Sherira Gaon, in his *Iggeret* (letter), explains the importance of the Synagogue of *Shaf ve-yateb* in Nehardea:

> Know ye, that at the beginning, when Israel went into exile during the exile of Jehoiachin, there were craftsmen and smiths and several prophets with them. They came to Nehardea, and Jehoiachin, King of Judah and his party built a synagogue and they set it on stones and earth which they had brought with them from the Temple [in Jerusalem], to take upon themselves the fulfillment of Scripture, "Your servants take delight in its [Zion's] stones, and cherish its dust" (Psalms 102:15), and they named that synagogue the Synagogue of *Shaf ve-yateb* in Nehardea, that is, the Temple journeyed and settled here.[11]

Rav Sherira Gaon claims that the foundation of this synagogue included earth and stones from the ruins of the First Temple which the exiles brought with them from Jerusalem. In this spirit, he also explains the name of the synagogue, '*Shaf ve-yateb*,' by the expression, "the Temple journeyed (Hebrew: נסע) and settled here (Hebrew: ישב, Aramaic: יתב)." This explanation is sort of a folk etymology, and *shaf ve-yateb* is simply the name of a suburb of Nehardea, a name which was also given to the synagogue within it.[12] It is clear that Rav Sherira Gaon's statements are not historically authentic, for at the time of Jehoiachin's exile, the Temple was still standing. Furthermore, Jehoiachin was thrown into prison and it is thus unlikely that he carried out any building projects in Babylonia, even if he received special treatment in prison. Indeed, scholars have argued that there is no evidence of the existence of any synagogues during the Babylonian Exile, and that their

---

[9] See B. Erubin 6b; compare B. Taa. 20b.

[10] B. Baba Batra 22a. Regarding the restoration of the academy at Nehardea, see also Y. N. Epstein, *Introduction to the Amoraic Literature* (Jerusalem, 1962), p. 129 (in Hebrew).

[11] Levin edition, pp. 72-73; M. Stern, "The Assyrian Jerusalem in a Fragment of the Work of Asinius Quadratus," *Zion* 42 (1977): 295-297 (in Hebrew).

[12] See note 5 above. Concerning the Synagogue of *Shaf ve-yateb* in particular and Babylonian synagogues in general, see also Krauss, pp. 214-223.

origins lie in the Second-Temple period.[13] Without doubt, then, there is considerable exaggeration in Rav Sherira Gaon's testimony about the antiquity of the *Shaf ve-yateb* Synagogue, and it includes a legendary element regarding the circumstances of its founding. But whatever the historicity of these claims, they certainly emphasize the importance which the Babylonian *amoraim* attributed to the antiquity of synagogues.

It should be noted that the *Shaf ve-yateb* Synagogue is the last-known remnant of the history of Jewish Nehardea. In his travel book, Benjamin of Tudela mentions nothing about Nehardea except *Shaf ve-yateb*: "And there is the synagogue that the Jews built out of Jerusalem earth and stones...they called it *Shaf-yateb* which is in Nehardea."[14]

The Babylonian Talmud, in tractate Megillah, also praises the synagogue at Hutsal. Rav Sherira Gaon, in his *Iggeret*, refers to this evidence and appends to it a disagreement among the *amoraim* about which of these two synagogues the Divine Presence desired as its place—the one at Nehardea or the one at Hutsal:

> And the *shekinah* was with them, as it is stated in [B.] Megillah: Where in Babylonia? Rav said, in the synagogue of Hutsal, and Samuel said, in the Synagogue of *Shaf ve-yateb* in Nehardea; and do not say here and not here, for sometimes it is here and sometimes here. Abbaye said, May I be rewarded, from a parasang away I come to pray there; and this synagogue of Hutsal is close to the Study House (*bet midrash*) of Ezra the Scribe and it is farther down from Nehardea.[15]

The tradition with regard to the importance of the synagogue of Hutsal, on account of the Divine Presence which resided there from the days of Israel's Exile at the end of the First-Temple period, fits in with other evidence which reflects the antiquity attributed to Hutsal. Rav Assi, a member of the first generation of the Babylonian *amoraim* and a native of Hutsal, rules that the Scroll of Esther read on Purim be read in Hutsal not only on Adar 14 but on the 15th as well, because it is one of the walled cities for which there is doubt whether it was surrounded by a wall in Joshua's time.[16]

---

[13] See S. Safrai, "The Synagogue," in S. Safrai and M. Stern, eds., *The Jewish People in the First Century*, vol. 2, Compendia Rerum Iudaicarum ad Novum Testamentum (Assen/Philadelphia, 1987), pp. 909-913. But see also L. I. Levine, "The Second Temple Synagogue: The Formative Years," in Levine, *SLA*, pp. 7-31.

[14] See Benjamin of Tudela, 69, p. 46.

[15] Levin edition, p. 73.

[16] B. Megillah 5b. From this we understand that the requirement of reading the Scroll of Esther in the synagogue on Adar 15 in cities having surrounding walls in the days of Joshua [rather than on the 14th, as in all other cities] also applies to cities outside the Land of Israel. Regarding other ordinances of Rab Assi in Hutsal, see B. Hullin 26b. In the Hamburg manuscript, this passage appears at 107a.

Another source attests to the prominence and the antiquity attributed to Hutsal:

> Said Rav Judah: Whosoever dwells in Babylonia is [accounted] as if he lived in the Land of Israel, as it is written, "Away, escape, O Zion, you who dwell in Fair Babylon" (Zechariah 2:11). Said Abbaye: We have a tradition that Babylonia will not experience the pangs [associated with the coming] of the Messiah applies to Hutsal of Benjamin, and they call it 'Refuge of Deliverance.'[17]

Abbaye's statement, which exempts Babylonia from the pre-messianic tribulations, is linked in this source to Hutsal. In addition to the importance and antiquity of the site, it seems that the link is based also on a folk etymology which derives the name Hutsal (הוצל) from the word 'deliverance' (הצלה).

Some scholars have attempted to differentiate the Hutsal in Babylonia from one in the Land of Israel. The latter was located in the tribal territory of Benjamin, on the basis of the above-mentioned source, where Hutsal is described as "Hutsal of Benjamin."[18] If this is the case, then this source is not speaking about the Babylonian Hutsal, even though there is no logic to link Abbaye's statement concerning the absence of pre-messianic tribulations in Babylonia to Hutsal. Furthermore, in the source which deals with Rav Assi's ruling about reading the Scroll of Esther in Hutsal of Babylonia there is a reference to the town as "Hutsal of the house of Benjamin."[19] As mentioned above, Rav Assi himself was a Babylonian *amora* from Hutsal. Thus we can assume that Hutsal always refers to the Babylonian Hutsal and the name "Hutsal of Benjamin," if authentic, probably derives from traditions that link the ancient inhabitants of Hutsal to the members of the tribe

[17] B. Ket. 111a. The first phrase appears in the Munich manuscript as, "Said Rab Judah in the name of Rab." The saying itself conforms to the views of Rab Judah. Compare B. Ber. 24b; B. Shab. 41a; B. Ket. 110b. See also note 19 below.

[18] See A. Neubauer, *La Géographie du Talmud.* (Paris, 1868; repr. Amsterdam, 1965), p. 152; J. Schwartz, *The Produce of the Land* (Jerusalem, 1900), Luncz edition, pp. 163-164 (in Hebrew); I. S. Horowitz, *Palestine and the Adjacent Countries* (Vienna, 1923; repr. Israel, 1970), pp. 73-74 (in Hebrew).

[19] It should be noted that these two sources, in some of the manuscripts, read only 'Hutsal' with no addition. In Abbaye's statement in B. Ket. 111a, "...applies to Hutsal of Benjamin," "...of Benjamin" does not appear in the Munich manuscript, or in Vatican 113. See also the parallel wording in *Midrash Haggadol* "applies to Hutsal, called 'Source of Deliverance'"(Leviticus 28:38, Steinsaltz edition, p. 714, and similarly in *Yalkut Hamakhiri* Zechariah 2:11; compare also *Kaftor Vaferah*, Luncz edition [in Hebrew], p. 171). In the ordinance of Rab Assi in B. Megillah 5b, "...Hutsal of the House of Benjamin," "of the House of Benjamin" does not appear in the Munich manuscript, Munich B, or London; the Oxford manuscript has "Hutsal of the House of Minyamin" and as does the margin of Munich B.

of Benjamin who supposedly settled in this area during the Babylonian Exile in the sixth century B.C.E.[20]

The statement of Rav Sherira Gaon quoted above provides an indication of Hutsal's location. It suggests that Hutsal lies south of Nehardea in the direction of Sura. This location helps explain the differences between Rav and Samuel mentioned by Rav Sherira Gaon. Samuel, the head of the Nehardea academy, pinpointed the location of the *shekinah* in the Synagogue of *Shaf ve-yateb*. Rav—who left Nehardea and founded the academy of Sura—wanted to become independent from Nehardea and for that reason identified the location of the *shekinah* as the synagogue of Hutsal, which was close to Sura and a place of antiquity and of prominence in its own right. The close connection between Hutsal and the academy of Sura and its sages finds expression in additional sources. Rav Hisda, head of the academy of Sura in the third generation of the Babylonian *amoraim*, bans the butchers of Hutsal.[21] Rav Aha of Hutsal heeds the halakic decision of Rav Ashi, head of the Sura academy during the sixth generation of the Babylonian *amoraim*, when the academy was located in Mata Mehasya.[22]

The sources tell of noteworthy activities by the sages at Hutsal to the extent that the impression was created that an independent *bet midrash* existed there. Among the sages who stayed at Hutsal and taught there, Rabbi Josiah is mentioned several times.[23] Various scholars have identified Rabbi Josiah as a *tanna* of this name who was a disciple of Rabbi Ishmael. In light of this, they have developed a theory about a group of Rabbi Ishmael's disciples who migrated to Babylonia after the Bar-Kokba rebellion. They established a *bet midrash* headed by Rabbi Josiah parallel to the *bet midrash* functioning at that time in Nisibis under the leadership of Rabbi Judah ben Betera. According to these scholars, the *bet midrash* in Hutsal took part in the literary creativity of the *tannaim*, including the redaction of parts of the

---

[20] If the Minyamin version is accepted (see preceding note), then it is conceivable that the tradition considers the original inhabitants of Hutsal to have been of the family of Minyamin the Levite, mentioned in the census of Hezekiah (2 Chronicles 31:15); also see J. Obermeyer, *Die Landschaft Babylonien* (Frankfurt am Main, 1929), p. 300, note 6, or among those listed with the priestly course Miyamin (1 Chronicles 24:9). See also A. Büchler, *Der galiläische 'Am-ha'Ares des zweiten Jahrhunderts* (Vienna, 1906; repr. Hildesheim, 1968), p. 322, note 2.

[21] B. Hullin 132b.

[22] B. Ker. 13b. On the location of Hutsal, its sages, and inhabitants, see Oppenheimer, Isaac & Lecker, pp. 160-164. Regarding the center at Mata Mehasya, see p. 421.

[23] B. San. l9a; B. Git. 61a.

Mekhilta of Rabbi Ishmael and Sifré to Numbers.[24] This theory lacks foundation, among other things, because of the basic argument that we should not identify Rabbi Josiah, the disciple of Rabbi Ishmael who flourished in the generation of Usha, with the Rabbi Josiah of Hutsal. In his *Iggeret*, Rav Sherira Gaon states, "And after Rabbi [Judah *ha-nasi*], there were tannaitic sages from there (the Land of Israel)...and from here (Babylonia) like Rabbi Josiah of Hutsal."[25] This means that Rabbi Josiah of Hutsal flourished after the days of Rabbi Judah *ha-nasi*, during the first generation of the Babylonian *amoraim*.[26] There is nothing in this to negate the possibility that there existed a *bet midrash* of this or another kind in Hutsal, possibly even during the tannaitic period. This possibility fits with the traditions regarding the importance of Hutsal and its antiquity, and from this point of view it may be appropriate to draw some lines of similarity between it and Nehardea. Still, it is a long way from this small similarity to a precise determination about the redaction of specific tannaitic literature in Hutsal.

In addition to the synagogues in Nehardea and in Hutsal, other synagogues in Babylonia had a historical tradition. These gained their reputations by association with biblical heroes found in Babylonia. One of these is the synagogue attributed to Daniel:

> Said Rav Hisda to Mari the son of Rav Huna the son of Rav Jeremiah bar Abba: It is said that you came from Barnesh [Khan Birnus] to the Synagogue of Daniel, a distance of three parasangs, on the Sabbath; what do you rely upon? Upon the *burgi* [isolated huts]? But said your father's father, in the name of Rav [that there are no] isolated huts in Babylonia?[27] He went out and showed him certain (ruined) settlements that were contained within seventy cubits and a fraction.[28]

This source reveals that amoraic sages walked on the Sabbath from Barnesh[29] three parasangs distant (about fifteen kilometers) in order to pray

[24] About the redaction of tannaitic midrashim by sages of Rabbi Ishmael's Academy in Hutsal, see I. Halevy, *Generations of the Founders*, vol. 4 (Jerusalem, 1967), pp. 679-681 (in Hebrew); J. Neusner, *A History of the Jews in Babylonia*, vol. 1 (Leiden: Brill, 1965), pp. 128-135, 179-187; B. Z. Eshel, *Jewish Settlements in Babylonia during Talmudic Times* (Jerusalem, 1979), pp. 106-107 (in Hebrew).

[25] Levin edition, p. 59.

[26] Y. N. Epstein, *Introduction to the Literature of the Tannaim* (Jerusalem, 1957), p. 570, note 179 (in Hebrew); I. Gafni, "The Academy in Babylonia," (Ph.D. dissertation, Hebrew University, Jerusalem 5739 [1979]), pp. 15-17, and bibliography.

[27] The Munich manuscript and other versions read "the father of your father," and this seems correct. See *Dikduke Soferim*.

[28] B. Erubin 21a.

[29] It is reasonable to identify Barnesh as modern-day Khan-Birnus located in the vicinity of Hilla. See Oppenheimer, Isaac & Lecker, p. 64.

at the Synagogue of Daniel on the outskirts of the city Babylon.[30] There is no reason to assume there was no synagogue at Barnesh itself, but rather that they perceived special merit in worshipping in an ancient synagogue associated with Daniel. It is possible that one can tie this to evidence in Arabic sources about pilgrimages of Jews and Christians on their festival days to Daniel's den in Babylon.[31] The 'historical perception' regarding the lion's den and other sites in the environs of the city Babylon finds expression in the Talmud as well:

> Rav Hamnuna preached: Whoever sees Babylon the Wicked should recite five benedictions—upon seeing Babylon, one says "Praised be He who destroyed Babylon the Wicked." Upon seeing the house of Nebuchadnezzar, one says "Praised be He who destroyed the house of the wicked Nebuchadnezzar." Upon seeing the Lion's Den or the Fiery Furnace, one says, "Praised be He who performed miracles for our ancestors in this place...."[32]

Daniel's synagogue, like other sites in the area of ruins of the city of Babylon, is mentioned as well by Benjamin of Tudela.[33] He mentions yet another synagogue associated with a biblical figure and which is found in the same vicinity: "And from there [from Kafri] three parasangs to the synagogue of Ezekiel the Prophet, of blessed memory, which is by the Euphrates River...."[34] Kafri was situated in the vicinity of Sura, and the synagogue ascribed to Ezekiel was located, by this evidence, at a distance of three parasangs from it, on the bank of the Euphrates.[35]

The sum total of the sources clearly shows the importance which Babylonian Jewry ascribed to specific ancient synagogues, and the traditions they associated with them in order to glorify that antiquity. The preference

---

[30] These amoraic sages were not concerned about violating the Sabbath limit prohibition, because of the ruins of settlements present by the road. Compare "Said Rabbi Simeon: It is possible to go from Tiberias to Sepphoris and from Tyre to Sidon [on the Sabbath] because of the caves and towers that are between them." Tos. Erub. 6:8; compare Y. Erub. 5, 22b.

[31] See Mas'udi, *Murug ad-dahab wa-ma'adin al-gauhar*, (in Arabic), Ch. Pellat edition, vol. 1 (Beirut, 1966-1974), p. 265 (=E. Barbier de Meynard and Pavet de Courteille edition [Paris, 1861-1877], vol. 2, p. 115); Qazwini, *Atar al-bilad wa-ahbar al-'ibad* (Beirut, 1960), p. 304 (in Arabic); al-Qurtubi, *al-Masalik wa-l-mamalik*, Nur Osmaniya manuscript, fol. 59a (in Arabic); Mustaufi, *The Geographical Part of the Nuzhat al Qulub*, (in Arabic), G. Le Strange edition (Leiden, 1915-1917), vol. 2, p. 44; at -Ta'alibi, *Timar al-qulub fi l-mudaf wa-l-mansub*, (in Arabic), Muhammad abu l-Fadl Ibrahim edition (Cairo, 1965), p. 233; ad-Dahabi, *Tadkirat al-huffaz*, vol. 1 (Hyderabad, 1956), pp. 92-93. On the den see especially al-'Umari, *Masalik al-absar*, (in Arabic), vol. 1, Ahmad Zaki Basha edition (Cairo, 1924), p. 232.

[32] B. Ber. 57b. Compare Y. Ber. 9, 12d. Regarding the archaeological remains of Nebuchadnezzar's summer palace, see Oppenheimer, Isaac & Lecker, pp. 54-55 and bibliography.

[33] See Benjamin of Tudela, 65, p. 42.

[34] See Benjamin of Tudela, 66, p. 43. See also Krauss, pp. 219 -220.

[35] See Oppenheimer, Isaac & Lecker, pp. 169-170.

for synagogues possessing historical associations is peculiar to the Jews of talmudic Babylonia and reflects their beliefs and manner of thinking. There is in this a certain similarity to the conceit regarding the purity of lineage which served as a criterion for determining the boundaries of Jewish Babylonia.[36] In this regard, the Jews of Babylonia viewed themselves as preeminent, even superior to the Jews of the Land of Israel. "Said Rav Judah in the name of Samuel: 'All the lands are as an *'issah* to the Land of Israel, and the Land of Israel is as an *'issah* to Babylonia.'"[37] Just as they traced synagogue origins to the early days of the Babylonian exile, so the purity of lineage is traced to the days of Ezra who, according to tradition, did not emigrate to the Land of Israel until he had refined Babylonian Jewry as pure sifted flour.[38]

An additional aspect of the extreme veneration of ancient synagogues is bound up with the connection these synagogues have with the Land of Israel. Despite their occasionally ambivalent relationship toward the Land of Israel, Babylonian Jewry safeguarded their strong and varied ties with it. The ancient synagogues with their roots in the Land of Israel—like the traditions about building the Synagogue of *Shaf ve-yateb* in Nehardea with stones brought from the Temple, or the connection of Hutsal and its synagogue with the exiles from the tribe of Benjamin—testify indirectly to the bonds between the Babylonian diaspora and the Land of Israel, and show the roots of the Babylonian Jewish diaspora in the Land of Israel.

[36] See A. Oppenheimer and M. Lecker, "Lineage Boundaries of Babylonia," *Zion* 50 (1985): 173-187 (in Hebrew).

[37] B. Kid. 69b and 71a; B. Ket. 111a. Compare the incident about Ze'iri who emigrated from Babylonia to the Land of Israel, but refused to wed the daughter of Rabbi Yohanan (B. Kid. 71b).

[38] B. Kid. 69b and 71b.

SECTION II

THE DEVELOPMENT OF ANCIENT SYNAGOGUES

THE STRATIGRAPHIC CHRONOLOGY OF THE GALILEAN SYNAGOGUE FROM THE EARLY ROMAN PERIOD THROUGH THE EARLY BYZANTINE PERIOD (CA. 420 C.E.)

DENNIS E. GROH

It was the scholars of the late nineteenth and early twentieth century who first noted the large number of apparently Jewish structures in the Galilee, which they termed 'synagogues.'[1] Since the days of Kohl and Watzinger, survey, architectural clearance, and stratigraphic excavation of such structures have proceeded to produce a large concentration of Jewish public buildings in the Galilee and Golan.[2] More recent scholarship has produced excellent summaries of the state of synagogue research, including the invaluable work of Rachel Hachlili.[3] Yet debates still continue in the field around a whole series of crucial questions: Is there a typological development of so-called 'synagogue' structures? Precisely when and where do certain structural and architectual elements appear? To what degree can we interpret how such structures were used when we continue to view them in architectural isolation, apart from their ancient village contexts? And, most important of all for purposes of this chapter, *precisely* when does each particular structure appear and how long (and with what changes) does a particular building continue in use? Although Hachlili has advanced us all to a great degree in this latter question, there is still considerable room for correction of and precision in the results she has presented. The sheer scope of her study has melded sites and structures with 'soft' (i.e., imprecise) publication—and hence imprecise dating—into her overall picture; her study has missed some

---

[1] Cf. Kitchener, 123-129; Kohl and Watzinger.

[2] See, for example, the map of synagogues concentrated in the Galilee and Golan in Hachlili, *Jewish Art*, p. 142. Her map should be corrected by moving the site of Marous (Meroth) to the East of Bar'am rather than the West, and Beth She'arim should be spelled as here. See also Susan Weingarten and Moshe L. Fisher, "Ancient Jewish Art: An Archaeological Perspective," *Journal of Roman Archaeology* 5 (1992): 444, n. 20. For a map showing a greater distribution of synagogues because it accepts architectural elements and parts of buildings as synagogues, see Z. Ilan, "Galilee, Survey of Synagogues," *EASI* 5 (1986): 35-37.

[3] The important summaries to date are: Gutmann, *Synagogue*; Gutmann, *Ancient Synagogues*; Hüttenmeister and Reeg; Chiat; Moshe Dothan, "Research on Ancient Synagogues in the Land of Israel," in Shanks and Mazar, pp. 89-96; Levine, *ASR* ; Levine, *SLA*; Hachlili, *Jewish Art*; and Hachlili, *Ancient Synagogues*.

very precise stratigraphic information, and, to a degree, has globalized the picture of the state of synagogue research, giving the impression that we know more than we do know.[4] This is not to negate what is her fine scholarly achievement, but rather to insist that we need to take a step back from it and come at the problem from another direction.

In this chapter I want to examine the chronology of the Galilean synagogue exclusively from the standpoint of stratigraphic archaeology. Sixteen years of excavation in both Upper and Lower Galilee have convinced me that only the precision of controlled scientific excavation and proper publication of those results will give us the precise starting points in our discussions of the chronology of Galilean synagogues. I want to confine myself to discussions of those Jewish public structures for which I have available to me, and (where possible) to the more general reader, balk sections, coins, and, especially, *pottery* taken in controlled excavation. As a specialist in Late Roman ceramics, I find pottery especially important. Coins alone (taken apart from sections and pottery) can be, and are, frequently deceptive in interpreting the chronological horizons and limits of a structure or site. One example may suffice.

The early modern excavations of the famous synagogue site Chorazin were published in 1973. In that report coin evidence indicated that, as Eusebius' *Onomosticon* testified, the site lay destroyed from the early fourth century C.E.; the latest coin dated from Theodosius.[5] Fortunately, the excavator, a skilled archaeologist, was wise enough to publish the pottery, which indicated the site continued on in the fourth, fifth, and sixth centuries C.E.[6] Subsequent excavations produced the 'coin-elusive' Byzantine city. Indeed, the sheer ubiquity, indestructability, and (when broken) worthlessness to ancient people makes ceramic evidence more valuable than coins to the modern excavator.

The almost obsessive preoccupation of archaeologists with inscriptions found in and on synagogue structures, by contrast, fails to provide sufficient basis for precise dating. Take the case of the latest synagogue structure at Nabratein. The inscription carved on the lintel, which dates to 564 C.E., is not only 'secondary' (e.g., carved on a previous structure's lintel), it gives no indication of the long history of that late building's usage. From stratigraphic excavation of that late structure, which includes proper recovery of

---

4 For inclusion of sites with imprecise publications, see the chart in Hachlili, *Jewish Art*, pp. 148-149; cf. p. 399 for the, e.g., dating of Gush Ḥalav II and Hammath-Tiberias IIA as "fourth century," with the discussions of these synagogues in the text below.

5 Z. Yeivin, "Excavations at Chorazin 1962-1964," *Eretz Israel* 11 (1973): 157.

6 The Chorazin pottery included fine wares of the following types, CRS Form 1 (late fourth century-ca. 475 C.E.); CRS 9 (ca. 550-600 C.E.); LRC Form 3 (early fifth-550 C.E.) and ARS Form 91A (late fourth-late fifth C.E.).

phases with coins and ceramics, we now know that the building was repaired and used through the seventh century C.E.[7] Our Galilean Jewish public buildings, contrary to early estimates of the length of their usage, are now showing hundreds of years of continuous occupation, and, thus, only stratigraphic procedures can untangle the history of such a long usage.[8]

Most problematic is the continuance of a method of dating synagogues by a scheme of architectural sequence pioneered by the great scholar E. L. Sukenik. Sukenik developed a dating typology in which the earlier basilica had no permanent place for the Ark in the wall facing Jerusalem, being facade-oriented towards Jerusalem and having a flagstone floor. In the next stage of development, called now a 'broadhouse,' an apse for the Ark was located in a long wall which faced Jerusalem, opposite to the entrance-way; and mosaic flooring replaced the older flagstone paving. The *terminus a quo* for this new type of synagogue was the first half of the fourth century C.E., though Sukenik seemed to have favored the fifth century for the actual appearance of such a synagogue.[9] That Sukenik model was refined to give a three-stage development of the synagogue: (1) a basilical type dating to the second and third centuries of the Common Era, followed by (2) Sukenik's fourth-century broadhouse type (supposedly 'transitional'), and finally (3) the full Byzantine synagogue with apse in the narrow end oriented toward Jerusalem.[10]

So much has changed since Sukenik's model was developed and refined. Both the actual location and actual orientation of synagogues seems to contradict the ancient literary laws by which modern scholars interpreted Galilean structures.[11] More importantly, stratigraphic excavation has flatfootedly destroyed the sequential development described above.[12] Yet that model of synagogue architectural dating and development has persisted in

---

[7] "En-Nabratein," p. 4 and Fig. 2 and 20-21; see also Dennis E. Groh, "Judaism in Upper Galilee at the End of Antiquity: Excavations at Gush Ḥalav and en-Nabratein," in *Studia Patristica* XIX, ed. by Elizabeth A. Livingstone (Leuven: Peeters Press, 1989), pp. 68, 70-71.

[8] Cf. the judgement of Kitchener in Kitchener, p. 126: "Thus we arrive at the conclusion that the Jewish influence which gave rise to these buildings was both extremely local and short-lived."

[9] Sukenik, *ASPG*, pp. 27-28, 69.

[10] Meyers, "Current State" p. 128.

[11] Availability of land and local topography seem to have dictated a synagogue's location often (as at Gamala, Khirbet Shema', Meiron), leaving the synagogue to be topped or overshadowed by houses on higher ground (against the Talmudic advice of Bavli, Shabbat 11a, and Tosefta, Megillah). Orientation of Jewish, Christian, and pagan structures is not as settled as scholars represent: cf. John Wilkinson, "Orientation, Jewish and Christian," and Sharon C. Herbert, "The Orientation of Greek Temples," *PEQ* 116 (1984): 16-30 and 31-34, respectively.

[12] Cf. Meyers (see n. 10 above); Rachel Hachlili, "The State of Ancient Synagogue Research," in Hachlili, *Ancient Synagogues*, p. 4; Seager, "Architecture," p. 85.

the training of archaeologists through three generations of faculty and students, primarily at the Institute of Archaeology of the Hebrew University in Jerusalem. Sukenik originated the model and Avi-Yonah embellished it.[13] In recent decades, Gideon Foerster has tried (with important modifications) to save it—especially the third-century date for the basilical Galilean Synagogue.[14]

Thus discussions of the late dating of the synagogue at Capernaum, whose stratigraphic evidence overwhelmingly supports Loffreda's post-370 C.E. founding date, continue to be clouded and muddied by supporters of the architectural development scheme, who insist that the synagogue is either earlier in date or employs earlier architectural elements in the later structure.[15]

In the present study, I am aiming at starting points—benchmarks, if you will—for a chronology of Jewish public structures in the Galilee and Golan. In this discussion, I intend to confine myself primarily to those structures which have been cleanly excavated and clearly published in a way that I can make sense of them for both myself and my readers. Specialists may therefore find their 'favorite' site ignored because of the state of the evidence or the state of publication of the evidence. In addition, I will not concern myself in this chapter about the precise usage to which a Jewish public building was put, that is, whether it functioned as a *bet tefillah* (House of Prayer), *bet knesset* (House of Assembly), or *bet midrash* (House of Study), but will concentrate on matters of the form or plan of the public structure.[16]

---

[13] Seager, "Architecture," p. 85, attributes the term "transitional type" for the broadhouse to Avi-Yonah.

[14] Cf. G. Foerster, "Notes on Recent Excavations at Capernaum," in Levine, *ASR*, pp. 57 and 59; "Synagogue Art and Architecture," in Levine, *SLA*, pp. 143-144.

[15] See n. 14 above; M. Avi-Yonah "Some Comments on the Capernaum Excavations," in Levine, *ASR*, pp. 60-62. The "earlier architectural elements" argument appears 'unkillable,' despite all the stratigraphic evidence to the contrary: cf. Hanswulf Bloedhorn, "The Capitals of the Synagogue of Capernaum—Their Chronological and Stylistic Classification with Regard to Development of Capitals in the Decapolis and in Palestine," in Hachlili, *Ancient Synagogues*, p. 52. Bloedhorn accepts Russel's hypothesized earthquake of 363 C.E. to explain the "reuse" of an earlier synagogue's architectural elements in the late synagogue at Capernaum (p. 52). Unfortunately, neither the excavators of the site nor the readers of the reports can find evidence of any such earthquake. Nor does any 363 C.E. earthquake appear at Tiberias, Hammath-Tiberias or Sepphoris; but mid-fourth century destruction at Sepphoris should be attributed to the results of the Gallus Revolt (based on the field books of the University of South Florida Excavations at Sepphoris: James F. Strange, Director; Dennis E. Groh and Thomas R. W. Longstaff, Associate Directors).

[16] For *bet tefillah* and *bet knesset*, see the references in Seager, "Architecture," p. 88 and nn. 30 and 31. Only one clear *bet midrash* has been found in Galilee. See Zvi Ilan, "The Synagogue and *Beth Midrash* of Meroth," in Hachlili, *Ancient Synagogues*, pp. 31-36 and plate XXIV. [See also Ilan's essay in the present volume—Eds.] The lintel from another has been found at Dabbura in the Golan Heights, see Dan Urman, "Jewish Inscriptions from

Furthermore, I do not intend to address questions of the architectural prototypes or origins of the synagogue structure.[17]

GALILEE AND GOLAN

While 'regionalism' is the order of the day in interpretation of stratigraphic finds, debate continues as to exactly what factors (e.g., geographic, political, economic, monumental) constitute a region. Though both Josephus and the Mishnah clearly conceive of Galilee as a well-defined region West of the Jordan; and Josephus, the Mishnah, and the Talmud divide it into Upper and Lower Galilees, these historical and archaeological distinctions are not quite so neat.[18] Earlier estimates of the "isolation" of Upper Galilee (and Western Golan) by Eric M. Meyers have been revised as trading patterns of Upper Galilean sites became clearer.[19] Moreover, although Josephus clearly does not list the Golan within the geographic borders of Galilee, Gamala in the Golan Heights is clearly under his command as "general of the Galilee."[20] A wider look at literary sources gives no greater clarity on the precise borders of Galilee, but shows rather the existence of informal rubrics and an expanding or contracting view of what constituted Galilee.[21] In the popular mind

---

Dabbura in the Golan," *IEJ* 22 (1972): 21-23 and "Jewish Inscriptions from the Village of Dabbura in the Golan," in Levine, *ASR*, pp. 155-156.

[17] Cf., e.g., E. Netzer, "The Triclinia of Herod as the Prototype of the Galilean Synagogue Plan," in *Jerusalem in the Second Temple Period. Abraham Schalit Memorial Volume* edited by A. Oppenheimer, U. Rappaport, M. Stern (Jerusalem: Yad Izhak Ben-Zvi/Ministry of Defence, 1980), pp. VII and 109-116 (in Hebrew) and "The Herodian Trichinia—A Prototype for the 'Galilean-Type' Synagogue," in Levine, *ASR*, pp. 49-51; G. Foerster, "Architectural Models of the Greco-Roman Period and the Origin of the 'Galilean' Synagogue," in Levine, *ASR*, pp. 45-51; N. Avigad, "The 'Galilean' Synagogue and Its Predecessors," in Levine, *ASR*, pp. 42-44; Sidney B. Hoenig, "The Ancient City Square: The Forerunner of the Synagogue," in *ANRW* 19.1, pp. 448-476.

[18] References and discussion in Eric M. Meyers, "The Cultural Setting of Galilee: The Case of Regionalism and Early Judaism," in *ANRW* 19.1, pp. 693-695 and Michael Avi-Yonah, *The Holy Land From the Persian to the Arab Conquest (536 B.C.-A.D. 640). A Historical Geography*, revised edition (Grand Rapids, MI: Baker Book House, 1966 [1977]), pp. 115, 134-135, 201.

[19] Eric M. Meyers, "Galilean Regionalism: A Reappraisal," in W. S. Green, ed., *Approaches to Ancient Judaism*, vol. 5, Brown Judaic Studies 32 (Chico, CA: Scholars Press, 1985), p. 115. And see below in this text at n. 30.

[20] See the excellent discussion by Dan Urman, *The Golan. A Profile of a Region During the Roman and Byzantine Periods*, BAR International Series 269 (Oxford: B.A.R., 1985), pp. 22-24.

[21] Cf. Günter Stemberger, "Appendix IV. Galilee—Land of Salvation?" in W. D. Davies, *The Gospel and the Land. Early Christianity and Jewish Territorial Doctrine* (Berkeley, Los Angeles, London: University of California Press, 1974), pp. 409-439; Seán Freyne, "Hellenistic/Roman Galilee," in *The Anchor Bible Dictionary*, edited by David Noel

the Eastern shore of the Sea of Galilee and the Golan seem to have been included in the term 'Galilee.'

Moreover, a continuous band of analogous material culture runs from Upper Galilee across the Jordan into the Golan as shown by synagogue and village architecture and art,[22] though that has been recently nuanced to emphasize distinctions between Galilean and Golani synagogues.[23] Also compelling for our inclusion of the Golan in our discussion of Galilean synagogues is the ceramic inclusion of the region within the Galilean sphere of trade and commerce. The so-called Galilean bowl is ubiquitous across both regions, but is not found in other regions of the country. More recent study on the close-commonality of clays and forms of the Galilee to those of the Golan by David Adan-Bayewitz has indicated that Kefar Hananiah ware from the Lower Galilee "...was plentiful at all Upper Galilee settlement sites excavated to date..."[24] Even though the Golan had its own locally made and distributed crude wares in the Roman and Byzantine periods, "...a significant minority of the cooking ware found in the Golan...was made at the Kefar Hananiah potteries."[25]

Scholarly knowledge of this unity was reinforced when, in 1989, James F. Strange, Thomas R. W. Longstaff and I identified and surveyed the previously unlocated Talmudic pottery-making site of Shikhin (Josephan 'Asochis').[26] It lies near Sepphoris on a previously unnamed tell. Wasters of the most characteristic Sepphoris forms were recovered from the kiln area of that site and subjected to neutron activation analysis by David Adan-Bayewitz. One example of Adan-Bayewitz's results will illustrate the close material-ties and trade-ties between the Galilee and Golan. Among the Shikhin 'wasters' was a storage jar with an everted rim and an inset neck, common in Galilean contexts from the late first century B.C.E. to around 250 C.E., of a ware type known now as Roman Galilee II.[27] Scientific analysis has shown that Roman Galilee II was manufactured at Shikhin in the Lower Galilee.[28] These jars have been excavated in Lower Galilee at Sepphoris, Hammath-Tiberias, Tabgha, Capernaum, and Khirbet Hazon; in

---

Freedman (New York/London, etc.: Doubleday, 1992), vol. 2, pp. 895-899, and "Galilee, Sea of (Place)," vol. 2, pp. 899-901.

[22] Eric M. Meyers, "Galilean Regionalism As a Factor in Historical Reconstruction," *BASOR* 221 (1976): 97, 99.

[23] Cf. Zvi Uri Ma'oz, "Ancient Synagogues of the Golan," *BA* 51 (1988): 116.

[24] Adan-Bayewitz, "Manufacture," p. 233.

[25] Adan-Bayewitz, "Manufacture," p. 230 (cf. pp. 198-199, 241).

[26] James F. Strange, Dennis E. Groh, Thomas R. W. Longstaff (with David Adan-Bayewitz), "The Location and Identification of Ancient Shikhin," *IEJ* (forthcoming).

[27] Adan-Bayewitz and Perlman, pp. 167-168.

[28] Adan-Bayewitz and Perlman, p. 168.

Upper Galilee at Nabratein and Meiron; and in the Golan at Sussita, Gamala, 'En Nashuṭ, and Dabiyya.[29] In addition to showing the ceramic links between Galilee and the Golan, Adan-Bayewitz's work further breaks down the earlier hypothesis of the "isolation" of both of the Upper Galilee from other regions and sub-regions of the North of Israel and between rural and urban centers in Galilee and Golan.[30]

While the trade pattern represented by pottery seems to move from the Lower Galilee to the Upper Galilee and Golan, without evidence of trade back to Lower Galilee, the impact of Galilee's influence represented by such trade is significant.[31] Thus it seems proper to study Galilean synagogues chronologically across both Galilees and the Golan's sub-regions. At the informal level (and for archaeologists, the most basic level) of material culture, tight regional lines drawn by ritual and political rule-makers were simply not observed.

FIRST-CENTURY SYNAGOGUES

A number of recent studies have struggled with the problem of identifying actual first-century or 'Second-Temple Period' synagogues.[32] Of the list of candidates, only two probably prove to be Jewish public structures that can yield significant plans for our purposes here—Migdal and Gamala. Two others have insufficient evidence to stand as first-century synagogues—Capernaum and Chorazin. The first-century synagogue identified under the late fourth-century synagogue at Capernaum amounts to only two large basalt walls parallel to the overlying late synagogue, some other walls, and some flooring.[33] A synagogue reported at Chorazin 200 m. west of the later

---

29 Adan-Bayewitz and Perlman, p. 167.

30 Adan-Bayewitz and Perlman, pp. 171-172; cf. n. 19 (above).

31 Both in the ceramic and architectural media Galilean imports prove of great significance. In the world of synagogue architecture, Galilean elements were adapted to the Golan (Ma'oz, see n. 23 above), whereas Golan crude wares similar to the Galilean forms were developed for the local market of the Golan: cf. Adan-Bayewitz, "Manufacture," pp. 198-199, 216.

32 Cf. especially, Marilyn J. Chiat, "First-Century Synagogue Architecture: Methodological Problems," in Gutmann, *Ancient Synagogues*, pp. 49-60; Lee I. Levine, "The Second Temple Synagogue: The Formative Years," in Levine, *SLA*, pp. 7-31; Lester L. Grabbe, "Synagogues in Pre-70 Palestine: A Reassessment," *Journal of Theological Studies* n.s. 39 (1988): 401-410 [Reprinted in the present volume—Eds.]; Paul Virgil McCracken Flesher, "Palestinian Synagogues Before 70 C.E.: A Review of the Evidence" in *The Ethnography and Literature of Judaism*, edited by J. Neusner and E.S. Frerichs, *Approaches to Ancient Judaism*, vol. 6 (Atlanta: Scholars Press, 1989), pp. 67-81. [A revised version appears in the present volume—Eds.]

33 Cf. James F. Strange and Hershel Shanks, "Synagogue Where Jesus Preached Found at Capernaum," *BAR* (Nov./Dec. 1983): 29-31. V. Corbo identified by means of his various

synagogue by J. Ory in 1926 has been accepted as a recent temple synagogue by G. Foerster,[34] but it is impossible to verify this stratigraphically.[35]

The first of the synagogue structures from the first century is that of Migdal, New Testament Magdala, where a small assembly hall structure has been identified and excavated. The building was a small, only slightly rectangular structure, measuring 8.16 m. x 7.25 m. on the eastern side.[36] The entrance to the structure, not recoverable by the excavators, was hypothesized to lie on the east side of the building.[37] On the north wall of the synagogue was a bank of five steps for seating the congregation, of which only four steps remained *in situ* (see PL. 1a).[38] Already in this first-century synagogue we can see the non-classical canons of building, so characteristic of the later synagogues, in the variation of the height (rather than the regularity) of the banked steps.[39] A colonade ran around the interior of the synagogue, though it remained *in situ* only on the south, east, and west.[40] At the corners were found the heart-shaped cornering bases for columnation (see PL. 1a) which was previously associated with the supposed Galilean basilicas of the third century.

The original floor was a basalt slab pavement, removed when the synagogue was reused; but some of it remained *in situ*—in front of the first step

---

trenches a perimeter wall 24.50 m. x 18.70 m. on the outside and 22.00 m. x 16.50 m. internally: "Resti della sinagoga del primo secolo a Cafarnao," *Studia Hierosolymitana* III, Studium Biblicum Franciscanum Collectio Maior 30 (Jerusalem: Franciscan Printing Press, 1982), p. 340 and "Miscellanea III. La Sinagoga del centuriano romano," in *La Terra Sancta. Studi di Archeologia. Atti del simposio "Trent `anni di Archeologia in Terra Sancta," Roma 27-30 aprile 1982*, Bibliotheca Pontificii Athenaei "Antonianum" 23 (Rome: Pontificium Athenaeum Antonianume, 1983), p. 110. Other walls related to this structure were uncovered, as well as the basalt courtyard bounded by the larger walls. This earlier structure, independent of the later synagogue excavated by the Franciscans, was begun in 63 B.C.E. and completed in the early first century C.E., a date they asserted paralleled that of the Magdala synagogue (see text below): Corbo, "Resti della synagoga," p. 339.

[34] "The Synagogue at Masada and Herodium," *Eretz Israel* 11 (1973): 308 and 224-228. The synagogue was reported (p. 227) in the Department of Antiquities of Palestine's file 120 for 1926; cf. James F. Strange, "Archaeology and the Religion of Judaism in Palestine" in *ANRW* 19.1, p. 656 and n. 38.

[35] Especially since the current excavator of the site considers Chorazin a city dating from the Mishnaic period and later: Zeev Yeivin, "Khorazin: A Mishnaic City," *BAAS* (1982-83): 46-48.

[36] Corbo, "Magdala," p. 366.

[37] At the point following after a rebuild of the wall for 2.0 m.: Corbo, "Magdala," p. 368.

[38] Corbo, "Magdala," p. 367.

[39] The steps vary in height as follows: 25 cm, 24.5 cm, 23 cm, 19 cm: Corbo, "Magdala,"

[40] Corbo, "Magdala." Rather than intuit a column on the N side of the colonade and speculate about how it would obscure the view of those on the banked seats, it seems better simply to eliminate it, as Strange (see n. 33 above), p. 29.

of the benching under the columns of the south wall, under the first column of the northwest.[41] Columns were set directly on the stone slab of the pavement without a stylobate.[42] Decoration of this small synagogue structure was austere—a neck-band, anuli, sea-urchin, and abacus being the only decoration recovered.[43]

Sometime in the first century, likely before 70, the floor was raised a few centimeters. The high water level of the site on which the synagogue was built, which in the early second century would result in its abandonment as a synagogue and its reuse as a water collector, may have been a factor in the raising of the floor of the synagogue.[44] Thus this structure, founded in the early first century C.E., continued in use until at least around 70 C.E.[45]

The second of the first-century synagogue structures appears in Gamala. At this Golan Heights site we have a sure *terminus* for a synagogue structure, 67 C.E. The site was destroyed by the Roman seige of that year and both survey and excavation have underlined the first Jewish war as the termination of that site.[46]

The synagogue building (19.60 x 15.10 m.) was divided by interior columnation on four sides (see PL. 1b) into a central nave (9.30 x 13.40 m.) with an aisle on each of the four sides.[47] Benched seating of basalt, which ran around the interior of the synagogue in the aisles, was preserved on the eastern side, where four steps of benching were preserved *in situ*.[48] Heart-shaped columns, as at Migdal, were found at the corners of the colonade, though, unlike Migdal, the main floor of the synagogue was earthen.[49] Additional columns to support the roof may have stood on a strip of stones found in the center of the nave (see PL. 1b).[50] Originally thought to be of Hasmonean founding,[51] the building cannot now be earlier than the age of Herod in its initial stage.[52] But its present plan clearly dates to the Zealot

---

[41] Corbo, "Magdala."

[42] Corbo, "Magdala."

[43] Corbo, "Magdala."

[44] Corbo, "Magdala" pp. 368, 370.

[45] Stanislao Loffreda, "Alcune osservazioni sulla ceramica di Magdala," in *Studia Hiersolymitana* (see n. 36 above), p. 339 and Fig. 1:1-6 for dating and pottery between the floors; p. 339 and Figs. 10.1 and 10.2 for the earliest synagogue.

[46] "Meiron," p. 7.

[47] Ma'oz, "Gamla," p. 37.

[48] Ma'oz, "Gamla."

[49] Ma'oz, "Gamla," p. 38; S. Gutman and H. Shanks, "Gamla, the Masada of the North," *BAR* 5:1 (1979): 19.

[50] Ma'oz, "Gamla," p. 38.

[51] Ma'oz, "Gamla," p. 35; S. Gutman, "The Synagogue at Gamla," Levine, *ASR*, p. 34.

[52] S. Gutmann [sic], "Gamla—1983," in *EASI* 3 (1984): 26.

period, and its channel connecting it to a nearby mikveh reinforces its identification as a synagogue.[53] A six-petaled rosette between date palms on a fragment of the lintel and the simple Doric capitals further indicate the restrained artistic embellishment of the early Galilean synagogue.[54]

The first-century Galilean synagogue structure seems to consist in a rectangular room with a benched interior, a colonade supporting the roof and (probably) no worship center or *bemah*. It is essentially a room to gather the community.[55]

A SECOND-CENTURY BROADHOUSE

Stratigraphically, the earliest appearance of a broadhouse synagogue occurs as a small structure found beneath subsequent synagogues at Nabratein. The structure, Synagogue 1, dates to Period II of the site, the Middle Roman era (ca. 135-250 C.E.).[56] The finding of this, the earliest broadhouse type yet discovered, seems to have thoroughly destroyed the older architectural-sequence model, as Eric M. Meyers himself has hinted.[57]

The 11.2 x 9.35 m. building was entered through the approximate center of the southern wall (see PL. 1c) but had a secondary entrance on the NE.[58] Stone benches were built along the walls on the east and the west, and traces of the cuttings for benching on the northern wall were found.[59] Though the presence of columns in the interior space of the synagogue cannot be established (plans showing such are conjectural), twin stone platforms, which flank the southern (main) doorway, were identified as *bemah*s.[60] Founded in the earlier second century, the synagogue continued in use until ca. 250, when it (as we shall see) was enlarged. The importance of Synagogue 1's discovery cannot be overestimated, since it not only is the earliest Galilean broadhouse type, but provides our first example of a permanent set of *bemah*s on the Jerusalem wall.

---

[53] S. Gutman, *Gamla* [Hebrew] (Tel Aviv: Hakibbutz Hameuchad, 1981), folded plan; "Gamla—1983," *EASI* 3 (1984): 26; Gutman, "Gamla," p. 32.

[54] Gutman, "Gamla," p. 34; Ma'oz, "Gamla," pp. 36, 39.

[55] Cf. Ma'oz, "Gamla," p. 41.

[56] "En-Nabratein," pp. 35-54.

[57] "The Current State of Galilean Synagogue Studies," in Levine, *SLA*, p. 132.

[58] "En-Nabratein," p. 40.

[59] "En-Nabratein."

[60] "En-Nabratein."

THE MID THIRD-CENTURY SYNAGOGUE

The mid third century inaugurated a boom in synagogue building in the Galilee, though many of the plans for these buildings can only be inferred from the synagogues of the subsequent period. At Nabratein, however, it is possible to recover the plan of Synagogue 2a in Period IIIa of that site (Late Roman, ca. 250-306 C.E.). Synagogue 2a gives us an example of a true basilical synagogue which appears for the first time at the mid third century.

Building 2a was oriented on a N/S axis with three columns on each side of the nave, dividing it off from the side aisles.[61] The building was lengthened, an exonarthex was added, and a permanent *aedicula* (Torah shrine) was constructed on the western interior *bemah*.[62] A fragment of the gable for the actual Torah shrine was discovered reused in Synagogue 2b of Period III (Late Roman, 306-350/63).[63]

Around the mid third century another synagogue was constructed at Gush Ḥalav of the basilical type with a single entrance in the south wall, similar to Nabratein.[64] The destruction and heavy rebuilding of this synagogue after the 306 C.E. earthquake makes a full reconstruction of the Period I synagogue difficult, but a basic plan of that synagogue can be recovered (see PL. 1d).[65] Here a four-columned nave, flanked by two side aisles with side-rooms on either side of the building, is oriented toward the interior south (Jerusalem) wall by a *bemah* just to the west of the single central doorway. Benching runs along the west wall and the north wall between the stylobates; and the synagogue has a small rear entrance into the western corridor at the rear.[66]

At nearby Khirbet Shema' an entirely different kind of synagogue is built in the late third century, a broadhouse synagogue. The massive destruction of this first synagogue at Khirbet Shema' by the 306 earthquake makes it extemely difficult to recover that synagogue's exact plan. But some clever excavating and publishing of results allows us to recognize a broadhouse building in the same general position and dimensions as the

61 "En-Nabratein," p. 36 and Fig. 2 on p. 38.

62 "En-Nabratein," pp. 42-43.

63 "En-Nabratein." For the ark, see also Eric M. Meyers and Carol L. Meyers, "American Archaeologists Find Remains of Ancient Synagogue Ark in Galilee," *BAR* 7 (1981): 20-39; E. M. Meyers, J. F. Strange, and C. L. Meyers, "The Ark of Nabratein—A First Glance," *BA* 44 (1981): 237-43. Since Synagogue 2b was rebuilt on the same plan as 2a, I will not discuss it again in the text. For the problem of terminating Period III, see Groh, "Chronology," pp. 83-84; and n. 15 (above).

64 *Gush Halav*, p. 120.

65 See the excellent reconstruction possibilities offered by Lawrence Belkin in *Gush Halav*, pp. 99ff.

66 See *Gush Halav*, Figs. 14-15 for block and isometric plans.

later structure. A bench ran along the long south (Jerusalem) wall, which bench was partly covered over when the foundation for an *aedicula* was added prior to the 306 destruction.[67] Synagogue I seems to have been a four-columned basilica. But unlike Nabratein, it conformed to the broadhouse type and was entered through a western doorway on which an eagle had been carved.[68]

Already we can see the great variety of types of Galilean synagogues, each of which is adapted to the tastes and topography of individual builders and communities. But the Meiron synagogue, erected in the last decade of the third century and undamaged by the earthquake of 306 C.E., underscores this point. A combination of factors—long occupation, centuries of pilgrim visitation to the site, and the clearing operations of Kohl and Watzinger—made this structure difficult to recover in its original entirety.[69] But an original plan has been recovered which shows a huge (27.5 x 28.4 m.) basilical structure oriented to the S (towards Jerusalem) by the three-door facade, which appears to have been the only entrance-way into the synagogue.[70]

The dating of the Meiron synagogue's founding is crucial, since much of the subsequent history of the structure has been obscured by the effects of nature and history. But the initial dating can be established by the stratigraphic excavation of Annex A on the east of the synagogue. This annex was bonded into the synagogue and, hence, was contemporary with it.[71] The 'critical' (i.e., 'dating') loci for Annex A are third/early fourth-century loci.[72] Locus 1008 produced the latest coin in this material, a coin of Probus of 276-282 C.E.—suggesting a late third-century date. Yet the excavators opt for a Stratum IV (250-365 C.E.) date, publishing fourth-century crude wares from loci higher up (Locus 1003) in support of the fourth-century dating.[73] Here the excavators seem a bit too conservative in their dating of the synagogue's founding. The coins should control and give pre-

[67] Meyers, *Khirbet Shema'*, pp. 49, 54. Fragments of the *aedicula* were dumped in the sub-floor fill of Synagogue II (p. 52; cf. p. 55).

[68] Meyers, *Khirbet Shema'*, p. 37 and Fig. 3.3.

[69] Cf. *Meiron*, p. 9.

[70] *Meiron*, pp. 10, 12. The entrance-way question is a bit obscured at Meiron because the NE corner, where another entrance may have been located, was "obliterated" (p. 12). For the plan, see p. 16.

[71] *Meiron*, p. 14. The principal excavators neglected to publish a photograph of that bond-joint, but it is just barely discernible in Photo 4, p. 10. However, I was a member of the senior staff of that expedition and was present to observe both the bonding of Annex A into the foundation platform of the synagogue and the excavation of the critical dating *loci*.

[72] MIII.1 *loci* 1003, 1004, 1008: *Meiron*, p. 16. The principal excavators call these *loci* "sealed," but I prefer the term "stratified" since the "seal" of a medieval foundation trench is not a perfect one.

[73] Cf. the locus list readings for III.1 on p. 251 and the pottery discussion on Pl. 8.19, pp. 127-128.

cision to the somewhat long and vague perdurance of crude ware forms, and the founding of the synagogue should be placed in the last decade of the third century, at the latest. The excavator's narrative remarks do indicate a *terminus a quo* at 280 C.E., but speculation about the relative completion of the synagogue *vis a vis* the annex is gratuitous.[74] Given the speed with which building operations proceeded in the Galilee at this time, the synagogue was likely in use before the turn of the century.[75] The peaking of the city commercially in the second half of the third century and the appearance of trade with (or rather from) the African ceramic factories, which evidence appears at Meiron precisely at the end of the third century, further confirm this dating.[76]

Meiron thus provides the earliest evidence—late third century—of the so-called 'Galilean' synagogue—a long basilica (eight columns on a side) with heart-shaped column bases at the cornering of the rear colonades, a three-door, facade-oriented structure with a columned portico on the front. The roof of the structure was tiled, but nothing can be known of the floor composition.[77] The peculiar construction, in which the synagogue was set on a bedrock platform extended to the east with a founding wall into which Annex A was bonded, assures us that this first plan was what the builders were stuck with, since change of plan in mid-construction would have been nearly impossible (or perhaps, at least, inconceivable). The fact that Meiron does not lie on the fault line which brought down a number of structures in the 306 earthquake and the synagogue's excellent construction mean we have its plan intact and need not infer it from destroyed remains recovered from under a subsequent synagogue.[78]

The synagogue at Ḥorvat 'Ammudim was built next, just at the turn of the fourth century, as both pottery and coins testify.[79] The plan cannot be completely determined; but the building was a basilical structure oriented by the short wall, in which a central doorway was constructed. Unfortunately, it was impossible to determine whether there were side doorways in the facade wall. The synagogue perhaps had benches around the interior sides, a Torah shrine; and was coverd by a tile roof.[80] Most important was the discovery of portions of a mosaic floor that originally covered the entire floor

---

[74] *Meiron*, p. 16.

[75] Here the immediate rebuilding without any signs of an abandonment period at Khirbet Shema', Nabratein, Gush Ḥalav and, perhaps, Hammath-Tiberias (see below) is significant.

[76] Cf. *Meiron*, p. 23ff.; p. 138 for MTS3.2 types A & B (ARS).

[77] *Meiron*, pp. 10, 17.

[78] *Meiron*, p. 17.

[79] Levine, "Ḥ. 'Ammudim," p. 6; Adan-Bayewitz, "Ceramics," p. 29.

[80] Levine, "Ḥ. 'Ammudim," p. 5; Adan-Bayewitz, "Ceramics," p. 25.

of the basilica.[81] It was of white tesserae, bordered with geometric designs in black, white, red, blue, and orange.[82] An Aramaic inscription in a mosaic medallion specifically mentioned the making of the mosaic pavement.[83] Ḥ. Ammudim thus is our earliest *clear* example of mosaic floor in the Galilean basilical synagogue, and represents the first instance in a synagogue building of the use of both stone decoration and mosaic in concert.[84] The excavators of the structure posited a short fourth-century occupation for it, but pottery from as late as the sixth century clouds that *terminus ad quem*.[85]

Before departing the third century, one additional synagogue structure needs to be located there. The first synagogue at Qaṣrin in the Golan Heights, which has recently been dated to the late fourth or early fifth century C.E., should be placed in the corpus of third-century synagogues. Dan Urman, the original excavator of Qaṣrin, dated the first phase of this synagogue from the beginning of the third century to the middle of the fourth.[86] Pottery from soundings inside this synagogue, which I read for Urman in 1975, was uniformly late third and early fourth century. Phase I of Qaṣrin consisted of a hall with two rows of basalt benches around all four walls. The floor of the hall was made of a thick plaster (ca. 10 cm), on which paver-sized panels had been drawn.[87]

SYNAGOGUES FROM 306—363 C.E.

The 306 C.E. earthquake in Galilee provided the occasion for the reconstruction and further embellishment of a number of synagogues. This gives an excellent view of the variety of synagogue structures in the first half of the fourth century. All of these buildings were built immediately after 306 C.E. without an intervening abandonment phase.

The third synagogue at Nabratein (Synagogue 2b) was rebuilt without changing the second synagogue's (Synagogue 2a) ground plan (see PL. 2a). The *bemahs* on the south wall were rebuilt, into one of which the fragment

[81] Levine, "Ḥ. 'Ammudim," p. 10.

[82] Levine, "Ḥ. 'Ammudim," p. 7-8.

[83] Levine, "Ḥ. 'Ammudim," p. 8-9.

[84] Levine, "Ḥ. 'Ammudim," p. 11. The first synagogue at Hammath-Tiberias is discounted because of major problems connected with that report (see text below), not the least of which is the assigning of a date in the first half of the third century based on architectural dating: cf. Dothan, *Hammath Tiberias*, p. 26.

[85] Levine, "Ḥ. 'Ammudim," p. 11; Adan-Bayewitz, "Ceramics," p. 24; and "Meiron," pp. 7-8.

[86] Urman, "Qaṣrin Inscriptions," p. 532.

[87] See Urman, "Qaṣrin Inscriptions."

of the Torah Ark of Synagogue 2a was placed upside down. While the roof tiles from the earlier structure were buried under the floor of building 2b.[88]

At Gush Ḥalav, significant repairs and reconstruction to the NE outer walls and the stylobate produced in Period II (306-363 C.E.) a simple basilical hall with several side chambers, the Western corridor likely belonging to this period.[89] The Period II synagogue (see PL. 2b) had a simple white mosaic floor as conjectured from the numerous tesserae (none *in situ*) found in excavating the structure.[90] Whether the heart-shaped corner column bases belong to the gallery or mezzanine level of this synagogue or to the stylobate of the post-363 C.E. synagogue is difficult to say.[91] In fact, the mezzanine at the north of the building can date from either Period II or III synagogue.[92] The *bemah* continued (likely) in use from Period I.[93] The roof of the building was tile.[94] The building was entered from the south (facade) doorway, passing under an eagle lintel, though a doorway in the NE corner continued to be used.[95] The column with the inscription of Yose bar Nahum was probably erected for this synagogue.[96]

At nearby Khirbet Shema', Synagogue 2 was erected just after the 306 C.E. destruction and continued to function until its destruction in 419 C.E. on the same broadhouse plan as Synagogue 1, but with several significant changes.[97] First, the new *bemah* on the south wall now had two levels and showed no signs or marks of having had an *aedicula* or Torah shrine on top of it, though the excavators waffle on whether there could have been a small shrine.[98] Second, the raised *bemah* focussing attention on the south wall more dramatically had its correlate in the two-tiered benches built on the north wall.[99] Third, though the posts of the West (eagle) doorway were rebuilt, the North doorway now came to be emphasized by a new lintel bearing a menorah.[100] All of these changes indicated to the excavators a heightened sense of liturgical practice within the synagogue. Moreover, the room inside the synagogue against the west wall was now frescoed (in red

---

[88] "En-Nabratein," p. 43.

[89] *Gush Halav*, pp. 2, 68, 74, 94.

[90] *Gush Halav*, 68; but cf. the contrary evidence on p. 79.

[91] Cf. *Gush Halav*, Figs. 16-17, pp. 69-70, 104.

[92] Cf. *Gush Halav*, p. 107. The NE walls, similarly, date to Period II or the subsequent rebuild after the 363 C.E. earthquake (p. 68).

[93] *Gush Halav*, p. 69, Fig. 16 and p. 79.

[94] *Gush Halav*, pp. 104, 115.

[95] *Gush Halav*, pp. 89-91.

[96] *Gush Halav*, p. 68; cf. p. 15.

[97] Meyers, *Khirbet Shema'*, pp. 65 and 83. For the earthquake of 419, see p. 38.

[98] Meyers, *Khirbet Shema'*, pp. 71-72; but cf. p. 79.

[99] Meyers, *Khirbet Shema '*, p. 68 and Fig. 3.2.

[100] Meyers, *Khirbet Shema'*, pp. 74-75.

geometric design) and its floor plastered (for the Torah scrolls to be stored in, the excavators hypothesized).[101]

Thus in the period 306-363 C.E., three Galilean synagogues of differing basilical plans, each of which utilized the topography and tastes of their particular community's location and practice, were built.

One other synagogue needs to be discussed, the Synagogue of Severos from Stratum IIa at Hammath-Tiberias. M. Dothan, the excavator, dated this synagogue to the period after the earthquake of 306 C.E.[102] This synagogue continued in use, he claimed, throughout the entire fourth century (latest coin 395 C.E.), with no evidence of any destruction, and was terminated 396-422 C.E.[103] But it is with the terminal date that the problem with Dothan's report comes into play; some of the fine-ware pottery adduced to illustrate the fourth-century usage of Stratum IIa are misidentified and actually derive from the fifth and sixth centuries.[104] What are we to make of this? Did the wrong pottery get published for Stratum IIa? Was the synagogue misexcavated? Coins seem to indicate a fourth-century date and a *terminus* in the early fifth century.[105] Perhaps only additional research can clarify this problem.

Dothan insisted the IIa synagogue had the same plan as a third-century synagogue (Stratum IIb) under it, but it seems best to work only with the fourth-century synagogue in the light of the problems of this report. What we have is a 'broad basilica,' that is, one nearly square, whose interior space was divided into "four aisles by three rows of columns."[106] The basilica was entered from the northerly side, whose three doorways were conjectured by Dothan.[107] On the south-east a series of communication rooms were created, just outside the nave. The floor of one of them (Room 35) was raised considerably (see PL. 3a).[108] Dothan considered this raised room to be the most important feature of this synagogue, for it represented to him one of the earliest permanent places for the Torah outside of the main hall and one

---

[101] Meyers, *Khirbet Shema'*, p. 79.

[102] Dothan, *Hammath Tiberias*, pp. 27, 67.

[103] Dothan, *Hammath Tiberias*.

[104] Dothan, *Hammath Tiberias*, p. 62 and n. 495. This note has earlier ARS and later CRS forms mixed up together. The stamp is ARS, but bowl references are to the early fifth-century LRC Form 3 and CRS Form 2/9, which at Capernaum has to be sixth century. Cf. Dothan's plate on Fig. 4, Nos. M & P where this sixth-century form appears. Barbara L. Johnson had also noticed that Dothan's Fig. 4 M, P really showed CRS Form 9, not ARS as he suggested in *Excavations at Jalme*, Gladys Davidson Weinberg, ed. (Columbia, MO: University of Missouri Press, 1988), p. 160, n. 35.

[105] Dothan, *Hammath Tiberias*, pp. 64, 66.

[106] Dothan, *Hammath Tiberias*, 27.

[107] Dothan, *Hammath Tiberias*, pp. 28-29; cf. M. Dothan, "The Synagogue at Hammath-Tiberias," in Levine, *ASR*, p. 69.

[108] Dothan, *Hammath Tiberias*, pp. 27-28.

of the earliest in a broadhouse or 'transitional' type synagogue.[109] Important to the art historian is the fact that the representational Helios mosaic and the fact that almost the entire nave was paved with polychrome mosaic, some 108 square meters.[110] Both the mosaic and its inscriptions in Greek, Hebrew, and Aramaic show the sophistication of the community, though mistakes in Hebrew indicate that clearly this was a Hellenized Jewish community in which Hebrew was a reminiscence.[111]

SYNAGOGUES FROM 363—420 C.E.

With two important exceptions this period is characterized by repairs to and refinement of already existing structures of the third (Qaṣrin) and early fourth centuries (the synagogues of Upper Galilee). The synagogue at Qaṣrin added a short *bemah* adjacent to the center of the southern wall. A mosaic floor, badly damanged by later phases of the building, was placed on top of the former plaster floor sometime after the mid fourth century.[112]

At Gush Ḥalav, the earthquake of 363 C.E. offered the community the opportunity to rebuild the *bemah* and raise it a step while diminishing its horizontal extent in the nave (see PL. 2b).[113] While the benching may originally have dated to the Period II synagogue, excavation established the southwest segment of the benching belonged to this Period III synagogue (see PL. 2b).[114]

But a stunning new synagogue appears precisely in this time period, the beautiful white limestone synagogue at Capernaum. Initially, the excavators held that the synagogue could not have been built before the middle of the fourth century.[115] Subsequent rethinking of the pottery and coins by these same archaeologists caused them to place the initial date of the building's founding even later: to the period ca. 390-450 C.E., or, more precisely, to the end of the fourth and early fifth centuries.[116] Objections to this late dat-

---

[109] Dothan, *Hammath Tiberias*, 32.

[110] Dothan, *Hammath Tiberias*, 30.

[111] Groh, "Chronology," pp. 87-89.

[112] Urman, "Qaṣrin Inscriptions," p. 532.

[113] *Gush Halav*, p. 68.

[114] *Gush Halav*, p. 78.

[115] Virgilio Corbo, Stanislao Loffreda, Augusto Spijkerman, *La Sinagoga di Cafarnao dopo gli Scavi del 1969*, Pubblicazioni dello Studium Biblicum Franciscanum, Collectio minor 9 (Gerusalemme, 1970), pp. 58-60; Virgilio C. Corbo, *Cafarnao I, Gli Edifici della Città*, Pubblicazioni dello Studium Biblicum Franciscanum 19 (Jerusalem, 1975), p. 168.

[116] S. Loffreda, "The Late Chronology of the Synagogue of Capernaum," Levine, *ASR*, pp. 52, 55.

ing fly in the face of thousands of readable coins, numbers of identifiable sherds, and good stratigraphic controls.[117]

Capernaum represents the 'classic' Galilean-type synagogue (in the earlier architectural typology): a flag-stoned floored, three-aisle basilical structure, oriented to the south (Jerusalem). The late date for such a synagogue type is paralleled by the excavation of another contemporary Galilean synagogue at Meroth (Khirbet Marus).

The synagogue at Meroth was founded in the late fourth and early fifth centuries.[118] A main basilical hall (18.0 x 11.5 m.) contained a central nave with two side aisles. Floor, wall, and columns were plastered and covered with red frescos in simple geometric design.[119] Various depictions, including both animals and men, were found among the many chunks of plaster.[120] Two platforms or two *bemah*s on either side of the main (south) doorway were discovered (see PL. 3b), the one on the west probably serving as the rest for a wooden ark.[121] There was an atrium or forecourt with a cistern, the first such found in a Galilean synagogue; stones from the arch over the central lintel apparently had carvings from signs of the zodiac.[122] And a piece (0.20 x 0.06 m.) of the central branch of a three-dimensional menorah was found in a debris-layer at the northwest corner of the building.[123] Whether the gallery belonged to this, or a later synagogue is difficult to say.[124]

CONCLUSIONS

Our survey of stratigraphically excavated synagogues, whose publication reports allow us to draw some firm conclusions, has focused on the synagogues of the early Roman through the early byzantine periods, the first century C.E. to 420 C.E. This period was chosen precisely because it is so formative for all manner of theories about the synagogue building and its usage. The great building boom of synagogues in the Golan Heights lies ahead, just in the next archaeological period; the great explosion of sixth-

[117] Cf. the objections of G. Foerster, "Notes on Recent Excavations at Capernaum," and M. Avi-Yonah, "Some comments on the Capernaum Excavations," in Levine, *ASR*, pp. 57-59 and 60-62, respectively, to Loffreda's evidence (n. 116 above).

[118] Ilan, "Meroth," p. 21; cf. "Khirbet Marus (Meroth) - 1985," in *EASI* 4 (1985): 65, 67; "Meroth (Kh. Marus) - 1986," *EASI* 5 (1986): 66. [Eds.—See Ilan's essay in this volume.]

[119] Ilan, "Meroth," p. 22.

[120] Ilan, "Meroth."

[121] Ilan, "Meroth."

[122] Ilan, "Meroth," pp. 21-22.

[123] Ilan, "Meroth," p. 23.

[124] Ilan, "Meroth," p. 22.

century construction and usage of synagogues in both Galilees is yet to come. But the early Roman—early Byzantine synagogues allow us to draw some precise conclusions about synagogues of this formative period and their features.

1. The earliest synagogues are essentially assembly halls with banked stone seating around the walls and have simple decoration (Migdal, Gamala).

2. The mid third century sees the first appearance of the basilical synagogue oriented by both its narrow (Nabratein, Gush Ḥalav) and its broad (Khirbet Shema‘) sides. The use of a basilical structure for the religious assembly of the Jewish community antedates Christian adoption of the basilical form by well over half a century.

3. The first instance of what has been called the Galilean-type synagogue—a basilical hall oriented towards Jerusalem by a three-door facade at its narrow end—make its first confirmable appearance at the very end of the third century (Meiron). It continues to be built in the late fourth and early fifth centuries (Capernaum, Meroth).

4. The 'broadhouse' or 'transitional' type of structure actually appears as early as the second century (Nabratein), continues in the mid third century (Khirbet Shema‘) and is represented in the fourth century (Khirbet Shema‘, Hammath-Tiberias).

5. The earliest datable synagogue mosaic floor found *in situ* (as contrasted with mosaic floors conjectured on the basis of disturbed tesserae uncovered in excavation) appears just at the turn of the fourth century in a basilical synagogue entered from the narrow end (Ḥ. ‘Ammudim). If the date of Hammath-Tiberias is sustainable as early fourth century, that synagogue represents the first representational mosaic floor.

6. A focus of attention towards the Jerusalem wall appears as early as the second century (the *bemah*s at Nabratein), and the first Torah shrine appears at that site in the mid third century. The raising of the *bemah* (Khirbet Shema‘) and/or the embellishment of it (Gush Ḥalav) appears to be a fourth-century phenomenon, as is the embellishment of a side room for possible Torah storage (Khirbet Shema‘).

7. Astrological representation in both mosaic (Hammath-Tiberias) and stone carving (Meroth), and the use of human figures (Hammath-Tiberias, Meroth) appear to be a fourth and fifth-century innovation.

8. Above all, this survey endorses the conclusions of the most recent synagogue scholarship that emphasize the individual planning and adaption of each structure to local topography and tastes.

ON THE SOURCE OF THE ARCHITECTURAL DESIGN OF THE ANCIENT SYNAGOGUES IN THE GALILEE A NEW APPRAISAL

YORAM TSAFRIR*

The remains of the ancient synagogues in the Galilee are silent witnesses to the flourishing settlement activity and artistic ability of the Jewish center in the Galilee during the formative period of talmudic literature. A debate has recently arisen over the dating of these synagogues. This debate has far-reaching ramifications for both the general study of Galilean Judaism and the more narrow discussion of synagogue architecture.

I

For many years, scholars have accepted the premise that, architecturally speaking, the ancient Palestinian synagogues are divided into three categories: "synagogues of the early type," "synagogues of the transitional type," and "synagogues of the later type."[1] According to this scheme, the 'early' structures are ascribed mainly to the second and third centuries C.E., the 'transitional' ones primarily to the fourth century, and the 'later' ones to the fifth through seventh centuries. Recently, various investigators have raised doubts about the validity of this basic division, and different opinions have been aired about the need to sever the connection between the different architectural types of the synagogue structures and their chronological definition as belonging to an 'early,' 'late,' or 'transitional' category.[2]

---

*An expanded version of a talk delivered at the Hebrew University in Jerusalem on March 19, 1981, on the seventh anniversary of the death of Professor M. Avi-Yonah, of blessed memory, and upon the publication of a book of his articles: M. Avi-Yonah, *Art in Ancient Palestine* (Jerusalem, 1981).

The essay was originally published as "On the Architectural Origins of the Ancient Galilean Synagogues," *Cathedra* 20 (July 1981): 29-46 (in Hebrew). It has been translated with the permission of the author and of Yad Izhak Ben Zvi. It was translated by Dr. Nathan H. Reisner.

[1] See, for example, Avi-Yonah, "Architecture." For a more general discussion, see M. Avi-Yonah, "Synagogues," pp. 32-33.

[2] On this problem see, for example, the articles published in the collection dedicated to the research of the synagogues in Israel, Levine, *ASR*. See especially, the introductory articles of Levine (pp. 1-10), and A. Kloner (pp. 11-18).

Although much has been written describing and classifying the various types of synagogues, we shall cite here only a few central characteristics unique to each of the three architectural types mentioned.[3]

The early group, according to the usual division, consists of Galilean synagogues. At the time of writing, this group includes about thirty synagogues, some of which are known from only a few remains. Together with similar synagogues from the Golan, there are close to fifty in this grouping. In the Galilee, the best known are the synagogues at Capernaum, Chorazin, Meiron, Bar'am, Ḥorvat 'Ammudim, Gush Ḥalav (Giscala), and Nabratein (Kefar Neburaya). In the Golan, the most studied are at ed-Dikkeh, Umm el-Qanaṭir, Qaṣrin, and 'En Nashuṭ. These synagogues were built out of hewn stone and decorated with stone carvings, most of which were placed, it seems, in the sections of the building facing the outside. The roof rested upon rows of columns—usually three rows placed parallel to the two lengthwise walls and the building's rear wall; in small buildings only two rows were set up running the length of the building. The building's main facade was erected facing Jerusalem, in a southerly direction, and it contained three entrances; in the small buildings, only one. This facade was the most elegant section of the structure.[4]

At the other end of the developmental continuum from the early synagogues are those designated 'late.' The exteriors of these synagogues are relatively modest and their plans in great measure remind one of a basilican church. Their floors are for the most part decorated with richly colored mosaics. In the direction of Jerusalem each has an apse with a *bemah* (raised platform) and the *aron ha-qodesh* (the Torah Ark) at the front of it; the entrances are situated conveniently and logically at the opposite side. Prominent in this group of synagogues are those of Bet Alpha, Ḥammat Gader, Na'aran, Bet-Shean, Ma'oz Ḥayyim, Ma'on (Nirim), and Gaza.[5]

The 'transitional synagogues' are those between the 'early' and 'late' categories. They have characteristics of both the early and late synagogues and do not adhere to a single plan.[6] Customarily counted among these are the

---

[3] See the concentration and classification of this literature in the extended bibliographical works of: Hüttenmeister and Reeg; Ruth P. Goldschmidt-Lehmann, "Ancient Synagogues in the Land of Israel," *Cathedra* 4 (1977): 205-222 (in Hebrew); and Levine, *ASR*.

[4] Among the basic works and summaries devoted to the Galilean synagogues, see first and foremost the original research of Kohl and Watzinger. See also E. L. Sukenik, "Ancient Synagogues around the Sea of Galilee," in S. Yeivin and H. Z. Hirschberg, eds., *Eretz Kinnarot* (Jerusalem, 1951), pp. 74-79 (in Hebrew); Avigad, "Synagogues"; M. Avi Yonah, "Architecture" and "Synagogues"; and Foerster, "Synagogues."

[5] See above, notes 1-2, and also the summarizing article of Avigad, "Bet Alpha," pp. 63-70 (in Hebrew).

[6] See above, notes 1-2, and also G. Foerster, "Ancient Synagogues in the Land of Israel," *Qadmoniot* 5 (1972): 38-42.

synagogues of Hammath-Tiberias, Bet She'arim, Khirbet Shema', and perhaps even the synagogue at Arbel.

A group unto itself, which apparently cannot be defined within the chronological parameters described above, is the group of synagogues in southern Judea such as Eshtemoa, Susiya, En-Gedi, and En Ramon.

Our discussion will focus on the Galilean synagogues of the early type. And even though our conclusions, which will be presented below, to a great extent reflect the attempt to support relatively conservative approaches as opposed to the innovative opinions that have been aired in other studies—it seems that there is no difference of opinion that there is room for a re-examination and re-appraisal of the subject.

II

Before one can discuss the matter of the origin and design of the synagogues, one must discuss their dating. The proper dating of the synagogues is of primary importance in locating the Jewish synagogue in its environmental context—the Jewish and the non-Jewish—and the cultural background of its world. It is the correct dating that allows us to discover what the architecture of the synagogues shared with the non-Jewish architecture and where it diverged; in what aspects it was in the forefront of its contemporary style and in what aspects it lagged behind; in what ways it was unique and in what ways it was not exceptional.

To our great sorrow, we have poor chronological data about the synagogues in general—unlike the public pagan structures, such as those in Syria and Hauran, whose inscriptions abound in dates, and unlike the church inscriptions that also have many dating indications. The Jews were very sparing with dates. Among the more than 150 inscriptions thus far discovered in Hebrew, Aramaic, and Greek, only a few have any indication of time.[7] On the lintel of a synagogue from Nabratein, Y. Avigad read "year 494 after its destruction," that is, 564 C.E.[8] Avigad thought that the date referred to the rebuilding of the synagogue and not the date of its first establishment. This opinion was not accepted by all.[9] But through recent excavations conducted at the site, it has become clear that this building had two periods of existence and that the inscription can only belong to the sec-

[7] See the collection of inscriptions in Greek in Lifshitz, and the inscriptions in Hebrew and Aramaic in Naveh, *Mosaic*.

[8] N. Avigad, "The Lintel Inscription of the Ancient Synagogue at Kefar Neburaya" *Yediot* 24 (1960): 136-145; and also Naveh, *Mosaic*, note 7 number 13.

[9] See, for example, Loffreda, "Capernaum," p. 37. See also Naveh, *Mosaic*, p. 4.

ond, later stage of its existence, as Avigad thought at the outset.[10] There are other synagogue inscriptions that lend themselves to dating. On a Gaza synagogue mosaic there is a date equivalent to 508-509 C.E.;[11] on a grille of an Ashkelon synagogue there is an engraved inscription from 604 C.E.;[12] on a synagogue inscription at Susiya an '*anno mundi*' ('Year of the Creation') date was found, but unfortunately the inscription was only partially preserved; the main section which contained the number of the tens and hundreds was in the destroyed section.[13] The oldest of the inscriptions is the Aramaic inscription from the Bet Alpha synagogue which in itself constitutes the cornerstone of the research. King Justin is mentioned in it, and Sukenik's opinion seems correct, that the reference is to Emperor Justin I, who reigned from 518-527, and not to Justin II, who reigned from 567-578.[14] But doubts do remain. The two possibilities direct us, in any case, to the sixth century. This same period of time also applies to the dating of the Northern (the Samaritan?) Synagogue at Bet-Shean, for the artisans who did the mosaic here are also the ones who worked at Bet Alpha.[15] At Gerasa in Arabia there is a synagogue the date of whose building is unknown, but it is known that in the year 530-531 it was already destroyed and that upon its ruins a church was built.[16]

It turns out that most of the inscriptions, except for the one from Nabratein, date synagogues of the 'late' classification. (The Nabratein inscription is not from the first stage of the synagogue's construction.) We therefore do not have from the inscriptions absolute dates for the Galilean group of synagogues on which this study focuses, namely, the early ones.

The dating of these structures, therefore, falls to the lot of the archaeologist, who uses finds from the excavations: potsherds and coins. As we know, the findings collected in the building's ruins generally represent the last stage of the structure's existence and therefore can tell us nothing about the date the structure was erected. More important than these are the findings gathered from beneath the floors or foundations of the building's walls, for these do indeed give us an approximate date of the structure's erection or, at least, a *terminus post quem*, i.e., the last possible date sometime after

---

[10] The existence of the two stages, the first from the third century C.E. and the second from the fifth century C.E., was clarified by the excavation that E. Meyers conducted at the site (summer 1980).

[11] A. Ovadiah, "The Synagogue in Gaza," *Qadmoniot* 1 (1968): 124-127. See also Lifshitz, number 739.

[12] Sukenik, "el-Ḥammeh," pp. 154-156; and also Lifshitz, number 70.

[13] See Gutman, Yeivin, and Netzer. Also see Naveh, *Mosaic*, number 76.

[14] See Sukenik, *Bet Alpha*, pp. 39-42; Naveh, *Mosaic*, number 43.

[15] N. Tzuri, "The Ancient Synagogue at Bet-Shean," *Erez Yisrael* 8 (1967): 6149-167, and particularly p. 157 (in Hebrew).

[16] G. Kraeling, ed., *Gerasa, City of the Decapolis* (New Haven, 1938), pp. 234-241.

which the building was erected. But we know that even this means does not offer absolute proof. More than once it happens (and this is particularly true with buildings that exist for scores and hundreds of years, such as those of which we speak) that restorations and reconstructions of parts of the building are done and old floorings are replaced by new ones. In these instances, items such as potsherds and coins get beneath the floors during the restoration and there is a danger that we might interpret findings that attest to the renewal of the building or its floors as if they indicate the period of its establishment.

Given the uncertain result of these dating methods, the value of general comparative research goes up. In particular, I refer to comparing the uncertain structures—in our instance, the Jewish synagogues or their architectural details—with other structures, be they Jewish or not, whose date is known. Of course, we must remember that comparative research also has its weaknesses. The main one is that we do not know how long it takes for architectural and artistic elements to move from region to region. We must also keep in mind that comparison never provides a sharp and absolute answer.

These difficulties have indeed caused the research of the Galilean synagogues to find itself in difficulty, with disagreement among the scholars sometimes outweighing their consensus. The main controversy is over the dating of the construction of the Galilean synagogues, especially the most magnificent of them—that of Capernaum—and also over the date of the Golan synagogues which are clearly similar to those of the Galilee from the architectural and artistic point of view.

Since the beginning of synagogue research, it was generally assumed that these synagogues were products of the second and third centuries C.E., that is, the period of the *tannaim* and the beginning of the period of the *amoraim*. This is the peak period of the creation of the halakah and its compilation in the Galilee.[17] A revolution took place upon the publication of the results of the excavations of Corbo and Loffreda at Capernaum.[18] and the first publications of the excavations of Z. Ma'oz at sites in the Golan.[19] These researchers claim, relying upon an 'independent' archaeological find of coins, that the structures they investigated should be dated later, to the Byzantine period of the fifth century C.E.

Due to the significance of this new dating proposal, the debate shifted from the limited scope of dating Galilean synagogues and became a testing ground for the validity of archaeological schools and even of research ap-

---

[17] See the works mentioned above in notes 1, 2, and 4, as well as M. Dotan, "A Study of the Ancient Synagogues in the Land of Israel," in *Thirty Years of Archaeology in the Land of Israel, 1948-1978 (The Aviram Volume)* (Jerusalem, 1981), pp. 91-98 (in Hebrew).

[18] See Loffreda, "Capernaum," pp. 37-42. See also Corbo, *Cafarnao*, vol. 1, pp. 113-170.

[19] Ma'oz, *Golan*, and also Ma'oz, "Synagogues."

proaches in general. Against an entire system, as it were, of historical, comparative, and artistic considerations which brought the scholars to a dating of the Galilean synagogues in the ranges of the second and third centuries C.E., the innovators came up with the one find or solitary findings that are 'independent'—'facts as given' so to speak. According to Corbo, Loffreda, and those who follow their lead the general outlook must yield to the unambiguous find that they have presented. In the opinion of other investigators, who cling to the 'conservative' point of view, the complete conception which has withstood the criticism of many tests, should also be preferred here and in similar instances. It should not be abandoned—at least not until all the possibilities of explaining the appearance of this exceptional datum in any way whatever that does not negate the entire structure are exhausted.

The last approach, which adheres to the 'over-all concept' and tends to prefer it over the 'decisive find,' as it were, is potentially dangerous and liable not only to bring about error but an intellectual freeze as well. And yet, as will become clear below, our intention is to adhere to this approach and defend it. We will argue that if all the other bases of the theory were re-examined and found valid, and if the general structure is still convincing and more fitting than the general structure the innovators suggest, it is better to maintain a general conception and seek a way to reconcile the contradiction between the new facts and the general concept so that the new information does not destroy the old structure. This seems to be the situation in the matter before us.

At Capernaum, thousands of coins of the fourth century onwards, including Byzantine ones, were discovered, most of them in two treasure-troves placed under the synagogue floor and its courtyard pavement. These, we know, are a proof of sorts that the building was also used in the Byzantine period. But the coins are not sufficient to indicate the period in which the synagogue was erected. More important than these, for purposes of clarification, is that the many coins of the fourth century were found scattered in the fill under the paving of the building to a considerable depth of a few tens of centimeters. Among these coins was found at least one from the beginning of the fifth century. The conclusions of the excavators, Corbo and Loffreda, are clear: the synagogue at Capernaum was built in the first half of the fifth century C.E.

A similar numismatic picture was discovered at a Golan synagogue. But for this site, only the conclusions have been published with the circumstances of the find still unpublished. Therefore we cannot analyze the find in detail.[20]

---

[20] See Ariel, "Ḥorvat Kanef." Among the 126 coins that have been identified, two are from the third century C.E. Most are of the fourth century and a few are fifth century. The

We find a different chronological picture in several other excavations. In the Lower Synagogue at Giscala,[21] at Meiron,[22] and at Nabratein—all structures that, by their form, belong to the 'early type.' Eric Meyers and his colleagues concluded, on the basis of the pottery and coin findings, that the synagogues were built in the second half of the third century C.E. At Nabratein, there may perhaps be a possibility of moving the date back to the first half of that century.[23] With regard to Ḥorvat 'Ammudim, which is also a classic synagogue structure of the early category, Levine dates its erection about the year 300.[24] At Khirbet Shema', whose synagogue structure approximates the 'transitional' category, the date favored by Meyers, according to the findings, is between 286-306.[25]

All the excavations have shown that the synagogue structures in the Galilee were in ruins for a lengthy period, and had served for tens or even hundreds of years. Some of them existed throughout the entire Byzantine period, or most of it. Several of them were destroyed and then rebuilt. The synagogue at Nabratein, for example, was in ruins for a long period, until it was rebuilt—as the inscription on its lintel attests—in 564 C.E.

The knowledge that the structures, which according to their construction belong to the 'early' type, stood for hundreds of years, can supply a certain explanation for the difficulties raised by the Capernaum find. It might be that this synagogue, indeed, was destroyed for some reason or other, (perhaps in the earthquake that occurred in the days of Julian "the Apostate" in 363, to which a number of sources attribute the destruction of the Temple in Jerusalem built by the Jews, and many other cities; and in one source that details the places destroyed, even 'Ein Gader' is mentioned, that is, the

---

date of the synagogue's establishment should be set, in the author's opinion, at the beginning of the sixth century C.E., based upon a coin of Anastasius (498-518) which was found in the fill beneath the floor. Since the article does not detail the circumstances of the find, but only sums it up, it is difficult to critique the discovery. But as a rule it seems difficult to defer this to the sixth century. This is also the feeling of excavator Z. Ma'oz, who indicates the absurdity of an unexamined reliance upon a single find. In our opinion it would be better to weigh the possibility that the building was built at an early period and that it was restored or had its floor replaced in the sixth century.

[21] See "Gush-Ḥalav," p. 233; and E. Meyers, "Gush Ḥalav," *Qadmoniot* 13 (1980): 41-43 (in Hebrew).

[22] See "Meiron," pp. 73-108; and E. Meyers, "Ancient Meiron—Five Seasons of Excavation," *Qadmoniot* 13 (1980): 111-113 (in Hebrew).

[23] Conveyed orally by the excavator, E. Meyers.

[24] Lee I. Levine, "The Excavations at Ḥorvat 'Ammudim," *Qadmoniot* 13 (1980): 107-110 (in Hebrew).

[25] See Meyers, "Khirbet Shema'," pp. 58-61; and Meyers, *Khirbet Shema'*, pp. 33-102.

nearby Ḥammat Gader).[26] When the synagogue stood in ruins, its paving stones were removed and broad gaps were opened in its foundations. When it was rebuilt at the beginning of the fifth century, the entire area was leveled with new filling to a depth of several tens of centimeters beneath the floor. It is in this fill that the later coins were found.[27]

This solution, as forced as it seems, is in our opinion more palatable and logical than to posit that the synagogue building at Capernaum was built in the fifth century. As we shall see below, in its plan, in its architectural facade, and in its architectural and artistic details—the carvings and the inscriptions—the synagogue fits the third century[28] and not the fifth.[29]

In the fifth century, on the other hand, in Capernaum itself, a few meters from the synagogue, an octagonal church was built that is representative of the prevailing fifth century Byzantine architecture which was 'introspective' and totally different in its characteristics. The explanation that these two structures—the synagogue and the nearby church—are a product of that self-same century seems most questionable.

It seems to us that pursuing this line of thought will also enable us to explain finding Byzantine elements in the Golan synagogues. It would be better to explain the finding of coins under the paving in a specific place as evidence of a restoration,[30] or the finding of a Byzantine basket-capital in the small portico of the synagogue at Umm el-Qanaṭir as if that entire front portico is a later addition, than to start with the assumption that they attest to the structures having been built for the first time at a later date.[31] However, since we do not yet have the finding itself before us in all of its

---

[26] S. P. Brock, "A Letter Attributed to Cyril of Jerusalem on Rebuilding of the Temple," *Bulletin of the School of Oriental and African Studies* 40 (1977): 276.

[27] Corbo and Loffreda try to attribute part of the coins to the layer of private buildings that were found beneath the synagogue; they argue that these structures existed until the fourth century and it was only thereafter that they were removed and a synagogue built in their place. This reconstruction, of course, nullifies the possibility of accepting the historic reconstruction that we proposed above—but a close study of the details of the dig in no way requires accepting their opinion that the private structures existed during the fourth century. Even they admit that the separation between the synagogue layer—Stratum B— and the civilian structures beneath them—Stratum A—is most difficult. See Loffreda in Levine, *ASR*, p. 55, as well as V. Corbo, "La sinagoga di Cafarnao," *Studia Hierosolymitana*, vol. 1 (Jerusalem, 1976), pp. 159-176.

[28] On the dating of the Capernaum capitals to the third century, see M. Fisher, "The Development of the Corinthian Capital in the Land of Israel from its Beginning until Constantine the Great," (Ph.D. dissertation, Tel-Aviv, 1979), pp. 323-334, and particularly p. 333.

[29] On this, see below.

[30] For the circumstances of the numismatic find at the synagogue of En Nashot, see Ma'oz, *Golan*, p. 24.

[31] See Kohl and Watzinger, pp. 126-134, and Ma'oz on the "almost certain" dating "to the sixth century or, at the earliest, the beginning of the fifth century," in Ma'oz, *Golan*, p. 21.

details it is impossible at this time to base the above premise on an analysis of the specific instance of each and every site.

Parenthetically, we must stress that finding specific architectural elements, such as Ionic or Corinthian capitals designed in a form far from the classical Roman prototype, need not necessarily be explained as if they are chronologically far from the classical period. One is not compelled to explain a simplified concretization of a capital or a lintel as if were an item necessarily produced in the Byzantine period. We are permitted to interpret these simplified folk elements (especially when they appear in basalt stone that is difficult to work) as revelation of art which Avi-Yonah, in his day, defined as "Oriental folk"[32] or "sub-classical" art.[33] This stream of art, as we know, co-existed with the "classical stream" throughout the Roman period and is not especially unique to the Byzantine period. In Qaṣrin and a number of other sites in the Golan a type of deteriorated lonic capital, characterized by an over-sized central 'egg' in the 'the eggs and darts' pattern on the echinus of the capital, was dominant. This capital, which seems to be almost a caricature of the classical Ionic capital, is routinely dated to the Byzantine period, on the basis of examples from Byzantine structures in Syria. It is also found in the city of Philippopolis in Hauran[34]—a city founded in the middle of the third century C.E.—which fell from its height not many years after it was established, although it continued to exist.[35]

In the interior sections of Syria, as we know, the architecture of the churches in the Byzantine period preserves many of the lines characteristic of the earlier Roman architecture. Especially outstanding are the ways of preserving the massive facade of the stone structures that characterized Syria, and the quality of the carvings in the decorated segments of the building. In this aspect the Syrian interior is outstanding in its conservatism. It is seemingly possible to point out this phenomenon and argue that in the Galilee as well, which is on the edge of the region of Syrian architectural influence, a similar process took place and we may therefore date the synagogues to the Byzantine period. But it seems to us that, at most, this phenomenon can explain the tendency in the fifth and sixth centuries to reconstruct several of the early synagogues in their early style of construction, or explain the con-

---

[32] M. Avi-Yonah, "Oriental Elements in the Art of Palestine in the Roman and Byzantine Periods," *QDAP* 10 (1942): 105-151; 13 (1948): 49-80; 14 (1950): 128-165. Reprinted in Avi-Yonah, *Art*, pp. 1-117. See also M. Avi-Yonah, *Oriental Art in Roman Palestine* (Rome, 1961), reprinted in Avi-Yonah, *Art*, pp. 119-211.

[33] M. Avi-Yonah, *The History of Classical Art* (Jerusalem, 1970), pp. 249-276.

[34] H. C. Butler, *Publications of the American Archaeological Expedition in Syria in 1899-1900, Architecture and Other Arts* (New York, 1903), photo on p. 379.

[35] Therefore we must emphasize that here too we do not have detailed knowledge of the source of the inscription, and yet its dating to the third century is the most plausible. It is possible that it belongs to later building.

struction from the foundation of some solitary buildings in the 'anachronistic' style (if we are indeed convinced that there is no other out but to agree with the late dating of their construction).

As a rule, it seems to us that in this phenomenon there is no possible contradiction to our conclusion, based upon the complete set of claims and considerations and on an architectural critique of the buildings themselves, that at least the great majority of the synagogue structures were established in the late Roman period nor, in the main, does it constitute any weakening of the conclusion that the Galilean synagogue type is the creative product of the late Roman period.

III

It is clear that the question of the dating of the early synagogues in the Galilee is only a necessary preliminary stage for clarifying the background of the growth of the synagogue. Though we have rejected the opinions that seek to move the synagogues of the 'early type' to the end of the fourth and to the fifth century C.E., we must verify one correction that arises from all of these excavations. For the time being, no remains from a synagogue built second century have been found. Of all the synagogues investigated recently, there is not a single one whose excavators place its construction earlier than the third century—usually in the second half or near the end of the century.

Where, then, did the Galilean Sages of the Mishnah, of the generation of Usha and their heirs, and Rabbi Judah the Prince, pray? While one may still expect to discover synagogue structures from the second century, we cannot ignore the quantity of accumulated findings we already have in favor of what might yet be discovered in the future. The archaeological finds known to us lead to a single conclusion, namely, prior to the third century synagogues did not exist as special structures, with external identifying signs, as in the third-century Galilean synagogues. The synagogues in which the *tannaim* prayed in the second century and even those used by the early *amoraim* were located in houses with the plan and facade of private homes. These buildings usually included one hall larger than the rest for study and prayer, and often had additional rooms which served the community. In terms later used to characterize the Christian community, one can say that this was a sort of 'religious community building'—*domus ecclesiae.*

Just as pre-Constantine Christian church structures were found that did not have a church facade of the accepted types, but rather a facade of a private home—such as the example of the Christian building at Dura-Europos[36] or the building in the 'sacred quarter' (*insula sacra*) at Capernaum[37]—it is possible to argue that the Jews also had similar structures in which their religious worship, prayers, and sacred studies were concentrated. When one compares the structure of the Christian *domus ecclesiae* of Dura-Europos with the synagogue there—both from the third century—the general similarity of the two is outstanding. Both have the facade of a private home with an interior courtyard, a hall for worship, and a number of additional rooms to serve the community.[38]

All this evidence shows that the Galilean synagogue is a third-century C.E. Jewish invention. This invention developed, as we shall see further on, against a background of the social reality of the third century and the background of that century's general architectural reality.

Our determination that there is no second-century structure among the Galilean synagogues—nor does there seem to be any expectation of discovering synagogues of the accepted pattern in this century—leads us to another conclusion: there are no architectural connections between the third- century synagogues in the Galilee and the synagogue structures of the Temple period. So far buildings at three sites have been discovered from Temple times that are thought to be synagogues, ones at Masada, Herodium,[39] and Gamala.[40] Since the first discovery at Masada, a few scholars have sought to identify a developmental link between the structures of the Second-Temple period and the later Galilean synagogues. From these attempts, two persuasive suggestions have emerged. One is that of Avigad, who sees the prototype of the column arrangement in the Galilean synagogues in the arrangement of the columns in the ancient synagogue at Masada.[41] And the other is the suggestion of Netzer, who connects the Galilean synagogue

[36] C. Hopkins, "The Christian Church" in *The Excavations at Dura-Europos, 5th Season* (New Haven, 1934), pp. 238-253. See also the reconstruction in R. Kravtheimer, *Early Christian and Byzantine Architecture* (Harmondsworth, 1965), fig. 1.

[37] Corbo, *Cafarnao*, vol. 1, pp. 59-74.

[38] The final basis for this premise will be found, of course, only with the discovery of a private Jewish structure from the second century or the beginning of the third century which served as a place of worship. This tradition continued into the sixth century, for we have found a prayer site within a private home constellation (the house of Leontes) at Bet Shean. See D. Bahat, "The Synagogue of Bet-Shean—Preliminary Survey," *Qadmoniot* 5 (1976): 55-58.

[39] Y. Yadin, "The Synagogue at Masada," in Levine, *ASR*, pp. 19-23; G. Foerster, "The Synagogue at Masada and Herodion," *EI* 11 (1973): 224-228.

[40] N. Gutman, "The Synagogue at Gamla," in Levine, *ASR*, pp. 30-34; Ma'oz, "Gamla."

[41] Avigad, "Synagogues."

halls with the reception halls (*triclinia*) in Herod's palaces, that are most similar in their plan.[42]

If we adhere to our conclusion that no synagogues were built as a building of a specific form during that intermediate period of 150-200 years between the Destruction and the appearance of the Galilean synagogues, we automatically dispose of the various theories that seek to connect the Galilean synagogue architecture with some kind of architectural prototype on the Second-Temple period. Therefore, since Jewish synagogues built as special structures were previously unknown, the third-century synagogue was not an adaptation or a copy of earlier forms but a totally new creation. The Christians, for example, had to wait another few decades—until Constantine in the first half of the fourth century—before they would forgo the modest 'church building,' the *domus ecclesiae*, for the basilica built solely for worship purposes.

Later on, the Christian basilica became a decisive influence on the design of the synagogue. This stage came in the fifth and sixth centuries, when the Jewish synagogues—those of the 'late type'—adopted many features similar to the church structure. The later synagogue would be influenced by the Christian church not only in the area plan and the character of the architectural ornamentation, but it would mainly take unto itself the emphasis on "internalizing the structure"—making the exterior of the structure relatively modest while enriching its interior. The modest facade of the synagogue of the Byzantine period is therefore not solely the result of the depressed economic situation or a desire to avoid angering the hostile Christian ruler, but derives above all from the dominant approach to the architectural design of structures for worship in the Byzantine world.[43]

In the third century, Roman culture, whose architectural styles were totally different, still predominated. Therefore the early synagogue facade created in this period is also absolutely different from the facade of the later synagogue. There seems to be no one who differs with Kohl and Watzinger that the synagogue structures of this period belong, at least in their general architectural design and the detail of the stone work, to the architectural world of Syria and Hauran (and to a certain extent also to the Gentile Galilee), that is, to the Provinces of Syria and Northern Arabia.[44]

Above, we sought to prove that the examples of the third-century Galilean synagogues do not stem from buildings of the Second-Temple period and, therefore, they are in the category of a Jewish 'invention' of the

---

[42] E. Netzer, "The Herodian Triclinia—A Prototype for the 'Galilean Type' Synagogues," in Levine, *ASR*, pp. 49-51.

[43] See Avigad, "Bet Alpha," p. 64.

[44] And see, especially, Foerster's discussion (Foerster, "Synagogues") that deals with the architectural details of each and every building.

third century. To further support this claim, we must examine the contemporary architectural sources because the possibility exists that third-century non-Jewish structural types might have been drawn upon or adapted to create the synagogues. Among prevailing scholarly views in this matter, two are primary. One is Foerster's suggestion that the Galilean synagogues develop from the ancillary courtyards—partially roofed by porticos—that were built in front of the facades of the Nabatean temples and other temples in Transjordan and Syria.[45] To be sure, these buildings were erected at an early period, but some of them continued to exist and it was still possible to visit them in the second and third centuries C.E. The second scholarly opinion stems from Kohl and Watzinger—which many scholars hold in full or in part—that the Galilean synagogues were mainly influenced by the secular Roman basilicas.[46]

Both of these suggestions provide a partial contribution to the question of the origin of the form of the synagogue, but neither explains what their proponents sought to explain. As we know, the Jewish architects were confronted with a challenge when they decided to erect a center for worship whose splendor would compete with that of the pagan temples. In contrast to the pagan temples (and to the Jerusalem Temple as well in its time), they sought to contain the worshipers within an interior hall. This Jewish innovation, as everyone knows, preceded the Christian church and the Muslim mosque. Other oriental religions, such as Mithraism, were organized in very small, intimate communities. Their assembly halls, therefore, were also small; they often were hidden in a subterranean structure, as befits the mystical content of the worship.

In the days of the Second Temple, the builders of the synagogues did not contend with the challenge completely, and contented themselves with the erection of structures that could hold the community within them, but did not vary in their form from the regular public and community buildings. At Masada and at Herodium, for example, the synagogues did not even stand as independent structures but were one area of a large structural complex. The need to build a grand, independent structure for the synagogue which would hold the community within it led the builders, by necessity, to the only feasible technical solution: supporting the roof on a network of beams resting upon the walls and interior columns. This is the reason we find a similarity to the Hellenistic (*bouleuterion* or *ecclesiasterion*) or Roman (secular basilica) prototypes, that influenced, as has been said, the structures of the

[45] Foerster, "Synagogues," pp. 56-80; as well as G. Foerster, "Architectural Models of the Greco-Roman Period and the Origin of the Galilean Synagogue," in Levine, *ASR*, pp. 45-48.

[46] Kohl and Watzinger, pp. 138-183. And also see about the difficulties raised by this suggestion in Avigad, "Synagogues"; Foerster (see note 45).

Temple period, and therefore the temptation is great to draw a comparison between the Galilean synagogues and the early synagogues of Temple times.[47] The Gamala synagogue (if it is a synagogue) is the only one which has four rows of columns within all its walls and, of all the buildings we know, it is the nearest in form to the Roman basilica.

But the Galilean synagogues of the third century, as Foerster has shown at length in his critique of Kohl and Watzinger, were not like the Roman basilicas, because they only had three rows of columns within, inside the three walls only (in the places where they made do with only two longitudinal columns, it was because of the narrow dimensions of the synagogue).[48] This contrasts with the Roman civilian basilica which was the most widespread type among the basilicas, and which always had four rows of columns, each one paralleling one of the structure's four walls. The design of the Roman civilian basilica's interior space, whether the building was long or wide, always emphasized the center of the structure, which was 'static' and enclosed within four rows of columns and emphasized by the elevated roof. Some of the basilicas—the 'palace basilicas'—that were not free-standing but were part of a large structure, did in fact have two lengthwise rows of columns or lacked columns altogether. But we do not find among them a basilica with three inside rows of columns as synagogues had (or as some of them would have had except that the dimensions were too narrow to allow for the row of columns across the width).

From the issue of the internal arrangement of the columns, Foerster's explanation is more acceptable. This is because the Nabatean temple courts arrange the columns within the three walls of the court facing the temple's facade. But the critics of this suggestion have properly pointed out its chief fault: only a small part of those courts were roofed, above the surrounding portico; they were not enclosed halls and the architectural rules relevant to the construction of such halls did not apply to them.

IV

After presenting the construction of the Galilean synagogues in the third century as more of an invention than an adaptation or copy, we are unable to point to an immediate source from which the builders drew their inspiration. How do we explain the distinctive elements of these synagogues—a covered structure with a gabled roof, within which three rows of columns were built parallel to its three walls, except for the facade? Without an immediate inspirational source, we must shift our area of investigation to the general

47 Yadin, "Synagogue"; Ma'oz, "Gamla."

48 Above, note 45.

constellation and source of inspiration which influenced the synagogue builders. As is known, the Jewish architects and artists of the third century had a great openness and readiness to absorbing artistic influences and motifs from the pagan environment. The first expression of this openness was the free use of human and animal likenesses, and even images from pagan mythology, in the Jewish synagogues and cemeteries.[49] We have no doubt that we have reflected here, first of all, the relative strengths of paganism and Judaism in the third century. In this period paganism was on the decline. The devotees of classical religion were disappointed and dissatisfied with the simplistic earthiness which characterized classical worship. The spiritual and religious message which they sought and the personal redemption which they longed for in the turbulent and very depressing period of crisis in the Empire, they were unable to find in classical paganism. Many were ready to seek their way in another source.[50] Sometimes this source was still within the realm of the classical religion, such as the sophisticated neo-Platonic school. But for the most part, many were attracted by the oriental mystery religions, or to Christianity or Judaism. Judaism, as opposed to paganism, was then at the peak of its power; the days of the rebellions were long past and the great stormy days of the stand against conquering Christianity had not yet begun. Palestinian Jewry was at the height of its spiritual power, consolidated, self confident, organized in its communities, and gaining adherents and esteem.

This readiness of Judaism to absorb artistic and decorative elements from its surroundings and from the outside world, feeling that they constituted neither danger nor a concession in the principles of faith, found its expression on lintels and architectural parts of the Galilean synagogues. There is no reason to assume that all these things did not also find expression in the structure's general facade.

Yet, with all of this, they took great pains to distance themselves from anything that, even if only in appearance, might be identified with pagan worship itself. The Mishnah tractate of Abodah Zarah (Idolatry) is replete with strict guidelines to guard against the danger of any contact with this impurity. Even the Talmud stresses the danger that a Jew might become confused between his synagogue and a place of idol worship, to teach us that

---

[49] Many articles have been devoted to this matter and there have been many attempts to explain it. First and foremost is the work of E. R. Goodenough, which collects the wealth of material and classifies it. Goodenough's analysis, as is known, has not been accepted by most of the investigators. Among the other central works we shall note only the basic writings of E. E. Urbach, "The Laws of Idolatry and the Archaeological and Historical Reality of the 2nd and 3rd Centuries," *EI* 5 (1959): 189-205 (in Hebrew); N. Avigad, "Image Art among the Jews," in *Beth She'arim*, vol. 3 (Jerusalem, 1972), pp. 201-208 (in Hebrew).

[50] See Peter Brown's excellent description of the perplexities of the period, in P. Brown, *The World of Late Antiquity* (London, 1971), pp. 11-96.

it was impossible to be entirely successful in the goal they sought to achieve—to erect an edifice in which no one would suspect anything whatsoever in it as having to do with a pagan structure.[51] This demand that the synagogue not be identified with the pagan temple (a position which would later on be taken by the Christians seeking to establish the form of their churches), was a basic condition for the planners. The Jews distanced themselves from the plan of the classic temple which was characterized by the construction, in its facade, of a magnificent *pronaos* of columns, often surrounded by peripteral columns on all sides.

The result that was realized in the Galilean synagogue most clearly illustrates the tensions between two diametrically opposite goals: the need to design a building whose main purpose is to make the interior space functional, and the accepted perception of the classical temple architecture—to design a building whose main impact is in its exterior. In worship at the classical temples, most of the adherents remained outside during the ritual worship. The courtyards were thus architecturally oriented outwards; temples were monumental structures that aimed to influence their surroundings. The revolutionary change in the world's religious architecture—the 'introversion' of the structures—would find its proper place only in the middle of the fourth century, with the construction of the first churches. Along with this process, as we have already indicated above, in the fourth and fifth centuries, we are witnesses to a change in the perception of the structure of the Palestinian synagogues. The main emphasis on the facade shifts from the exterior to the interior—along with the rise of church architecture and the decline of the classical temples.

The basis of this change is not 'imitation,' but a general change of values that occurred in architecture and its intellectual perception in general. The decision to imitate or not was a matter of the individual architect's free choice. But the change in the general world of values which encompassed world architecture and art—Jewish Palestinian art in particular—was a matter against which its creators were not likely to contend. And it is doubtful whether at the time they were at all aware of the sharp change taking place that we, at a great remove in time, easily discern.

The two poles we mentioned above, the functional need to emphasize the interior against the universal tendency of religious architecture to stress the exterior, constituted a kind of 'conflict of interest' which gave birth to the Galilean synagogue. Just as the beauty and grandeur of the pagan temple was in its facade that the believers looked at from the court and sanctified themselves before it and before the temple of the god who was beyond it inside, so was the beauty and grandeur of the synagogue in its facade, its

[51] B. Sabbat 72b.

gables, the decorated alcoves, the friezes, the ornamented lintels and, above all, the gates and windows, richly designed in the spirit of the 'Roman baroque' which characterized the public and religious construction in Syria.[52] They gave the facade a grand exterior but, along with it, guaranteed the absence of surrounding columns and especially in the facade (except for the uncharacteristic low *pronaos* at Kefar Bar'am), so that the synagogue did not have a classic pagan temple facade. For this reason it was impossible to 'correct' the obvious flaw in the interior organization of the Galilean synagogue where people entered via the facade and, within the building, had to turn around toward the facade to face the direction of prayer as other people continued to enter and leave through it; and no fitting place was found therein for the Torah Ark. The desire to have the grand facade of the building—which, like the temples, necessarily was the facade of the entrance—face the direction of prayer, that is, toward Jerusalem, was decisive, even at the cost of the discomfort in organizing the prayer ceremonial inside.

Only later on, after the change in the architectural values came about, was it possible to shift the entrances from the facade to one of the side walls, as we find in the buildings of the 'transitional type,' or, better yet, to the opposite wall. But the synagogues of the category designated 'early' that are in the Galilee and the Golan, headed by the most magnificent building of them all at Capernaum, cannot possibly be extracted from their temporal background, the third century, or at the latest, the beginning of the fourth century C.E.

---

52 See Foerster, "Synagogues"; likewise about the 'oriental baroque' style in the Roman world, in M. Lyttleton, *Baroque Architecture in Classical Antiquity* (London, 1974).

DATING SYNAGOGUES WITH A 'BASILICAL' PLAN AND AN APSE

GIDEON FOERSTER*

Corbo and Loffreda have advanced some revolutionary conclusions about the synagogue of Capernaum, based on their excavations which began in 1969. Even though their conclusions have not been wholly accepted, they have caused a change and a renewed attitude among archaeologists and historians towards the history of the Jewish settlement in Israel during the rabbinic period. The two archaeologists conducted a systematic stratigraphic excavation for the first time at the Capernaum synagogue, a synagogue that is both the most splendid and the best-known of all Galilean synagogues. The excavation's results were published with exceptional speed[1] and questioned what used to be commonly accepted, namely, that the Galilean synagogues were established a few decades after the crystallization of the growing Jewish settlement in Galilee following the Bar Kokba War.[2] The theory was that the magnificent Galilean synagogues had been constructed at the end of the second and the beginning of the third centuries C.E. This period saw a conjunction of several favorable, historical factors: it was during the rule of Rabbi Judah the Patriarch and the Severan dynasty which was well-disposed to him, and it was the period when the Jews established themselves in the Galilee after the profound trauma following the Bar Kokhba War. This chronological framework furthermore fit well with the style of architectural plans and decorations of the Galilean synagogues in that period.[3] In contrast

* This essay was originally published in A. Kasher, A. Oppenheimer, and U. Rappaport, eds., *Synagogues in Antiquity* (Jerusalem, 1987), pp. 173-180 (in Hebrew). It has been translated with the permission of the author and of Yad Izhak Ben Zvi. It was translated by Ms. Bati Leviteh.

[1] V. Corbo et al., *La Sinagoga di Cafarnao dopo gli scavi del 1969*, SBF Collectio Minor, vol. 9 (Jerusalem: Francescani, 1970); idem, *Cafarnao I: Edifici della Città*, SBF Collectio Maior, vol. 19 (Jerusalem: Franciscan Printing Press, 1972); idem, "Edifici antichi sotto la Sinagoga di Cafarnao," in E. Testa et al., eds., *Studia Hierosolymitana*, vol. 1 (Jerusalem: Franciscan Printing Press, 1976), pp. 159-176; idem, "Sotto la Sinagoga di Cafarnao un'insula della città," *LA* 27 (1977): 156-177; V. Corbo, "Resti della Sinagoga de primo secolo a Cafarnao," in E. Testa et al., eds., *Studia Hierosolymitana*, vol. 3 (Jerusalem: Franciscan Printing Press, 1982), pp. 313-357.

[2] Thus, for instance, see the articles of A. Oppenheimer, "The Rehabitation of the Jewish Settlement in the Galilee," and of L. I. Levine "The Time of Rabbi Yehuda ha-Nasi" & "Eretz Israel in the Third Century" in Baras, *Eretz Israel*, vol. 1, pp. 75-143 (in Hebrew).

[3] G. Foerster, "The Ancient Synagogues of the Galilee," in Levine, *GLA*, pp. 289-319.

to this interpretation, Corbo and Loffreda argued, on the basis of their excavations, that the construction of the Capernaum synagogue began in the middle of the fourth century C.E. and was completed in the second half of the fifth century.[4]

Since the beginning of the 1970's, various scholars have conducted excavations and stratigraphic examinations of several Galilean synagogues (Gush Ḥalav, Meiron, Khirbet Shema', Ḥorvat 'Ammudim, Chorazin and Ḥorvat Nevorayah [=Nabratein]). The excavators of these synagogues have concluded that their construction was complete by the second half of the third century C.E.[5] Thus only the Capernaum synagogue remains dated to the fifth century.

It should be noted that the building of a synagogue often continued for a long time; we should distinguish between the early years of building and the final period, for between them certainly many years passed. This way we reach the dating suggested by historical and artistic analysis.[6]

In the excavations of the synagogues at Hammath-Tiberias, Rehob, Ma'oz Ḥayyim and Ḥammat Gader, clear indications were found that the buildings erected during the third and fourth centuries went through considerable changes in both decoration and architectural plan over the long years they served their congregations.[7] Furthermore, we can now learn more about the construction of synagogues in the third century from the new

---

[4] See above, note 1.

[5] Gush Ḥalav: See "Gush Ḥalav." In the excavators' opinion, the building was completed in 250 C.E.

Meiron: See *Meiron*. The date was determined by a coin of Probos (276-282 C.E.), which gives, according to the excavators, a *terminus ante-quem* dating of the synagogue; in our opinion, the synagogue could be dated even earlier.

Khirbet Shema': See Meyers, *Khirbet Shema'*. The building was destroyed in 306 C.E. and was certainly constructed some decades earlier.

Ḥorvat 'Ammudim: See Levine, "Ḥ. 'Ammudim." The completion of the floor was dated to the third century C.E.

Ḥorvat Nevorayah (Nabratein): See "En-Nabratein." At stage II of the settlement—the first synagogue was dated to the years 135-250 C.E. Stage III was identified as 250-363 C.E., the excavators observed two phases in this stage. Note that the site's name was fixed by the Committee of Names as 'Ḥorvat Nevorayah,' and is identified as such on the historical sites list and on modern maps. This uniformity should be kept.

Chorazin: Z. Yeivin, "The Excavations at Chorazin in the Years 1962-1964," *EI* 11 (1973): 144-157, and especially p. 157 (in Hebrew).

[6] Corbo and Loffreda argue that the synagogue at Capernaum took one hundred years to build!

[7] Hammath-Tiberias: See Dothan, *Hammath-Tiberias*.

Rehob: See F. Vitto, "The Synagogue at Rehob," in Levine, *ASR*, pp. 90-95; "Notes and News," *IEJ* 30 (1980): 214-217.

Ma'oz Ḥayyim: Tzaferis, "Ma'oz Ḥayyim."

Ḥammat Gader: Foerster, "Ḥammat Gader," pp. 11-12.

excavations in Judea—specifically at En-Gedi[8] and Ḥorvat Rimmon[9]—although their plans lack the necessary clarity.

In contrast to the variety of plans reflected in the third- and fourth-century Galilean synagogues, there is a prominent group of synagogues based on a single design. These are dispersed from Tiberias southwards, along the Bet-Shean and Jericho valleys and also on the Judean plain. The design of these synagogues centers around a rectangular longitudinal building with an apse in the wall directed towards Jerusalem. They are decorated with floor mosaics. The uniformity of the group and its wide dispersion witness to an influential source, namely, church architecture of the fifth and sixth centuries. Indeed, this model indicates, in our opinion, a clear chronological framework. Among the synagogues of this type, sometimes designated 'basilical type with an apse' (טיפוס באסיליקאלי עם אפסיס), are at least two that have indubitable chronological identifications, namely, datable inscriptions that were found in them. The dedicatory inscription in the synagogue of Beth Alpha relates to 'King Justinus,' probably Justin I who ruled in the years 518-527.[10] The inscription also mentions the craftsmen Mariannus and Hanina, whose names also appear on the floor of the Samaritan synagogue at Bet-Shean.[11] This allows us to date the building at Bet-Shean to the beginning of the sixth century. This firm dating enables us to correct the dating of the excavator, who assigned it to the end of the fourth or beginning of the fifth centuries.[12]

A dated dedication was also found at the synagogue excavation at Gaza-Maioumas. This is a broad, large building with five aisles, unlike the usual buildings with three aisles. The excavator reconstructs an apse in the wall directed towards Jerusalem, although this is uncertain. This splendid building is dedicated to the wood traders Menachem and Jeshua, who donated its construction in the year 561 (by the Gaza reckoning [=508/9 C.E.]).[13] Close to this building, geographically and artistically, is the synagogue at Ma'on, whose plan is that of a basilica with an apse.[14] Its decoration, as has been

---

[8] D. Barag et al., "The Second Excavation Season at the Synagogue of En-Gedi," *Qadmoniot* 5, no. 2 (1972): 52-53 (in Hebrew).

[9] A. Kloner "The Synagogue of Ḥorvat Rimmon," *Qadmoniot* 17, nos. 2-3 (1984): 65-71, and especially pp. 66-67 (in Hebrew).

[10] Sukenik, *Bet Alpha*, pp. 39-42.

[11] See Tzori, p. 159.

[12] Tzori, pp. 149-154. There is no justification to suggest different building phases and thus no chronological development can be ascertained.

[13] See Ovadiah, "Gaza," pp. 195-196.

[14] S. Levi, "The Ancient Synagogue at Ma'on (Nirim). (First review of the excavations)," *EI* 10 (1961): 77-82 (in Hebrew). M. Avi-Yonah, "The Mosaic Floor of the Synagogue at Ma'on (Nirim)," *EI* 10 (1961): 86-93 (in Hebrew).

noticed by other scholars, resembles that of the mosaic in the nearby Shellal Church, which also has a dedicatory inscription dated to 565 C.E.[15]

The synagogue of stratum 1/b at Hammath-Tiberias—a large, majestic basilical structure with an apse in the wall directed towards Jerusalem—was built according to a new plan on top of the previous synagogue—the well-known Hammath-Tiberias synagogue. The earlier structure was destroyed and abandoned, according to Dothan, between 396 and 422. Although the later synagogue has not yet undergone final publication, it seems to us—from the style of its mosaic remains and from historical considerations—that the building was not rebuilt prior to the beginning of the sixth century.[16]

The synagogues discovered at Ḥammat Gader and Ma'oz Ḥayyim had also a basilical plan with an apse. The stratigraphy of both buildings dates the synagogues to the sixth century.[17]

The synagogue at Ḥammat Gader was uncovered in 1935 by Sukenik,[18] who dated it to the fifth century,[19] but Avi-Yonah, referring to its style, revised the date to the sixth century.[20] In a later excavation of the synagogue in 1982—after removing the mosaic pavement for preservation—were found two earlier stages in the history of the synagogue's building that had not been noticed by previous excavators.[21]

The earliest stage is characterized by simple white mosaic, in the center of which were found the remains of a black-and-red frame. The plan of this building is unclear, but it seems that it was a public building that was similar, but not identical, to the two succeeding stages. In the second stage, the plan was fixed (since it was preserved in the third stage) except for a few elements—important in themselves—that were added or taken away during the building's last stage. The building was paved with local-stone tiles, placed in an ornamental style. At the hall's center a square frame was contoured carpet-like by quadrangular and triangular tiles (sort of *opus sectile*). Adjacent to the hall's south wall, the foundations of a raised platform were exposed. It was here that the main finds of the synagogue were discovered, mostly sherds of oil lamps and other vessels from the end of third or beginning of fourth century. The latest coins that could possibly be ascribed to this stage are those of Constantine II, who ruled until 361 C.E.

---

[15] Trendall, *Shellal*, pp. 12-13.

[16] M. Dothan, "The Synagogues at Hammath-Tiberias," *Qadmoniot* 1, no. 4 (1969): 122-123 (in Hebrew). See also Dothan, *Hammath-Tiberias*, p. 67.

[17] Sukenik, *el-Hammeh*. And more recently, see Foerster, "Ḥammath Gader."

[18] Sukenik, *el-Hammeh*, pp. 80-81.

[19] Tzaferis, "Ma'oz Ḥayyim."

[20] *NEAEHL*, vol. 2, p. 568.

[21] Foerster, "Ḥammath Gader."

During the third stage the mosaic floor was laid and an apse was added in the southern small room of the building, at the width of the central hall. The mosaic is about 20 cm above the previous tile-floor, and was laid over several plaster layers founded upon a sand layer.[22] Above the early *bemah* we exposed from the second stage of the building, a platform surrounded by a screen had been already exposed by Sukenik. A staircase led to the platform and the apse. Fifty years after the upper *bemah* had been discovered, only a little of it was left. By checking the material that could be saved from the mosaic bedding, it seems that it was probably laid in the sixth century.

Similarity in measurements, plan, and development of the Ḥammat Gader synagogue can be observed at the synagogue discovered at Ma'oz Ḥayyim and published by Tzaferis.[23] The synagogue at Ma'oz Ḥayyim was first built in the fourth century. It was a small rectangular building paved with stone tiles, with the *bemah* located at the southern side directed towards Jerusalem. At the second stage, the hall was widened to the north, an apse was added at its southern end, and a mosaic floor was laid on above the earlier tile floor. The excavator dates the mosaic floor to the first half of the fifth century according to stylistic considerations, but this date should be revised to the beginning of the sixth century, according to the same criteria. The first mosaic was replaced by a second, and constitutes the main change at the building's final stage.[24]

From the buildings analyzed above, it can be argued that synagogues built according to a basilical plan with an apse were not constructed prior to the early sixth century C.E. This does not imply, of course, that all the synagogues of this period had apses. Indeed, several synagogues dated to the sixth century lack an apse—whether or not they are based on a basilical plan.

In the synagogues with the apse, it seems that the apse replaced the niche which appeared in other synagogues. In the apse was kept the Ark containing the Torah scrolls. In synagogues where the apse was spacious enough, it probably also served as the sitting place of the congregation elders, as did the *presbyterium* in churches—but we have no evidence of such a use.

To the synagogues analyzed so far—which point to a wave of building and renovation in the early sixth century—we could add newly rebuilt syna-

---

[22] Foerster, "Ḥammath Gader."

[23] Tzaferis, "Ma'oz Ḥayyim."

[24] Tzaferis, "Ma'oz Ḥayyim" pp. 224-225. The three-dimensional meander pattern that includes various descriptions, is present, in our opinion, only in clear contexts of the sixth century at Shellal (see Trendall, *Shellal*, plate 11).

Ḥorvat Susiya: S. Gutmann et al., "Excavations of the Synagogue at Ḥorvat Susiya," *Qadmoniot* 5, no. 2 (1972): 47-52, see especially p. 41 and its photograph (in Hebrew).

Ḥorvat Berakot: Y. Tsafrir et al., ""The Church and Mosaics at Horvat Berachot, Israel," *DOPapers* 33 (1979): 302-309, fig F, pl. 1b..

gogues and the final phases of synagogue constructions that were repaired and changed, such as in Na'aran, Rehob, Bet-Shean, Ḥorvat Susiya, Eshtemoa and En-Gedi.[25] In the second half of the sixth century, the synagogues of Ḥorvat Rimmon and Ḥorvat Nevorayah were renovated,[26] and new synagogues were erected in Jericho and Tiberias.[27]

From all of this evidence, a most interesting archaeological picture appears, which identifies two main periods of construction and repair of synagogues after the Bar Kokba War. During the first period—in the third and fourth centuries C.E.—synagogues were erected all over Israel. Most of them were constructed in the third century and were modified during the fourth century. The second period essentially began after a gap of over a hundred years; it comprised the end of the fifth and the beginning of the sixth centuries. This second phase affects the whole country—as we have documented—with new buildings erected and old synagogues repaired.

The obvious decline and gap in synagogue construction from the second half of the fourth century until the end of the fifth—which we noticed in the archaeological finds mentioned up to now—is easily explained by the distress that afflicted the Jewish settlements in Palestine. The decline in construction began with the difficulties following the failure of the revolt in the time of Gallus Caesar[28] and increased after the failure of Julian the Apostate's plan to rebuild the Temple.[29] It should be remembered, that in 363 the great earthquake occurred, causing the destruction of twenty-three towns across the land.[30] In the same period—primarily at the end of the fourth and the beginning of the fifth century—the Christian rule over the

---

[25] Na'aran: *NEAEHL* vol. 3, pp. 1075-1076..

Bet-Shean: See Tzori, p. 159; and also N. Tzori, "The House of Kyrios Leontis at Beth-Shean," *IEJ* 16 (1966): 123-134; D. Bahat, "The Synagogue at Bet-Shean—First Review," *Qadmoniot* 5, no. 2 (1972): 55-58 (in Hebrew).

Ḥorvat Susiya: see above, note 24.

Eshtemoa: Z. Yeivin, "The Synagogue at Eshtemoa," *Qadmoniot* 5:2 (1972): 43-45 (in Hebrew). Avian does not indicate a date, but it seems to me that the mosaic is from the sixth century.

En-Gedi: See above, note 7.

[26] Ḥorvat Rimmon: see above, note 8.

Ḥorvat Nevorayah: see above, note 5. And also N. Avigad, "A Dated Lintel Inscription of the Ancient Synagogue of Nabratein," *Rabinowitz Bulletin*, vol. 3, pp. 49-56..

[27] Jericho: *NEAEHL*, vol. 3, pp. 695-696..

[28] Y. Geiger, "The Revolt in the Days of Gallus and the Episode of the Temple's Construction in the Days of Julian," in Baras, *Eretz Israel*, vol. 1, pp. 202-208.

[29] Ibid, pp. 208-217.

[30] S. P. Brock, "A Letter attributed to Cyril of Jerusalem on the Re-building of the Temple," *BSOAS* 40 (1977): 267-286; G. Foerster, "An Earthquake on the 19th of Year 363 and its Historical and Archaeological Meaning," in *The Eighth Archaeological Congress in Israel* (Jerusalem, 1981), p. 20 (in Hebrew); K. W. Russel, "The Earthquake of May 19, A.D. 363," *BASOR* 238 (1980): 47-64.

country strengthened, evidence to which is the fanatic asceticism movement that spread Christianity by enforcement and terror, and also institutionalized persecution. One of the latter's expressions is the intensive religious legislation, which among other actions actually canceled the office of the Jewish Patriarch.[31]

A series of laws during this period directly concerned the institution of the synagogue. It starts with an exemption from the obligation to accommodate soldiers given to the synagogue in Trier between the years 368-373 during the reign of Valentinian II.[32] In 393, Arcadius and Honorius forbid the looting and demolishing of synagogues, a protection that indicates, of course, that synagogues were indeed harmed.[33] In 397, a similar law was legislated.[34] A law protecting synagogues and forbidding their seizure was legislated in 412 by Honorius and Theodosius II.[35] In 420, these two rulers also decided to establish another law for the protection of synagogues and dwelling places against unlawful burning.[36] A law from 423 widens the scope by discussing compensation to those damaged by the illegal looting of synagogues and turning them into churches as well as penalties for stealing holy vessels. It also banned the building of new synagogues and promulgated an order to maintain the former ones as they were.[37] In 438, Theodosius II and Valentinian III declared the confiscation new synagogues built against the law, and levied a fine of 50 gold pounds against their builders. At the same time, it emphasized that permission was given for repairing synagogues that were about to collapse.[38] Indeed, by the end of the fourth and beginning of the fifth centuries, many synagogues had been damaged, both physically and by seizure and transformation into churches. This

---

[31] Z. Rubin, "Spreading of Christianity in Israel from the Days of Julian until the Period of Justinian," in Baras, *Eretz Israel*, vol. 1, pp. 234-251 (in Hebrew); Y. Dan, "Eretz Israel in the 5th and 6th centuries," in Baras, *Eretz Israel*, vol. 1, pp. 273-275 (in Hebrew).

[32] Linder, no. 14, pp. 116-118 (Codex Theodosianus, 7:8:2, ed. Mommsen, p. 327).

[33] Linder, No 21, pp. 137-138 (Codex Theodosianus, 16:7:9, Mommsen, p. 889).

[34] Linder, No 25, pp. 143-144 (Codex Theodosianus, 16:8:12, Mommsen, pp. 889-890). This law was directed to Praetorium Prefect of Illiricum.

[35] Linder, No 40, pp. 190-192 (Codex Theodosianus, 16:8:20, Mommsen, p. 892).

[36] Linder, No 46, pp. 205-208 (Codex Theodosianus, 16:8:21, Mommsen, p. 892).

[37] Linder, No 47, pp. 208-209 (Codex Theodosianus, 16:8:25, Mommsen, pp. 893-844). The absolute prohibition of building new synagogues, along with the indication to maintain their form unchanged, should be emphasized. The intention is, certainly, to preserve the decorations and plans of existing buildings.

[38] Linder, No 54, p. 245-235. (Theodosius II, *Novella* [=*Breviarium*, 3], ed. Meyer & Mommsen, pp. 7-11; also in, *Codex Justinianus*, 1:9:18, ed. Krueger, p. 62).

happened in Calinicum,[39] Odessa,[40] Asia Minor, Alexandria,[41] and Constantinople.[42] In Rome, the synagogue had been burnt down.[43]

The archaeological evidence from the fifth century also witnesses to the seizure of synagogues of Gerasa in Trans-Jordan[44] and Ephainea in Syria,[45] and their subsequent transformation into churches. No similar phenomenon has been found in Israel. It seems, however, that the general decrease of Israel Jewry after the 363 earthquake and continuing into the fifth century—a fact supported by archaeological finds—reflects similar processes in Israel. This decline derived from the strengthening of Christian rule in Israel and the pressure that followed. The partial revival in synagogue construction in the sixth century stemmed from the weakening of the Christian rule in Israel on the threshold of the Muslim conquest.

[39] In the year 388, according to the legends of Ambrosius, Archbishop of Milan, see Parkes, pp. 166-167, pl. XVI, col. 1101.

[40] In the year 411, see Parkes, pp. 236-411.

[41] Linder, p. 206.

[42] Parkes, in 442; the synagogue in the copper market, p. 238. See also Linder.

[43] Linder, p. 137, according to Ambrosius' report.

[44] C. H. Kraeling, ed., *Gerasa: City of the Decapolis* (New Haven: ASOR, 1938), pp. 234-241. The dating of the church erected above the synagogue is 530/1. There is no way to know when the synagogue was constructed and demolished.

[45] The report on the synagogue was not published. For the latest reference to this case, see J. Napoleone-Lemaire & J. Ch. Balty, *L'Eglise a Atrium de la Grand Collonade* (Bruxelles: Centre belge de recherches archeologiques a Apamee de Syrie, 1969), pp. 9-10. There is a promise to publish the excavations done at the synagogue.

THE DIASPORA SYNAGOGUE: ARCHAEOLOGICAL AND EPIGRAPHIC EVIDENCE SINCE SUKENIK

ALF THOMAS KRAABEL*

I. INTRODUCTION: RESOURCES

Epigonoi usually deserve their reputations. The three persons from whom this study takes its beginnings would not be pleased with the narrowness of the topic, since all three saw that distinguishing 'Diaspora' from 'Holy Land' was a most imperfect way of dividing up the Judaism of the Greco-Roman world. Eliezer Lipa Sukenik (1889-1965), Erwin Ramsdell Goodenough (1893-1965) and Michael Avi-Yonah (1904-1974) knew that the Diaspora was not itself a religious and cultural unity, still less was it out of touch with Syria-Palestine.[1] However, the study of post-Biblical Judaism, and particularly the archaeology thereof, has taken some unexpected turns in the two generations since E. L. Sukenik's 1930 Schweich Lectures;[2] the field is almost certain to continue to expand, with new excavations and investigations of other sorts. This is a proper time to survey the archaeological and epigraphic evidence presently available, and draw some tentative conclusions about these Diaspora buildings and the 'Jews in a gentile world' who use them—hopefully, without losing sight of the larger Judaism mentioned above.

Since the 1930s, most of the new information about the ancient synagogue has come from what is now the State of Israel: the 1973 edition of S. J. Saller's catalogue lists evidence from 131 sites, M. Avi-Yonah's *Ariel* article of the same year examines a score of the best-preserved examples in some detail, and every year additional evidence is uncovered, preliminary

---

* This essay originally appeared in H. Temporini and W. Haase, eds., *Aufstieg und Niedergang der römischen Welt: Principat, Religion (Judentum: Allgemeines; Palästinisches Judentum)*, Bd. 19.1 (Berlin and New York: Walter de Gruyter, 1979), pp. 477-510. It is reprinted by the permission of the author and Walter de Gruyter & Co.

1 Their bibliographies reveal the range of their interests; these are listed in the bibliography under Ben-Horin (Sukenik), Kraabel (Goodenough) and Salzmann (Avi-Yonah).

2 Sukenik, *ASPG*, to which the title of this essay refers. In spite of the many other things Sukenik wrote on synagogues afterward, it is this book which determined the image of its topic for at least a generation.

notices thereof appearing promptly in *Israel Exploration Journal*.[3] These buildings are quickly visited and easily compared with each other, and members of the archaeological community in Israel (along with some American archaeologists) are rapidly assembling a full picture of the religious architecture of what is sometimes called early rabbinic Judaism. Inevitably, these advances stimulate questions about the situation outside the Holy Land in the same period.

In the Diaspora, the work goes more slowly.[4] There have been spectacular discoveries, Dura and later Sardis chief among them; the result, more than once, has been to explode carefully assembled hypotheses about 'Diaspora Judaism,' theories based on scraps of excavated evidence and tantalizingly vague or remote literary references from the rabbis, from hostile Church Fathers or from uncomprehending pagan writers.[5] Thus, while the number of ancient synagogues known from the Diaspora is only a small fraction of those identified in the tiny State of Israel, a single building in, say, Yugoslavia or Greece will have much greater impact on the understanding of ancient Judaism; the handful of sites discussed below will repay close attention, if we do not try to assemble from them another sweeping picture of what 'normative' Judaism might be.[6]

The last major development since the 1930s in this field is a change in the relation of literary to non-literary evidence, due in large part to archaeological advances. For the Judaism of the earlier, 'Biblical' period, there has been for nearly half a century no question but that the Hebrew Bible can only be understood against the background of the much larger *Umwelt* known chiefly through the evidence produced by excavation. In the neighboring fields of New Testament studies and patristics, such an approach, long overdue, is only beginning to take hold. And the study of post-Biblical Judaism has been dominated literally for centuries by the sheer bulk of the rabbinic literature, from which have been produced pictures of a 'normative Judaism' which now turns out to be anything but the entire story. Thus ar-

---

3 Avi-Yonah, "Synagogues"; Saller, *Second Revised Catalogue*.

4 Sukenik had hoped to survey systematically the ancient synagogues of the Mediterranean world with the aid of the Louis M. Rabinowitz Fund for the Exploration of Ancient Synagogues (Sukenik, "The Present State," p. 22), but the three *Bulletins* published on this fund (1949, 1951, 1960) report only on synagogues excavated in Israel.

5 In some ways the greatest distortion (although always "well documented") occurs in the crypto-Nazi statements of Gerhard Kittel, e.g. in Kittel, "Kleinasiatisches Judentum," cf. W. F. Albright, "Gerhard Kittel and the Jewish question in antiquity," in W. F. Albright, *History, Archaeology and Christian Humanism* (New York, 1964), pp. 229-240. In general, however, I have in mind the careless statements about the "syncretism" or even "apostasy" of Diaspora Jews, as found still in the more derivative handbooks; on the matter, see Kraabel, "*Hypsistos*"; Kraabel, "Paganism."

6 The phrase is of course most closely associated with G. F. Moore, see the partly autobiographical comments in Goodenough, vol. 1, pp. 16-32.

chaeological discoveries turn out to have implications for the understanding of literary texts which at first appeared wholly unrelated to them, as the amulets, the papyri, the inscriptions, the mosaics and the buildings reveal a Judaism greatly more complex than the one we thought we saw in the rabbinic literature alone.[7]

Out of this wealth of evidence for ancient Judaism, this paper will review one segment: the Diaspora synagogue buildings[8] excavated or reinterpreted since 1930.[9] Inscriptions mentioning synagogues not yet located will be brought in only as they illuminate the present topic. The sites are arranged in a geographical order, east to west.

Of reference works and recent general studies the following should be noted: E. R. Goodenough's mammoth, idiosyncratic and indispensable *Jewish Symbols in the Greco-Roman Period* (thirteen volumes, 1953-1968). The articles in: Pauly-Wissowa, *Real-Encyclopädie der klassischen Altertumswissenschaft* (1932, by. S. Kraus); *The Interpreter's Dictionary of the Bible* (1962, by I. Sonne); Kittel's *Theological Dictionary of the New Testament* (1964 in the German; 1971 in English, by W. Schrage); *Encyclopedia Judaica* (1971, by M. Avi-Yonah); *New Catholic Encylopedia:*

---

[7] Of the three men, Goodenough went farthest with 'non-literary' evidence, and (deservedly at times) received the most sceptical response from his colleagues, see Smith, "Jewish Symbols." Sukenik was the earliest, and understandably had the greatest difficulty in freeing himself from earlier views, as for example in the debate over the presence or absence of a permanent Torah shrine in the Capernaum synagogue. In *ASPG* (pp. 18f., 52f.) he accepted the hypothesis of the earlier excavators that a stone shrine had stood before the main (south) doors of the building in its later phase. In "The Present State" he has revised his view, after a fresh examination of the site; now the stone fragments once thought to be from a Torah shrine are actually part of the exterior façade—there never had been a permanent shrine in the building, a conclusion which "agrees completely with the Talmudic statements that the Torah scrolls had no fixed place within the prayer-hall" (p. 19). Goodenough (vol. 1, p. 181 note 17a) and Sonne ("Synagogue," p. 488) attack this procedure as, in the latter's words, an attempt "to adjust the archaeological data to assumed rabbinic implications." Still later developments complicate the debate: Ostia (see below) furnishes a clear example of a permanent Torah shrine added to an existing synagogue in a manner which blocks one of its main doors-exactly the procedure Sukenik was rejecting for Capernaum in "The Present State" (cf. p. 18)!

[8] *synagogē* may mean the community rather than the building, e.g. Lifshitz, no. 100 (Berenice, Cyrenaica). On the words used to indicate the building in antiquity, see Sonne, "Synagogue," pp. 477f., and Hengel, "Proseuche" passim.

[9] Hence the omission here of sections on other Diaspora synagogue buildings mentioned by Sukenik, Goodenough or Avi-Yonah, e.g. Hammam Lif in North Africa, Apamea in Syria (Saller, *Second Revised Catalogue* no. 10) and Aegina in Greece. The Aegina synagogue mosaic was removed and repaired in 1966, cf. *Deltion* 22 (1967) B. Chronika, pp. 19f., 161, plates 19a, 19b, 122a; comparison of plan 1 (20), giving the condition of the mosaic in 1966, with earlier plans shows the floor has deteriorated greatly in recent times. Earlier plan reproduced by Sukenik (*ASPG*, plan XI), Goodenough (vol. 3, no. 881) and Avi-Yonah ("Synagogue: Architecture," p. 600); see also Sukenik, "The Present State," pp. 20f. and fig. 6.

Supplement 1967-1974 (1974, by A. T. Kraabel); and *The Interpreter's Dictionary of the Bible: Supplement* (1976, by E. M. Meyers).[10]

For inscriptions, the pioneer work is *Corpus Inscriptionum Iudaicarum* (volume one, 'Europe,' 1936; volume two, 'Asia-Africa,' 1952), edited by J.-B. Frey. *CII* is marred by errors and omissions, however; many of the flaws in the first volume are corrected in Baruch Lifshitz's 100-page "Prolegomenon" to the 1975 reprint. The second volume, even less satisfactory than the first, should be read along with the reviews, particularly that of J. and L. Robert in *Bull. épigr.* 1954 no. 24. For new inscriptions, and new interpretations, the annual review by the Roberts in *Bull.epigr*' under the heading "*inscriptions gréco-juives*" is absolutely indispensible. Lifshitz's *Donateurs et fondateurs dans les synagogues juives* is a very useful collection of inscriptions relating to the construction, furnishing and rebuilding of synagogues.

Comprehensive surveys of the ancient synagogue are rare, and S. Krauss' *Synagogale Altertumer* is still essential; his article in Pauly-Wissowa is a condensation. The first chapter of R. Wischnitzer, *The Architecture* reviews more recent evidence and draws sound conclusions.[11]

For each of the seven buildings below, major publications and particularly useful reference works will be listed, accompanied by a discussion of the issues raised by the finds for the history of religions and, in particular, for Diaspora Judaism. For plans, detailed measurements and full discussion of finds, the reader is referred to the items in the bibliography. (Strictly speaking, analysis of the Miletus and Priene buildings by the archaeologists responsible for them has not progressed beyond what Sukenik described in 1930; however, the Sardis discoveries require that the evidence known in 1930 be reviewed for these neighboring sites.)

---

[10] *Fasti Archaeologici* (*FA*) is essential for information on new finds and interpretations, but it can be a bewildering tool for this particular topic; thus in the 1969-1970 edition, the latest available at this writing, the annual Sardis report in BASOR is no. 3609 ('Prehistoric and Classical Greece: Regions and Sites'). Bruneau, *Recherches sur...Delos*, is no. 6111, and reviews of Goodenough are no. 5123f. ('Hellenistic World and the Eastern Provinces: History and Civllization: Religion and Mythology'). Floriani Squarciapino's article on an *archisynagogus* inscription from Ostia is no. 8004 ('Roman West: Roman Civilization and Art: Epigraphy'). Finally, two entries on 'Holy Land' synagogues are in the section 'Christianity and Late Antiquity': no. 12893 is an earlier edition of the Saller catalogue ('Civilization and Art: Architecture: Synagogues') and no. 13699 a brief survey by Avi-Yonah ('Regions and Sites: Israel'). There are cross-references only occasionally.

[11] One recent survey with a promising title is a disappointment: *The Jews in the Roman World*, by M. Grant; time after time the archaeological evidence readily available is ignored.

II. DURA

The Dura(-Europos) synagogue was discovered in 1932 by an expedition sponsored by Yale University and the French Academy of Inscriptions and Letters;[12] the excavators' final report on the building is C. H. Kraeling, *The Synagogue*. Dura was a trading outpost on the Euphrates River, subject to a rainbow of cultural influences, and under Seleucid, then Parthian, then Roman domination. The Roman army held control during the time the synagogue was in existence, but lost the town to the Sassanians in AD 256; the synagogue was preserved only because it had been buried under hastily constructed fortifications just prior to the last Sassanian attack.

Of the seven sites here examined, Dura is the farthest from Rome, with the greatest admixture of elements from outside the Greco-Roman sphere. Fortunately, it is an extensively excavated and well documented site; if its colorful and often clashing religious and cultural mosaic has not been completely explained, it is at least fully documented.

Goodenough devoted the last section (volumes 9-11) of his *Jewish Symbols* to the Dura synagogue; he saw it as "a sort of Rosetta Stone" for the understanding of ancient religious symbolism, and Avi-Yonah was correct in calling the three Dura volumes "the final—one may even say the crowning—section of the whole."[13] The two men jointly authored the lavish *Encyclopedia Judaica* entry on the synagogue. The collection edited by J. Gutmann, *The Dura-Europos Synagogue*, includes useful discussion and new comparative material four decades after the initial discoveries. For the religious situation in ancient Dura, see the standard reference works, e.g. *Reallexikon fur Antike und Christentum* (1959, by O. Eissfeldt); on the synagogue, the entry in *Reallexikon zur byzantinischen Kunst* (1966, by J. Gutmann) is particularly well done. Reviews of Goodenough are listed by Morton Smith in Smith, "Jewish Symbols," pp. 66f., and again in Goodenough, vol. 13, pp. 229f.; note particularly that of E. Bickerman, "Symbolism." The building itself, reconstructed, is now a part of the National Museum, Damascus.

In the middle of the third century AD the synagogue complex took up much of a city block, next to the west wall in a residential quarter, not far from the main city gate. Originally the Jewish community had used a private dwelling as their place of assembly; by the end of the second century this had been remodelled into the earlier synagogue, which was rebuilt again in AD 245, a decade before the final destruction of the town.

---

[12] After a visit to the site, Sukenik was able to include a brief discussion in "Ancient Synagogues," pp. 82-85.

[13] Avi-Yonah, "Goodenough's Evaluation," p. 118.

The synagogue in its final form was not easily identified as such from outside; it could be entered only through a complex of some nine rooms, forming with the synagogue the Jewish community center for the town. The synagogue proper includes a forecourt open to the sky, and the 'house of assembly,' a rectangular room 14 x 8.7 m from floor to ceiling. It is wider than it is deep, a 'broadhouse' in plan, a design infrequent in Palestinian synagogues; of the seven Diaspora buildings treated here, only Dura is a broadhouse.[14] The 'house of assembly' was provided with two entrances (from the forecourt) in its long east wall, one in the center, a smaller one at the south end. A Torah Shrine was attached to, and extended into, the west wall, the one closest to Jerusalem. Two-level masonry benches were attached to all walls of the room, interrupted only by the two doors and the shrine.

But the most spectacular, most controversial and most discussed element of the entire complex is the paintings which covered all four walls of the 'house of assembly,' and the front of the Torah Shrine. Some reproduce Biblical stories (The Exodus, Elijah reviving the widow's child, Samuel anointing David), others display puzzling symbolism (The Open Temple /The Closed Temple), all display a bewildering mixture of costume (Persian caftan and trousers, Greek *chiton* and *himation*, perhaps a Jewish prayer shawl with *zizith* or ritual fringes), imagery (Biblical, mythological, astrological, apotropaic) and languages (legends and graffiti in Aramaic, Greek, Middle Persian and Parthian). Most scholars agree that there is a unifying general theme for the paintings, but disagree as to what it might be—and a few insist there is no single central idea at all.[15] The Jews of Dura were neither heretical nor esoteric,[16] but the kind 'Judaism' which might provide the theology for the paintings is much debated, Kraeling, for example, assuming that the source is the rabbinic Judaism of Palestine and Babylonia, Goodenough insisting on a hellenized, 'mystic' Diaspora Judaism with equal fervor, others (e.g. Bickerman, Avi-Yonah, M. Smith) suspecting that their dichotomy was unnecessarily severe. To judge from the first four decades, it is unlikely that there will ever be a single universally accepted explanation; from Kraeling and Goodenough we have the evidence in great detail, but Dura remains a 'source' for ancient Judaism more puzzling than the Dead Sea Scrolls, and no less important.

---

[14] On this form, see Goodenough, vol. 1, pp. 225-237; Avi-Yonah, "Synagogue: Architecture," p. 597f., Kraabel, "Synagogues, Ancient," p. 437f.

[15] See the summary in Gutmann, "Die Synagoge," pp. 1236-1238.

[16] See M. Simon, "Synagogues."

III. SARDIS

Sardis and Dura are the two most important discoveries in Diaspora Judaism since 1930, each contributing as much to the understanding of this area as the Dead Sea Scrolls have for Palestine. There are other similarities between the two sites as well: both were excavated as a part of a larger project in archaeology, so that we have the context for each building; thanks to the two expeditions, we know a very great deal about Roman Dura and Roman Sardis, and the place of the synagogue communities within those settings. In all probability, these are the synagogues for their sites: in the third century AD it is unlikely that there were other Jewish communities for Dura and for Sardis than those represented by these two excavated structures. Thus if either seems strange in any particular—architectural, theological, social—the strangeness is due to our previous lack of knowledge of Judaism along the Euphrates or the Pactolus, the famous gold-bearing river of Croesus; for Sardis and for Dura, the buildings, inscriptions, art reveal their normal, standard, even every-day Judaism, no esoteric or heretical conventicle. Further, the members of both communities knew they were Jews, knew what it meant to be loyal to this tradition, and so presumably knew how to break with that tradition, had they wished.

One older way of explaining a newly identified and seemingly aberrant form of a particular religion was to claim that this new piece of evidence reveals a group which has unwittingly apostatized or assimilated; they have abandoned their religion, whatever it might be, without knowing it. In the case of ancient Judaism, it would be said that a group had allowed itself to become 'hellenized' or 'paganized' without realizing what had been lost. That explanation, always at least arrogant as applied by the modern scholar, will not work for either of these two sites; the Sardis and Dura Jews may surprise us in their ways of being Jewish, but if so, I suspect they would be surprised at our surprise. After all, they were what Judaism was for their locations; if they are not a norm, they are at least 'working definitions,' the only ones now available for their specific areas—for this is the last point they have in common: each reveals an important Judaism about which only scraps of information had been available previously.[17]

But the sites have great differences at the same time. Remote Dura (like Qumran!) is on the fringe of the Empire, scarcely touched by much of what was central to the life of the Roman world; Sardis had been a city since before the Trojan War, known later to Alcman and Sappho, Aeschylus and Euripides, Herodotus and Plato.[18] Gyges and Croesus, the first and last of

[17] Further on the comparison of the Sardis and Dura synagogues, Seager, "The Architecture."

[18] The literary references are collected in Pedley, *Ancient Literary Sources on Sardis.*

the Mermnad dynasty (ca. 680-ca. 547 BC), are familiar from Greek and Latin literature. After Croesus' famous misinterpretation of the Delphic Oracle, and the fall of his kingdom, Sardis is for two centuries the western capital of the Persian Empire, so threatening to the Greeks; and the city maintains its stature thereafter under Seleucid, then Pergamene, then Roman rule.[19]

The first Jews known to have visited Sardis are "the exiles of Jerusalem who are in Sepharad" (Obadiah 20 in the Hebrew Bible); Sepharad is the Hebrew and Aramaic name for Sardis, to which these refugees came after their city was destroyed by the Babylonians in 587 BC.[20] There are Jewish permanent residents in Sardis by the end of the third century BC, if not before, and a politically powerful Jewish community by the first century BC.[21] Josephus preserves two documents (*Ant.* 14.235, 259-261) which guarantee Sardis Jews a *topos* ('place') of their own in the city; this *topos*, possibly a section of a public building, was surely their religious and community center, the predecessor of the building discussed below.[22]

The synagogue was discovered in 1962 during excavations being carried out by Harvard and Cornell universities and under the direction of G. M. A. Hanfmann. A year-by-year account of the excavations overall is available in Hanfmann, *Letters*, a sector-by-sector summary in Hanfmann and Waldbaum, *Survey*; annual reports are printed in *BASOR*. A. R. Seager has published two substantial studies of the architecture of the synagogue, "The Building History" and "The Architecture." The final publication of the building is A. R. Seager et al., *The Synagogue*, in preparation; until it becomes available, the best sources of plans, photographs and reconstruction drawings of the building are *Letters* and *Survey*. Goodenough was able to include some preliminary comments on the synagogue in volume twelve of his *Jewish Symbols* (1965); he saw in the new data confirmation of some of his hypotheses, and his delight is obvious.

The Sardis synagogue is not a building, but only one segment of a mammoth structure, a monument of Roman Imperial urbanism, the Sardis gymnasium complex, often not quite accurately called the 'Marble Court.'

[19] Further on the history of the city, Hanfmann, "Sardis und Lydien"; Mitten, "A New Look"; Hanfmann and Waldbaum, "New Excavations."

[20] For Sepharad, see the biblical dictionaries and lexica, and especially Rabinowitz, "Sepharad." For a review of the sites in Asia Minor mentioned in the Old Testament and Apocrypha, see Simons, *The Geographical and Topographical Texts*, chapter 31. For a general description of the three Anatolian sites (Sardis, Miletus and Priene) as they are today, see Bean, *Aegean Turkey*.

[21] Josephus, *Ant.* 12:147-153; 14:235, 259-261; 16:171. On the first text, see Robert, *Nouvelles Inscriptions*, pp. 9-21; Hanfmann and Waldbaum, "New Excavations," pp. 318f.; Applebaum, "Legal Status," pp. 431f. and Applebaum, "Organization," pp. 468-473.

[22] On *topos*=synagogue, Hengel, "Synagogeninschrift," p. 173; Sonne, "Synagogue," p. 477; Krauss, pp. 24f.

Sardis was devastated by an earthquake in AD 17; the gymnasium is a major part of the rebuilding afterward. The center of the excavated area is an open *palaestra*, square, its colonnaded sides roughly east-west and north-south; in the original design, the entrance to the complex was a gate in the middle of the east side of the *palaestra*, with the Roman baths proper on the west—strictly speaking, the multi-storied Marble Court is the formal entrance from the *palaestra* to the baths. On the north and south sides of the *palaestra* were parallel halls, each with three large rooms opening into the *palaestra* and serving perhaps as its dressing rooms or *apodyteria*. Apparently the north hall remained in this form, but the south hall was extensively remodelled in about the second century; the openings into the *palaestra* were sealed, the interior north-south walls removed, and an *exedra* was added at the west end of the long room thus formed—the result is a structure which closely resembles the usual Roman civil basilica.[23]

These alterations may have been carried out in order to produce a synagogue; it is more likely, however, that this space too was originally public, and was turned over to the Jewish community only later—thus it was probably not designed to serve as a religious structure. In the second half of the third century, however, already decorated with mosaics and revetments some of which are still in place, it is in the possession of the Jewish community and functioning as their synagogue; remodelled once or twice more, it became the building excavated and reconstructed by the Sardis expedition. It was still attached structurally to the gymnasium complex, but could be entered only from outside that complex. Attached to its south wall and the continuation of that wall (as the south wall of the gymnasium complex) are over two dozen small shops (some of them owned by Jews) facing out on the main street of the Roman city.

The present interior plan of the synagogue dates from the fourth century; the *exedra* has become an apse, and the east-west dimension from the apse to the front steps is nearly 100 meters. The width is nearly 20 meters. There is one north-south crosswall, separating the main hall (60 meters long) from an *atrium*-like forecourt over 20 meters long. The forecourt, colonnaded on four sides, open to the sky in the center, has entrances on three sides: triple doors leading in from the street on the east, triple doors opening into the main hall on the west, a single subsidiary entrance through the shops on the south.[24]

The interior of the main hall is dominated by massive shapes: six heavy piers line the north wall, another six the south wall, supporting the roof at least 20 m. above the floor. A pair of substantial stone shrines or *aediculae*

[23] Seager, "The Building History."

[24] The triple door is common in Palestinian synagogues and tombs; Goodenough rightly stresses its symbolic value; see Goodenough, Index.

flanks the central entrance on the east. The apse at the west is a *synthronon*, large enough to seat seventy or more on a three-level semi circular bench. Before the apse stands the 'Eagle Table,' in shape and positioning resembling nothing so much as an altar; its top is a two-ton slab (an architectural fragment from an earlier building), its two supports are decorated with Roman eagles clutching thunderbolts. The eagle carvings (also in re-use) are well preserved, in high relief, but the head of each has been knocked off. The table is flanked by pairs of stone lions, Lydian, sixth-fifth century BC, in re-use. Precisely in the center of the main hall stands a platform or *bema*, probably the last important feature to be added to the room.

The floors are elaborate designs in mosaic, floral or geometric patterns, no animal or human shapes; each section includes an inscription giving the name of the donor. The walls are decorated with carefully cut pieces of marble (*skoutlosis*). The ceiling is painted. The overall effect of the colors, the shapes and the great space—illuminated with many lamps—must have been awesome.

There are over seventy Greek inscriptions from the synagogue; one group has already been published by Robert in 'Nouvelles inscriptions' (available also in Lifshitz). They are chiefly donors' records and tell a great deal about the Jewish community and some of its important members, less about its theology. The most important text for the history of religions is also one of the latest; it describes one member of the community as a priest and *sophodidaskalos* ("wise teacher" ? "teacher of wisdom"? rabbi?).[25] There are only two legible inscriptions in Hebrew (in addition to a few fragments and one graffito from outside the synagogue); one is *shalom* ("peace!"), the other appears to read "Verus" and has been understood as a reference (perhaps part of a dedication) to Lucius Verus, emperor with Marcus Aurelius AD 161-169.

For the most part the above information has been available in print for a very few years, but it has already prompted vigorous discussion, not only on the building (to which we are restricted in this paper), but also on the Sardis Jewish community within a much greater gentile population,[26] and on Sardis Judaism and its relation to pagan religions and to Christianity.[27] My own tentative answers to the major questions are as follows; they are provisional, since the research and synthesis are far from over, and they concern only Sardis—conclusions on the entire topic will be found at the end of this paper.

---

[25] *BASOR* 187 (1967): 29 and figure 48.

[26] On the legal status and organization of the Sardis Jewish community, see Applebaum, "Legal Status," pp. 447-450, and Applebaum, "Organization," pp. 477-485.

[27] On pagan religions, see Kraabel, "*Hypsistos*," and Kraabel, "Paganism." On Christianity, see Kraabel, "Melito"; Wilken, "Melito"; and, generally, Johnson, "Asia Minor," and Johnson, "Unsolved Questions." On Sardis Jews, pagans and Christians in the later periods, see Foss, *Byzantine and Turkish Sardis*.

The building is a synagogue-basilica not by design, but because this is what the Sardis Jews were presented with; when this kind of ancient religion puts such a building to use, this—we now know—is how it was done. Later, when ancient Christianity is given the opportunity to construct churches at public expense, they will take the same form. Sardis is not the first large synagogue-basilica; the Alexandria *diplostoon*, destroyed under Trajan, is earlier—it is quite likely that such buildings as these are the pattern for the later Christian basilica-churches.[28]

The building had three uses: religious services, education and community meetings; given the size of the main hall, two or perhaps all three could have gone on at the same time.[29] The apse benches must have been reserved for community leaders, the 'elders'; such special seating arrangements must have been common, witness the "seventy-one golden chairs" for the elders in the Alexandria synagogue, and the "Seat of Moses" mentioned in the New Testament gospels. During the service, the apse and the Eagle Table are the focus of worship; the table served as a monumental and imposing lectern, probably not (*pace* Goodenough) for cult meals. The scrolls of the Torah were stored in one of the *aediculae* at the east end of the main hall, at least in the last phase; these shrines were not a part of the earliest phase of the synagogue—in Sardis as in Ostia, a permanent and impressive container for the scriptures was added to a room which had not previously required it. In both cities, the addition was sometimes awkward; in Sardis, it required that the scrolls be brought from the aedicula at the east or 'Jerusalem' end of the hall, to the table nearly 45 m. away—and then returned to the shrine again after reading.

Classes in the scripture and its interpretation could have taken place anywhere in the building; when the *bema* is installed in the center of the hall, it is probably for this purpose, for it is closely associated with the *sophodidaskalos* inscription. The building is also the successor to the *topos* mentioned in Josephus, where Sardis Jews "decide their affairs and controversies with one another" (*Ant.* 14.235); it is the community center, of great importance in the Diaspora.

For the understanding of Greco-Roman religions, Sardis presents us with an image of Jews and Judaism never as clearly attested before: still a minority, but a powerful, perhaps even wealthy one, of great antiquity in a major city of the Diaspora, controlling a huge and lavishly decorated structure on 'Main Street' and able to retain control of it as long as the city existed. (This is perhaps the strongest evidence of the power of this Jewish commu-

---

[28] For the literary evidence, see Goodenough, Index.

[29] Using the standards of modern church and synagogue architecture (assuming benches or pews), a room the size of the Sardis main hall would provide space for just under 1000 persons.

nity. Synagogues were frequently taken over by Christians in late antiquity; the Sardis building would have made a fine church, but not one piece of evidence for Christianity has been found within it.) From Rome and other ancient cities we have long had the picture of Jews as just one eastern minority, often a despised minority, in a large urban population; for some sites that picture is still valid, but the Sardis evidence shows that there are dramatic exceptions.[30]

IV. MILETUS?

If the Jewish evidence at Sardis is unmistakable, the meager data at Miletus are much more typical for the Jewish community of a large Diaspora city. Josephus records a decree, not later than the first century BC, which guarantees to the Jewish community certain religious rights; these had been under attack by gentile Milesians. The picture is similar to what we assume of other Jewish communities protected by the various decrees Josephus records: a group of Jews of some political influence, not always on good terms with their gentile neighbors.

The most famous piece of evidence from Miletus is the inelegant inscription or graffito which reserves fifth-row seats in the huge Miletus theater for "the Jews, also known as 'those who fear God'" (*CII* 748).[31]

Miletus thus has about as much evidence for Judaism as Sardis had produced before 1962; both are major Anatolian cities, and might be expected to have had similar Jewish communities and even similar synagogues. Early in this century the German excavators of Miletus thought they had located the remains of such a building; first publication of the evidence was by A. von Gerkan, in Gerkan, "Synagogue in Milet."[32] It has been accepted as a synagogue by Sukenik (and discussed as such in *ASPG*), by Avi-Yonah[33] and apparently by Robert;[34] Goodenough in his *Jewish Symbols* held that the evidence is too ambiguous to make a judgement.

The Miletus building is a small oblong room, 18.6 m X 11.6 m, with a peristyle court at the side; it incorporates in its foundation a monument of the Flavian period, and thus could not have been built until time had passed

[30] Leon, *The Jews of Ancient Rome*.

[31] Discussed in the context of the new Sardis evidence in Robert, *Nouvelles Inscriptions*, pp. 41f., 47. On the Miletus hypsistos inscriptions sometimes mislabelled as Jewish, see Kraabel, "*Hypsistos*," especially p. 89.

[32] Final publication was by A Von Gerkan, *Milet*, 80-82 with Abb. 19 (reconstruction of the plan) and Tafel I, 2 and XI ('Erhaltungszustand'); he also published "Synagoge in Milet" with essentially the same text and the clearest plan of the site. See also Goodenough, vol. 2, p. 78; vol. 3, no. 880, and Sukenik, *ASPG*, pp. 40-42.

[33] Avi-Yonah, "Synagogue: Architecture," p. 699.

[34] Robert, "Inscriptions grecques," p. 45 note 4.

sufficient for the monument to fall into ruin. Two or three construction periods are evident from the excavations, the earliest in the third or early fourth century; the evidence is too complex for certainty.

But is it a synagogue? That is far from proved. The complex was not fully excavated; perhaps half of the main room and less than a sixth of the courtyard was exposed fully. This is indicated by convention in the plan published by von Gerkan and reproduced by Sukenik and by Goodenough: the unexcavated but "suggested" features are more lightly drawn in. This 'restoration' was done on the basis of synagogue plans from Palestine, as given in H. Kohl and C. Watzinger, *Antike Synagogen*, which had just been published![35] In actuality much of the restoration was conjectural, and no Jewish evidence was found in or near the complex.[36]

The Priene and Sardis synagogues show that Palestinian building styles are not always reproduced in Asia Minor;[37] some Jewish evidence is to be expected, particularly when the Miletus excavators (unlike those at Priene) thought they had a Jewish building. We may speculate as to whether the Miletus building would ever have been designated a synagogue if the Kohl and Watzinger publication had not been available! The present evidence does not warrant including Miletus in a list of Diaspora synagogue sites.

V. PRIENE

The Priene synagogue was identified as a 'house-church' by its excavators, T. Wiegand and M. Schrader, *Priene*, but was later recognized as a synagogue, and described as such by V. Schultz, *Altchristliche Städte* II, p. 2 (1926), and then by Sukenik, in *ASPG* and Goodenough, *Jewish Symbols*. Interestingly, the most recent survey of Priene, M. Schede, *Die Ruinen*, continues the Wiegand-Schrader identification, which the Jewish evidence from the site has proved incorrect.

The synagogue, located in a rebuilt house of the hellenistic period, is a slightly irregular rectangle measuring 10 m. east-west and 14 m. north-south. A Torah-niche 1.50 m. wide by 1.50 m. deep is set in the east wall, the side closest to Jerusalem. The excavators dated the remodelled structure as no later than the fourth or fifth century, but they were surely influenced

35 As von Gerkan states ("Synagoge in Milet," p. 181).

36 The present writer visited Miletus just half a century after this complex had been excavated; the site of the building is much overgrown and marked by no identifying sign, but the exploratory trenches of the excavators are clear enough, and correspond to those indicated in the published plans of the building. Apparently little or nothing has been done since the publication of the final report in 1922 to make the identification of the structure more certain. The 'synagogue' is not mentioned in the official guide to the site, M. Baran, *Guide to Miletus* (Ankara, 1965), though the complex appears (unlabelled) in plan 3.

37 As von Gerkan realized ("Synagoge in Milet," p. 181).

in this by their identification of it as a 'house-church.' A likely parallel in plan if not in dating is the Dura synagogue; in both locations, the synagogue proper is a remodelled house, and the adjoining rooms at Priene might have been used for community functions and perhaps as a hostel.[38]

The evidence which proves the building a synagogue is clear enough, but the published descriptions are incomplete; four items are involved: 1) A rather clumsy relief, showing a *menorah*, its central shaft or 'arm' flanked by spirals representing the ends of rolled Torah scrolls;[39] an *ethrog* (citron fruit) is depicted at the left, and at the right a *shofar* (ram's horn) and then a *lulab* (palm branch)—all familiar Jewish symbols. This plaque was taken by the excavators to Berlin, with the consequence that it was often photographed and became quite well known.[40] 2) Another relief of somewhat better workmanship was found on the floor of the synagogue, in front of the Torah-niche. All representations of it are dependent on Wiegand-Schrader and show a *menorah* flanked by peacocks and (between the left peacock and the *menorah*) a *lulab*. However, an object between the *menorah* and the right peacock was omitted;[41] at first glance, it resembles a human figure with an elongated head, but is more likely an oddly shaped *ethrog* or perhaps what Goodenough called a *Rübe*, "a sort of root vegetable which tapers to a point below and has long leaves on top."[42] I suspect that the confusion arises from the fact that neither the ancient stone cutter (a gentile perhaps) nor the archaeological draftsman understood what was to be symbolized; one produced an unrecognizable shape, and the other omitted it from his sketch.

Also found on the synagogue floor were 3) a large ablution basin[43] and 4) a stele on which a *menorah* had been cut with light but regular lines; the carving is well-centered on the stone, but was apparently only a pattern for a

---

[38] Cf. Avi-Yonah, "Archaeological Sources," p. 54.

[39] Y. Shiloh, "Torah Scrolls."

[40] Published originally in Weigand and Schrader, *Priene*, Abb. 582 (= Goodenough, vol. 3 no. 872). In vol. 2, p. 77, Goodenough considers the *shofar* "some kind of circumcision knife" but he later changed his mind, cf. vol. 13, p. 215.

[41] The plaque was recovered and photographed by the present writer during an examination of the synagogue on 10 August 1966; it was in two pieces, as the original report records, Weigand and Schrader, *Priene*, p. 481. One fragment had remained in the main room of the synagogue, the other was found in the room just to the right (south) of the Torah niche.

[42] Goodenough, vol. 4, p. 146; the clearest example is vol. 3 no. 814, a drawing from the Torlonia catacomb in Rome.

[43] The basin (also still on the site in 1966) appears in Sukenik's plan as a small circle near the niche, but it is not labelled or mentioned in the text (*ASPG*, p. 43, fig. 12). Goodenough reproduces the original plan from Weigand and Schrader, *Priene*, as vol. 3 no. 879; there the basin is clearly labelled and a number of other details included which are omitted in Sukenik's sketch.

more elaborate design which was never finished—only three arms of the *menorah* are represented.[44]

Priene is a hellenistic city which never experienced the overlay of massive Roman structures so familiar from other sites in western Asia Minor; the synagogue in its present form is probably from the time of the Roman Empire, but there is no reason that a Jewish community could not have existed there earlier. The building is small but so is the city; this may well have been the only synagogue in Priene in its time.

VI. DELOS

The building on Delos discussed briefly in Sukenik, *ASPG*, has now been published fully by Phillipe Bruneau, *Recherches* (1970); if it is a synagogue, it is the earliest to be excavated yet, but its identification is hotly debated. Plassart, the original excavator, considered it a synagogue; he was followed by Sukenik, *ASPG*, by Frey (*CII* 726-731) and by Kittel.[45] In 1935 Mazur, *Studies*, rejected the identification; her arguments convinced Sukenik to reverse his position in "The Present State" (1949). Goodenough reviewed the debate in *Jewish Symbols*, vol. 2 and was not convinced by Mazur.[46] Lifshitz reprinted the Delos inscriptions in *Donateurs*, Avi-Yonah also includes the building in his lists of synagogues, and Hengel assumes the same in his writings cited in the bibliography. Wischnitzer, *The Architecture*, agrees with Mazur. Bruneau reviews the debate in detail, publishes the evidence completely—including the results of his own work in 1962—and concludes that the structure is most likely a synagogue, in use as such during the first century BC and the first two centuries of our era.[47] For documentation and secondary literature, the reader is referred to his thorough presentation.

The evidence that Jews lived on Delos in the first century BC is indisputable: Josephus gives two decrees protecting their rights (*Ant.* 14. 213-216 and 231f.), and the two epitaphs cited as *CII* 725 are almost certainly Jewish. The points of debate have rather been five: the plan of the building, the absence of obvious Jewish symbols, the terms (*theos*) *hypsistos* and

---

[44] Mentioned in Weigand and Schrader, *Priene*, p. 481, but with no reference to the fact that the "seven-branched candlestick" is incomplete. It remains in the synagogue also, just in front of the niche.

[45] Kittel, "Kleinasiatisches Judentum," p. 16.

[46] His marginalia reveal the difficulty he had with the problem, see Goodenough, vol. 12, p. 215.

[47] Bruneau also lists himself as being in agreement with Robert regarding the epigraphic evidence, *Recherches*, pp. 486-488, cf. Robert, *Bull. epigr.* 1971 no. 456.

proseuche in the inscriptions found in the building, and the presence of lamps with pagan motifs in the building.

Like the later Dura, to which Bruneau frequently compares it, the Delos structure is a complex of rooms in a residential area. The main room is 16.90 m. north-south, 14.40 m. east-west; in a later stage it was divided with an east-west wall. Marble benches are placed along the north half of the west wall, interrupted by a fine white marble throne complete with marble footstool and recalling the throne provided for the priest of Dionysus in an ancient Greek theater! It is often identified as a 'seat of Moses.' A series of smaller rooms was discovered south of the main room, one of them containing the opening of a cistern which extended back under the main room. A roofed portico runs north-south on the east. Nothing in this design obviously suggests a synagogue, or prevents that identification. There is no permanent Torah shrine or niche, but one is not to be expected at this early date.[48]

Jewish symbols proved that the Sardis and Priene buildings were synagogues, and the Miletus structure was considered doubtful in part because it lacked them. However, the Delos building is much earlier than all of these, and the lack of symbols should not be over-emphasized; as Goodenough stated in his discussion, "there is no reason to think that we should have found specific Jewish symbols, since from that early time we have found Jewish symbols in the proper sense nowhere else."[49]

The term (*theos*) *hypsistos*, "highest god," occurs in four *ex voto* inscriptions found in the building. This is a common designation for God in the Septuagint, but it is not always to be taken as such; it often refers to one or another pagan deity, even in areas in the Diaspora with large Jewish populations.[50] In later times, say, the third century AD, the term is avoided in Diaspora Jewish inscriptions lest it be misunderstood, but the individuals in Delos who set up these texts might well be using the terms as Septuagint language, oblivious to the danger of 'syncretism'—indeed it could be argued that this danger is perceived only later, after the destruction of the Jerusalem Temple, as Judaism becomes more decentralized and Diaspora Jews more sensitive to the religious language of their gentile neighbors.[51]

The term *proseuche* which appears in *CII* 726 was originally taken to mean 'synagogue' and was a major factor in Plassart's identification of the

[48] Bruneau's description, plans and photographs give a complete picture; his discussion of orientation (*Recherches*, p. 490) perhaps goes beyond the evidence.

[49] Goodenouch, vol. 2, p. 73, cf. Hengel, "Proseuche," p. 166, and Hengel, "Synagogeninschrift," pp. 173-176.

[50] Kraabel, "*Hypsistos*."

[51] Note however Bruneau's comments on the date of 'Inscriptions de Delos' no. 2331(= *CII* 727), no. 2332 (= *CII* 730) and no. 2333 (= *CII* 731) in Bruneau, *Recherches*, p. 484.

building. Hengel argues in 'Proseuche' that the term is particularly appropriate as a designation for a synagogue while the Jerusalem Temple is still standing; it suggests the synagogue is (only) a 'house of prayer,' in no sense a rival for the Temple.[52] Mazur, *Studies*, argued that the word rather meant 'prayer' and did not refer to the building at all.[53] Bruneau inclines to the translation 'prayer' but argues that the term is Jewish in either case; he cites Robert in support.[54]

The lamps are some sixty in number, approximately half from the first two centuries of our era, the rest somewhat earlier. Not one bears a Jewish symbol; lamps with such symbols are rare in any case, and particularly in the earlier periods. But some of the Delos lamps show clearly pagan symbols, including deities; these appeared to Goodenough to present the strongest evidence against calling the building Jewish.[55] However, in the absence of any other 'pagan' materials among the finds, these are perhaps not an insurmountable problem; those who favor simple and 'clean' arguments would be happier without such evidence, but it has become clear that the Delos situation is not a simple one.

My own suspicion, after reviewing the earlier debate and all that Bruneau has presented, is that we are in fact dealing with a synagogue on Delos, the earliest excavated anywhere. The building is the sort one would expect from this early period: a converted residence, little more than an assembly hall, with no permanent Torah shrine and no Jewish symbols. I suspect that it would be anachronistic to expect either the art of Dura or the architecture of Sardis. But if that is true, it will be difficult to identify any early Diaspora synagogue; the specificity of religious imagery, epigraphic formulae and architectural features will not be found because it probably did not yet exist. We may have to be content with the kind of 'ambiguous' evidence a Delos presents.

The inscriptions after all may offer the best argument. As Bruneau emphasizes, they refer to a *theos hypsistos*, never a *Zeus hypsistos*; they do not offer an obviously pagan use of the term at a time when references to one or another pagan deity as *hypsistos* are not uncommon. The epitaphs mentioned earlier, *CII* 725a and b, are actually demands for divine vengeance, since they commemorate two young women who had been murdered; the language is formal and strongly reminiscent of the Septuagint: the deity is ὁ θεὸς ὁ ὕψιστος, "the highest God" (cf. *CII* 769) and there is a

[52] Hengel, "Proseuche," pp. 166-169; Hengel, "Synagogeninschrift," pp. 173-176. Cf. Krauss, pp. 93-102; the section heading ('Die Synagoge-Ersatz fur den Tempel') states a central thesis of this book.

[53] Mazur, *Studies*, p. 21.

[54] Bruneau, *Recherches*, p. 488, citing Robert, "Inscriptions grecques," p. 44 note 7.

[55] Goodenough, vol. 2, pp. 74f.

later appeal to κύριε ὁ πάντα ἐφορῶν καὶ οἱ ἄγγελοι θεοῦ, "Lord! You who watch over all things!—and you angels of God!"[56] I suspect that it is this same deity who is referred to in abbreviated fashion in the other inscriptions as *hypsistos* or *theos hypsistos*. The term *proseuche* here is not unambiguous either, but with Robert and Hengel I suspect it also is Jewish.

Further data may be found by the Delos excavators, but I suspect that the evidence which will make a more positive identification of the Delos building will be found elsewhere, in excavations which uncover other synagogues built while the Second Temple still stood, or in the reexamination of the reports of digs already completed, where—as at Priene—synagogues are to be found by means of a more accurate labeling of buildings which their excavators never suspected were Jewish.[57] For Delos for the present, I find Bruneau persuasive.

VII. STOBI

Systematic excavation of the synagogue(s) of Stobi in modern Yugoslavia did not begin until 1970, but important information had been available for four decades before that, thanks to the 1931 discovery of *CII* 694, a late-third century inscription in which the wealthy donor Klaudios Tiberios Polycharmos describes extensive construction work done at his expense on the synagogue and related structures;[58] the 'holy place,' a *triklinion*, a *tetrastoon* and 'upper chambers' are all mentioned as parts of this complex in the thirty-three line text. Before the present excavations, headed by James Wiseman (Boston University) and Djordje Mano-Zissi (University of Belgrade), it was thought that a fifth-century structure previously excavated was the Stobi synagogue, and plans of this basilica as a 'synagogue' still appear in recent publications, e.g., Wischnitzer, *The Architecture*. The new archaeological evidence makes clear however that the fifth-century building is a church, and that the remains of the synagogue or synagogues of Stobi are in earlier strata beneath.[59]

---

[56] On angels, see Simon, "L'angelolatrie," pp. 123f., and Hengel, "Synagogeninschrift," p. 166 note 32.

[57] Private homes which were used by Jewish communities occasionally or regularly but without architectural modification may never be identified, any more than the earliest Christian 'house churches.' In this case *synagogē* would mean 'assembly' rather than 'building'; the evidence presented in this paper suggests that this was the case for Dura, possibly for Priene and probably for Stobi, where the Polycharmos inscription appears to reflect a later stage of that practice. Cf. Hengel, "Synagogeninschrift," pp. 159-165.

[58] For an excellent review and analysis of the site and excavations until the Second World War, see E. Kitzinger, "A Survey"; pp. 129-146, 159f. (bibliography) are on the 'synagogue' and inscription.

[59] Hengel also had realized that the fifth-century building had to be a church, not a synagogue, see Hengel, "Synagogeninschrift," pp. 146-150, cf. Wiseman and Mano-Zissi, "Excavations 1970," p. 406, note 82.

The published reports on the entire site from the present excavations are Wiseman and Mano-Zissi, "Excavations 1970," "Excavations 1971," "Excavations 1972," "Excavations 1973-1974" with the most substantial treatments of the synagogue in "Excavations 1970" (pp. 406-411) and "Excavations 1971" (pp. 408-411). Summary descriptions with bibliographies are given in Wiseman's *Stobi* for the 'synagogue basilica' (pp. 30-33) and the Jewish and later Christian 'House of Psalms' (pp. 34-36). The Polycharmos inscription is treated in Sukenik, *ASPG*, and by Lifshitz in *Donateurs* and in his introduction to the new edition of *CII*, but the most thorough discussion of the text and much else important for our topic is Hengel, "Synagogeninschrift." Since 1974, the synagogue excavations have been supervised by Dean L. Moe, whose assistance in this section is gratefully acknowledged.[60]

It is likely that the area now being excavated by Moe contains whatever remains *in situ* of the synagogue of the Polycharmos inscription. At this writing it appears that there are three buildings, one above the other: the fifth-century basilica (a church, formerly misidentified as a synagogue) which deliberately supplants a fourth century synagogue (anti-semitism at Stobi?), below which is the still earlier synagogue of Polycharmos, "the father of the synagogue in Stobi"—a title given him in *CII* 694 and in several fresco fragments from the new excavations.[61] Hengel has analyzed the elements of the Polycharmos synagogue as described in *CII* 694;[62] he concludes that the building had been Polycharmos' private dwelling, which he had turned over to the Jewish community with the proviso that he and his heirs retain possession of "all the upper rooms" (*ta hyperoa panta*), where presumably they continued to live. 'The holy place' mentioned in the inscription is the synagogue proper; since the destruction of the Jerusalem temple, the central meeting room of the synagogue has taken on an increasing sanctity, as reflected 1) in the terms used to describe it, 2) in its being restricted more and more to 'religious' use solely, 3) in its decorations and embellishments, e.g., Jewish symbols, Torah Shrine—and in the case of Stobi, in the desire of Polycharmos to live in immediate contact with 'the holy place.' The *tetrastoon* and the *triklinion* are distinguished in the text from 'the holy place,' but are surely related to it in usage; the former, a kind of hall usually with four rows of columns, would most likely be used as a

60 Moe graciously agreed to review this section, and provided a copy of an initial draft of his article, which appeared subsequently as "The Cross and the Menorah," *Archaeology* 30 (1977): 148-157.

61 Wiseman and Mano-Zissi, "Excavations 1970," 408 and pl. 90, fig. 21; provisionally on the phasing, pp. 408-411.

62 Hengel, "Synagogeninschrift," pp. 173-176, cf. footnote 52 supra.

study room and guest-house.[63] The *triklinion*, strictly a small dining room with three couches, is here probably the common dining room, used by the Jewish community much as were the dining hall and kitchen found attached to the Ostia synagogue (see below).[64]

None of the features of the Polycharmos synagogue described in *CII* 694 has been identified as yet in the present excavations; indeed, between this building and the fifth-century church[65] uncovered a half-century ago there is a fourth-century synagogue yet to be excavated fully! The main hall of the Christian building measures 14.20 m. x 19.20 m., excluding the apse. Just south of this Christian basilica with its attached rooms is a large residence, the 'House of Psalms,' which communicated with the church and at an earlier stage with the later synagogue;[66] this residence and the later synagogue may be an even more substantial replacement of the earlier structures mentioned in the inscription. What the excavations have revealed to this point is as follows:

The earlier synagogue had frescoed walls; the frescoes (fragments of which have been found) are geometric in design and several times repeat the legend Πολύχαρμος ὁ πατὴρ εὐχήν. "Polycharmos the father, (has fulfilled his) vow" (or, "has paid his pledge").[67] Dimensions and other features have yet to be determined, but the references to Polycharmos make it quite probable that this building and that described in *CII* 694 are one and the same.

The later synagogue had a mosaic floor of geometric design and walls decorated with frescoes, "all geometric and painted in a variety of bright colors." The main room is approximately 7.90 m. x 13.30 m. "A rectangular brick and concrete foundation stands against the E(ast) wall on the axis of the room"; since this is the wall closest to Jerusalem, this structure may well be the base of a Torah shrine. "A layer of flat stones may well have served as the foundation for a bench" along the south wall.[68] (The plan and mosaic immediately suggest the synagogue at Aegina in Greece; its dimen-

[63] On the synagogue's educational uses, Sonne, "Synagogue," p. 487, and generally, Hengel, *Hellenism*, pp. 65-83. On the Stobi synagogue as guest-house, Klein, "Neues zum Fremdenhaus." On new evidence for both uses, Meyers, *Khirbet Shema'*, pp. 85-87.

[64] Hengel, "Synagogeninschrift," pp. 167-172, with many references and parallels (and some understandably outdated information on Sardis, e.g. note 84).

[65] Originally and mistakenly called a synagogue, later (e.g. Wiseman, "Stobi") 'the synagogue basilica,' now (Wiseman and Mano-Zissi, "Excavations 1973-1974," pp. 146f.) 'the Central Basilica.'

[66] Wiseman, "Stobi," p. 35, cf. pp. 31-36. The relation of Central Basilica and House of Psalms is strikingly illustrated in Wiseman and Mano-Zissi, "Excavations 1973-1974," p. 146, fig. 32, an aerial photograph taken via balloon.

[67] Wiseman and Mano-Zissi, "Excavations 1970," p. 408 for the Greek text and a different translation, pl. 90, fig. 21 for the fresco fragments.

[68] Quotations from Wiseman and Mano-Zissi, "Excavations 1970," p. 410, cf. Wiseman, "Stobi," 30-33.

sions are 7.60 m. x 13.50 m., almost exactly those of the Stobi building.)[69] The most recent evidence suggests that this building, kept in good repair and even improved by alterations, was in regular use by the Jews of Stobi right up until it was "deliberately supplanted by the new basilica."[70] As Christianity gained political power, Christians destroyed some synagogues and pagan temples, and turned others into churches. Stobi now provides an example of what appears to be a third kind of Christian 'triumphalism': the synagogue property is expropriated, and the synagogue replaced on its original (and long-held) site by the new church. "One gets the impression both of painstaking efforts and of considerable expense undertaken to replace a seemingly still adequate and usable building."[71]

For our purposes, this site is quite important: two early synagogues and a church in one location, the stratigraphic record amazingly complete, the excavation carefully and knowledgeably done—most promising for the understanding of Diaspora synagogue architecture as well as for the history of religions in the Roman Empire!

VIII. OSTIA

Except for the one review article by Fausto Zevi (Zevi, "La sinagoga") and the useful *Encyclopedia Judaica* entry by A. M. Rabello, the bibliography on this building is all under the name of its excavator, Prof. Maria Floriani Squarciapino, director of the Ostia excavations.[72] Excavations and restoration of the building were completed in two years, 1961-1962; her article in *Archaeology*, "The Synagogue," is the most readily available summary, although its documentation and detail leave something to be desired.

The building as restored is dated to the fourth century; not surprisingly, it is a complex of rooms, 36.60 m. x 23.50 m. The synagogue proper is a near-rectangle, 24.90 m. x 12.50 m., and includes an entrance area, then—at a slightly higher level—a four-columned inner gateway and finally the main hall. Parallel to this, and immediately south of it, is another rectangle whose units include a kitchen, its oven and storage jars still in place, and a larger room which could have been used for study, as a hostel, and surely as a dining hall.[73] The third part of the building is a vestibule which runs

---

[69] On Aegina, see note 9 supra.

[70] Moe, "Cross and Menorah," p. 153.

[71] Moe, "Cross and Menorah," p. 153.

[72] Meiggs was able to include a brief summary of her work in the second edition of his *Roman Ostia*, pp. 587f., and Wischnitzer provides a good introduction and the clearest plan in *The Architecture*, pp. 5-7. I cannot explain why the Mindis Faustos inscription was not included in Lifshitz or mentioned in his introduction to the reprinting of *CII*.

[73] Cf. footnote 63 supra.

roughly north-south, at right angles to the synagogue proper and the kitchen-dining-hall; three doors lead from the vestibule to the synagogue, two more into the kitchen, and one, on the north, to the street outside.

The synagogue proper is strikingly odd, with two phases immediately obvious to the modern visitor. In the earlier phase there were three doors into the main hall; someone entering through the center door would pass between two pairs of columns, surely in re-use, set in a square pattern, and so large as to dominate the building. One passed to the left or the right of this 'square' of columns to enter the main hall through a side door. Thus originally there were three doors from the vestibule to the entrance area of the synagogue proper, and three more doors (one flanked with the columns) from the entrance area into the main hall of the synagogue. The west wall of the main hall (the wall opposite that containing the four columned door and its two lesser companions) is bowed outward slightly; fastened to it is a low platform, like a shallow stage—this is the *bema*, over half as wide as the hall itself. The floor of the main hall is *opus sectile*.

The early plan is clear: the main hall was built as a meeting room (witness the curved *bema*-wall), that is, it was a synagogue from the beginning, provided with a *bema* on the west wall and a monumental, four columned entrance arrangement on the east wall.

The later stage is attested by the massive Torah shrine which now dominates the reconstructed building; it is a kind of 'apse,' built of regular courses of brick and tufa-block, which completely blocks the southernmost of the three entrances to the main hall. It is at the back of the main hall, on the wall opposite the focus of worship, and immediately recalls the two aediculae added to the back of the Sardis synagogue. In both buildings, the shrines are on the wall closest to Jerusalem. The shrine at Ostia is a bold, if architecturally asymetrical, indication of the increasing importance of the scriptures in Diaspora Judaism, and at the same time provides the strongest clue to the purpose of the Sardis shrines. The three shrines (two at Sardis, one at Ostia) each incorporate a pair of small columns, and each is approached via a small flight of stairs; in general, all three manifest the salient features of the Torah shrine familiar from Jewish art, but the Ostia evidence in particular shows how important such a shrine had become, and the lengths to which Diaspora Jews would go in order to include one in their building.

The Torah shrine at Ostia, when viewed from the front, also recalls the apse of the typical Byzantine church, and the apse-like Torah shrine of such late synagogues as that at Beth Alpha in Israel. At Beth Alpha, however, the apse is formed in an exterior wall and projects in the customary fashion; it is visible from outside the building. At Ostia the Torah shrine is free-standing, and contained wholly by the building. At Side in Pamphylia (Asia

Minor) the Torah shrine may have been called the *simma* (= *sigma*?), because its shape in plan recalled the lunate form of the Greek letter *sigma*, which looked like our letter C (*CII* 781).[74] The apse-like shape in any case is well known from later synagogues; its replication at Ostia must be deliberate, since in this situation the community could have created nearly any kind of structure to house the Torah. The design of the building would have allowed that freedom.

The term used at Ostia, however, is not *simma*, but *keibotos* (=*kibotos*), 'ark,' a word heavy with meaning in Jewish Greek, where it is used for the ark of Noah and the Ark of the Covenant as well as the Torah shrine.[75] The relevant section of the Ostia inscription is as follows:...τὴν κειβωτὸν ...νόμῳ ἁγίῳ..., the donor, Mindis Faustos, is providing "the ark for the holy Law."[76] The *keibotos* in question may be an earlier container for the Torah rather than the present shrine, since the inscription (dated late second or early third century by Squarciapino) had been used to repair the floor of the present building. It is unlikely that a donor inscription for a shrine still in use would be treated in such a fashion!

Beneath this fourth century building the excavator has identified an earlier structure of similar plan, including the four-columned entrance, but lacking the large dining hall; this, she says, is also a synagogue, and from the first century. This would suggest the following chronology: first century: synagogue with benches and perhaps a *bema* but without a Torah shrine. Late second or early third century: remodeling, including the addition of the *keibotos* of Mindis Faustos. Fourth century: rebuilding produces the present structure, but without the present Torah shrine. Later in the fourth (?) century: the present shrine is added. But a number of questions arise:

The first century building: it would be no surprise to learn of a Jewish community in Ostia, with a synagogue, at this early date; except for this building, the only evidence for the existence of a Jewish community in Ostia is epigraphic, and meager at that,[77] but a large community in nearby

---

[74] The excavator (Squarciapino, "The Synagogue," p. 198) refers to the Side inscription, which had already been interpreted in the same fashion for Side by Goodenough, vol. 2, pp. 82f., with a reference to Beth Alpha. But *simma* might mean apse in the sense of hemicycle or *synthronon* (as at Sardis), so Frey in *CII* and Lifshitz, no. 36. On the Jewish inscriptions of Side, Robert, "Inscriptions grecques," pp. 36-47, is valuable and thorough.

[75] On the common Jewish and gentile use of this word (due perhaps to common or conflated Flood legends) at Apameia Kibotos (!) in Phrygia, Asia Minor, see Kraabel, "*Hypsistos*," p. 85, and "Paganism," pp. 23f.

[76] Squarciapino, "La Sinagoga," pp. 314f. The text begins with the Latin religious-political formula *pro salute Aug(usti)*! the remainder is in Greek, not Hebrew as Rabello has it in Rabello, "Ostia."

[77] *CII* 533f. and Lifshitz's addition in "Prolegomenon," *CII* 534a. Add the new *archisynagogus* inscription described in the excavator's 'Plotius.'

Rome is early and well known.[78] But would a first century synagogue contain something so 'Temple-like' as that four-column entrance? Perhaps, but a simpler design would be more likely.

The Torah shrines: the Mindis Faustos *keibotos* is tantalizing; here we have a shrine from a building at the center of the Roman Empire, exactly contemporary with that at Dura on the extreme eastern border—but what did it look like? And where was it located? The later shrine is also confusing. It appears wholly an afterthought, blocking the south door as it does. But then there must have been some Torah shrine for the first stage of the fourth-century building, replacing the earlier *keibotos* of Mindis Faustos. But where was it and what did it look like? If it were part of the fourth-century design from the start, we would expect it to fit less awkwardly than does the present shrine. Or did the Mindis Faustos shrine remain for a time before it was replaced (and the inscription re-used)? Or, finally, might the present shrine have been a part of the fourth-century structure from the beginning (contrary to the account given above) ? If the Ostia Jews were determined to retain a three-door entrance with the four columns from an earlier building, and had also decided to include in the new structure a monumental shrine to replace the Mindis Faustos *keibotos*, they might have come up with the present pattern. In that case, the present shrine would look awkward because it was inserted into an entrance of the earlier building—although it was in the fourth-century plan from the first. In that case there would have been no 'second' Torah shrine later than the Mindis Faustos *keibotos* but earlier than the present one (that 'second' shrine for the first phase of the fourth-century building has always been hypothetical—there is no archaeological evidence for it). And then there would be only one known phase, not two (as above), for the present building.

(It may be of some small comfort in the midst of these uncertainties to learn that Ostia would have been a problem to Sukenik—and was probably a bit of a disappointment to Goodenough. In writing about the hypothetical Torah shrine at Capernaum, Sukenik had questioned that hypothesis in part because "it seemed strange to build an elaborate portal and then to block it up."[79] But this is exactly what happened at Ostia!—and thus the Capernaum hypothesis has at least one clear piece of 'parallel' archaeological evidence to back it up. Goodenough gave Ostia much less attention than it deserves from anyone interested in Diaspora synagogues; the evidence had started to appear while he was working on Dura and was all available by the time he wrote the last volume of the *Jewish Symbols*—yet his index gives only a few references to the building and his statements about it are meager indeed. He calls it a 'plain' building, and I suspect that it was not as rich in sym-

[78] Leon, *The Jews of Ancient Rome*.

[79] Sukenik, "The Present State," p. 18.

bols as he would have wanted—hence in *Jewish Symbols* he all but ignores it.)

IX. SOME CONCLUSIONS

Happily, it is too early to generalize on the above in any great detail. From Stobi, Sardis and hopefully Ostia there is more to learn, and more Diaspora synagogues are surely to be discovered—in the squares and trenches of the excavator, and perhaps also in the already published reports of other 'Prienes.' But the following comments may be made, by way of summary:

1. The shape and materials of the Diaspora synagogue will be determined first by local custom and conditions; there is no one 'canonical' pattern, as a glance at the plans of the buildings discussed here instantly shows. The walls of the Ostia synagogue resemble other Ostia walls, the plan at Sardis is determined in large part by the overall design of the gymnasium complex, the shape of the Delos building is determined by the functions it had to serve at its early date—and the list could be extended.

2. But then the attempt of Sukenik and others to see each synagogue as some variety of 'basilica' must be abandoned; only confusion is created by trying to force each new building into this too-narrow pattern. Sukenik described the Priene building as a typical synagogue, "consisting of a fore court and a basilica."[80] Avi-Yonah states that "Delos, Priene and Miletus follow the basilica plan,"[81] indeed the Miletus building was originally identified as a synagogue in part because it somewhat resembled a basilica—and similar conclusions were drawn for the fifth-century basilica at Stobi which is clearly a church. The buildings of Diaspora Judaism show great architectural variety; they are just not that much alike—contrast Sardis with Dura, Ostia with Priene. To continue to make the normative pattern the 'basilica' confuses, rather than clarifies.

3. Thus it follows that no chronological list of stages of synagogue design can be drawn up for the Diaspora, although some such staging is possible for the 'Holy Land,' a tiny and homogeneous area by comparison, where Jews—much the majority in the population—would have quite different requirements of their religious buildings.[82]

4. But that means that we cannot date a Diaspora synagogue by its plan; in the continuing debate over 'dating by architecture' vs. 'dating by stratigraphy,' the first alternative is clearly not permissible. A synagogue built in

---

80 Sukenik, *ASPG*, p. 43.

81 Avi-Yonah, "Synagogue: Architecture," p. 599.

82 The desire to establish architectural stages for the Diaspora seems to lead Avi-Yonah astray in "Synagogue: Architecture," pp. 599f. and "Archaeological Sources," pp. 54f. Generally on staging, see Kraabel, "Synagogues, Ancient," pp. 437f.

the Diaspora in AD 200 might look like Sardis, or Dura, or something presently unknown.

5. Rabbinic statements about synagogue architecture and usage are not concerned with the Diaspora, surely not with that part of the Roman Empire west of the 'Holy Land,' thus they are largely irrelevant. Sukenik in particular was wont to follow rabbinic patterns and norms; these now turn out to be inapplicable to our topic.

6. Because of the Jews' minority status, the Diaspora synagogue may be concealed or at least deliberately inconspicuous, e.g., Dura, Ostia and probably Priene. But that is not always the case, e.g., Sardis and possibly Stobi. This too will depend on the local situation.

7. The Diaspora 'synagogue' will be a complex of several rooms, witness every building discussed above with the possible exception of Sardis. The synagogue outside the 'Holy Land' is the community center for a minority group faced with preserving its identity in a Gentile culture. This will make the synagogue more important for a Diaspora Jew than for the Jew of, say, Tiberias, but it will also expand its functions. The synagogue may include a school, a hostel, a dining hall, even a kitchen—and, as at Stobi, the donor and his family may live upstairs! We can predict that a group of rooms, not just a single 'sanctuary,' will likely be discovered at Stobi, and elsewhere in the Diaspora as well.[83]

8. Early Diaspora synagogues, those of the second Temple period, may be expected to be particularly difficult to identify—see the discussion of the Delos building. They are not as differentiated in their uses as are the later buildings, nor will there be obviously Jewish symbols present. They existed in some numbers surely; the literary evidence is overwhelming—but their functions and features are not wholly clear, and their religious uses may have been less central while the Temple still stood.

9. Finally, one general progression can be identified without contradicting what was stated in no. 3 above: over time the 'sanctity' of the synagogue will increase, particularly after the destruction of the Jerusalem Temple and the realization that it will not be rebuilt. The synagogue will become more than a *proseuche*, a 'prayer house'; it will become a *sancta sinagoga* (Hammam Lif), a 'holy place' (Stobi), even 'the most holy synagogue' (Side, *CII* 781, cf. *CII* 754). 'Secular' functions will be restricted to side rooms if such are available. The scriptures will be housed in impressive and permanent shrines. The use of religious symbols will increase. As Krauss and Hengel have stressed, more and more the synagogue will become a replacement for the lost Temple, and will acquire some of its functions,

[83] Thus the entire 'context' of the synagogue ought to be excavated, a practice no less valuable in the 'Holy Land'; for a recent example of a Galilean synagogue excavated in context, see Meyers, *Khirbet Shema'*.

characteristics and aura. Indeed, this may have started earlier in the Diaspora than in the 'Holy Land'; Diaspora Jews must have begun to learn to live 'without' the temple even before it was destroyed, just because for most of them it was so far away. At the same time, it seems likely that an increase in formal and liturgical practices in Diaspora synagogues was prompted in part by similar practices in other religions nearby; in some locations Christianity may have been an influence on Diaspora Judaism at this point, but it is perhaps more often the case that both these 'Biblical' religions were each influenced independently by the worship practices and on occasion the theologies of their pagan neighbors.[84]

Diaspora Judaism will never come fully into focus as long as it is seen chiefly either as an extension of the religion of the 'Old Testament,' the Hebrew Bible, or as an aspect of the rabbinic Judaism whose literature is available in such abundance. It is both of these, of course, but it is also a religion of the Roman Empire, not mindlessly mixing with Cybele or Dionysus or Christianity, but not sealed off from them either, nor oblivious to the values they contained and the aid they offered. Isis, Mithras, Christianity, Judaism—all of these changed as they expanded beyond their respective homelands and 'holy lands' and moved into the Roman world. As this 'gentile' context is taken more fully into account, Diaspora Judaism begins to fit together; it is only within that context that the Diaspora synagogue—in its many shapes and locations and with its several purposes—will finally be understood.

X. APPENDIX: COMPARISON OF BUILDING PLANS

As might be expected, the six Diaspora synagogues have less in common than would a representative half-dozen such buildings from Palestine; the reasons for this architectural variety are social, economic and political as well as religious, and will be explored further in a paper scheduled for presentation in late 1979.[85]

The plan makes some preliminary comparisons possible; in schematic fashion it shows the six buildings at the same scale and orientation. For the sake of presenting a manageable single plan with all six sites represented, side rooms, late additions and adjacent structures have been omitted. This makes some distortion of the evidence inevitable, since it eliminates the multi-roomed 'synagogue complex' present at Dura and Ostia, and the

[84] This may be particularly true when—as at Sardis—some of the earliest Jewish immigrants come from among the 'exiles' of Babylonia rather than directly from the 'Holy Land,' cf. Kraabel, "Paganism."

[85] [The article appeared as "Social Systems of Six Diaspora Synagogues," in Gutmann, *Synagogues*, pp. 79-91—Eds.]

Roman gymnasium and baths of which the Sardis synagogue is a part. This schematic drawing is no substitute for more complete plans published by the excavators; the concern here is rather with the relative sizes, the shapes and the orientation of the buildings.

The plan was prepared by Sylvia Ruud (Ancient Studies, University of Minnesota) with funds provided by the College of Liberal Arts and the Department of Classics of the University of Minnesota.

1. Sardis

Niches and passageways behind the *synthronon* (at the west end) are shown to illustrate something of the pre-synagogue phase of the apse area; they were not visible while the building was a synagogue. The narrow east west room just south of the apse is also a remnant of the earlier design; probably it was used by the synagogue community "for the storage of sacra used in worship" (Goodenough). The Eagle Table is shown as an open rectangle before the apse; the twin *aediculae* are represented as open squares on the east wall of the main hall, on either side of the center door. The peristyle forecourt was roofed on four sides but open in the center. There were three entrances into the forecourt on the east and one between two shops on the south; three more doors led from the forecourt into the main hall. The beginnings of the walls of the shops which lined the outside of the south wall are shown at the bottom of the Sardis plan; at the extreme right are the bases of a colonnade which began at the front of the synagogue porch and continued northward the length of the east side of the gymnasium complex. That complex extended for a great distance north and west of the synagogue.

2. Priene

The forecourt is on the left, the main room on the right, with the Torah niche in its east wall. The two stylobates in the main room are not quite parallel, being closer together on the east than on the west; the only column found in situ is shown on the north stylobate. A bench runs along the main room north wall. It is probable that some of the rooms which surrounded this synagogue were also controlled by Priene Jews.

3. Dura

The plan is of the last phase of the building: forecourt with columns on the right, main room on the left, with its Torah niche on the west wall and benches on all four walls. The other rooms linked to the synagogue are east of the forecourt; one passed through these rooms and then through the forecourt to reach the synagogue proper.

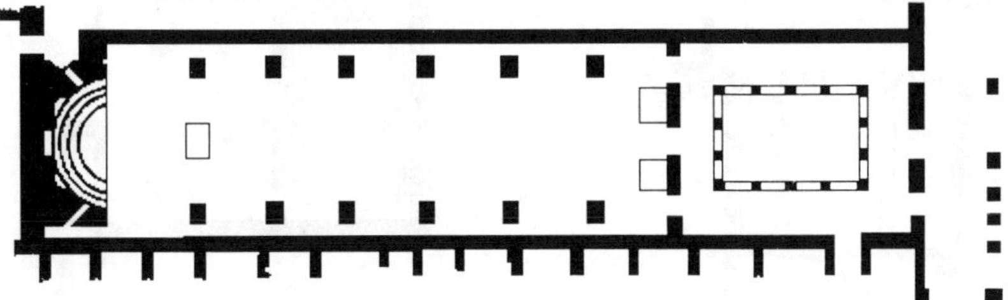

FIG. 1 Plans of Diaspora synagogues.

4. Delos

The plan is of the earlier phase; later the single large room with its three entrances in the east wall was divided by a wall running east-west, blocking the central entrance on the east. Extant benches are shown on the west, north and south walls of the main room, and just outside its north door; the famous Delos 'seat of Moses' is in the center of the bench on the west wall. Remains of the portico to the east of the main room are shown in outline, but the complex of small rooms south of the main room has been omitted.

5. Ostia

The plan is of the last phase of the building, with the Torah shrine or *keibotos* (=*kibotos*) in place. The long axis of the building is parallel to the street outside; the synagogue complex was entered from the street through a single door on the north-northeast, at the arrow. The main room is on the left, with the *bema* shown on its curved west wall; the entrance area at the Opposite end of the main room was dominated by four massive columns set in a square. In the last phase the Torah shrine was attached on the south to the south wall of the main hall and on the north to the southwest entrance column, thus blocking the south entrance between the main room and the forecourt; the plans shows the curved back of the shrine, opening west, and the steps and pair of small columns in front of it. The kitchen of the synagogue was located south of the forecourt, and the dining hall south of the main room.

6. Stobi

The plan is of the later synagogue (supplanted by a church in the fifth century); elements of the building of Polycharmos have been found beneath it. The *bema* is represented by an open rectangle at the east; just south of it a bench runs east-west in an inset in the south wall.

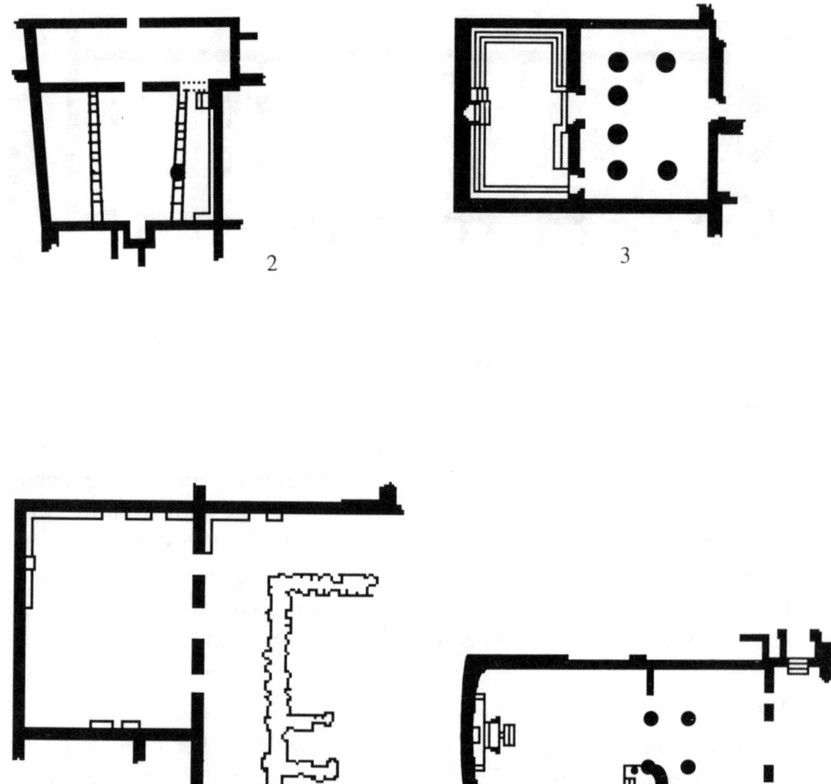

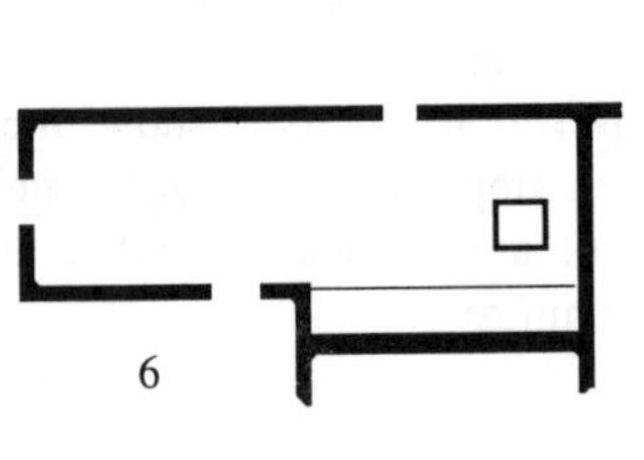

FIG. 2 Plans of Diaspora synagogues.

XI. ADDENDUM: A SYNAGOGUE IN THE ATHENIAN AGORA?

Early in 1978 I learned from G. M. A. Hanfmann of new evidence for a synagogue in the center of ancient Athens. Homer A. Thompson, Field Director Emeritus of the Agora Excavations, has graciously provided the following details:

In the summer of 1977 a small fragment of wall revetment was recovered from a tray of potsherds gathered originally by Prof. Thompson in 1933; the piece of Pentelic marble bears an incised *menorah* and, to the right, a palm branch or *lulab*. Dimensions: height 8.5 cm., width 8.0 cm., thickness 1.0-1.3 cm. The pottery and the marble fragment were in a late fourth—early fifth century context on the west side of the Agora a few meters to the north of the northeast corner of the Metroon.

Thompson notes that the plaque represented by this fragment apparently came from a curvilinear frieze, conceivably from an arcuated doorway or niche; he assumes that it is from a building which had been erected after the sacking of Athens by the Heruli in A.D. 267 and which had been damaged subsequently during the invasion by the Visigoths under Alaric in AD 396.

Very tentatively Thompson advances the hypothesis that a part of the Metroon (second century BC) may have become a synagogue in its latest phase. "This building had suffered severely in AD 267, but its northern two rooms were reconditioned subsequently, and continued in use at least into the 5th century. Some damage may have been done in AD 396; at any rate the mosaic floor in the second room from the north was laid ca. AD 400 (the latest coin from under it is of Arcadius 295-408). The large north room in its latest form had the scheme of a basilica with a semicircular apse protruding from its west end; inside the apse was a bench made of marble seat blocks salvaged from some Hellenistic exhedra." On the Metroon and the excavations considered here: H. A. Thompson, "Buildings on the West Side of the Agora," *Hesperia* 6 (1937): 115-217, especially 195-202; H. A. Thompson, *The Athenian Agora: A Guide to the Excavation and Museum* (Athens, 1976), p. 33, fig. 10 (=p. 27, fig. 37 of the following work; the plan shows the 'basilica' within the Metroon), p. 65; J. Travlos, *Pictorial Dictionary of Ancient Athens* (London, 1971), pp. 352-356.

This building as reconditioned is contemporary with the Sardis synagogue (section III, supra) and resembles it in several ways: both are centrally located in major cities of the Roman east, each results from the conversion of a previously 'pagan' structure, both are basilicas with apse and *synthronon* on the west wall, both are paved with mosaic from which 'pagan' motifs are conspicuously lacking. Each building at first impression suggests a "Christian basilica in reverse," i.e. with apse to the west, not the east; but there is no evidence of Christian use for either building (cf. *Hesperia* 6 [1937]: 212 note 1).

In July 1978 I was able to inspect the revetment fragment and the excavated Metroon. The fragment is no chance splinter of marble; it appears to have been deliberately if crudely broken out of a larger piece so that the *menorah* could be preserved, perhaps as a keepsake or souvenir, or for architectural reuse. The foot of the *menorah* was lost thereby, but at least the most distinctive feature is there, viz. the seven arms. I suspect that the person who squared the piece off to its present shape was working with broken revetment to begin with—otherwise he would have kept more of the design. The fact that there is nothing on the left to balance the palm branch to the right suggests that this *menorah* may have been one of a pair, or at the least that it was part of a larger design. Thompson notes that the broken edges of the marble are very fresh, and the scrap was found lying in loose accumulation of ca. AD 400 without any sign of re-use.

Thompson's cautious hypothesis is tempting: the revetment is obviously from a building, the symbols argue that the building belonged to Jews; such embellishment is conceivable in a private home, but more suited to a public building—and for the Jews of the Diaspora, the likely public building is a synagogue. The condition of the fragment suggests that it had not traveled far from wherever it was first used; the closest suitable building is the reworked Metroon. And the parallels with the Sardis synagogue are striking indeed. The remains and the excavation records deserve very close reexamination with Thompson's hypothesis in mind.

The excavated synagogue closest to Athens is on the island of Aegina, see note 9 supra; it is contemporary with the Metroon-basilica but the two structures have exactly opposite alignments: the Aegina synagogue has its apse on the east side, not the west as in the Agora building. There is epigraphic and literary evidence for Jews in Athens from the fourth century BC on, see *CII* 712-715, *CII* 715a-i (in Lifshitz's "Prolegomemon" to the 1975 reprint) and L. B. Urdahl, "Jews in Attica," *SymbOslo* 43 (1968) 39-56 (with the extensive critique by Robert in *Bull. epigr.* 1969, no. 206)—but until now no archaeological evidence for a synagogue.

SECTION III

SYNAGOGUES AND SETTLEMENTS

REPORTS AND ANALYSIS

ARCHITECTURAL PLANS OF SYNAGOGUES IN THE SOUTHERN JUDEAN HILLS AND THE 'HALAKAH'*

DAVID AMIT**

In the Southern Judean Hills four synagogues of the talmudic period have been discovered. These are the synagogues of Eshtemoa, Susiya, Ḥorvat Maon and 'Anim. The first of these, Eshtemoa, was discovered and excavated in the mid-thirties. After its excavation and the publishing of its plan, the investigators expressed their opinion about its architectural uniqueness. At that time, the accepted research divided the ancient synagogues into two groups: early and late. The Eshtemoa synagogue was defined as 'transitional,' between the two.[1]

More than a generation later, after the synagogue at Susiya was excavated, it was possible to see the great similarity between the two. Now, scholars speak of the South Judean Hills synagogues as an architecturally unique group. In 1987-1990, the late Zvi Ilan and the author excavated the synagogues of Maon and 'Anim. It became clear that these two are similar to—yet also different from—the first two. But the architectural characteristics common to these four differentiate them as a group from the other synagogues discovered in Israel. (See map in FIG. 3.)

We shall discuss the distinctive architecture of the four synagogues in this article and attempt to identify their source. First, however, we shall briefly review each of the four synagogues involved, emphasizing the architectural details which will provide the basis for our subsequent discussion.

THE SYNAGOGUE AT ESHTEMOA

In 1838, Edward Robinson identified the village of Sammu in the South Hebron Hills as the biblical Eshtemoa (Joshua 15:50, 21:14; 1 Samuel

---

* This article is an expanded version of the author's lecture at a symposium held on Sivan 27, 5750 (June 20, 1990) under the auspices of the Center for the Study of Eretz-Israel and its Settlement, of Yad Itzhak Ben Zvi and the Hebrew University, and devoted to the memory of Dr. Zvi Ilan, of blessed memory. I wish to express my appreciation to L. Levine, G. Foerster, E. Netzer, S. Wolff, Z. Safrai and R. Reich for their comments. A Hebrew version of this article appeared in *Cathedra* 68 (1993), pp. 6-35.

** Translated by Dr. Nathan H. Reisner.

[1] For a concise summary of the traditional division mentioned, see M. Avi Yonah, "Synagogues," *EAEHL*, pp. 1129-1132.

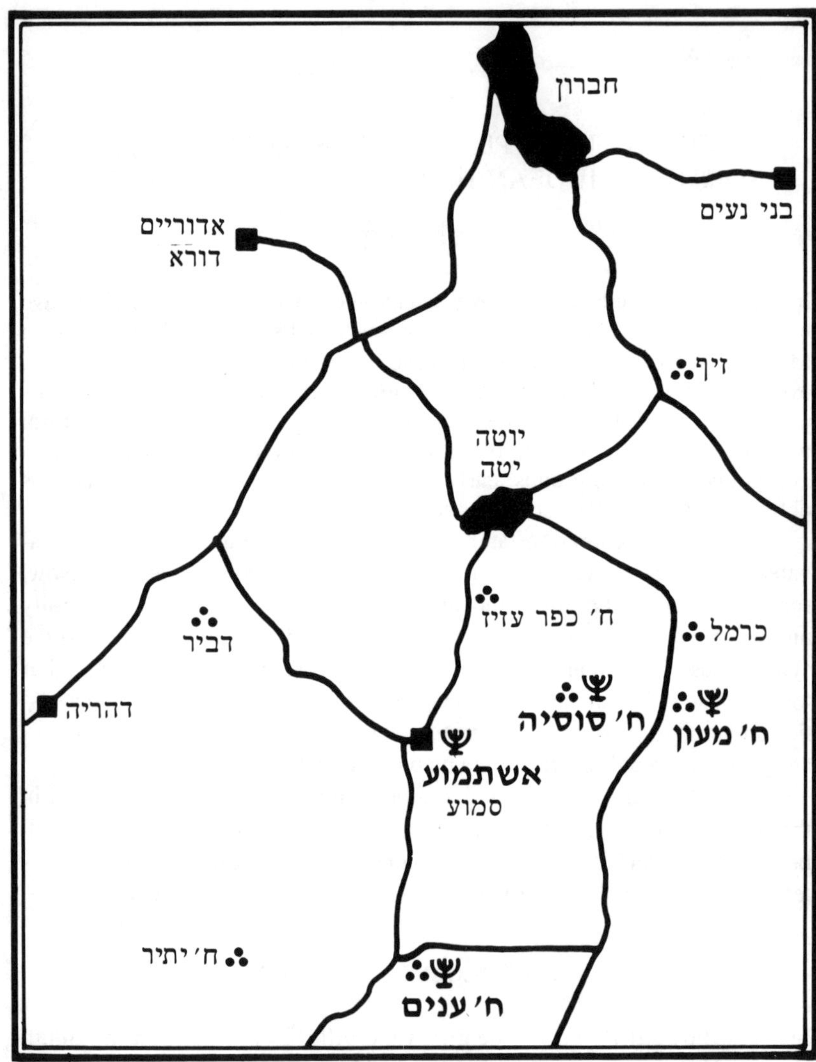

FIG. 3 Southern Judean Synagogues

Synagogues
1. Eshtemoa אשתמוע
2. Ḥorvat Susiyah ח׳סוסיה
3. Ḥorvat Maon ח׳מעון
4. Ḥorvat ʻAnim ח׳ענים

Towns and Villages
5. Hebron חברון
6. Yattah יוטה
7. Benei Naim בני נעים
8. Dura דורא
9. Dehiriyah דהריה

Architectural Sites
10. Zif זיף
11. Karmel כרמל
12. Devir דביר
13. Ḥ. Kefar Aziz ח׳כפר עזיז
14. Ḥ. Yatir ח׳יתיר

30:28; 1 Chronicles 4:17 & 19, 6:42).[2] Eshtemoa is also known from the later periods; it is mentioned in Eusebius' *Onomasticon* of the fourth century C.E. as "a very large village of Jews in the South."[3] The site is also mentioned in the Palestinian Talmud (Nedarim 7:16, 40a).[4] Different investigators who visited the village in the course of the nineteenth century and the beginning of the twentieth identified many remains from the rabbinic period including stone bas-reliefs of *menorot* and other art objects. But it was only toward the end of 1934, in the course of a visit there by L. A. Mayer and A. Reifenberg of the Hebrew University in Jerusalem, that they discovered the remains of the ancient settlement's synagogue. About a year later, the two began an archaeological excavation of the site, uncovered substantial portions of the structure, and managed to make out its plan in detail.[5] Because of the Arab uprising that broke out at that time, the work was stopped. Only after the Six Days' War was the excavation completed under Z. Yeivin's direction.[6]

The synagogue had the shape of a broad rectangle oriented from east to west, its inner dimensions about 20 x 10 meters. Its facade had an entrance porch (narthex) reached by three steps via an expanse paved with large stones. The entrance floor was decorated with a colored mosaic, of which all that has survived is a picture of a tree in five colors and a dedication inscription in Aramaic.

The facade wall has been preserved to a height of about 2 meters and has three entrances to the hall. The middle entrance is wider than the two side ones (which today are sealed). The entrances are decorated with a protruding frame. Unlike the eastern wall, the western wall has been preserved to a height of 8 meters or more.

The focal point of the synagogue was in the northern wall facing Jerusalem. It has a central alcove which served to hold the *aron ha-qodesh* (the Torah Ark) and two smaller alcoves that apparently served for the menorahs. In front of the central alcove, a *bemah* (platform) protrudes from the wall and at its center there apparently was a series of steps by which one went up to the Torah Ark. On the left part of the *bemah*, Mayer and Reifenberg discovered a Hebrew inscription. The stones bearing the inscription were removed and disappeared in the time between the two excavations.

Two benches, one above the other, were built along the length of the northern and southern walls. On the northern wall, only the segment be-

[2] See Robinson, vol. 1, p. 494.

[3] See the *Onomastikon*, p. 86.

[4] See S. Klein, ed., *The Settlement Book*, vol. 1 (Jerusalem, 1939; repr. 1978), p. 16 (in Hebrew).

[5] See Mayer & Reifenberg.

[6] See Z. Yeivin, "The Synagogue of Eshtemoa," Levine, *ASR*, pp. 120-122.

tween the *bemah* and the eastern wall survived; on the southern wall, the benches are interrupted by a *mahrab* that was built here when the building became a mosque (in the days of Saladin, according to local tradition). It seems that the building was covered by a broad double-sloped tile roof. The roof was placed upon a wooden frame which rested upon the north and south walls.

The synagogue floor was covered with a colored mosaic, only sections of which have remained. These include examples of floral and geometric patterns.

THE SUSIYA SYNAGOGUE

The existence of the ancient synagogue at Ḥorvat Susiya was already suspected in the thirties from a survey conducted there by Mayer and Reifenberg when they uncovered the synagogue at nearby Eshtemoa. However, it was only in 1970, in light of new surveys conducted in the region, that its excavation was begun by Shemarya Gutman, Ze'ev Yeivin and Ehud Netzer.[7]

The site contains the synagogue building itself and the large courtyard entrance east of it. The courtyard was connected and paved with large rectangular stone slabs. Stoas enclosed it on three sides. Five long steps led from the courtyard to the entrance portico of the synagogue. (See PL. 4a.)

The building was divided into three parts: the entrance to the east, a long narrow wing to the south, and the prayer hall to the north. At the southern end of the entrance there were stairs that led to the second story which was over the south wing. The hall was two stories high, about 8-9 meters. Three decorated entranceways led from the entrance to the prayer hall. The middle entranceway was larger than the side ones. The hall's dimensions are 9 x 16 meters.

The entrance, the hall, and the southern stoa of the courtyard were paved with colored mosaics that included diverse artistic themes: a Torah Ark, and menorah, a zodiac, Daniel in the lions' den (?), as well as images of winged figures, various fruits and rich and variegated geometric patterns. The mosaic floors also included four dedicatory inscriptions in Hebrew and Aramaic.

On the hall's northern wall, which was double the thickness of the other walls, there were two *bemot*. Due to the great destruction, the alcove of the holy ark above the main *bemah* was not found, but clear signs of its existence were discovered.

The main platform underwent many transformations and at the height of its glory, it was entirely encased in gray marble, and a semi-circular staircase was added on each side. Many sections of the marble latticework that encir-

[7] See Gutman, Yeivin, and Netzer.

cled the *bemah* have survived (among them even inscriptions dedicated to donors). The secondary *bemah* found east of the main *bemah*, is one of the outstanding innovations in the Susiya synagogue. It was originally shaped as a cube, but changes were made during the years of the synagogue's existence.

Along the length of the hall's three walls—in the south, west and north—there is a continuum of three benches, one above the other, until the main *bemah*. The synagogue had a tile roof, as attested by the many fragments found in the excavation. The roof rested on the walls alone, for the hall had no columns.

The synagogue was established toward the end of the fourth century or the beginning of the fifth century C.E. and existed until the eighth century C.E.

THE MAON SYNAGOGUE

Ḥorvat Maon lies on a high mound in the southeast Hebron Hills on the edge of the Judean Desert. At the top of the hill, the tell of biblical Maon was identified (Joshua 15:55; I Samuel 23:24-25; 25:2) by E. Robinson, who also was the first to describe the remains at the site.[8] After him, different researchers, among them V. Guérin, Sh. Gutman, and Y. Hirschfeld, described the Iron Age remains found at the top of the tell and the remains from the settlement of the Roman and Byzantine periods on its slopes. Prominent among the latter were remains on the northern slope of a public building made of large hewn stones, thought to have been a church. This structure was excavated in 1987-1988 by Z. Ilan and the author in view of their hypothesis that it was an ancient synagogue.[9] (See FIG. 4.)

The synagogue that was uncovered is a long north-south structure facing Jerusalem. (See PL. 4b.) Its dimensions are 10.5 x 15.5 meters, and its walls, about a meter thick, are of hewn stone. In its first stage, the building had three entrances in its long eastern wall and it apparently had a gabled tile roof. It was paved with a mosaic floor. Sections of two benches remained along the length of the building's walls. In the northern wall there was an alcove for the holy ark which protruded from the wall. This building, it seems, was established during the second half of the fourth century or the beginning of the fifth. (See FIG. 6.)

[8] See Robinson, vol. 2, p. 204.

[9] See Amit and Ilan, as well as Z. Ilan and D. Amit, "Maon (in Judea)," *NEAEHL*, pp. 942-944. The final report of the excavations will appear in *Atiqot*.

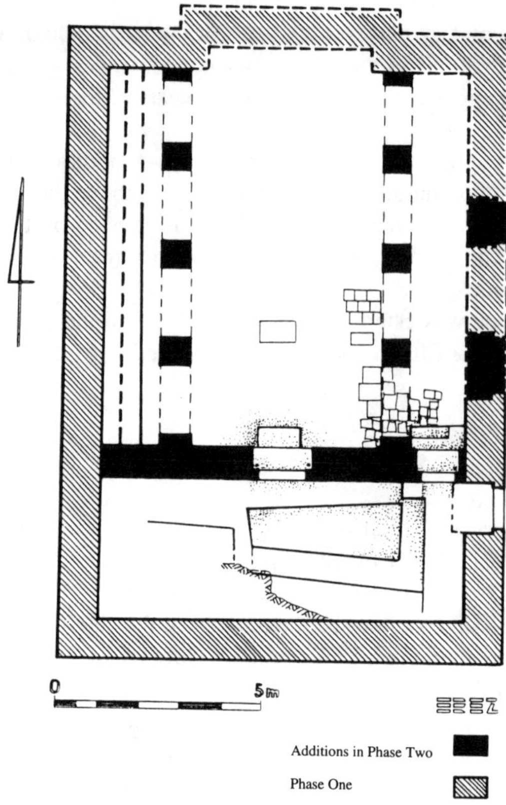

FIG. 4 Ḥ. Maon: Plan of Synagogue

During the building's second stage, apparently in the sixth century, significant changes were made. The prayer hall was reduced 3.5 meters by building a wall in its southern part with two entrances in it. The area taken from the hall now served as a vestibule. This may also have been used as a classroom after a stone bench was added along the length of the new entrances' wall. (See FIG. 7 and PL. 5a.)

The western part of the vestibule apparently served as the synagogue storeroom. The entrance to the vestibule was through the eastern wall's south entranceway which was in continuous use from the previous stage. Square columns with arches were now erected in the prayer hall itself and its roof rested upon them. The mosaic floor which had been damaged was completed with square stone paving. This building lasted until the seventh century C.E. when it was abandoned.

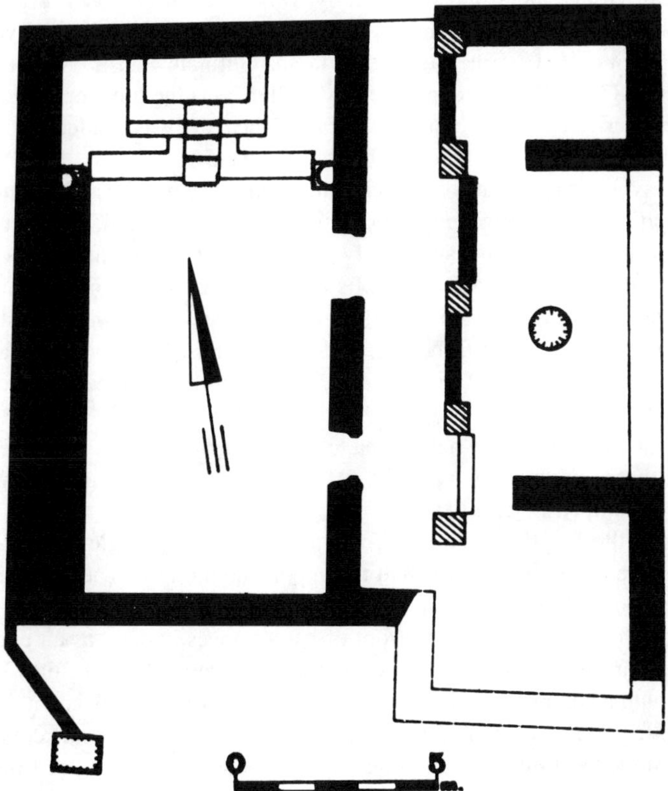

FIG. 5 Ḥ. 'Anim: Plan of Synagogue

THE 'ANIM SYNAGOGUE

Ḥorvat 'Anim is about 19 km. south of Hebron, within the area of the Jewish National Fund's Yattir Forest. The Arabic name of the ruin, *Khirbet Ghuweine et-Taht* (*el-Gharbiyeh*), its geographic location and the ceramic finds there, led to its identification with 'Anim of the biblical period (Joshua 15:50).[10] The site is also identified with the western Anaia of the Roman-Byzantine period about which Eusebius wrote: "and in the South there is another large village of Jews called Anaia, nine miles south of Hebron."[11] This is to distinguish it from the eastern Anaia, which was a contemporary

[10] See Robinson, vol. 1, p. 494.

[11] See the *Onomastikon*, p. 26.

Christian village identified with nearby *Khirbet Ghuweine el-Fawqa (esh-Sharqiyye)*. The remains at the site were surveyed and described by various investigators: V. Guérin, M. Kochavi, Sh. Gutman, and Z. Meshel. But only in 1987, in a survey conducted by Z. Ilan, was the location of the synagogue discovered.[12] Thereupon an archaeological dig was conducted there in 1988-1989 by Z. Ilan and the author.[13] (See FIG. 5.)

The synagogue contains a prayer-hall, an entrance portico and a courtyard to which rooms are attached on both sides. The prayer-hall, rectangular in shape, with exterior dimensions of 14.5 x 8.5 meters, is oriented from south to north, that is, toward Jerusalem. Its walls are built of hewn stone and are preserved to a height of 3.5 meters. Its two entrances are on the east side. They survived to their full height, with their lintels. Its floor was made of square stone slabs. Beneath it, signs were found of the existence of an earlier mosaic floor.

About a quarter of the hall's area, at its northern end, was set aside for a *bemah* that took up its entire width. At its center, against the northern wall, was the Torah Ark. (See PL. 6b.)

Along the length of the western wall there was a single stone bench. There were no columns in the hall to support the tile roof. There apparently was a wooden gable frame that rested upon the outer walls. (See PL. 5b.)

In the facade of the hall, in front of its entrances, there was an entrance portico (narthex) whose width was about 2 meters. (See PL. 6a.) It was paved with a colored mosaic that contained geometric designs and a dedicatory inscription. A row of columns separated the portico from the courtyard which stretched to its east and contained a connected plaza (7 x 4 meters) paved with stone, a well, and rooms attached on the north and south which served various communal needs. According to the finds discovered during the dig, the synagogue is dated to the fourth through seventh centuries C.E.

THE TYPOLOGICAL ASPECT

The information that existed on the synagogues of the South Judean Hills prior to our excavations at the synagogues of Maon and 'Anim was primarily based upon the synagogues of Eshtemoa and Susiya. Their great similarity in plan, on the one hand, and, on the other hand, the difference between these plans and that of everyone of the dozens of synagogues known to us across the country, led to the logical conclusion formulated by Kloner,

---

[12] See Z. Ilan, "A Synagogue Hidden in a Forest," *Teva' va-Aretz* 29, no. 7 (1987): 28-31 (in Hebrew).

[13] See Z. Ilan and D. Amit, "Horvat Anim—Synagogue," *EASI*, 7-8 (1988-1989): 6-8; D. Amit, "'Anim, Ḥorvat," *NEAEHL*, vol. 1, p. 62. The final report will appear in *Atiqot*.

that the synagogues at Susiya and Eshtemoa "represent a separate grouping, apparently typical of this geographic region."[14]

Y. Tsafrir, who also considers this group as "a group unto itself," notes that "apparently it cannot be defined by chronological criteria" that relate to the northern synagogues.[15] Tsafrir's observation, in its general context, touches upon the basic questions of synagogue research, which should be briefly discussed before we return to the specific topic of our essay. In the study of ancient synagogues, for some time, the weight which had previously been given to chronological criteria has diminished. The hard and fast division of synagogues into early and late has given way to a set of criteria no longer dominated by chronological considerations but which also incorporate regional, economic, social, and other considerations.

As more synagogues have been uncovered, it has become all the more clear how greatly the schematic picture which the investigators sought to draw at the start of the research has become complex and multi-faceted, and how much the attempt to set a clear typology with well-defined lines, has fallen upon difficulties and limitations.[16] Despite these complexities, one should not hasten to conclude that there is no longer room for any attempt to fix a typological chronology for ancient synagogues by examining the connection between them. This tendency, which arose in the wake of the publication of the Franciscan Fathers' new excavations at Capernaum, is an attempt by scholars to avoid the problems with which they are being confronted by evolving research.[17]

Our generalization about ancient synagogues also applies to our treatment of the four in the South Judean Hills when we test the validity of the typology formulated above by Kloner and Tsafrir. The question we faced after the excavations of the Maon and 'Anim synagogues was whether we could also, now, still allow ourselves to define the synagogues of the South as a separate group? We shall examine this in breadth (the stylized typological aspect) and in depth (the chronological aspect) integrating and intersecting the cross-sections of both aspects.

Kloner characterized the synagogues of Susiya and Eshtemoa architecturally as follows:[18]

a. wide buildings.
b. entrances in the eastern wall

---

[14] See Kloner, "Synagogues," p. 11.

[15] See Tsafrir, p. 168.

[16] For an up-to-date discussion of the problems connected to the architecture of the synagogues in light of the modern discoveries, see Seager, "Historiography."

[17] On the problem and its ramifications, see Tsafrir, pp. 170, 171, and also, "The Synagogue at Meroth, the Synagogue at Capernaum, and the Dating of the Galilean Synagogues—a Reconsideration," *EI* 20 (1989): 337-344 (in Hebrew).

[18] See Kloner, "Synagogues," note 14.

c. a platform with an alcove for the Torah Ark, on the northern wall facing Jerusalem.
d. a mosaic floor.
e. hewn-stone construction.
f. a wooden ceiling and tiles.
g. no pillars to support the roof.

An examination of these characteristics, even superficially, indicates the different weight that should be given to each of them in characterizing the group. Components (d), (e) and (f) are common in many synagogues with different plans and there is no point therefore, in treating them as typological characteristics. Even component (c)—the platform and alcove for the holy ark—is not particularly unique and its like can be found even in northern synagogues, except for its location in the northern wall required in synagogues south of Jerusalem, (more on this later).

There remain, then, three outstanding characteristics: the buildings' width, entrances on the short eastern wall, and the absence of columns to support the root. The three together, as far as we know, occur only in the synagogues of Susiya and Eshtemoa—and this indeed makes them an architecturally unique group.

A comparison of the Maon and ‘Anim synagogues with these two indicates one clear difference: the structures at Maon and ‘Anim are built long (rather than wide). On the other hand, in the first stage at Maon, and at ‘Anim, there are two similar characteristics: the entrances on the eastern wall (though here, in the nature of things, it is not the short wall) and the absence of columns in the hall to support the roof.

In our opinion, the existence of two such outstanding characteristics in the four synagogues under discussion, is sufficiently significant to categorize them as a separate typological group, in spite of the difference between them as far as the third characteristic.

To reinforce the validity of this determination, let me restate it in a negative form. The existence of only one clear architectural characteristic in a number of buildings is not enough to distinguish them as a group, but the presence of two clear characteristics provides ample demarcation of a distinctive group. Therefore, we cannot, for example, include the synagogues of Eshtemoa and Susiya in a group with the synagogue of Khirbet Shema‘ even though the three are built in the width.[19] Likewise, we cannot include in a single group, for example, the synagogues of Ḥorvat Sumaqa, Ma‘oz Ḥayyim and Maon, even though all three have their entrances on the east wall. Thus, we can conclude that within the general grouping of the South

---

[19] On this H. Shanks has put it well, "If unity is the primary characteristic of basilican-plan synagogues, diversity is the essential quality of broad-house plan synagogues." See H. Shanks, *Judaism in Stone* (Tel-Aviv, 1979), p 97.

Judean Hills synagogues, despite the difference in details, there are grounds for seeing them as a unique group, as we have tried to prove, for we can now discern two subtypes: the broad type (Eshtemoa and Susiya), and the long type (Maon and 'Anim).

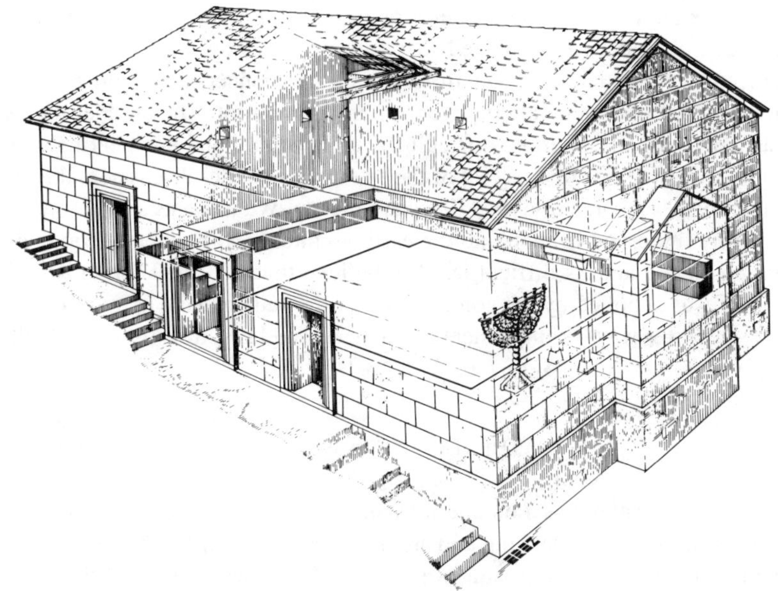

FIG. 6 Maon synagogue: Reconstruction of First Phase

An examination of further components that differentiate the two types shows that those of the wide type are larger and more complex than those of the long type, and are richer in decorated stone and artistic items.

This difference can be explained against the background of the different types of settlement to which the synagogues of the two secondary types belonged. On the one hand, the wide type, large and wealthy, represents large settlements, Jewish towns with hundreds of households such as the historical sources (for Eshtemoa)[20] and the archaeological evidence in the area indicate Eshtemoa and Susiya to have been.[21] On the other hand, the long type,

---

[20] See above, notes 3-4.

[21] On Eshtemoa, see: F. M. Abel and A. Barrois, "Sculptures du sud de la Judée: es-Semou," *RB*, 38 (1929): 585-589; B. Z. Luria, *Gelilot ba-moledot* (Jerusalem, 1956), pp. 249-267 (in Hebrew). In 1969, S. Gutman surveyed the village thoroughly and discovered new details. His survey report is in the Archives of the Israel Antiquities Authority and has not yet been published.

On Susiya, see A. Negev, "Excavations at Carmel (Kh. Susiya) in 1984: Preliminary Report," *IEJ* 35 (1985): 231-252.

the simple small building, represents small rural settlements such as Maon and 'Anim that counted only a few dozen households.[22]

It is almost certain that the architectural development of the unique structure described here—that is, a hall whose entrances are on the east wall and without interior columns—is not the result of purely stylistic influences, even though they too play a role in its design. From an engineering standpoint, it should be emphasized that forgoing the row of columns in the hall's space posed a significant difficulty for the planners and builders which necessitated finding an alternative support for the roof. The broader the expanse of the hall, the more difficult the architectural and engineering challenge. At Eshtemoa, the largest of the synagogues under discussion, the hall encompasses an area of over 270 square meters. We must seek a reason sufficiently important to motivate the early architect and builder to cope with the challenge and its difficulties. We believe that, first and foremost, this reason was supplied by the combination of the Judean halakic tradition and the search for ways to implement it practically and functionally in the building's plan.

THE HALAKIC ASPECT[23]

Talmudic literature has a number of halakhic discussions with direct implications for the basic planning and architectural design of the synagogue. For the purposes of our discussion, we shall focus on two topics: (1) the direction of prayer, (2) the location of the entrances.

(1) Direction of Prayer

This question is primarily discussed in two places in the Babylonian Talmud, the tractates of Berakot (and its parallels) and Baba Batra. In the Mishnah, Berakot 4:5-6 lists instances of a man who is traveling when the time for prayer arrives.

[22] In a comprehensive survey which we conducted at Ḥ. 'Anim, at the same time as the excavation of the synagogue, we counted about fifty family dwellings. (The report of the survey will be published along with the excavation report, see above, note 13.) Hence Eusebius' statement that Anaia is "a very large village of Jews" (see note 11) was exaggerated. At Maon, where the present settlement covers a considerable portion of the remains of the ancient settlement, it is difficult to carry out a precise survey, but it seems that the situation is the same and even tends to lower numbers. See also Amit and Ilan, pp. 116-117.

[23] We have been greatly assisted in the writing of this essay by Ginzberg, *Commentary*, even more than we have been able to note in the marginal notes below. Our friends Dr. Menahem Kahana and Rabbi Elhanan Samet were kind enough to read the rough draft of this chapter and offered important comments. For this, we are sincerely thankful to them.

> If he was riding on an ass, he should dismount [to say *tefillah* ("Prayer," i.e., the Eighteen Benedictions)]. If he cannot dismount he should turn his face [toward Jerusalem]. If he cannot turn his face, he should direct his heart toward the Holy of Holies.
> If he was journeying on a ship or a wagon, or a raft, he should direct his heart toward the Holy of Holies.

According to the Mishnah, then, one should direct prayer toward the Holy of Holies. In the *baraita* commenting on this passage, found in various versions in the Tosefta, and in the Palestinian and Babylonian Talmuds, as well as in the Midrashim,[24] this is cited in greater detail. Here is the formulation in Sifré Deuteronomy 29, (p. 47 in the Finkelstein edition):

> They who stand [in prayer] outside the Land [of Israel] turn their faces toward Land of Israel and pray, as is said, "and they pray to You in the direction of their land" (I Kings 8:48).
> They who stand in the Land of Israel turn their faces toward Jerusalem and as is said: "and they pray to You in the direction of the city" (2 Chronicles 6:34).
> They who stand in Jerusalem turn their faces to toward the Temple and pray, as is said: "and they pray toward this House" (2 Chronicles 6:32).
> They who stand in the Temple direct their hearts toward the Holy of Holies and pray , as is said: "and then they pray toward this place" (2 Chronicles 6:26).
> If they are standing in the north, they turn their faces toward the south; in the south, they turn their faces to the north; in the east, [they turn] their faces toward the west; in the west, [they turn] their faces toward the east. [Thus] all Israel are found praying towards one place.

We cite the Sifré text because it (as in the Palestinian Talmud) reads: "they turn their faces," which is similar to the expression at the beginning of the Mishnah "he should turn his face." It is clear that turning the face is not something wholly external but expresses an internal intention, as indicated by the expression "he direct his heart" which is at the end of the Mishnah. This is identical to the parallels of the *baraita* in the Tosefta, the Babylonian Talmud and elsewhere.[25]

In sum, the geographic-geometrical picture that emerges from the above sources reveals that one central point constitutes the main focus for the complex of orbits encompassing it. On every occasion of prayer, one's direction should be toward the central point. The angle of direction is relative and depends upon where one is standing.

In the Mishnah (BB 2:9), we read, "A tannery may be set up only on the east side of the town. Rabbi Aqiba says: 'It may be set up on any side save the west but it may not be within a distance of fifty cubits.'" And in the

[24] For a detailing of the parallels, see *Tosefta Berakhot*, Lieberman edition, p. 15, note 65.
[25] See Lieberman, *Tosefta ki-fshutah*, Berakot, p. 44.

Tosefta (BB 1:8, p. 131 in the Lieberman edition), and also in the Palestinian Talmud (BB 4:9, 13a) this is quoted with a slight variation and the addition of the motivation. The Tosefta formulation reads: "Rabbi Aqiba says that in every direction it must be at a remove of fifty cubits except in the west *because [the wind from that side] is constant.*"

Rabbi Aqiba, who lived in Palestine, meant that the prevailing winds in Palestine are from the west; the smells of a tannery located on the west side of a settlement would thus be spread over the whole town. To those who lived in the Land of Israel, this meaning was understood by all.[26] However, in Babylonia, where the wind patterns are different, the Babylonian *amoraim*, Rava and Rav Nahman attached a spiritual meaning to Rabbi Akiba's words. In the Babylonian Talmud (BB 25a), they explained that Rabbi Aqiba meant that the west wind is "constantly with *shekinah*," or in a more apt version that appears in some manuscripts, is "constantly with Prayer."[27] That is, in light of the west's additional sanctity one should not set up a source of stench on that side. This interpretation should be viewed in light of the Babylonian's designation of *eretz yisrael* as '*ma'arava*' ('the west').

In a continuation of that Bavli passage, various opinions of the Sages—*tannaim* and *amoraim* of Palestine and Babylonia—are expressed about the direction of Tefillah and location of the *shekinah*. Their words reflect two basic outlooks presented in the following table:[28]

In the West	Everywhere
Rabbi Aqiba (in the Babylonian explanation)	Rabbi Ishmael
Rabbi Joshua ben Levi	Rabbi Oshaiah
Rabbi Abbahu	Rav Sheshet

The practical ramification of this discussion about the direction of Tefillah/ and location of the *shekinah* finds expression in the comment of "Rabbi Joshua ben Levi: 'Come let us be grateful to our forefathers who informed us of the place of Tefillah,'" and in the opinion of Rav Sheshet which can be deduced from an actual incident. When the time for the Prayer came "Rav

[26] See Lieberman, *Tosefta*, Baba Bathra, p. 335.

[27] See *Diqduqei Soferim*, ad loc.

[28] It should be pointed out that Rabbi Aha bar Jacob also participated in the discussion. Attacking the homily of Rabbi Joshua ben Levi who interpreted Nehemiah 9:6, "and the host of heaven prostate themselves before You" to mean that the *shekinah* is in the west and this is the place of prayer, he argued that from this verse one could also reach the opposite conclusion ("and perhaps it is like a servant who, upon receiving a reward from his master, backs away, bowing"). Some of the *Rishonim* ("the early authorities") tried to conclude from this that an opinion also exists that the *shekinah* is in the east. However, a careful reading of Rabbi Aha's words proves that he did not intend that at all. He only wanted to protest Rabbi Joshua ben Levi's homily. See also Ginzberg, *Commentary*, vol. 3, p. 375.

Sheshet said to Shemaiah: 'Stand me in any direction except east, and not because the *shekinah* is not there but because the heretics teach that.'"[29]

At the end of that segment (B. BB 25b), they resume the discussion on the directions for the Tefillah and the focus shifts to practical matters, even though it relies entirely upon Palestinian sages' statements that were originally in no way related to prayer. Two opinions are cited. Rabbi Isaac states, "Let him who wishes to become wise—face south, and to become rich, north." That is to say, in the Babylonian opinion, one who prays may choose which of the two directions he pleases. The second opinion comes from Rabbi Joshua ben Levi, "One should always face south, for if he becomes wise, he will also become rich." Since this sage held that the *shekinah* is in the west, how can he now say that one should always pray facing south? The answer given is that "he should face sort of sideways," that is, he should stand in a kind of position between south and west.[30]

To sum up, the geographic-geometrical picture that emerges from B. Baba Batra is completely different from that depicted in B. Berakot. In Bavli Berakot, the directions for prayer were related to the points of the compass, relative and conditioned upon where the one praying stood in relation to a defined focal point. In Bavli Baba Batra, as it were, a two-fold picture is presented. On the one hand, we find an open system where no direction is obligatory and there is no focus—the basic concept being that "the *shekinah* is everywhere." On the other hand, we find a set of lines whose directions are absolute with the main one being west toward a spiritual focal point—"the *shekinah* is in the west"—but alongside this set, we also find south and north, or both together, with a line between them running south-west.

The only apparent connection between the discussion in B. Baba Batra and the halakah in B. Berakot is contained in the statement of Rabbi Hanina in Baba Batra. He says to Rabbi Ashi, "Like you who live in the north of the Land of Israel who face south." That is to say, that from Babylonia, perceived as being north of the Land of Israel, and relying upon the words of the prophet, "From the north shall disaster break loose" (Jeremiah 1:14), one should turn in prayer in the direction of Palestine. Hence the conclusion that there is a relative, not absolute, direction as emerged from the course of the discussion previously. Still, Rabbi Hanina does not base his statement upon the explicit halakah in B. Berakot.

Can we really draw two such entirely unrelated pictures, two such diametrically opposed basic concepts? This is astonishing, first and foremost,

---

[29] On the essence of the '*minim*' (heretics), see Ginzberg, *Commentary*, vol. 3, pp. 372-375. For a different opinion, see Urbach, *Sages*, p. 62, note 99.

[30] In the commentary attributed to Rabbenu Gershom: "In no way at all is the direction south nor is it north." For the various possibilities of interpreting the concept, see Ginzberg, *Commentary*, vol. 3, pp. 390-391.

from the internal talmudic aspect. After all, the halakah in B. Berakot, whose essence is already in the Mishnah and is detailed in a *baraita* that is in the Tosefta and the two *talmudim* and the *midrashim*, is always presented as a set tannaitic halakah, with none taking exception. How, then, could the seemingly practical-halakic discussion in B. Baba Batra have been held almost totally ignorant of this explicit law?

The Tosafists to B. Baba Batra 25a, beginning "Face me in any direction," raise this problem saying: "None of these *amoraim* were aware of what was taught in B. Berakot (30a) that a person must pray facing Jerusalem." They explain the difference of opinion among the *amoraim* as based upon such a difference among the tannaim. That is to say, the halakah in M. Berakot is only one opinion, upon which Rabbi Haninah, at the end of the discussion in B. Baba Batra, relied. In opposition to this, stood Rabbi Ishmael's opinion that "the *shekinah* is everywhere" and upon which the other *amoraim* based themselves, arguing that one may pray in any direction.[31]

The third opinion—"the *shekinah* is in the west"—relies upon the words of Rabbi Aqiba as they were interpreted by the Babylonian *amoraim*.

Still, it is clear that this explanation is far-fetched and that the weight and unambiguous meaning of the halakah in M. Berakhot give it clear priority over the opinions cited in B. Baba Batra which are subject to interpretation as to their practical implications.[32] This conclusion, apart from additional questions which will arise, is tenable only if we assume that what we have here is a difference between various halakic traditions.[33] It seems to us, therefore, that the Baba Batra discussion, even if it is focused on the direction of prayer, rests upon various statements whose original meaning was unrelated to this and hence is also not directly concerned with the halakah but with the theoretical-philosophical question of the place of the *shekinah*. The single practical matter is connected with Rav Sheshet and, as a matter of fact, no conclusion can be drawn from it because of the sage's special circumstances, namely, that he was blind and therefore any direction was acceptable to him.[34]

The opinions at the end of the segment—both Rabbi Isaac's "Let him who wishes to be wise, face south, and to be rich, face north," and Rabbi Joshua's "Always face south"—should be seen as a continuation of the folk-

---

[31] Menahem Kahana suggested that the fact that only Babylonian Amoraim express this opinion perhaps is indicative of an internal Babylonian motive in their struggle against the Land of Israel. Urbach, *Sages*, pp. 61-63 presents another interpretation.

[32] To emphasize this point one should also note that in Bavli Berakot the law is dependent upon explicit verses, whereas in Bavli Baba Bathra the entire matter is built upon an interpretation of the dictum of Rabbi Aqiba.

[33] And see Ginzberg, *Commentary*, vol. 3, pp. 384-386.

[34] And see Ginzberg, *Commentary*, vol. 3, p. 389.

loristic discussion preceding them. That discussion revolved around the characteristics of the four points of the compass and the natural forces in the Land of Israel. Hence, in actuality, only Rabbi Hanina's statement touches upon the practical question of the direction of prayer, but it, as has been said, agrees with the halakah in B. Berakot. This latter is the only unit that has practical ramifications for the form of the synagogue and the design of its plan, for it determines the direction of prayer and thus the orientation of the building: towards the Land of Israel in general, then towards Jerusalem, the Temple mount, and ultimately the Holy of Holies.

This conclusion contradicts the opinion which has gained some acceptance in the commentaries and in the research. As a result of this there are practical ramifications for determining that "the *shekinah* is in the west."[35] Below we shall return to this question and attempt to prove that the accepted understanding has no solid basis.

(2) The Synagogue Entrances

In Tosefta, Megillah 4(3):22 (Lieberman, *Tosefta*, Moed, p. 360) we read, "Synagogue entrances are opened only to the east as we have found in the Temple which was open to the east, as it is written: 'Those who were to camp before the Tabernacle, in front—before the Tent of Meeting, on the east'" (Num. 3:38).

This indicates that the halakah relies upon the shape of the Tabernacle in the Temple. It oriented the synagogue's entrances out of a desire to preserve this shape, since the synagogue is in a sense the substitute for the Tabernacle, a "miniature sanctuary." But the commentators and the researchers have already dwelt upon the actual intent inherent in this law.[36] It has to do with Judaism's age-old struggle against the pagan concept, which in its later development takes on a Christian garb, that the worshipper should face the east. An expression of this struggle already exists in the Hebrew Bible, in the vision of Ezekiel, who sees an abomination taking place in the Tabernacle: "about twenty-five men, their backs to the Temple of the Lord and their faces to the east; they were bowing low to the sun in the east" (Ezekiel 8:16-17).[37]

---

[35] See the opinion of the Tosafists and, likewise, Urbach, below, in the discussion of the synagogue entrances.

[36] The first who made a point of this was Y. Schorr in his edition of Rabbi Judah ben Barzilai of Barcelona's twelfth century *Sefer ha-Ittim* (=*Book of the Times*) (Cracow, 1902), p. 273, note 121 (in Hebrew). And see Lieberman, *Tosefta ki-fshutah*, Megillah, p. 1200.

[37] And apparently the words are directed in contradiction to the verse in Numbers 3:38 which is the source for the law in the tosefta above, for that verse has "Moses and Aaron and his sons attending to the duties of the sanctuary" while standing "before the Tabernacle, in front."

In this context, the Mishnah describes the procession of the celebrants at *simhat bet ha-sho'evah* (the Feast of Water Drawing) approaching the eastern gate of the Temple Mound: "...they turned their faces to the west and said: 'Our fathers when they were in this place turned with their backs toward the Temple of the Lord and their faces toward the east, and they worshipped the sun toward the east; but as for us, our eyes are turned toward the Lord'" (M. Sukkah 5:4). E. E. Urbach has pointed out that Rabbi Joshua ben Levi's statement in the matter of the place of the *shekinah* in Baba Batra: "Come and let us be grateful to our forefathers who let us know the place of prayer" recalls the words of the celebrants: "Our fathers when they were in this place, etc."[38] These words of Rabbi Joshua ben Levi's represent, as you will recall, the opinion that "the *shekinah* is in the west," as against the opinion that "the *shekinah* is everywhere." It is very likely that this tradition of the *shekinah*'s being in the west indeed developed as a counter to the pagan and Christian concept that considered the east as "the place of the *shekinah.*"

We shall focus on two quotations from the matters detailed above to demonstrate this

1. In B. Baba Batra, Rav Sheshet's statement to his assistant supports the view that "the *shekinah* is everywhere," still reveals a reluctance about praying to the east because "the heretics teach that."[39] Urbach theorizes that the very fact that a position developed that "the *shekinah* is everywhere" was a reaction to the claims of those heretics he sees as Judeo-Christians.[40]

2. In the Palestinian Talmud, tractate Berakot, preceding the halakah about the directions of prayer, and in relation to the text of the Mishnah (M. Ber. 4:5) which reads "If he was riding on an ass...if he cannot dismount he should turn his face [toward Jerusalem], says Rabbi Jacob bar Aha: 'It is taught there that one faces in no direction but east.'"[41]

We can sum up, therefore, and say that it may indeed be that the halakah about setting the synagogue entrances in the east was intended to dissuade the heretics who prayed toward the east, since locating the entrance in the east creates a situation in which one who enters the synagogue must turn his back to the east.[42] The question that arises from this is whether the fact that the worshipper entering the synagogue is facing west, which is a result

---

[38] See Urbach, *Sages*, p. 62.

[39] And see note 29, above.

[40] See Urbach, *Sages*, pp. 61-63.

[41] For the substitute versions "one does not turn/one turns"—see Ginzberg, *Commentary*, vol. 3, pp. 370-372. And also see the *Penei Moshe* commentary ad loc., which cites "they turn."

[42] Against this we should note that there was a similar situation in which the worshipper's back faces the sacred focal point upon entering Galilean synagogues, where the entrances were in the south, toward Jerusalem.

of the halakah in the Tosefta, as well as the determination of a few Sages that "the *shekinah* is in the west," compels the conclusion that the direction of prayer was westward? In other words, are the laws about the entrances and the direction of prayer interdependent? The Tosafists (to B. Erubin 18b, item "and not the rear of the synagogue"), in relating to Tosefta Megillah, explain, "and it seems that this *tanna* holds that the *shekinah* is in the west."

Urbach, following their lead, states definitively, "The view that 'the *shekinah* is in the west' is reflected in the halakah that determined the form of the synagogue structure: 'The entrances of the synagogues are to be made only towards the east.'" Indeed, this ruling governed the construction of many synagogues that were uncovered both in the Land of Israel and in the Diaspora, such as that at Dura-Europos.[43] We have already noted earlier that the discussion in B. Baba Batra about the location of the *shekinah* is essentially theoretical, and we have now also shown its polemical significance against the heretics. These two factors render it difficult to reach a practical conclusion concerning the direction of prayer in the synagogue. As for Urbach's determination about the archaeological evidence, a deeper examination of the matter will show that one is not dealing with many synagogues. And even for those few that do have eastern entrances, there is little indication that the prayers of their congregants were directed toward the west. On the contrary, there are many proofs that they prayed in another direction—toward Jerusalem—which is 'a relative direction' depending upon the synagogue's location relative to Jerusalem, in keeping with the halakah in M. Berakot.[44]

In this vein, even the example of Dura-Europos cited by Urbach fails to support his position, because Dura-Europos is northeast of the Land of Israel and hence prayer there is toward the southwest, again in keeping with the halakah in M. Berakhot, and not because the *shekinah* is in the west.[45] In our opinion, the archaeological evidence actually proves that there is no connection between the law about entrances being in the east and the direction in which one prays the Tefillah. That is to say, what we have are two laws that are independent of each other:

1. The law in Mishnah Berakot about directing prayer toward the focal point of Jerusalem and the Temple, whose architectural realization depends upon the site of the synagogue in relation to that point.

---

[43] See Urbach, *Sages*, p. 62 [For the plan, see figures 1 and 2—Eds.]

[44] Urbach's interpretation serves as the basis for the opinion which has gained a foothold in the archaeological research, according to which in various synagogues the direction of prayer was westward, and only at a later stage was it diverted toward Jerusalem.

[45] In this connection it is difficult to accept Kraabel's categorical determination that "Rabbinic statements about synagogue architecture and usage are not concerned with the Diaspora." See Kraabel, pp. 500-505.

2. The law in Tosefta Megillah about setting synagogue entrances in the east.

It is worthy of note that even Maimonides, unlike the Tosafists, found no connection between the two halakot.[46] In the *Mishneh Torah* (Hilkot Tefillah 5:3), the law from Berakot is cited about directing prayer toward the Land of Israel first, then Jerusalem, the Temple mount, and the Holy of Holies. And in Hilkot Tefillah 18:2, the law from the Tosefta Megillah about the entrances in the east is quoted without making it contingent upon the location of the synagogue in relation to Jerusalem.[47] This means that the law about the entrances is not dependent upon the location of the synagogue in relation to Jerusalem and the direction to which the worshippers turn their faces.

THE HALAKIC RAMIFICATIONS OF THE ARCHITECTURAL PLAN

As we indicated at the end of our discussion of the typological aspect, we believe that basic to the design of the plans of the synagogues in Judea were the two fundamental laws which we have just treated at length: the law on the direction of prayer, and that of setting the entrances in the east. Before we deal with the practical application of these laws in Judea, let us examine their validity in other parts of Israel. The law that one should pray in the direction of Jerusalem took hold in the great majority of synagogues in the Land. With a few minor deviations here and there, they are Jerusalem-oriented.[48] In early synagogues of the Galilean type, the facade wall—in which the entrances were located—is oriented southward. By contrast, the late synagogues with the basilica plan have the entrances in the north; it is the southern wall with the apse and the Torah Ark that faces Jerusalem. On the other hand, few are the synagogues whose entrances are in the east.

In most of the synagogues, the entrances are on the same axis as the structure. In the Galilean synagogues, for example, the axis is north-south. This, then, is the axis of entrance and prayer. Even the rows of columns that divided the building's space into a central hall and two side areas were on that axis and merged architecturally with the internal flow within the synagogue.

Even in the 'deviant' synagogues, where the entrances were in the east, it is difficult to determine whether this was done out of halakhic principle, or

---

[46] See S. Goren, "Synagogue Entrances," *Mahanayim* 95 (1965): 9-14 (in Hebrew).

[47] Rabbi Isaac Alfasi, who preceded Maimonides, also followed this system. Ginzberg (*Commentary*, note 28, p. 393), however, criticized both their interpretations of the Tosefta in light of the archaeological finds known in his day, and wrote, "and the ancient synagogue entrances are 'witnesses to the contrary' concerning this interpretation."

[48] About exceptions in this sense, see below.

because of constraints of the place and other circumstances. In the north, this concern applies to the synagogues of Arbel, Ḥammat Gader, Ma'oz Ḥayyim, and perhaps, also, Hammath-Tiberias (the synagogue of Severus), as Ze'ev Weiss suggests.[49] In the first two instances, Sukenik has already shown that it was a result of topographical necessity and not principle.[50]

Outside of these, it should be noted that the synagogues of Sumaqa, Ḥusifa in the Carmel, and the synagogue of Japhia in the Lower Galilee, are 'deviant' in their orientation, for they are built on an east-west axis, and their prayer direction was apparently eastward, even though Jerusalem is south of them. Sukenik tried to cope with the difficulty of the unusual direction of these synagogues and explained that those on the Carmel, because of their proximity to the sea, were considered as western Eretz-Israel and therefore Jerusalem was, as it were, east of them.[51] Sukenik attempted to apply this explanation to the Japhia synagogue as well, although it is distant from the sea, and overcame this problem pilpulistically. According to him, it is possible to also include Japhia in the coastal region since it is still included within the territory of Zebulun of whom it is written: "Zebulun shall dwell by the seashore" (Gen. 49:13).[52] In our opinion, these forced explanations are very hard to accept. In the absence of any indications to that effect, it is also difficult to accept Goodenough's explanation that the Japhia synagogue was a wide structure with its Torah Ark on the south wall facing Jerusalem.[53]

In all of the above instances we have seen that Sukenik tried to find many different reasons for setting the entrances in the east and did not think that it was done for halakic reasons in compliance with Tosefta Megillah. In his perception, the law in the Tosefta was not relevant to the synagogues in the Land of Israel, and thus he followed in the footsteps of earlier investigators of the beginning of the twentieth century. The first of these was W. Bacher, who claimed that the *baraita* in question relates to the synagogues in Babylonia and the other places east of the Land of Israel in which, indeed, the prayer is oriented west, in the direction of Eretz-Israel, and therefore the entrances should be placed in the east.[54] S. Krauss continued in this way and

---

[49] See Z. Weiss, "The Synagogue at Hammath-Tiberias (Stratum II)," *EI*, 23 (1992): 320-326 (in Hebrew).

[50] See E. L. Sukenik, *The Ancient Synagogue of El-Ḥammeh* (Jerusalem, 1935), p. 168. As for the synagogue at Arbel, Kohl and Watzinger showed that the exception to the 'standard' plan was due to topographic circumstances. See Kohl and Watzinger, p. 60.

[51] See Sukenik, *El-Ḥammeh*, p. 170.

[52] See E. L. Sukenik, "The Ancient Synagogue at Yafa near Nazareth—Preliminary Report," *Rabinowitz Bulletin*, vol. 2, p. 24.

[53] See Goodenough, vol. 1, p. 216.

[54] See W. Bacher, "Synagogue," in J. Hastings, ed., *A Dictionary of the Bible*, vol. 4 (Edinburgh, 1902), p. 639.

raised various historical motives as the background to the halakah in the Tosefta about the entrances in the east.[55] Kohl and Watzinger also resolved the contradiction between the halakah in the Tosefta and the archaeological picture revealed by their excavations in this manner.[56]

Franz Landsberger, in an article published in 1957, argued against the stand taken by Bacher, Krauss, Kohl and Watzinger.[57] First, he contended that the halakah's reliance upon the location of the entrances in the Tabernacle attests that this is not a specific instruction, limited to the circumstances of Babylonia and the like, but a principle instruction for synagogues in general. In his opinion, the basis for this law is the desire to use the plan of the Tent of Meeting as a model, since the Second Temple, which lay in ruins, was no longer a suitable symbol. The direction, then, was not sacred; rather, adherence to the plan of the Tent of Meeting was imperative. And since its entrance was in the east, it should also be that way in the synagogues. Landsberger, then, moves the date of the law back to the destruction of the Temple (the year 70 C.E.), or thereabouts. He then surveys the synagogues that were known to him in which the entrances are found in the east (as stated, in the mid-50's): Arbel, Ḥammat Gader, Ḥusifa (in error, for its entrances are in the west; others also made this mistake), Sumaqa, Japhia (where the entrance was apparently to the west and therefore the synagogue is irrelevant to this discussion) and Eshtemoa. He differs with the practical-functional reasons put forth in every instance to explain the entrances set in the east. To sum up, based upon all the data, Landsberger's conclusion is that even in instances where the entrances were apparently located in the east for circumstances unrelated to the halakic tradition, these circumstances postdate the basic motivation which flowed from the halakic tradition of the model of the Tabernacle entrances and thus are additional to it.

In the generation that has elapsed since Landsberger's publication, additional synagogues have been uncovered whose entrances are in the east: Ma'oz Ḥayyim and Ḥorvat Susiya. Furthermore, of central importance to our interests, synagogues were discovered from the Second-Temple period at Masada, at Herodium, and apparently even at Gamala. This last datum made it possible to test Landsberger's theory. G. Foerster, in his discussion of the synagogues at Masada and Herodium followed in Landsberger's steps and argued that the fact that the direction of the entrances in the structures of the Second-Temple period is the same as that of the Temple entrances shows that these structures were planned according to the most sacred site in Israel,

55 See Krauss, pp. 223-230. See also J. Braslavi, "Symbols and Mythological Figures in the Early Synagogues of Galilee," in Hirschberg, p. 112, note 36.

56 See Kohl and Watzinger, p.139.

57 See Landsberger, p. 188.

when it was still standing on its mound.[58] According to Foerster, the synagogues at Masada and Herodium, as well as at Magdala and perhaps even at Chorazin, attest to the fact that the source of the halakah in the Tosefta Megillah is in the tradition that began in the days of the Second Temple.

Like his predecessor, Foerster also thought that this tradition was preserved in a number of synagogues of later periods: those on the Carmel and surrounding areas (Sumaqa, Ḥusifa, and Japhia),[59] those in South Judea (Eshtemoa and Susiya), and perhaps even the supposed synagogue at 'David's Tomb' on Mt. Zion.[60] Though at first glance it seems that Landsberger's theory has withstood the test of what actually exists, as Foerster tried to prove, a more critical examination indicates a number of weaknesses in their suggestion.

First, of the four synagogues with eastern entrances assigned to the Second-Temple period, only two, that is, Masada and Herodium, can be spoken about with any certainty. As for the structure at Magdala, E. Netzer has proven convincingly that it was not a synagogue but a well-house.[61] Incidentally, the building's entrance is in the north, not the east. The Chorazin building is difficult to relate to because its location today is unknown; except for its short description from 1926, there is no extant plan or photograph by which to judge its nature.[62]

At Masada and Herodium, the synagogues were Herodian *triclinia* that through internal architectural changes were converted by the Zealots to their new purpose. At Herodium, indeed, the entrance to the hall faces precisely to the east, but at Masada it faces southeast. If the tradition of entrances to the east were already extant and in force, the Zealots could have selected a building facing exactly eastward, of which there were not a few at Masada.[63]

As has been said, a public building of the Second-Temple period, supposedly a synagogue, has also been uncovered at Gamala, but its entrance is

---

58 See Foerster, "Masada & Herodion."

59 As I noted above, at Huseifa and Japhia the entrances were to the west and not to the east. Foerster also accepts Goodenough's opinion (Goodenough, vol. 1, p. 216) that these three synagogues were broad-houses whose focal point was on the south wall facing Jerusalem, see Foerster, "Masada & Herodion," p.11, note 28.

60 See J. Pinkerfeld, " David's Tomb—Notes on the History of the Building," *Rabinowitz Bulletin*, vol. 3, pp. 41-43. For an extended discussion of the details of this structure, see: Y. Tsafrir. "Zion—The Southwest Mound of the City of Jerusalem and its Place in the Byzantine Period," (Ph.D. thesis, Hebrew University of Jeruslam, 1975), pp. 197-205 (in Hebrew). We will not discuss this structure here since we have great doubt about its identification as a synagogue.

61 E. Netzer, "Was the Nymphaeum at Magdala Used as a Synagogue?" in A. Kasher et al., eds, *Synagogues in Antiquity* (Jerusalem, 1987), pp. 165-172 (in Hebrew).

62 See Foerster, "Masada & Herodion," p. 8.

63 E. Netzer, "The Herodian Triclinia—A Prototype for the 'Galilean-Type' Synagogue," in Levine, *ASR*, p. 51, note 5.

oriented not eastward but southwest.[64] Hence, of the three structures known to us and thought to be synagogues of Second Temple times—at Masada, Herodium and Gamala—only in one instance, that of Herodium, do the entrances face east. We can understand this in light of what has already been mentioned, that these structures were built with local improvisation and the adaptation of an ancient building to new needs, and its incorporation into a given architectural complex. Ehud Netzer and Zvi Ma'oz having already realized this, also rejected the attempt to link the entrances of the Second-Temple period's synagogues and the halakah in the Tosefta.[65] Now, having seen that the archaeological evidence is insufficient to prove the existence of the halakic tradition about the entrances from the Temple days, it is also difficult to prove its existence in the generations after the Destruction on the basis of those lone synagogues in the north of the country. These have entrances in the east and at least for part of which it has been proven conclusively that the reason was functional and not halakic.

Against this background, all the more outstanding is the phenomenon that the entrances in all four of the South Judean Hills synagogues are in the east. There is no other obvious reason for this and, therefore, it must be halakic. In our opinion, the halakic tradition whose roots were in the Temple and whose beginning was immediately after the Destruction, as Landsberger suggests, was preserved over the generations among the residents of southern Judea, while in the Galilee it was forgotten or never recognized at all.

The relative proximity of southern Judea to Jerusalem and the connection the southern Judeans felt with it, along with its being a rather isolated region far from the centers of foreign culture, brought about a much greater adherence to the traditions of the past from Second-Temple days and led to a decided conservatism. This was expressed, for example, in the extreme care exercised by the Judeans in laws of the priestly tithes, hallowed things, and forfeited properties (M. Hagigah 3:4; M. Nedarim 2:4); in preserving Hebrew as the spoken language as is proven by the synagogue inscriptions;[66] and by the continuation of the burial practices that characterized the Second-Temple period, that is, the gathering of bones in ossuaries even till the fourth century.[67] In light of this, even the great care to set the synagogue entrances in the east—"for we find that the Tabernacle was open to

---

[64] See Gutman, "Gamla"; Ma'oz, "Gamla."

[65] See Ma'oz, "Gamla," p. 40; Netzer, note 63 above.

[66] See S. Safrai, "The Synagogues South of Mount Judah," *Immanuel* 3 (1973-1974): 47-48.

[67] See N. Avigad, "Jewish Rock-cut Tombs in Jerusalem and in the Judaean Hill-Country," *EI* 8 (1967): 135-137 (in Hebrew); A. Kloner, "The Jewish Settlement in the Judean Lowlands in the Period of the Mishnah and the Talmud (after the Bar Kokhba Rebellion) According to the Archaeological Findings," M. Broshi et al., eds., *Between the Hermon and Sinai—Memorial to Amnon* (Jerusalem, 1977), pp. 191-193 (in Hebrew).

the east"—can be attributed to the linkage of the area's residents to Jerusalem and the Temple, and their close adherence to the customs of their fathers. It may be that along with the historical reason there may also have been the actual reason—to dissuade the heretics who bowed to the east—and all this against the background of the existence of a Christian population in South Judea, neighboring the Jewish settlements, and even in mixed settlements where Jewish communities existed. This arises from the literary sources headed by the *Onomasticon* of Eusebius who, already in his days (end of the third and start of the fourth centuries) lists two Christian settlements, Yattir and (eastern) Anaia,[68] and is verified by the discovery of many churches at regional sites.[69]

Setting the Judean synagogue entrances in the east forced the flow of those entering the synagogue into an east-west axis. On the other hand, the synagogue's focal point—the *bemah* and/or the alcove of the Torah Ark—was set in the northern wall, facing Jerusalem, and the prayer axis was south to north. That is to say, the worshipper was required to perform a ninety-degree turn after entering the synagogue hall.

We have, then, two intersecting axes—the east-west entrance axis and the south-north prayer axis. The excavators of the Susiya synagogue were already aware of the problematics of this arrangement and expressed it well, "In the Susiya synagogue, like the synagogue at Eshtemoa, one can find a contradiction between the direction of the building, which is clearly a long one with an east-west axis, and its facing toward Jerusalem, northward, which turns the hall itself into a wide one."[70] John Wilkinson suggested an explanation of his own for the "architectural contradiction," depending upon Urbach's interpretation above. In his opinion, in the synagogues where the entrances were in the east, such as those of Eshtemoa and Susiya, they first prayed toward the west according to the concept that "the *shekinah* is in the west." Only at a later stage, did they change the direction and shifted it toward Jerusalem by adding a *bemah* and Torah ark in that direction. The main basis of this theory is dependent upon an architectural analysis that Wilkinson made of the Eshtemoa synagogue's north wall. According to him, at first there was nothing special about this wall, and benches were built along its entire length; only at a later stage were the platform and holy ark set into it.[71] The first excavators of the Eshtemoa synagogue, Mayer and

[68] *Onomastikon*, 26:13, 108:1. See also J. Schwartz, "The Jewish Settlement in the Region of Judea and the South Coast in the Third and Fourth Centuries," in Baras, *Eretz Israel*, p. 193.

[69] See M. Kochavi, "The Land of Judah," in M. Kochavi, ed., *Judaea, Samaria and the Golan: Archaeological Survey 1967-1968* (Jerusalem, 1972), p. 24 (in Hebrew).

[70] See Gutman, Yeivin and Netzer, p. 48.

[71] See J. Wilkinson, "Orientation, Jewish and Christian," *PEQ* 116 (1984): 17-30. See also Seager's passionate critique in Seager, "Historiography," p. 87.

Reifenberg, had already pointed out the 'seam' between the western wall and the northern one.[72] But this should not be taken as evidence of different chronological stages, as Wilkinson did, but rather as technical stages in the construction of the site. Mayer and Reifenberg, and—following their lead—the last excavator of the site, Ze'ev Yeivin, even dwelt upon the changes that took place in the unit of the *bemah* and the Torah Ark in the course of the building's existence, primarily the enlargement and expansion of this region.[73] Still, there is no doubt that already at an early stage of the building a Torah Ark was placed in the center of the northern wall which indicated the direction of prayer toward Jerusalem. The development of platforms and Torah arks in the synagogues was an independent phenomenon with no connection to the change of the direction of prayer.[74] Now, when we also know that the synagogues of Maon and 'Anim are long buildings, and yet even there we have the aforementioned architectural arrangement, that is, an east-west entrance axis and a south-north prayer axis, it seems that the ground has been completely cut out from beneath Wilkinson's theory. We have proof that this architectural arrangement was planned from the start and is not the result of improvisations and later changes in the given structure. In our opinion, this arrangement, at the basis of whose planning lies, as it were, the above-mentioned 'contradiction,' is the architectural answer to the two halakic dictates which guided the planners and builders of the synagogues in Judea.

We theorize that the ancient architect coming to plan the building in light of these givens anguished over the problem of the axis on which he should place the rows of columns needed to support the roof. His decision is surprising in its originality: he decided to place no columns at all in the hall's expanse since placing them in one of the two possible axes would impede the 'free flow' along the opposing axis. This is unlike what we find in the Galilean synagogues where the entrance axis, the prayer axis, and the columns axis were parallel and overlapping one another.

An exception to this rule in the Galilee is the synagogue at Khirbet Shema', which has no parallel among the country's synagogues.[75] It can

---

[72] See Mayer & Reifenberg, pp. 316-317.

[73] See Mayer & Reifenberg, pp. 318-319; Z. Yeivin, "The Synagogue at Eshtemoa—Final Report," *Atiqot* (in preparation). Our thanks to Dr. Yeivin for permission to quote from the report even though it is not yet unpublished.

[74] And see in this matter G. Hütenmeister, "The Holy Ark and the Development of the Ancient Synagogues," *Proceedings of the Eighth World Congress of Jewish Studies*, vol. 1 (1984), pp. 1-6 (in Hebrew); Z. Weiss, "The Location of the 'Shaliaḥ Tzibbur' During Prayer," *Cathedra* 55 (1990): 8-21 (in Hebrew).

[75] This determination of ours does not take account of the suggestions of Goodenough (vol. 1, p. 216) and of Foerster ("Masada & Herodion," p. 11, note 28) in relation to the synagogues of Sumaqa, Ḥusifa and Jafia, for their suggestions have no basis in the findings at these sites.

serve as the "exception that proves the rule" and as the 'touchstone' negatively illustrating our argument. The two rows of columns that were erected in this wide space on an east-west axis, 'clash' with the prayer and main entrance axis and certainly caused difficulties for the activities in the synagogue hall. The problem of supporting the roof without columns in the Judean synagogues was solved by 'thickening' the north and south walls to three meters and more. How unusual and unexpected was this solution of 'removing' the columns from the expanse of the hall can be learned from the reactions of Mayer and Reifenberg, the excavators of the first synagogue of this group. They decided, in the absence of the columns in the hall, that "the columns upon which the roof rested were entirely destroyed."[76]

And indeed, the facades of the synagogues at Eshtemoa and Susiya with their three entrances—the main one in the center and the secondary ones at the sides—are similar in form to the facades of the synagogues with hall interiors that are divided into three sections.

In these synagogues, then, the 'broad house' model developed whose architectural significance was that the entrance axis (east-west) was 'preferred' over the prayer axis and the building was planned accordingly. It seems that this model was suited to the needs of the large settlements and allowed for a more complex building containing additional rooms for the various communal needs.

The wide model, albeit with columns, is known from a number of synagogues in the Land of Israel and the Diaspora of the period under consideration, and it raises various questions outside the parameters of this discussion.[77] In the small settlements of Maon and ''Anim they made do with a building humble in its dimensions and its plan, and therefore they apparently continued to use the routine long-house model.

As for the chronological framework, the developmental process of the types of Judean synagogues as presented here apparently began in the fourth century and continued in the fifth.[78] This was the same time that the Christian basilica model was being absorbed and adopted in the northern synagogues.[79]

[76] See Mayer & Reifenberg, p. 319.

[77] See L. A. Mayer, "Broad-house in Jewish Religious Art," *EI* 5 (1958): 238-239 (in Hebrew); H. Shanks, *Judaism in Stone* (Tel-Aviv, 1979), pp. 97-104.

[78] Since the complete reports of the excavations of the synagogues at Eshtemoa and Susiya have not yet been published, we do not have clear chronological data about them. However, for the synagogues of Maon and 'Anim we have proof of their establishment at the time indicated here.

[79] See Tsafrir, pp. 183-184, 289.

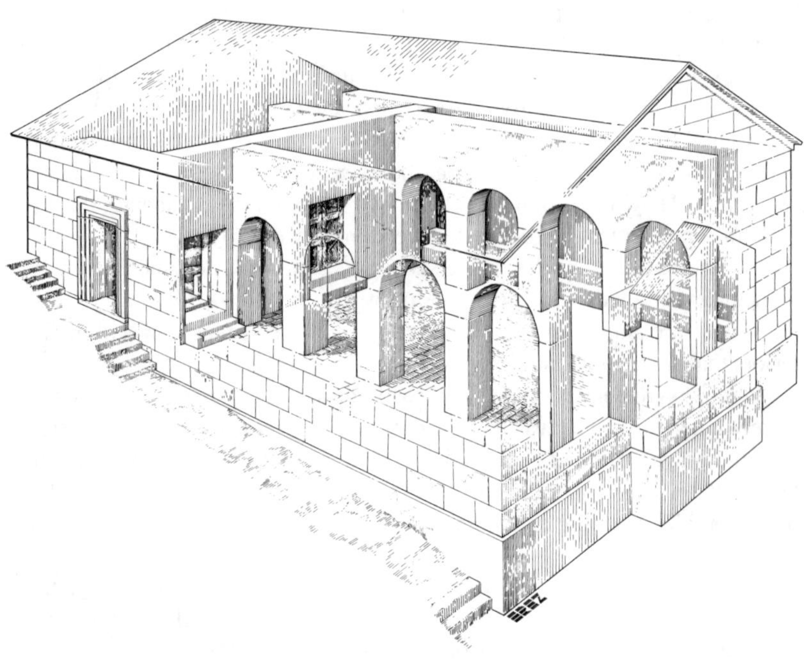

FIG. 7 Maon synagogue: Reconstruction of second phase.

The later stage in the Maon synagogue, (and similarly the later stage in the synagogue of Ḥorvat Rimmon[80] and apparently also at En-Gedi),[81] testifies that the independent and unique position of the Judean type, at least at this site, did not last long. During the last phase of the Byzantine period (the sixth and seventh centuries) this model made way for the basilica one which, in the other parts of the country, was already dominant in synagogue architecture. By contrast, in the wide synagogues of Susiya and Eshtemoa and the long synagogue at 'Anim, the original plan was preserved in spite of the basic renovations and interior changes that were made in these structures in the course of their prolonged existence.

---

80 See A. Kloner, "The Synagogues of Horvat Rimmon," in Hachlili, *Ancient Synagogues*, pp. 43-48 pl. XXV-XXVII.

81 See D. Barag, Y. Porath and E. Netzer, "The Synagogue at 'En-Gedi," Levine, *ASR*, pp. 116-119.

THE SYNAGOGUE OF ḤORVAT SUMAQA, 1983-1993*

SHIMON DAR & YOHANAN MINTZKER

Sumaqa was a Jewish village from the Rabbinic Period, located on Mount Carmel, two and a half kilometers south of Dalyat el-Carmel and five kilometers west of the summit of Mt. Carmel (*Deir el-Muḥraqa*) (Map ref. 1539-2307). The settlement was built on a rocky hill, 350 m. above sea level. Sumaqa had no perennial water source, so its inhabitants depended on rain water, collected in hewn underground water cisterns. The built-up area of the village was about 30 dunams (3 hectares) in size. The village's buildings were built of fine hard limestone quarried near Sumaqa.

The settlement is surrounded by a dozen workshops (their function not yet certain), half a dozen agricultural installations, oil and wine presses hewn into the rocks, and over 20 rock-cut burial caves.

EARLY EXPLORATIONS

The first scientific description of Ḥorvat Sumaqa was done by the British Survey of Western Palestine.[1] Their account identified the site as important, stating that it had numerous structures. The most prominent of these was the remains of an impressive building, identified by the surveyors as the village's synagogue. The British surveyors suggested, on the basis of the visible facade as well as of architectural details which have since disappeared, that the building was a synagogue of the type found at Bar'am and Meiron.[2] Other surveyors and scholars visited Sumaqa at the end of the nineteenth and the beginning of the twentieth century; among them were the Frenchman Victor Guerin, the Englishman Sir Lawrence Oliphant, and the German Graf

* Excavations were conducted from 1983-1993 under the auspices of the Land of Israel Studies Department of Bar-Ilan University, with the participation of the Carmel Field School of the Society for the Protection of Nature. The work was directed by Professor Shimon Dar, with Azriel Siegelmann and Dr. Yohanan Mintzker.

This study was supported in part by the Dr. Irving and Cherna Moskowitz Chair in Land of Israel Studies.

[1] C. R. Conder and H. H. Kitchener, *The Survey of Western Palestine*, vol. 1 (London 1881), pp. 318-320.

[2] *EAEITHL*, s.v. vol. 3, "Kefar Bir'am," pp. 704-707; "Meiron," pp. 856-862.

von Mülinen.[3] In 1905, the German scholars H. Kohl and C. Watzinger carried out excavations in the synagogue. Their excavation seems to have been rather limited, however, for their suggested reconstruction was based primarily on analogies drawn from the Galilean synagogues with which they were familiar.[4]

In more recent times, the area around Sumaqa was surveyed as part of the work of the Archaeological Survey of Israel; the survey was carried out by the northern team headed by Ya'aqov Olami.[5]

FIG. 8 Ḥ. Sumaqa: Aerial view, 1986.

1. The synagogue.
2. The oil press.
3. The underground cistern.
4. Dwelling quarters.
5. Workshop.

---

[3] M. V. Guerin, *Description Geographique, historique et archeologique de la Palestine. Galilee, 1-2* (Paris, 1880), pp. 297-298. L. Oliphant, *Haifa, or Life in Modern Palestine* (Edinburgh, 1887), pp. 94-95. Mülinen, Graf von, "Beitrage Zur Kenntnis des Karmels," *ZDPV* 31 (1908): 157-160.

[4] Kohl and Watzinger, pp. 145-147.

[5] H. P. Kuhnen, *Nordwest-Palastina in hellenistisch-römischer Zeit. Bauten und Graber im Karmelgebiet* (Weinheim, 1987), p. 89, taf. 6:2, 15:3, 24, 47:2, 52:3. H. P. Kuhnen, *Studien zur Chronologie und Siedlungsarchäologie des Karmel (Israel) zwischen Hellenismus und Spätantike* (Wiesbaden, 1989), p. 348, taf. 67:2. See also A. Kloner and Y. Olami, *Atlas of Haifa and the Carmel* (Haifa, 1980), pp. 38-43 (in Hebrew).

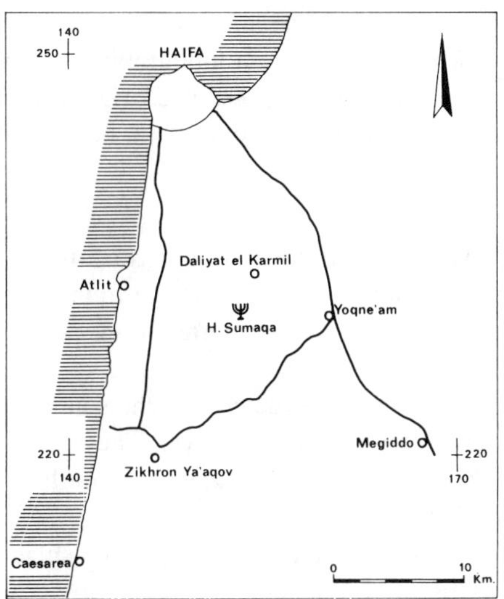

FIG. 9 Map of Carmel, with Ḥ. Sumaqa indicated.

THE IDENTIFICATION OF THE SITE

Sumaqa, or *sumaq* in Aramaic, is a bush today known as 'tanners sumaq' (*Rhus coriaria*). It was used up to modern times as a base for spices, medicines, and tanning.[6]

Several rabbinic scholars appear in talmudic literature with the name of *sumaq* or a name derived from it. S. Klein has argued that some of the scholars originated from the village of Sumaqa on the Carmel.[7] These include: Hilfi ben Samqai, referred to in Gen. R. 51:2; R. Tiifah Semuqa in Y. Dem. 3:4, 14a (Tiufah in Y. Yeb. 43b); and R. Abba Semuqa in Y. Ber. 9:1.

THE EXCAVATIONS OF 1983-1993: PRELIMINARY REPORT

The archaeological probes of Kohl and Watzinger were inconclusive, and as we studied the site we decided that their plan was based on too many unproved hypotheses. We figured as well that a scientific excavation would be a long process. Eleven seasons later, with only half of the synagogue excavated, we know we did not underestimate our task.

[6] D. Gera, "Tryphon's Sling Bullet from Dor," *IEJ* 35, nos. 2-3 (1985): 153-163.

[7] S. Klein, *Galilee* (Jerusalem, 1967), p. 129 (in Hebrew).

The synagogue was built on the southern slope of a hill. Phases of destruction and reconstruction built up a topography which was more than 3 meters higher in the north than the presumed original floor, whereas in the south it was necessary to dig down about 2.5 m. below this same level.

Description of the Excavations

We began our excavations with the eastern part of the synagogue, along its facade. We then moved to the south, where we found the foundation of the southern wall. In the 1990 season, we started to investigate the western part of the synagogue. (See FIG. 11.)

Since the synagogue was constructed into the southern face of a hill, the builders took steps to keep the building level. They cut into the bedrock on the building's northern side (wall W2) and built up the foundations on the southern side (wall W9). (See PL. 8b.)

The synagogue walls were constructed of large ashlar stones, shaped by combed-chisel dressing and assembled with fine joints without mortar. In the facade (the eastern wall, W1), we found evidence of three doors. The main entrance and the northern door were almost completely preserved (missing parts could be reconstructed from the description in *The Survey of Western Palestine*). The northern jamb of the southern door was found, but not *in situ*. The southern part of this facade wall was completely missing, while its northern part survived comparatively well. It should be noted that at the north end of this wall, where the building is cut into the hill, its lower part is dressed bedrock. In the interior, the walls were most probably plastered. (See PL. 7b.)

A sloped plaster revetment helped us reconstruct the northern wall (W2), which was built upon an artificial terrace cut into the bedrock. The terrace is about 125 cm. high. The southern wall (W9) was a different story. Initially, we found no traces of construction in the south. It was a hard decision to undertake excavations in the southeastern (L158) and southwestern (L157) corners, but it was worth it. We discovered in both *loci* the first course of ashlar stones—beautifully dressed like those in the eastern wall (W1)—built into a foundation trench cut out of the bedrock. On the northern side of the southern wall, directly upon the sloping bedrock (L280), we discovered a large accumulation of stones, with many architectural fragments.

Many surprises waited for us at the western wall (W15), where we found incomplete stages of construction. In the southwestern corner (L157), the bedrock was terraced in preparation for laying the foundation stones. In the northwestern corner (L171), we found two courses of stones; the southern part of these was never continued, and the northern part was built inside a natural cavity in the rock.

Sometime after the synagogue's initial construction, an east-west wall (W6) was added within the building, close to and paralleling the northern wall. This secondary wall was composed of many architectural fragments in reuse; it was built against the northern jamb of the facade's northern door and was finished with a new door jamb. This shows clearly that this wall was built at a time when the original building was altered. The inner surface of the wall was plastered, as well as a bench (W10) which was built against it on the southern side. (See PL. 8a.)

Inside the synagogue, a plastered, level floor stretches from the northeast corner (L386) to the southeast corner (L156) and then across toward the western wall, ending before reaching it in a room at L381. Indeed, in the west the plaster floor does not extend into the southwest corner, set off by locus 13 and the interior wall of W4. In the northern part of the room, the plaster of the floor climbs up to cover the bench at W10 and the lower part of the secondary wall W6. In the east, it ends against the facade wall (W1). In the southern side of the room, the plaster floor ends in a straight line (L6). The floor was built in three layers: (1) stone soling, (2) rammed lime with nicely crushed stones about 20 cm. thick, and (3) a hard lime plaster finish, about 86 mm. thick.

As of 1993, we do not know whether the plastered floor covers any earlier phases of construction, such as stylobates or column foundations. Nor have we arrived at a final conclusion about the relation between the floor and the five grooved columns which remain upright.

Reconstruction of Phases I to III

We discovered that there were three main phases of occupation of the site. (See FIG. 10.) Our reconstruction of the synagogue is based on a synthesis of two major components:

1. Analysis of the archaeological evidence.
2. A full inventory of architectural and ornamental fragments and debris.

Analysis of the many fragments and debris of columns revealed that two sets of Ionic columns existed in the first phase of the synagogue. The two sets of columns were identical in style, but differed in size. In our reconstruction, we suggest that the larger columns were placed inside the synagogue's main room, while the smaller ones were erected in the narthex (L285, L286, L287).

We were lucky enough to find architectural fragments which helped us work out a hypothetical reconstruction of the facade: lintels of doors, a conch which was the decoration used for the lintel of a window, a frieze which gave us the head angle of the gable, several types of cornices, and fragments of a three-dimensional statue of an eagle which might have stood above the lintel of the main doorway.

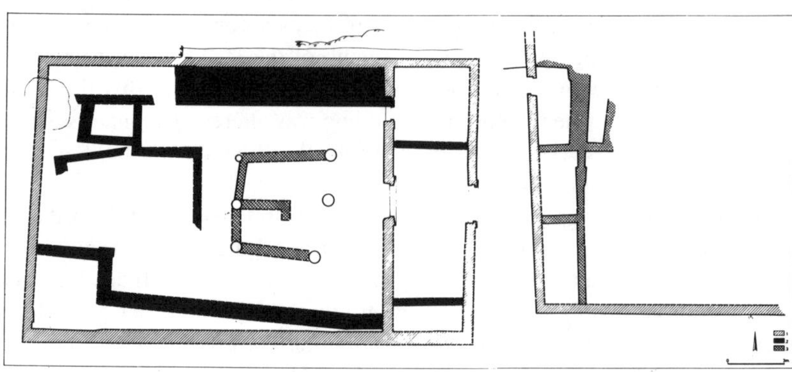

FIG. 10 The three phases of the synagogue's occupation.

In the present stage of research, we believe that the building of Phase I had a basilical plan, measuring 14.80 x 23.80 m. with the narthex, and that the synagogue adjusted itself to the difficult topography by quarrying in the north and adding fill in the south. Indeed, it is theoretically possible that Phase I was planned on a grand scale, but went through alterations in the course of its construction, and the original basilica-type structure was made smaller. The existence of a narthex that hides the imposing facade of this structure is puzzling. (See PL. 7b.) This phenomenon desires further study.

Phase I of the synagogue apparently belongs to the third century C.E., on the basis of pottery, coin finds, and architectural analysis. The site yielded a number of city coins of the second-third century C.E., several fragments of eastern *terra sigillata*, and the nozzle of a Herodian lamp. These finds suggest that there had been settlement on the site of the synagogue in the late second century C.E. Architectural and stylistic parallels show that this synagogue is similar to the Galilean synagogues of the older type, such as Bar'am, Meiron, Khirbet Shema', Gush Ḥalav and Chorazin.[8]

This first building was probably destroyed deliberately during the fourth or early fifth century C.E. The reason for the destruction could stem from local disturbances or from political persecution by the Christian Byzantine

[8] G. Foerster, "A Basilica Plan as a Chronological Criterion in Synagogues," *Synagogues in Antiquity*, A. Kasher et al., eds. (Jerusalem, 1987), pp. 173-179 (in Hebrew).

rulers against the Jewish communities in Palestine.[9] It is also possible that the Samaritan revolt, which spread even to the vicinity of Mount Carmel, was responsible.[10]

The building of Phase II went under extensive architectural modifications. The northern interior wall (W6) and its southern counterpart in L158 narrowed the original plan of the hall to the size of 10 x 15 m. approximately. The facade with the narthex was used in Phase II, but one of the side entrances was narrowed. Benches were added along the plastered walls, like the bench in the north (W10).

The western part of the synagogue was set apart from the main room by a wall, part of which was discovered in L381. This part of the synagogue was probably a courtyard with small rooms, like L384 in the northwest corner and L359 south of it.

Two *menorot* may also belong to this second phase. One was scratched on the front of the facade and the other on a building stone found in the excavation.[11]

Phase II can be dated to the fifth-seventh centuries C.E. The pottery and the coin finds point to the late Byzantine period. A small hoard of six Byzantine coins was discovered under the slabs in the room in the northeast corner (L286). The earliest coin was from Justin II (565-578 C.E.), and the latest was from the time of Heraclius (610-641 C.E.), minted in 618/619 C.E. We are not yet sure what kind of synagogue existed in Phase II, and there is a possibility that in the long period of Phase II, the building was used for different purposes.

It seems that in the early Moslem period the synagogue and its vicinity was abandoned. Phase III—the latest one in the history of the building—thus belongs to the Middle Ages, 11th-15th centuries C.E. (See PL. 9b.)

The residents of this building in the Middle Ages used only parts of it. Kitchenware, animal bones and ovens were found in the partly used eastern hall. (See PL. 9a.) The building did not serve as a synagogue during this

[9] G. Foerster, "The Synagogues in Galilee," in A. Shemueli et al, eds., *The Lands of Galilee* (Haifa, 1983), vol. 1, pp. 231-256 (in Hebrew).

[10] M. Avi-Yonah, "The Samaritan Revolts against the Byzantine Empire," *EI* 4 (1956): 127-132 (in Hebrew); J. Ben-Zvi, *The Book of the Samaritans*, rev. ed. (Jerusalem, 1970), pp. 97-98 (in Hebrew); S. Dar, "Archaeological Evidence on the Samaritan Revolts of the Byzantine Period," in D. Jacoby, Y. Tsafrir, eds., *Jews, Samaritans and Christians in Byzantine Palestine* (Jerusalem, 1988), pp. 228-237 (in Hebrew); Leah DiSegni, "Rebellions of Samaritans in Palestine in the Romano-Byzantine Period," in A. Crown et al, eds., *A Companion to Samaritan Studies* (Tübingen, 1993), pp. 199-201.

[11] S. Dar, "The Synagogue at Khirbet Sumaqa on Mt. Carmel," in *Synagogues in Antiquity*, A. Kasher et al, eds., (Jerusalem, 1987), pp. 213-230 (in Hebrew); S. Dar, "Horvat Sumaqa: Settlement from the Roman and Byzantine Periods," *BAIAS* 8 (1988-9): 34-48. *Menorot* were also found in nearby burial caves, see PL. 7a.

period. The Middle Ages inhabitants preferred the eastern buildings opposite the synagogue (L355, L387).

The roof of phases II-III was probably supported by six pillars, four of them grooved. It seems that these grooved pillars were brought to the synagogue from the nearby workshops, and do not belong to the original building.

During the Middle Ages, the vicinity of Sumaqa belonged at first to the Crusaders, but following military defeats it was handed over to the Mamelukes.[12] The site appears to have remained deserted during the Ottoman Period.

[12] D. Barag, "A New Source concerning the Ultimate Borders of the Latin Kingdom of Jerusalem," *IEJ* 29 (1979): 197-217.

FIG. 11 Ḥ. Sumaqa: Map of excavation indicating loci.

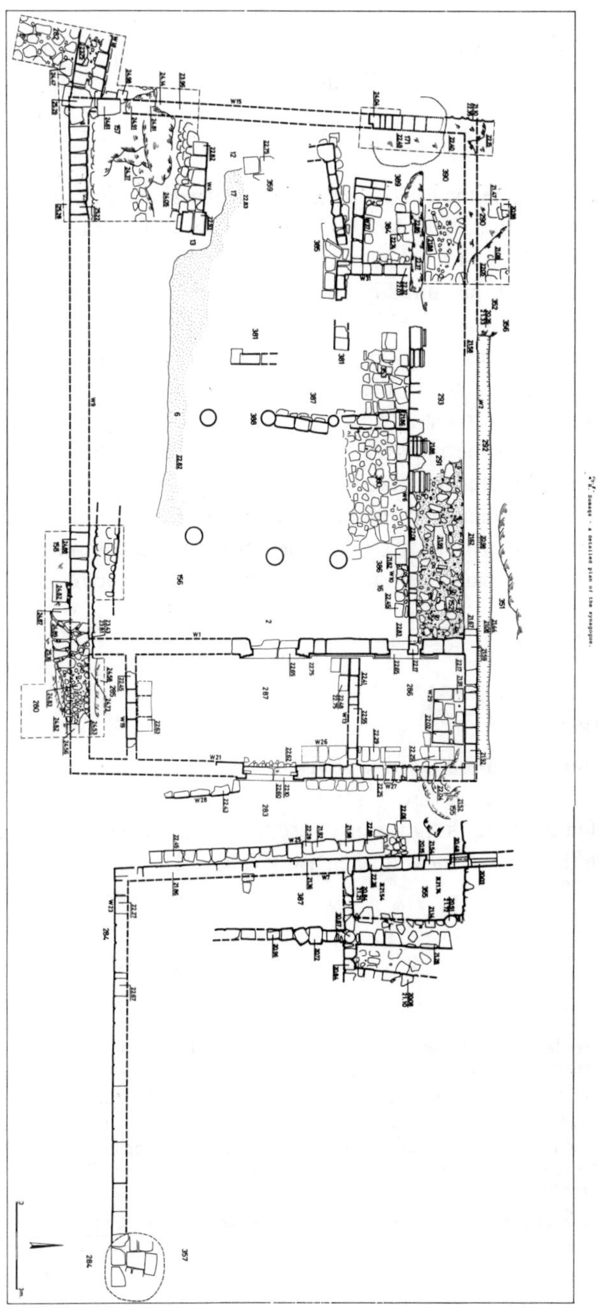

ANCIENT SYNAGOGUES IN THE EASTERN LOWER GALILEE*

ZVI GAL

In the decades since the 1920's, remains of several ancient synagogues have been discovered in eastern lower Galilee. Many of these have basalt lintels decorated with seven-branched menorahs and other Jewish symbols. Most of the material which has already been published from this area is related to synagogues of the type called 'Galilean' and has been dated to the second and third centuries of the common era. In an archaeological survey which was conducted by the author in the basalt plateaus of this region (the Issachar plateaus) further discoveries were made. Together with previous finds, these shed new light on the nature of Jewish settlement in the area.[1] These remains are closely related to those of the nearby Bet-Shean and Harod valleys. This essay will discuss finds at the more important sites in the eastern lower Galilee surveyed by this writer and then analyze their implications for our understanding of Jewish settlement and synagogues in the region.[2]

FINDINGS

Saronah (R.P. 1949-2355)

A basalt lintel decorated with a seven-branched menorah, on either side of which are two standing birds, was found in the ruins of the Arab village of Saronah. On the lintel's right side a rosette appears, which presumably had a parallel on the left side now broken away (FIG. 12).[3]

---

* This article was first published in Ely Schiller, ed., *Zev Vilnay's Jubilee Volume* (Jerusalem, 1984), pp. 263-266 (in Hebrew). It is translated with the permission of the author, the editor, and Ariel Publishing House. It was translated by Ms. Bati Leviteh.

[1] The survey was conducted by the writer on behalf of the Israel Archaeological Survey Association, with the help of the Gilboa field school of the Society for the Protection of Nature. A previous survey of the area was made by N. Tzori. See N. Tzori, *Naḥalt Issachar* (Jerusalem, 1977) (in Hebrew).

[2] See map in FIG. 18. The region under discussion lies in southeastern Galilee.

[3] E. L. Sukenik, "Remains of an Ancient Synagogue in Saronah near Yavniel," *Zion* 5 (1933): 93-97 (in Hebrew).

FIG. 12 Lintel from Saronah.

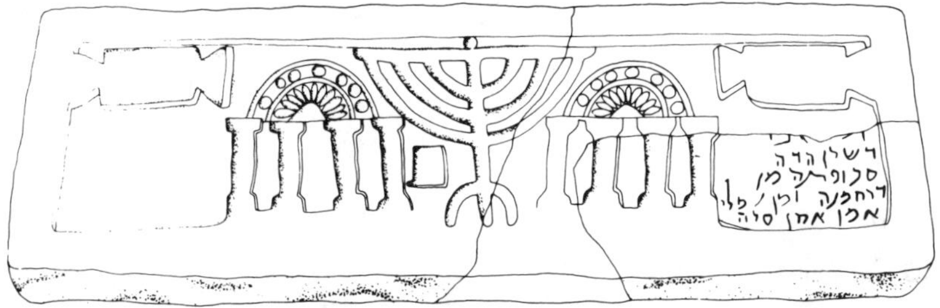

FIG. 13 Lintel from Kokav Ha-Yarden.

Kokav ha-Yarden

Several stones decorated with floral and geometric patterns were found in the ruins of the Crusader fort. These stones were originally part of a synagogue at this site.[4] The most important find was a basalt lintel with a seven-branched menorah at its center. On either side of the menorah appears a relief of a colonnade, topped by a conch-like decoration. The lintel also contained a dedicatory inscription in Aramaic and two *tabula ansata* (FIG. 13). The ancient settlement of Kokav ha-Yarden was located on a natural terrace at the foot of the Crusader fort. On this terrace the remains of a building which can be identified as a synagogue were exposed. These remains included broken basalt columns and an Ionic capital. The remains were dated to the second and third centuries C.E. and associated with a Galilean-type synagogue.

Danah (R.P. 1928-2244)

Several years ago a basalt lintel was found in the ruins of the Arab village of Danah. In its center appears a seven-branched menorah with incense shovels on either side (FIG. 14).[5] This survey has located several more items

[4] M. Ben-Dov, "Remains of a synagogue in Kokav ha-Yarden and the location of Grophina in the Gilead," in *The Land of Samaria* (Jerusalem, 1973), pp. 86-98 (in Hebrew).

[5] G. Foerster, "A Menorah on a lintel from Danah," *Atiqot* 3 (1966): 66-67 (in Hebrew).

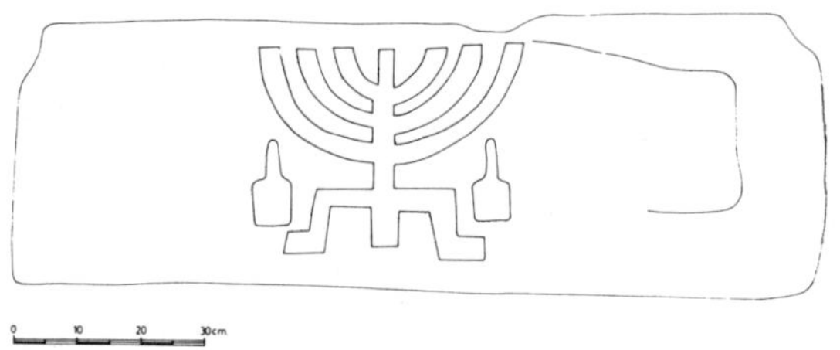

FIG. 14 Lintel from Danah.

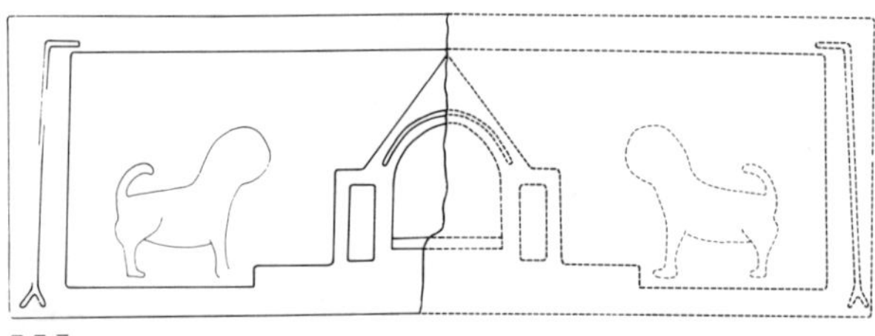

FIG. 15 Lintel from Danah.

belonging to the synagogue, among them basalt columns, column bases, and a broken lintel. The lintel is 0.7 m. in length and 0.5 m. high. A relief representing a colonnade topped by a gable adorns this lintel. To the left of this decoration there is a worn relief that can be identified as the figure of a lion facing toward a central opening. It may be concluded that this lintel was decorated with reliefs of lions facing a central opening from either side (FIG. 15).

Decorations of lions facing each other are not common in Galilean synagogues, and are particularly rare on lintels. Single parallels of this lintel type are known from Umm el-Amed[6] and Ḥorvat Sumaqa.[7] The stone with a lion relief from Nabratein might belong to this lintel type.[8] In contrast to this, facing lion decorations were common in the mosaic floors of synagogues of the 'late' type.[9]

Kafra (R.P. 1965-2220)

Pieces of columns and capitals were found at this site during the present survey. Among them was a basalt stone with a serrated profile. This stone was decorated with a relief showing a seven-branched menorah accompanied

---

[6] Goodenough, vol. 3, fig. 509.

[7] Goodenough, vol. 3, fig. 536.

[8] Goodenough, vol. 3, fig. 523.

[9] For examples, see Beth Alpha, Ḥammat Gader, Hammath-Tiberius, Na'aran, and Ma'on.

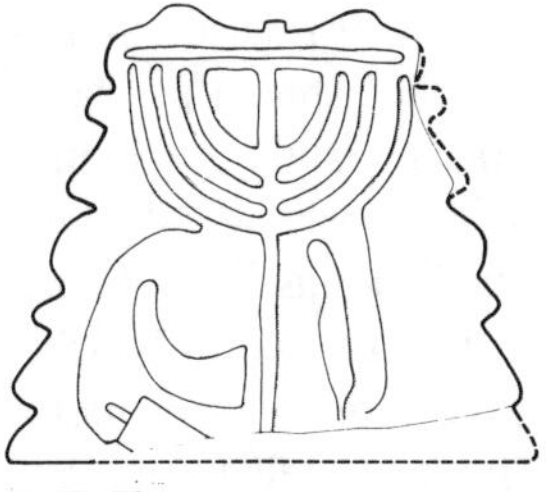

FIG. 16 Lintel from Kafra.

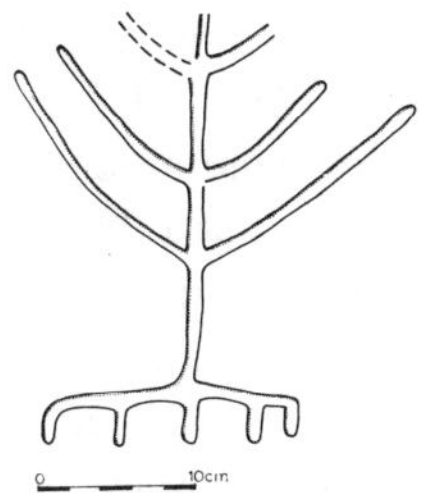

FIG. 17 Lintel from Kh. Riv.

by a shofar, a *lulav*, and an incense shovel. It is possible that the stone was part of a Corinthian capital which supported the lintel above the synagogue entrance. The lower part of the stone, triangular in shape, is broken away, making it impossible to recover the shape of the menorah's base. The branches, however, are clearly connected by a horizontal line. Although this stone has an unusual shape, its motifs are common ones on synagogue lintels and in mosaic floors (FIG. 16).

Khirbet Riv (R.P. 1943-2262)

A carved lintel showing a seven-branched menorah in relief was found in the opening of a large cave at this site (FIG. 17). Although the branches of this menorah are similar to examples found at Bet She'arim, the base, which has four legs, is of an uncommon design.[10] The cave in which the lintel was found might have been used in its earliest phase for burials and later enlarged for a different use. It is more probable, however, that the cave was originally used as a dwelling.

ANALYSIS

Many lintels decorated with menorahs and other Jewish symbols are known to us. Some of these are found at the entrances to burial caves (such as the one found in Tamrah in the western Galilee) while others adorn synagogue entrances.[11] Of the latter, several are known. A lintel was found at Japhia, on which is engraved a menorah with a rosette on the right and on the left,[12] while Nabratain unveiled a splendid lintel portraying a menorah decorated with a laurel. This was accompanied by an Aramaic inscription dating the

[10] N. Avigad, *Beth-Shearim*, vol. 3 (Jerusalem, 1971), p. 198, note 12 (in Hebrew).

[11] N Avigad, "Jewish Art Remains in the Galilee," *EI* 7 (1969): 24-28 (in Hebrew).

[12] L. H. Vincent, " Vestiges d'une Synagogue Antique a Yafa de Galilee," *RB* 30 (1921): 434-438.

lintel to the sixth century C.E.—although Avigad correctly regards the inscription as a later addition.[13] In the synagogue of Khirbet Shema', excavators found a menorah-decorated lintel, dated to the fourth century.[14] A similarly decorated lintel from Ḥorvat Kishor in the Shephelah was dated to the fifth century.[15] Other lintels are known from sites like Tiberias,[16] the Golan Heights,[17] and Eshtemoa.[18] The different lintel dates, besides that of Khirbet Shema', were suggested according to stylistic and typological considerations; it may be possible to date the eastern lower Galilee lintels to the fifth century and sixth century, according to Professor A. Negev's classification.[19] It is noteworthy that menorah-decorated lintels are not common in the Galilee, and neither are the shofar, *lulav* or shovel decorations, which appear only seldom—mainly on capitals as at Capernaum and 'En Nashuṭ.

The objects that were found in the survey sites have many similarities to the architectural style of the so-called Galilean synagogues, but the motifs appearing on them are widespread in mosaic floors of synagogues known as 'late' type. These are a group of lintels originating in a given area, and in spite of the difficulty of dating them because they are only survey finds, we cannot ignore the question of these finds' relation to the mosaic-floored synagogues found in the nearby Bet-Shean valley. Six mosaic-floored synagogues are presently known in the Bet-Shean and Harod valleys:

(1) Beth Alpha[20]
(2) Tel Menorah, near Tirat Zvi[21]
(3) Bet-Shean, outside of the Byzantine city wall[22]
(4) Ma'oz Ḥayyim[23]
(5) Rehob[24]

---

[13] N. Avigad, "Dating the Inscription of the Lintel from the Ancient Synagogue at Nevoraya," *Yediot*, A, 35 (1960): 136-145 (in Hebrew).

[14] *Khirbet Shema'*, p. 175.

[15] A. Kloner, "A Lintel with a Menorah Relief from Ḥorvat Kishor in the Shephelah," *Qadmoniot* 9 (1976): 81-82 (in Hebrew).

[16] G. Foester, "Some Unpublished Menorah reliefs from Galilee," *Atiqot* 7 (1974): 77-80 (in Hebrew).

[17] Goodenough, vol. 5, figs. 577, 578, 581.

[18] *Qadmoniot* 5 (1972): 45 (in Hebrew).

[19] A. Negev, "The Chronology of the Seven-Branched Menorah," *EI* 8 (1967): 193-210 (in Hebrew).

[20] Sukenik, *Bet Alpha*.

[21] S. Goldschmidt, "Remains of a Synagogue at the Tel of Kefar Qarnaim" *EI* 11 (1973): 39-40 (in Hebrew).

[22] N. Zori, "The Ancient Synagogue at Bet-Shean," *EI* 9 (1967):146-167 (in Hebrew).

[23] V. Tzaferis, "The Ancient Synagogue at Ma'oz Ḥayyim" *Qadmoniot* 8 (1974): 111-113 (in Hebrew).

[24] F. Vitto, "The Ancient Synagogue at Rehob," *Qadmoniot* 8 (1974): 119-123 (in Hebrew).

(6) Bet-Shean, a chapel in the House of Leontis, within the boundaries of the Byzantine city[25]

The analysis of the synagogues in the northern valleys and the basalt plateaus of the Lower Galilee is integrally linked to an understanding of the mutual relations between the plateaus and the Bet-Shean and Harod valleys. These relations originated in the different ecological conditions of the two geographical regions, and existed throughout the history of ancient settlement in those areas. The lower Galilean plateaus are characterized by their vast basalt covering that formed rocky ground which was difficult to cultivate. These plateaus are almost entirely lacking any year-round water source, and are bisected to a considerable depth by the wadies of Yavniel in the north, Tabor in the center, and Issachar in the south. In the bottom of these wadies are several springs, which comprise the area's only water sources. Stretched out around the basalt plateaus are the valleys of Jordan, Bet-Shean, Harod and Jezreel with their fertile soil and plenitude of water sources. These factors contribute to establish dense settlement and support it through all of the ancient periods.

The results of the archaeological survey reveal that the Issachar plateaus were a marginal area whose settlement was connected to conditions in the valleys.[26] This means that the development of the settlement in the marginal area was influenced by factors that affected the ancient settlement of the valleys, like the security conditions, economical stability, and perhaps also socio-ethnic processes. Thus the history of ancient settlement in the Issachar plateaus and its archaeological remains could be described as a reflection of the ancient settlement history in the nearby valleys. This concept of settlement in the Issachar basalt plateaus is the key to understanding the archaeological remains of the different periods.

From the theory outlined above, we can surmise that the unprecedented expansion of settlement in the valleys during the Roman-Byzantine period caused a similar phenomenon in the eastern lower Galilee. Furthermore, the archaeological finds indicate that this settlement was ethnically uniform; it combined a network of Jewish settlements in the valleys of Bet-Shean and Harod with the marginal area in the Issachar plateaus.[27]

Based on the regional characteristics described above, the comparison between the remains of the Jewish settlements in the valleys and those of

---

[25] D. Bahat, "The Synagogue at Bet-Shean—a Preliminary Review," *Qadmoniot* 5 (1972): 55-58 (in Hebrew).

[26] Z. Gal, *Ramat Issachar—Ancient Settlement in a Marginal Area* (Tel Aviv, 1980) (in Hebrew).

[27] Several names of Jewish settlements in the valleys and the basalt plateaus are known in Jewish sources: Tiv'on, Ginegar, Gevul and Sargonim. All of these are in complete antithesis to the large urban center at Bet-Shean/Scythopolis, which was a gentile enclave within the heart of the Jewish rural settlement.

the Issachar plateaus raises a significant phenomenon in the geographical history of the two areas. In the valleys, there are synagogues with mosaic floors, dated to the fifth and sixth centuries, while on the plateaus, the remains of synagogues are apparently similar to second- and third-century Galilean synagogues. This diversity creates a situation in which, for the first time in the history of the area, there was a period of prosperity in the valleys (the largest until that time) that did not affect the marginal area of the Issachar plateaus. It seems that when the eastern lower Galilee (the Issachar plateaus) had a large Jewish population in the second and third centuries C.E., the valleys were not occupied simultaneaously. And vice versa—when the valleys were settled by Jews in the fifth and sixth centuries, the basalt plateaus were not likewise settled. The solution to this conundrum lies in the overlapping of the construction date of mosaic-floored synagogues in the valleys with that of the building of the so-called 'Galilean' type synagogues in the Issachar plateaus.

In light of the finds discussed above, the mutual relations between the valleys and their marginal areas, and possibly also the decorative motifs (shofar, shovel, and *lulav*) found in them, it is argued that the lintels found in the survey of the Issachar plateaus originated in later fourth- and fifth-century synagogues. This conclusion balances the understanding of the valleys' and the Issachar plateaus' archaeological finds and their historical significance. It leads to the possibility that some of the Galilean synagogues could be dated to the fourth or fifth century. This conclusion is supported by the results from the Khirbet Shema' excavations[28] and by new finds from Capernaum.[29] Furthermore, the date is similar to that of the construction of several mosaic-floored synagogues in some of which parts of floors earlier than the fifth or sixth centuries were exposed.

To conclude, it seems that the analysis of ancient settlement patterns in the eastern lower Galilee—beginning with the ecological conditions and continuing with the settlement-geographic characteristics of the area—could be of considerable importance in issues only indirectly connected to the subject itself. It has been shown how regional characteristics produce different architectural styles and establish local traditions and customs expressed in the styles of synagogue construction. It now seems that the settlement-geographical considerations behind the understanding of the settlement patterns in the Issachar plateaus should be added to the new and variegated criteria of synagogue classification. In this light, the traditional classification of ancient synagogues should be reexamined.

---

28 See *Khirbet Shema'*, p. 175.

29 Loffreda, "Capernaum."

FIG. 18 Map of southeastern Lower Galilee

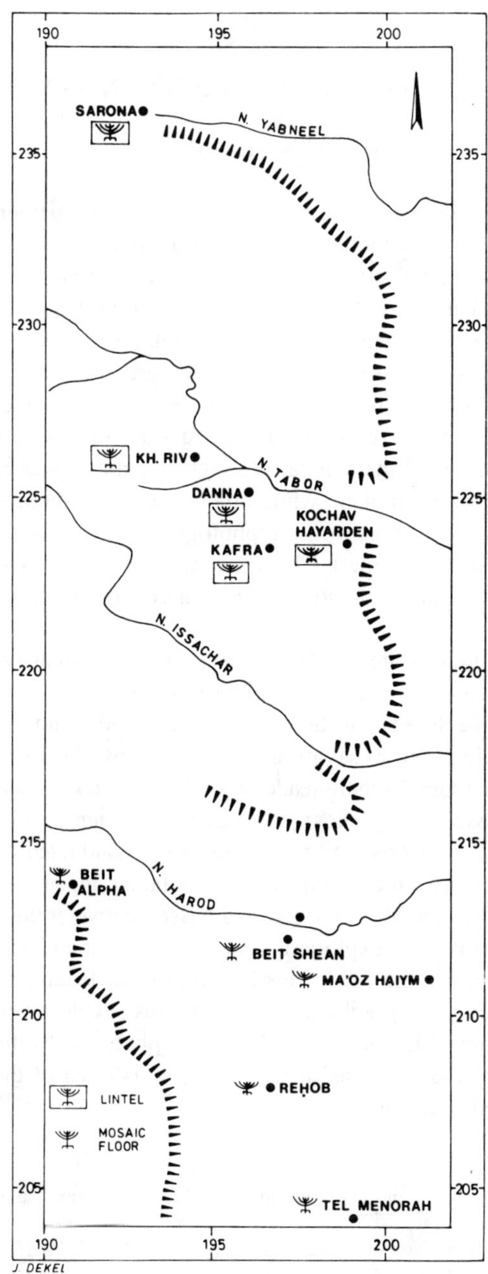

EARLY PHOTOGRAPHS OF GALILEAN SYNAGOGUES

DAN URMAN*

In 1990, when I was a visiting professor at the Department of Western Asiatic Archaeology of the University of London, I worked at the Library and Archives of the Palestine Exploration Fund on a number of occasions. On one of my visits there, Shimon Gibson—who at that time was working on the reorganization, identification, and cataloguing of the Fund's photograph collection—showed me a group of photographs of ancient synagogues in the Galilee. Some of these had been published and some had not. The photographs had been taken in the 1860's and the 1870's by P.E.F. personnel.[1] The condition of their negatives—glass plates—was not the best: a few of the plates were broken, while others were scratched. At my request, Mr. Gibson prepared prints of these photographs for me and, with the gracious consent of Dr. Rupert Chapman, the Executive Secretary of the Palestine Exploration Fund and Mr. Shimon Gibson, I am publishing them here.

These photographs are of obvious importance, primarily as historical documents revealing the archaeological circumstances of Galilean synagogues during the surveys at these sites in the 1860's and1870's. This was before the exploratory excavations conducted by the expedition of the Deutschen Orient-Gesellschaft headed by H. Kohl and C. Watzinger in 1905. Following the exploratory excavations of the Germans, additional excavations, conservation efforts, and restoration were conducted at these sites in the twentieth century which completely altered their appearance. It should be pointed out that in the 30 years that had passed between the surveys of the P.E.F. personnel and the exploratory excavations of the Germans, there had also been changes in the field. This becomes clear from a comparison between the P.E.F. photographs and the Germans' exploratory excavations; some archaeological items seen in the P.E.F. photographs disappeared and were lost before the Germans' activity. Below is a list of the photographs with a few added comments:

---

* In memory of my friend and colleague Zvi Ilan. This essay was translated by Dr. Nathan H. Reisner.

[1] See C. W. Wilson, "Notes on Jewish Synagogues in Galilee," *PEFQS* (1869): 37-42; H. H. Kitchener, "List of Photographs taken in Galilee, with Descriptions," *PEFQS* (1878): 134-141.

Plate 10a—Arbel (Arbela): looking from south to north over the remains of the synagogue that remained *in situ*. It seems that this photograph, like #2, was taken during the brief examination conducted there by C. W. Wilson in 1866. It is interesting to note that this photograph was also published by Watzinger (see Kohl and Watzinger, p. 61, Fig. 114). He pointed out that when they were working there, the column standing on the left side of the photograph was then lying on the ground.

Plate 10b—Arbel (Arbela): looking from north to south at the remains of the entrance and columns that survived *in situ*. To enhance the photograph, a number of decorated archaeological items were placed in the foreground that were not found *in situ* but which were apparently collected in the general area of the ruins. Among the items, it is possible to make out three Corinthian capitals (one of them smaller than the other two), an Ionic column, parts of column drums, a column base (apparently the one that was later published in Kohl and Watzinger (p. 66, Fig. 121), a cornice fragment (lying between the two large Corinthian capitals), as well as a lintel (?) fragment with a triglyphon decoration (standing atop the Ionic capital, cf. Kohl and Watzinger, p. 69, Fig. 131). Between the two columns standing *in situ*, it is also possible to discern a half-colonette that was also published by Watzinger (p. 68, Fig. 129). Finally, let us note that in front of the seated man it is possible to clearly make out the mounds of earth of the exploratory excavation conducted at the structure by C. W. Wilson in 1866.

Plate 11a—Bar'am: looking south-west to north-east at the facade and the remains of the porch of the structure designated as 'the Great Synagogue' (to differentiate it from 'the small synagogue,' the remains of which are about 400 meters north of it—see Photo. #7). Regretfully, the negative of this photograph is cracked and defective. Nevertheless, the reader can see that when the photograph was taken, an Arab family had built a house—whose roof was made of wooden boards, reeds, and pressed earth—in the midst of the ancient ruins. Above the lintel of the western window, it is possible to discern a stone which served as a pulley-block to fasten the roof of the Arab building. A comparison of this photograph with those taken there in the course of the twentieth century (Kohl and Watzinger, p. 95, Fig. 182 and N. Avigad, "Bar'am," in *NEAEHL*, vol. 1, p. 149) shows that in the nineteenth century, the east window lintel was still intact. It may be that the lintel was broken at the start of the twentieth century when the Arab house situated in the ancient structure was dismantled.

Plate 11b—Bar'am: looking from south-west to north-east at a segment of the facade wall from the porch in front of it to the Great Synagogue.

Plate 12a—Bar'am: looking from south-east to north-west upon the remains of the Great Synagogue and the Arab structure that was built within it during the nineteenth century. To the right of the Arab structure, it is possible to make out a corner column standing *in situ*, in its full height, in the northern part of the synagogue hall.

Plate 12b—Bar'am: looking at the central entranceway in the wall of the southern facade of the Great Synagogue structure. Note that the residents of the Arab house made secondary use of the ancient building stones. To our regret, the glass negative of the photograph is also cracked and defective.

Plate 13a—Bar'am: looking from north to south at the remains of the 'small synagogue.' As we know, these remains disappeared from the area at the end of the nineteenth century (see Watzinger's testimony in Kohl and Watzinger, p. 89). Yet in 1966, as part of a survey of the abandoned Arab villages in Galilee (unpublished), the location of the 'small synagogue' could be discerned and it was possible to make out the stones of the threshold of the entranceway visible in the photograph, as well as the fragment of the 'heart-shaped' corner-column. Other architectural items from the structure were found incorporated in secondary use in the house of the Arab village.

Plate 13b—Capernaum: a general view of the area of the ruins of the synagogue in the 1860's.

Plate 14a—Capernaum: a view of a number of decorated architectural items found near the ruins of the synagogue by C. W. Wilson and R. E. Anderson, when they conducted a brief exploratory excavation there in 1866. It appears that the photograph was taken near the west wall of the building complex, and it is possible to see that a number of the small items were deliberately set there to enhance the photograph. Prominent on the left is a frieze fragment decorated with a row of acanthus leaves, and on the fragment's right end, there appears the famous relief of a temple resembling a wheeled chariot that many investigators assume is a Torah ark.[2] Above this fragment, two more fragments from the same acanthus leave decoration can be seen. Standing above them, atop an inverted Corinthian capital, there appears an item with a conch decoration. The latter item was attributed by Kohl and Watzinger to one of the building's windows (Kohl and Watzinger, p. 8), as was the item with the double half-colonette with Corinthian capitals that appears in the center of the photograph.

Plate 14b—Capernaum: a view of the various decorated architectural items that were found in the ruins of the synagogue structure in the 1860's.

Plate 15a—Chorazin: a view of decorated architectural items in the area of the ruins of the synagogue before its excavation.

Plate 15b—Chorazin: part of a gable on which there is a relief of a lion. This photograph was published at the time by R. A. S. Macalister in *A Century of Excavation in Palestine*, first published in London in 1925 (in

---

[2] For an extended discussion of this frieze, see Goodenough, vol. 1, pp. 187-188.

the second edition, the photograph appears between pp. 314-315). In the discussions of Chorazin in recent decades (see, for example, Z. Yeivin, "Chorazin," in *NEAEHL*, vol. 1, pp. 301-304), this item is not mentioned and seems to have escaped the notice of more-recent scholars.

Plate 16a—Meiron: looking from south to north at the remains of the synagogue's facade wall. A comparison of this photograph (whose negative is flaking) with that published by Kohl and Watzinger (Kohl and Watzinger, p. 93, Fig. 163) shows that in the period between the P.E.F. surveys and the German expedition at the site, three of the five parts of the cornice that were set atop the lintel of the central entranceway of the facade wall have vanished.

Plate 16b—Nabratein: the lintel of the entrance to the synagogue, as it was found by the P.E.F. personnel.

SECTION IV

THE SYNAGOGUE'S NATURE AND THE JEWISH COMMUNITY

THE COMMUNAL FUNCTIONS OF THE SYNAGOGUE IN THE LAND OF ISRAEL IN THE RABBINIC PERIOD

ZEEV SAFRAI*

The synagogue (*bet kneset*) is one of the main institutions characteristic of the public and religious life of the Jewish people from as early as the Hasmoneans.[1] During the Hasmonean and Rabbinic periods, the *bet ha-kneset* was the most prominent—and often the only—public structure in the Jewish cities of Israel and the Diaspora. In this article we shall attempt to review the synagogue's communal functions, and especially its role in the civic affairs organized by the autonomous Jewish leadership. These functions will include without distinction both organized civic activity and regular public activity. But we shall not address synagogue prayer, for it alone would take up the entire essay.

This topic is a chapter in a much broader subject—communal and civic activities in the Jewish town. We shall not be able to treat all of these questions. The Jewish community of this period was very developed and the matters that the community leadership handled were varied: education, charity, internal security, water supply, sewage, economic and other services.[2] Within this constellation of responsibilities, the *bet ha-kneset* played an important role and we shall attempt to clarify and detail its functions.

The primary function of the *bet ha-kneset* was not as a place of public prayer but as a place for the reading and study of Torah. From the generation

---

* This essay was originally published as "Communal Functions of the Synagogue in Eretz Israel during the Mishnaic and Talmudic Periods," in S. Schmidt, ed., *Festschrift for M. Wizer* (Jerusalem: Yavneh, 1981), pp. 230-248 (in Hebrew). It has been translated with the permission of the author. It was translated by Dr. Nathan H. Reisner.

1 There is an abundance of literature on synagogues in the Land of Israel and the nature of this institution. For the first attempt to discuss the matters treated here, see Krauss, especially pp. 102-198. For a survey of the main literature, see R. P. Goldschmidt, "Ancient Synagogues in the Land of Israel," *Cathedra* 4 (1977): 205-221 (in Hebrew). For a list of the synagogues in the Land of Israel, their description and what was found in them, see Hüttenmeister and Reeg, and Safrai, *Compendia*. See also Chiat, *Handbook* and Ilan, *Synagogues*.

2 The term 'Jewish town' refers to the Jewish rural settlement and the Jewish communities in the mixed Gentile cities. The communal services in the Jewish town were very developed, see Safrai, "Town"; Z. Safrai, "On the Margin of the Rehob Inscription," *Zion* 42 (1977): 19-22 (in Hebrew); Z. Weinberg, "Organisation der jüdischen Ortsgemeinden in der Talmudischen Zeit," *MGWJ* 41 (1897): 588, 604, 639-660, 671, 681; and Safrai, *Community*.

of Yavneh onwards, prayer began to assume a more and more important place in Jewish religious life. Assumedly, the more important prayer became, the more important a place it came to occupy in in the synagogue activities. An expression of the importance of prayer in the synagogue is the plan of the synagogue's central hall. There is no doubt that most of the synagogues faced Jerusalem.[3] Indeed, the structure came to be considered as a place of prayer *par excellence*. But this was of consequence only during the time of prayer, and—in the final analysis—the time of prayer formed only part of the synagogue's many hours of activity. Torah study occupied the largest amount of time.

TORAH STUDY

Torah study was the chief and foremost purpose of the synagogue.[4] For example, in the Theodotos Inscription discovered in Jerusalem, the founder of the synagogue proclaims that he built the structure for "reading the Torah and studying the commandments."[5] Study of the Torah is one of the important characteristics of the Jewish people in the Rabbinic period; it is almost impossible to exaggerate its importance and influence upon the life and character of the people.[6] Most of the organized activities of Torah study took place in the synagogue. Let us examine each in turn.

(1) The homily (*derashah*)—The homily took place in the synagogue mainly on Sabbaths and Festivals. The homily provided a kind of folk academy, and the Sage conducted a lesson lasting a number of hours. For the ordinary populace this was their only study after leaving school.[7] A large audience attended the homily and it could be held only in a large hall or outdoors. It is impossible to know whether or not the homily was occasionally delivered outside the synagogue. It is clear, however, that it generally was given in the synagogue. There are no indications that this activity was organized by the city institutions.[8]

---

[3] There are a number of unusual synagogues whose direction of prayer is not toward Jerusalem (Hulda, Japhia, Beth-Shean) but this is not the place to discuss it. On the structure of Hulda, see Kloner, *Hulda*.

[4] Safrai, "Town," pp. 927-933.

[5] S. A. Cook, "The Synagogue of Theodotos at Jerusalem," *PEF* (1921): 22-23; G. M. Fitzgerald, "Theodotos Inscription," *PEFQS* (1921): 175-181; *SEG* 8 (1937), no. 170.

[6] Safrai, "Town," pp. 927-933.

[7] I. Heinemann, *Public Homilies in the Talmudic Period* (Jerusalem: Mosad Bialik, 1971) (in Hebrew).

[8] There are a number of testimonies to the fact that the town leadership concerned itself with bringing a *darshan* (preacher) to the town. See the sources mentioned in note 77. Similarly M. Abot 6:9 (in the printed texts); Tana Devei Eliyahu 11. All the sources speak of

(2) The Sabbath Torah reading—One of the ancient customs was to read the weekly Pentateuchal portion "twice [in the] original and once [in the Aramaic] translation." Needless to say, this also took place in the synagogue.[9]

(3) Learning and instruction in the synagogue—In the Land of Israel, there was no 'yeshiva' institution such as existed in Babylonia or medieval Europe. In the Land of Israel, a sage sat with his students in an unorganized fashion wherever he saw fit. The learning process was also the process of arriving at legal decisions. Those with legal questions appeared during the periods of study and presented their problems. The matter was presented to the students for discussion and the decision was made by a vote of the sages in the group.

As I stated, the study of Torah took place everywhere. A. Buchler collected many indications that, in general, it was the practice to study outdoors, often beneath a tree or in the shade of a structure.[10] Yet it seems that in the period of the *amoraim*, it was customary to study in the synagogue or the *bet midrash* ('house of study'). Only the large settlements had a *bet midrash,* and if there was a sage in the small settlement (most sages were township dwellers), he functioned in the synagogue. R. Abbahu, for example, often sat in the *kenishta "maradeta*" in Caesarea,[11] while R. Yohanan

---

the concern to bring a preacher and not of the on-going organization of the homilies themselves.

[9] Safrai, "Town." In the synagogue, semi-ritualistic readings were also read, such as the recital of Hallel on Passover Eve for whoever is incapable of reading it; see Tos. Pes. 10:8.

[10] A. Buchler, "Learning and Teaching in the Open Air in Palestine," *JQR* n.s. 4 (1914): 485-491. Rabbi decreed that one should not study in the marketplace (B. Moed Qatan 16b) and apparently his main purpose was to object to this practice. It is interesting that his pupil and colleague R. Ishmael b. R. Jose did not heed his words and ruled on a wedding contract in the marketplace. Assumedly Rabbi was primarily opposed to issuing rulings in the marketplace, his argument being that it was probably impossible to take all of the possible considerations into account in such a place. See Y. Ketubot ch. 13, 35d. Rabbi's reason for the prohibition is not clear. It might be that he was interested in strengthening the order and organization of the court and the place of study. Nor is it impossible that it was Rabbi's efforts that caused the concentration of of the learning in the synagogue.

[11] For a list of the instances, see Hüttenmeister and Reeg, entry: Caesarea. At Caesarea, an inscription was found dedicating the synagogue in honor of the head of the synagogue, Marutha. So the synagogue was called 'Marutha.' Palestinian sources mention a synagogue in Caesarea called 'Maradeta' (Mardeta), and various scholars have proposed theories about the origin of this name (see Hüttenmeister and Reeg, entry: Caesarea). It is clearly, however, nothing but a corruption and the synagogue is named after its head.

sat in the synagogue at Ma'on or Caesarea.[12] This happened at other synagogues as well.[13]

The activities of the Sages were not organized by the local community, yet it is clear that they fit into the community's organization. The following passage illustrates this clearly.

> R. Berechiah went to the synagogue of Beth-Shean. He saw a man washing his hands and feet (with water) out of its (the synagogue's) *gorna* (reservoir).[14] Said he to him: "You are not permitted (to do this)." The next day the same man saw R. Berechiah washing his hands and feet from the reservoir. Said the man to him: "Rabbi, for you it is allowed but for me not?" Replied R. Berechiah: "Yes." "Why?" asked the man. He replied: "Thus said R. Joshua b. Levi: 'The synagogues and the Houses of Study are for the Sages and their disciples.'"

The cistern at the synagogue was certainly municipal property originally intended to serve all who all who came to the synagogue or all of the town's residents, but the community placed it at the disposal of the Sages since they were the regular users of the synagogue. This is somewhat reminiscent of the academy in the ancient Greek city. The philosopher received no remuneration from the city, but the city placed the structure (that is, the academy) at his disposal.[15] Similarly, there is no hint that a sage received any payment whatsoever from the city institutions—he was even forbidden to accept payment for the teaching of Torah—but the city placed the structure at his

[12] B. Yebamot 65b. It is told of R. Ammi and R. Assi that even though they had thirteen synagogues, they prayed only among the columns (B. Ber. 8a & 30b); and B. Shab. 10a. And they apparently did not study in the synagogue or at least in the place befitting them in this structure. On study in the synagogue, see also Deuteronomy Rabbah 8ff.

[13] Thus, for example, we find the Sages sitting and eating in the synagogue, and it turns out to be in the middle of their study. See Y. Berakot ch. 2, 5d; Y. Shab. ch. 1, 3a. "Our Teacher (R. Judah ha-Nasi) was sitting and studying the Torah in front of the Babylonian Synagogue in Sepphoris" (Genesis Rabbah, 33:3), and also see B. BQ 99b; B. Hullin 97a; Y. Meg. ch. 1, 70a; Genesis Rabbah 70:8; Leviticus Rabbah 35:12; and many other examples.

[14] The '*gorna*' does not seem to be a *mikveh*, because a *mikveh* has its own designation. Likewise, it is not an ordinary cistern which would not be called a 'reservoir.' It might be that the reference is to a practice alluded to in *The Laws of the Land of Israel from the Geniza* (M. Margalioth, ed. [Jerusalem: Mosad ha-Rav Kuk, 1973], pp. 131-132 [in Hebrew]) "and if, because of our sins, we do not have the Temple Mount, we do have a 'miniature sanctuary' (i.e. the synagogue) and we must conduct ourselves with sanctity and awe as is stated (in the Torah), 'and you shall venerate My sanctuary.'" Therefore, the Rishonim installed in all the synagogue courtyards basins of fresh water for the ritual laving of hands and feet. If this be the case, we are speaking of a small water installation, but it is not a regular *miqweh*. *Gorna* (reservoir) is a Greek term for a kind of water basin and it reasonable to assume that the basins mentioned are those very *gorna*. See Sokoloff, *Dictionary*, p. 129. Unmistakable basins are found at the En Gedi synagogue. They are stone installations in the form of an open pot that were installed in the courtyard of the synagogue entrance.

[15] In the Roman period, the matter changed and the philosopher became a salaried municipal functionary.

disposal and set aside part of the synagogue's auxiliary installations for that purpose.[16]

(4) Individual Torah Study—an individual wishing to study would come to the synagogue either to study by himself, with others, or with a sage.[17] As we have implied, all the evidence regarding the rabbis' study of Torah in the synagogue is from the amoraic period only.[18] It was in this period that the ideology of Torah study in a closed structure developed. Rabbi Yohanan preached, "And Rabbi Yohanan says, a covenant was made for study in the synagogue, and it will not be quickly forgotten."[19] Further on in the passage, in an interpretation by another rabbi, the humble student is praised; this may represent a disagreement with R. Yohanan's interpretation regarding study in the synagogue. Additional interpretations from the amoraic period emphasize the importance of studying in a building, although the synagogue is not mentioned. In the course of those interpretations we also find hints of earlier, opposing interpretations, preferring study outside.[20] All the evidence regarding *batei midrash* is from the amoraic period, as well. The process of introducing the study of Torah in closed structures is connected to social processes among the rabbis. This is, of course, beyond the scope of the present work, and here we will just note that the role of the synagogue changed between the tannaitic and the amoraic period. We will return to this issue later.

(5) *bet ha-sefer* and *bet ha-mishnah*—the most institutionalized forms of studying Torah were the *bet ha-sefer* and the *bet ha-mishnah* for the children and the young. Operating the educational system was one of the clear functions of the city leadership.

---

[16] This is not the place to deal with this serious problem.

[17] B. Ber. 14b and 6a. The sages are commendatory: "Hence they said that every ten men who enter the synagogue are accompanied by the *shekinah* (the Divine Presence), as is stated: 'God stands in the divine assembly.'" The context concerns ten men who enter to study and judge, see Mekilta de-Rabbi Ishmael, Jethro 11 (S. Horowitz & I. A. Rabin, eds. [Jerusalem: Sefer Wahrman, 1960], p. 243). It is interesting that the Mekilta seems to cite a mishnah (the phrase "hence they said" is usually a quotation from the Mishnah). The reference is to M. Abot 3:6, which speaks only of "ten who are sitting and studying the Torah" (without any explicit mention of the synagogue). The prooftext in both instances is "God stands in the divine assembly." (Ps. 82:1) The similarity is also prominent in the continuation of the passage. Therefore, any ten studying are in the synagogue. In the Babylonian Talmud, the verse is interpreted as referring particularly to prayer (B. Ber. 6a), but Babylonia and the Land of Israel are separate entities, and we shall treat this below. Talmudic literature contains the requirement to go to the houses of prayer and the houses of study. The combination proves that the intent is to attend primarily for study, not for prayer, especially as we have stated that the place of prayer in the synagogue was secondary. See, for example, Genesis Rabbah 60:6, 67:3, and 42:2.

[18] See note 10, above.

[19] Y. Ber. 59a.

[20] Tanhuma Buber, Bechukotai 4; Tanhuma Bechukotai 3.

The city's compulsory education consisted of three levels:

a. It was the parents' duty to send their children to the *bet ha-sefer* (the elementary school). This is a *mitzvah* (a religious commandment) and there is no evidence that the city was asked to compel performance of this obligation, nor was there any need to do so.[21]

b. The city was obligated to provide an instructor and a place for study, and to supervise the instruction.

c. Funding the educational system.

Although we shall not deal here with the details of the educational system, we must establish a number of principles. The sources mention three types of institutions of learning: (1) the *bet ha-sefer*, in which the *sefer*, the Book of the Torah, was studied; (2) the *bet ha-mishnah*, in which they studied Mishnah; and (3) the *bet ha-talmud* in which the talmud was studied. The talmud study was done in the presence of and at the direction of a sage. And as stated heretofore, this study was not institutionalized. The *bet ha-sefer* was much more widespread than the *bet ha-mishnah* and the 'rule' of compulsory education apparently applied only to the elementary level.

Large communities could afford separate schools, but in most communities the school was in the synagogue. Many sources mention the presence of pupils or of the *sofer* (the elementary school teacher) in the synagogue. Furthermore, discussion about the school often relates to the synagogue as self-understood with no need for specific mention. Thus, for example, it is reported that R. Joshua b. Levi brought his son to the synagogue himself. This Sage motivated his action with: "Is it of slight significance that it is written (in the Torah) 'And make them known to your children?'" (B. Kidd. 30a). In the continuation of the passage, this verse is interpreted as the source of the obligation to teach one's son Torah. If, then, it be the case that bringing one's child to the synagogue is in order that he learn Torah—and the Jerusalem Talmud also asks the same question—is it permitted to pass through the synagogue vestibule? In the continuation of the discussion it becomes clear that the concern is lest this disturb the group of students (Y. Megillah ch. 3, 64a). And there is much similar evidence, part of which will be cited in the course of the discussion below.[22]

In M. Shabbat 1:3, the *hazzan* (pl. *hazzanim*) is mentioned, not the *sofer* (pl. *soferim*), as the one who is with the pupils on Sabbath eve in the synagogue. To be sure, it is not stated specifically that studies in the synagogue framework are being spoken of there. However, the example cited of who is with the children indicates the possibility that the *hazzan* was filling the role

[21] On the educational system in the Jewish city, see S. Safrai, "Education and the Study of Torah," *Compendia Rerum Judaicarum*, vol. 2 (Assen: Van Gorcum, 1976), pp. 945-970. On education not being forcibly imposed, see Y. Kidd. ch. 1, 61a.

[22] Such as Genesis Rabbah 65:19, 26:4, and 52:4 .

of the *sofer.* The *hazzan,* in this instance, is fulfilling a function in the complex of the communal activities implemented in the synagogue. It may be that this was the situation in the small communities. Similarly, it might be that what we have here is an early law. The Mishnah opens with the phrase "In truth they said," and it might be that this is an indication of an early redaction.

Only the *bet ha-sefer* is connected with the synagogue, not the *bet ha-mishnah.* The difference is emphasized in the Midrash: "to set up *soferim* in the synagogues from the tribe of Simeon and teachers of talmud and Mishnah from the tribe of Levi in the Houses of Study."[23]

To sum up, in the city the synagogue served as the main locus for the study of Torah on all its levels: private study, the Sage's study, the folk academy, the organized study of Torah in the *bet ha-sefer*, and even textual study in the framework of prayer.

BET HA-DIN (THE COURT)

In the Jewish town there were three kinds of courts (*batei din*):[24]

a. The "private" *bet din* (court) of a sage who was a member of the Sanhedrin. This *bet din* was a city institution. Its authority was very broad but the appointment of the *dayyan* (judge, pl. *dayyanim*) was not based upon the communal institutions but upon the authority and prestige of the Sanhedrin.

b. The city *bet din* appointed by the local community. This court did not enjoy religious authorization but rather the authorization of the community.

c. The non-rabbinic (lay) *bet-din*. Arbitrators were sometimes appointed by disputants to deal with and decide a specific problem.

As we have said, at least from the beginning of the amoraic period the Sage sat and taught in the synagogue. He studied and taught where the *bet din* sat. Clearly, then, the court proceedings were generally conducted at the synagogue. It is reasonable to assume the the city courts also sat in the synagogue. This claim, however, is difficult to prove for a number of reasons:

---

[23] Genesis Rabbah 97:1 and see Albeck's notes to the passage, (J. Theodor and Ch. Albeck, *Bereshit Rabbah*, second ed. [Jerusalem: Sefer Wahrmann, 1965], p. 1207 [in Hebrew]). It should be noted that according to the ms. 3 version of the Midrash Tannhuma (S. Buber, ed. [Vilna, 1885], part 1, p. 70) the Hebrew word *hamas* (lawlessness) in the phrase "their weapons are tools of lawlessness" (Gen. 49:5) is interpreted as an acronym for *hazzanim*, *melamedim*, and *soferim.* The reference apparently is to the blessing (the curse?) that there were *soferim* and teachers of Mishnah. And the Midrash adds *hazzanim* as well. If this is so, then here, too, the *hazzan* joins the list of the teachers in the school.

[24] G. Alon, "The *Strategoi* in the Palestinian Cities during the Roman Epoch," in *Jews, Judaism and the Classical World* (Jerusalem, 1977), pp. 458-475. See also Safrai, *Community*, chap. 2.

a. When a Sage sits as judge, there is no way to know whether he is only acting as a Sanhedrin member, or as a member of a town *bet din*. (It turns out that a Sanhedrin member interested in this also received a municipal appointment.)

b. Most of the items mentioned in the talmuds are decisions of the Sages, for understandable reasons.

c. When a court is mentioned with no further identification, there is no knowing which court is involved.

Some evidence indicates that legal proceedings took place in the synagogue. For example, the sources cited about the Sages sitting in the synagogues deal, in part, with legal rulings. The fifth-century Christian writer, Chrysostom, relates that the Jews take oaths in the synagogues;[25] Jesus warns his disciples that they will be turned over to the Sanhedrin and flogged in the synagogues;[26] Paul attests to his having himself flogged Christians in synagogues,[27] and that this flogging was the court's punishment, which was probably meted out where the court sat. Paul himself was apparently not a Sanhedrin member. One may assume that he gained prestige by virtue of his being a representative of the leadership in Jerusalem, but the legal power was in the hands of the local *bet din*. These things occurred in the Diaspora, that is, where there were no Sanhedrin members functioning, for the Sanhedrin functioned only in the Land of Israel, and these were local courts only, which, according to this evidence, functioned in the synagogue.

Important evidence lies in the tale of the man who deposited money with Bar Tamalion, and when he requested his money back Bar Tamalion claimed that the money had already been returned. The depositor therefore asked that Bar Tamalion take an oath—a ritual that must be performed in the synagogue.[28] The synagogue is simply mentioned as the place where the oath took place. Presumably the reference is to the *bet din* that sat there. The reference here is not to an ordinary court, since the very decision about the oath had already been decided upon by the two earlier. Furthermore, Bar Tamalion appears not only as a cheat but also as one who is "anxious to swear." One would conclude that the oath itself was superfluous and certainly not ruled

---

[25] John Chrysostom, *Orat.* I. Needless to say, according to the halakah there is no oath except within the framework of a legal decision. See also Krauss, p. 188.

[26] See Krauss, p. 186. Matt. 10:17, Mark 13:9, Luke 21:12.

[27] Acts 22:19. See also Epiphanius, *Haeres* 30:11; Eusebius, *History of the Church*, vol. 12, #16.

[28] Pesikta Rabbati 22, The Ten Commandments, 1, p. 113a; Midrash HaGadol, Exodus, Jethro 20:7. The story also occurs in B. Nedarim 25a and refers to Rava. The story *per se* is also known in non-Jewish literature and the mention of the synagogue as the place where one swears seems incidental. And see S. Lieberman, *Greeks and Hellenism in the Land of Israel* (Jerusalem, 1963), pp. 100-101, note 129 (in Hebrew).

necessary by a court of a Sanhedrin member.[29] If that be so, the court sitting in that synagogue was a local one that only decided Torah matters.

Clear proof of the connection between the organized court and the synagogue is the fact that the *hazzan* was the one who flogged the guilty.[30] It reached such a point that the midrash claims that the officials mentioned as carrying out the decisions of the magistrates are the *hazzanim*: "these magistrates are the *dayyanim* and these officials are the *hazzanim*."[31] The *hazzanim* are part of the regular staff of the court and the *dayyan is* responsible for their salary.[32] In another source, the Sages condemn the *dayyanim* who have become the "rod of their *hazzanim*."[33] Spoken of here, then, is a court that serves as an instrument of the relatively low-rank officials of the local community. In all these instances the connection with the *hazzan* attests that the court is functioning in the synagogue. Moreover, the *hazzan* was a city official (*parnas*, pl. *parnasim*); hence the assumption that the court in question is the town court.

In the Beth She'arim synagogue, an inscription was found which apparently marked the seat of the 'arbitrator' (*borrer*). Since his name is not mentioned at all, it is not the seat of someone who just happened to fill that role. This is the official seat of the one holding that post. In our discussion of the judicial system in the Jewish city (alluded to above), we suggest explaining this term as referring to a member of the town court. Even if this explanation be imprecise, it is clear that the arbitrator is part of the local community's system of justice.

Presumably, the inscription did not indicate the arbitrator's seat only during prayer but his place during communal events as well. Indeed, he would

---

[29] According to the Pesikta, Bar Tamalion claimed that the money had been returned, and this claim requires an oath. However, according to the Midrash HaGadol he denied it all (in this midrash the hero is anonymous), and clearly does not have to take any oath at all. It seems to us that the Pesikta version was corrected to have it conform more to the Halakah. Otherwise, one cannot see Bar Tamalion as rushing to swear but rather as a person obeying the Law. And see Lieberman on this passage. It should be noted that one should not assume that the oath simply took place in the synagogue without a *bet din* (a court). Otherwise, there is no significance to the synagogue. And see Krauss, pp. 187-188. Yet, it is also possible to swear where there are Torah Scrolls.

[30] M. Makkot 3:12, and many parallels.

[31] Midrash HaGadol, Deuteronomy, 16:18. In this spirit one should understand the homilies wherein the 'officials' are *parnasim*. (Tanhuma Buber on Shofetim 3, and Tanhuma, Shofetim 2). In the Aramaic targums, the Hebrew *shoter* is translated as *sarkan* which means an 'official' (*parnas*). The function of the *shoter* requires further clarification, but this is not the place for it.

[32] Midrash HaGadol, Exodus, 21:1 and B. Shabbath 56a. In this instance the example is of the sons of Samuel whose halakic status is unclear. The rule not to pay the *hazzanim* too much is addressed, generally speaking, to the *dayyan* (the judge) and it is logical to assume that this primarily means the city judge, for not every Sanhedrin member was a *hazzan*. And see also B. Sanhedrin 17b.

[33] B. Shab.139a.

have especially occupied this seat when he carried out his duties. Otherwise, the name of the office-holder would have been mentioned, not just the office. It is difficult to assume that every *parnas* had a fixed place for prayer by virtue of his function. It is possible that the *parnasim* did have personal marks of honor, but not seats reserved for them because of their role. Everything above proves that the arbitrator functioned in the synagogue in the hall itself, or in one of the structure's side rooms.

To sum up, all the organized courts operated in the synagogue and the synagogue 'apparatus' was in actuality available to the court in order to enforce its decision or to see to the court's needs. This institutional structure will return in other contexts. For the rabbinic court we have evidence only from the amoraic period. For the local (community) court, we have information also from the first century, second century, and later.

THE HOSTEL

Within the synagogue or connected to it, a hostel for wayfarers was often operated. R. Abba bar Kahana tells of a group of rowdy hired laborers at Kefar Hittin that used to eat in the synagogue and throw the bones on the *sofer*. But when one of them was about to die, he deposited his will with that same *sofer*.[34] According to the story, the mistreatment occured every Friday. On a regular weekday, the *sofer* was found in the synagogue because he taught there; but his presence there on the eve of the Sabbath is strange. Perhaps the text needs correction, or it might be that the school also operated on Friday, as we saw in M. Shab. 1:3. In any case, it is clear that both the *sofer* (and his pupils) as well as the laborers were to be found in the synagogue.[35]

This combination of hostel and *sofer* in the synagogue is also found in Y. Megillah ch. 3, 74a. R. Immi instructed his *soferim* that if a person

---

[34] Genesis Rabbah 65:16; Krauss, pp. 195-196; Klein, *Land*, pp. 107-108. According to Klein, the *hazzan* had a residence in the synagogue; however, a *hazzan is* not a *sofer*. Furthermore, the *hazzan*'s residence is mentioned almost entirely in the Babylonian sources. See, for example, B. Erubin 55b, with Tos. Erub. 6:4; B. Yoma 11b; and, especially, Deuteronomy Rabbah 7:2. But see Tos. Maas. 2:2. A second proof that Klein brings is from the inscription at Kefar Ramah published by Izhak Ben-Zvi, see I. Ben-Zvi, "A 3rd Century. Aramaic Inscription in Rama," *JPOS* 13 (1933): 94-96. It explicitly mentions a 'guest house.' However, the inscription has been examined again recently by Naveh and it contains no indication of these words at all. See Naveh, p. 33. In the Vatican ms. of Genesis Rabbah 65:16, it says that the event took place at a place called '*bei zara*' which apparently is the name of the community's hostelry.

[35] One should assume that these laborers were not residents of the city, otherwise they would be eating at home. Furthermore, when one of them was dying, he would summon his family. The absence of family and the emphasis on the friends attests to the fact that outside laborers are being spoken of.

comes who knows little Torah, he along with his mule and his clothing should be accepted. The picture here is that the *sofer* sits in the synagogue and the travelers who reach the synagogue warrant his attention as a matter of course. It turns out that the hostel generally did not provide food; but if one learned in the Torah arrived, he should be given special attention, including food and personal service. The leadership probably allotted a special budget for this purpose.

The synagogue's role as a hostelry also appears in an account about R. Meir who lodged at an inn "in the south." The innkeeper (conspiring with a band of bandits operating in the area) tried to persuade him to start out at night. R. Meir objected, claiming that he had a friend sleeping at the synagogue. In the end, it turned out that R. Meir had outwitted the innkeeper.[36] This city had an inn near it and a synagogue which included a hostel. Presumably, the synagogue provided hospitality for the poor, while the wealthier slept at the inn. (This is probably a late story about a sage from the second century.) Talmudic literature has additional references to hostels at synagogues.[37]

The hostel at Kefar Hittin was inside the synagogue building, and this is borne out by the last story. Yet in the Theodotos Inscription, the hostel is presented as a structure found attached to the synagogue but not within it, for it says: "He built the synagogue...and the hostel and the rooms and the water installations." The assumption, then, must be that there were different customs about this and no single, set practice. (Rooms for guests excavated near synagogues will be further discussed below.)

CHARITY

One of the Jewish town leadership's chief areas of activity was charity. Taxes were imposed for that purpose and an apparatus was set up for the collection of funds and their distribution. One way of gathering the money was the 'allocation' (*psikah*). This was done at a community meeting at which the purpose or specific need for the funds was announced and everyone present contributed as he saw fit. Sometimes a person was 'pledged' even without his consent.[38] Since most of the city's communal assemblies were held in the synagogue (prayer, preaching, and public meetings), as we shall

[36] Genesis Rabbah 92:6.

[37] See Klein, *Land*, pp. 107-108.

[38] I have dealt with this issue more extensively in my article, "Security." See also Krauss, pp. 191ff.

see, it was natural that the 'allocation' also generally took place in the synagogue.[39]

The synagogue became synonymous with the place for giving charity, or more precisely, for announcing the giving of charity. As Jesus said, "Thus, when you give alms, sound no trumpet before you, as the hypocrites do in the synagogues and in the streets" (Matthew 6:2). Clearly Jesus is alluding to the accepted custom of giving charity publicly in the synagogue. Further evidence comes from the Tosefta, which rules that "guardians (of orphans)...do not allot them charity in the synagogue." This implies that ordinary allocations were made in the synagogue.[40] The Tosefta also relates, "Thus was R. Simeon b. Eleazar wont to say: ('The house of Shammai say) that charity for the poor is not allotted in the synagogue...on the Sabbath. and the House of Hillel permit it."[41] This passage further indicates, therefore, that the ordinary allocation of charity is implemented in the synagogue. This source speaks not only of a regular allotment but of imposing such a charity allotment upon the community (according to the Munich ms. on the Gemara at this passage), that is, imposing a tax upon the community.[42]

Some activities were conducted in the synagogue because that is where the community gathered. Indeed it can be argued that giving charity is not connected to the synagogue as an institution; the link appears only because it happens to serve as the place the public gathers to study and pray. There is some support for this claim in that the allotment was occasionally announced in the *bet midrash* and that the collectors of charity funds circulated and gathered the monies in streets and residential courtyards.[43] There is no doubt that sometimes community gatherings at the synagogue provided the reason for the allotment in the synagogue. The following story is an example of this:

> A certain Babylonian came to the Land of Israel and R. Berechiah knew that he was a bastard. The Babylonian came to him and said: "Give me charity." R. Berechiah replied: "Go away now but come tomorrow and we will make a

[39] Part of the allocations were made on the Sabbath, when people gathered in the synagogue for prayer, a homily (above), and a general meeting (below). Of course, this in and of itself raises certain halakic problems. See also note 41 and Z. Safrai, "Financing Synagogue Construction in the Period of the Mishnah and the Talmud," in A. Kasher et al, eds., *Synagogues in Antiquity* (Jerusalem: Yad Izhak Ben Zvi, 1984), pp. 77-96 (in Hebrew).

[40] Tos. BB 8:4; Tos. Ter. 1:10; Y. Ter. 40b; B. Gittin 22a.

[41] Tos. Shabbat16(17):22, and B. Shab. 12a. On imposing a tax on the community, see above, note 38.

[42] Safrai, "Security," pp. 80-82.

[43] Tos. Demai 3:20; Y. Demai ch. 3, 23b; Y. Horayot ch. 3, 48a; Leviticus Rabbah 5:4; Deuteronomy Rabbah 4:8.

> public allotment...." The next day he came and found him at the synagogue sitting and preaching.[44]

In this case, it is clear the allotment occured in the synagogue because the community was gathered there for a sermon. It is interesting that the Jerusalem Talmud's version of this story fails to indicate that the sermon was in a synagogue. The original version is difficult to ascertain, but even if the original version did not specify the location, it is logical to assume that the person who corrupted the text knew that the ordinary allocation was in the synagogue; it would be hard to argue that such information was known to a later scribe. Therefore it appears that if there was an addition, it had already been done by the editor of the midrash and it attests to the reality of its day.

For a number of reasons it appears that the allocation was occasionally part of the community activities organized at the synagogue:

a. Apparently a sizable portion of the charity activities were organized by the community and hence the unavoidable claim that these organized activities were also centered in the synagogue where most of the allotments were made.

b. Some sources (cited above) speak of the imposition of a tax upon the community in the synagogue, and this certainly is an organized community action.

c. The *hazzan* of the synagogue appears as a collector of the monies pledged at the time of the allocation.[45] Generally the charity collector (*gabbaei tzedaka*) or the community leaders (*parnasim*) are those who have the task of collecting the monies, for they are town and community officials.[46] But it seems that the synagogue's *hazzan* also fulfilled this function in certain situations. Presumably, in large communities, the collection apparatus was independent, but in smaller ones it was also the task of the synagogue's *hazzan.*

To sum up, most of the charity allocations were made in the synagogue because that was where the community normally gathered and because community meetings for distributing charity and setting the charity taxes were held there. The synagogue as an institution was sometimes part of the city's charity system and synagogue officials also functioned as part of this system. This was also the case with the court structure and the education system. The *hazzan*, as part of his synagogue functions, also served as a

---

[44] Leviticus Rabbah 32:7; Y. Qid. ch. 3, 64c.

[45] Leviticus Rabbah 16:5; Ecclesiates Rabbah 5:3 and Midrash Tehillim on Psalm 52:1 *shaliah tzibbur* instead of *hazzan.*

[46] Such as Tos. Demai 3:20; Y. Demai, ch. 3, 23b; Tos. Megillah 3:4 and parallels; Tos. BM 3.9; B. BB 80b; B. BM 38a; B. Pes. 13a; Tos. Sheqalim 2:8.

teacher and as an officer of the court.[47] The *sofer* likewise functioned in a similar manner. He was not a synagogue employee, but a municipal official who worked at the synagogue and was responsible for hospitality within the synagogue's framework.

PUBLIC AND COMMUNITY MEETINGS

Public meetings were held at the synagogue. Although the functions and authority of such gatherings is not within the scope of this discussion, it is clear that the meeting was an organized institution which occasionally involved itself with the implementation and authorization of activities of the municipal management.[48] Josephus tells of a public meeting that took place in the Tiberias synagogue at which the subject under discussion was the conduct of the struggle against the Romans. The meeting began on the Sabbath and was continued the next day.[49] The Bavli provides other support for this observation in the names of Palestinian sages.

> And R. Eleazar said: "We allocate charity for the poor on the Sabbath." And R. Jacob bar Idi said that R. Yohanan said, "We save an immediately endangered human life (*pikuah nefesh*) and the lives of many on the Sabbath and go to the synagogues to supervise public affairs on the Sabbath." [50]

[47] See above, notes 27, 41; M. Shab. 1 :3. The source of the word is Akkadian and means an appointed functionary. In our literature the *hazzan is* mentioned in many contexts. *hazzanim* are first mentioned in connection with the Temple. Another *hazzan is* Baitos ben Zonin who was *hazzan* of the Sanhedrin or of the House of the *Nasi*. However, this term is mainly used reference to the synagogue *hazzan* who is the synagogue's general *factotum* and, as we shall prove below, also served in communal city functions within the framework of his function in the synagogue. And see different discussions, above and below, on the matter. It would seem that the *hazzan* fulfilling the general communal functions might not be the synagogue *hazzan*. Nevertheless he did fulfill functions that were not directly connected with the synagogue, such as Tos. Sukkah, 4:11-13 and the sources in my notes 27, 41, and 64. Moreover, in the later tannaitic literature there is not a single clear mention of a *hazzan* who does not function in the synagogue. It seems, then, that in this period the term became applied exclusively to the synagogue functionary.

[48] See Safrai, *Community*.

[49] Josephus, *Vita*,. 54.

[50] B. Shab. 150a; B. Ket. 5a. Rabbi Eliezer's opinion differs from that of Bet Shammai (above, note 41). "Saving the lives of many" [*pikuah rabbim*] seems to mean discussing important public issues that are not literally and immediately 'life saving.' The term *pikuah is* borrowed. *Pikuah nefesh* is a term which comes from the case in the Mishnah which deals with the question of whether it is permissible to *p-k-h* [to uncover] a pile of rubble on the Sabbath in order to save the life of someone buried under it. Thereafter, the term became more general to mean any life-threatening situation. The term "to uncover community matters" is a bit strange since, in the terminology of the sages, the root *p-k-h* has no sense of criticism/supervision. And apparently this was changed because of the *pikuah rabbim* coinage. See the following note.

If that is so, then important public affairs such as described by Josephus b. Mattathias are dealt with in the synagogues.

In a similar vein, we should understand the law which forbids the eulogy of an individual in the synagogue but which permits and even terms it most proper to deliver a "public eulogy." The distinction between the two lies the the importance of the deceased individual to the community.[51] At any rate, despite the conflicting version in the Tosefta, the sources indicate that the synagogue served as a central place of assembly for eulogies and the comforting of mourners. It may be that all the sources actually refer to the eulogy "of many," but it is also possible that the early religious practice that appears in the Tosefta was expanded. As early as the Mishnah, which serves as a basis for the Tosefta,[52] as well as in many other sources, there is repeated mention, in general terms, that "the synagogue that was destroyed...there shall be no eulogizing within it."[53]

G. Foerster argues that the architecture of the synagogue is derived from the community centers in Syria whose primary function was as a public gathering place.[54] There is no doubt that this was indeed one of the synagogue's main purposes as demonstrated and verified by this combination of sources.

THE COMMUNITY OFFICES

Apparently the synagogue was where the city's *parnasim* and functionaries regularly sat. According to the Mishnah, the difference between city and village is that in the city there are *'asarah batlanim* ("ten idlers") (M. Megillah 1:3) and the talmuds explain that this refers to "ten people who are relieved of their work [so that they can go] to the synagogue."[55] Krauss dwelt upon

---

[51] Tos. Meg. 3(2):7. The version of the Vienna ms. (2:8) is of interest. "They should receive a public eulogy [*hesped shel rabbim*]." This sentence does not have a parallel in Y. Meg. ch. 3, 74a. In B. Meg. 28a there is a detailed discussion about what a "public eulogy" is. And see Lieberman, *Tosefta,* Megillah, pp. 1163-1164, who suggests differentiating between a synagogue of the "many" [*rabbim*] of which these laws speak, and a synagogue of the individual [*yahid*]. It should be pointed out that term *rabbim* often refers to many people, but sometimes it means the community in the organized sense of the word. The *hesped shel rabbim,* then, is a eulogy which is of communal interest and it is to such a eulogy that the above-mentioned section in the Babylonian Talmud refers.

[52] See M. Meg. 3:3 and Y. Meg. ch. 3, 74a.

[53] Such as tos. Sanh., ch. 6; Pes. ch. 8, 36b; Neg. 7:11. See also Sofrim 19:12; 23d; and other sources.

[54] G. Foerster, "Ancient Synagogues in the Land of Israel," *Qadmoniot* 5 (1972): 38-42 (in Hebrew).

[55] Y. Meg. ch. 1, 70a; B. Meg. 5a; Krauss, p. 105. Krauss mentions a synagogue in Tiberias whose name was the *Boule* Synagogue; in our opinion this was the synagogue in which the *boulé* of Tiberias sat. We are not sure that this interpretation is compelling. The

the importance of this evidence and worked hard to attempt to link the "ten idlers" with the town leadership. Most of the Rishonim (the early talmudic commentators) and Krauss were influenced by the reality of the medieval Jewish community. This Jewish community abounded in Jewish scholars who studied in the synagogue and did not work. As early as Rashi, these were already identified with the "ten idlers." Krauss, therefore, tried to connect the "ten idlers" and the *hever ha-ir.* This reality of a community that does not work and devotes itself to the study of Torah was almost non-existent in the Land of Israel in the ancient period. Even the greatest of the sages worked for their living. Furthermore, at least in the days of the *tannaim*, the sages did not tend specifically to study in the synagogue, and certainly there was not a place for study in every community but only where there were ordained sages. Generally speaking, it is difficult to match this explanation with the reality of the rabbinic period. It seems to us that S. Safrai is correct in explaining that, based upon the traditions in the midrashim and geonic literature, that the reference is to the ten *parnasim* of the town.[56] The difference, then, between town and village is that the village, because of its smaller, poorer population, did not have public institutions. All the town functionaries regularly sat in the synagogue, and the synagogue is their ordinary location. In the Beth She'arim synagogue, inscriptions were found for the seats of the 'arbitrator' and the one responsible for public sales (or properties). We examined this evidence above and saw that it attests to the fact that these appointees functioned at the synagogue. We have indicated elsewhere the close connection between the town court and the communal leadership, and in practice the arbitrator is a member of the city leadership (one of the city notables).[57] This then is further proof that the synagogue served as the office for the community administration and its various *parnasim.*

OTHER ACTIVITIES

According to the Babylonian Talmud and a passage in the Tosefta, eating was forbidden in the synagogue proper but permitted in the side rooms. In

---

name could have been given even if a number of the Council [*boulé*] members happened to pray and study in this synagogue.

[56] Safrai, "Town," p. 232 and Safrai, *Community*, chap. 2. It should be noted that a *hever 'ir* existed only in the large central communities, whereas the "ten idlers" indicate it as city rather than a village. The term "a large city" mentioned in these sources is used in contrast to "a small city," that is, that it is a village, not a town. The entire matter of the terms used for settlements requires a detailed study out of place here.

[57] Above, note 24.

the Land of Israel, it was customary to hold festive meals celebrating the performance of a *mitzvah* there, most commonly that of the New Moon.[58] There are a number of proofs for this, such as: "R. [Judah the *nasi*] said: 'Money may be lent at interest to *mitzvah* associations [specializing in the performance of a specific *mitzvah*] and for sanctification of the new moon. R. Yohanan used to go to the synagogue in the morning, collect crumbs, eat them and say: 'May my portion be with those who ate here in the evening.'"[59] And so does R. Hiyya bar Ba (in the name of R. Yohanan) instruct the synagogue of Kafra (near Tiberias) to partake of the New Moon Meal before evening, when there still is a bit of light.[60] From both sources it is clear that the New Moon Meal was regularly held at the synagogue.

In the synagogue at Qaṣrin, an inscription mentioning "*revua*" was found. It is difficult to interpret this word, but apparently it refers to a place where feasts are held.[61] According to the Tosefta, as previously noted, it was possible to hold feasts only in the secondary rooms or in the gallery, but in some of the sources the synagogue as such is mentioned, as if the feasts were held in the main hall. As in the case of the eulogy of an individual, passages in Tosefta Megillah and in the Bavli contradict the implications of the more general versions in the sources. We have no way of explaining this discrepancy.

Many activities were held at the synagogue because it was a popular gathering place. Thus, for example, one who sought testimony in his favor was liable to have those present in the synagogue swear that "if you have any evidence relating to me you will come and testify for me."[62] It is logical that this action be done at the synagogue because the public was there. The synagogue is also cited as an example of a place where a married woman and a strange man are likely to meet by accident (or not) and that it be halakically permissible.[63] Announcements of lost items were made in the

---

[58] Above, note 51. A festive meal on the beginning of the new month was one of the important components of this holiday. See Masseket Soferim 19:9; Y. MQ, ch. 2, 81b: B. Sanhedrin 70b.

[59] Y. MQ ch. 2, 81b; Y. San. ch. 8, 26b. The Feast of the New Month was held in the evening (also see note 58). Assumedly this occurred when R. Johanan was along in years since when he was active he would participate, if he wished, in this *mitzvah*-celebrating meal. Hence sages did eat in the synagogue. See, for example, Y. Ber. ch. 2, 5d.

[60] Y. Taa. ch. 4, 68b.

[61] I. Meitlis, "The Significance of the '*revua*' in Qaṣrin," *Tarbiz* 53 (1984): 465-466 (in Hebrew) .

[62] M. Shebuot 4:10; Sifra 52 (Parashat Vayyiqra Dibura Dehobah 8:5) and parallels.

[63] Y. Sotah ch. 1, 16c. According to the halakah a husband may forbid his wife to meet with a specific man. Yet, he cannot prevent them from meeting at the synagogue since the entire community comes there. And see S. Safrai, "Was there a Women's Section in the Synagogue in the Ancient Period?" *Tarbiz* 32 (1963): 329-338 (in Hebrew).

synagogue following the destruction of the Temple.[64] Likewise, other public announcements such as about a woman who has 'rebelled' against her husband, a son who neglects his father, and a son who has been barred from inheriting his father.[65] The *anshei ha-ma'amad* (the division of Israelites assisting the priests on duty) who were the representatives of the city and the region, also sat in the synagogue.[66] On the mosaic floor of the synagogue at En Gedi there is a long inscription containing a number of declarations of importance in the life of the community that have no direct relationship to the synagogue. In all of these instances, the synagogue serves as the place for informal public assembly. This function has been treated and mentioned above.

We shall now examine some of the archaeological examples that support our conclusions, and prove that various communal structures were found within the synagogue or connected to it.[67]

Beth Alpha—a collection box with coins in it, which may have belonged to the city. A similar box was found in the synagogue at Ma'on. A slightly different box was found at En-Gedi.

Beth Yeraḥ—The synagogue is in the context of a group of public buildings (a Roman stronghold, a magnificent bathhouse, and a church). This is clearly the settlement's public area, and the synagogue is incorporated in this entity.

Beth-Shean—Many auxiliary rooms at various periods. There is a clearly evident process of how their number grew. Various utensils such as pails were found in some of them.

Beth She'arim—In this large township were two synagogues. Near the western one, there were rooms north of the synagogue, directly adjacent to it. A bathhouse or furnace also stood beside the synagogue. Near the eastern synagogue was a cistern, a *miqweh* (perhaps more than one), a public street, and another public building with a sitting room (perhaps a *bet midrash*).

En-Gedi—A collection box, many auxiliary rooms, lavers, a large courtyard. West of the synagogue, beside the prayer hall, an unfurnished building served as a hostel, or a room for offices.

---

[64] B. BM 28b.

[65] Y. Peah ch. 1, 15d; Y. Qidd. ch. 1, 61c; Pesikta Rabbati 23-24; Krauss, p. 186. It could be that a kind of reception for the groom was held in the synagogue, see Yalkut Shimoni, I Kings, 13 ch. 201; Sofrim 19:12. See also note 76 below.

[66] B. Taa. 27b. The presence of the 'many' in the synagogue is the real background of the expression "the sitting in the synagogues of those making their pilgrimage to the Land" (M. Abot 3:10 and parallels).

[67] To move the discussion, we will not deal at length with the literature on the synagogue. Anyone so minded can turn to the bibliography of R. P. Goldschmidt (above, note 1), Hüttenmeister and Reeg, or Ilan, *Synagogues*. Occasionally the material has not received full publication, and particularly the additional structures were not mentioned in the brief repots of ongoing excavations. In these cases, my discussion is based upon site visits.

Eshtemoa—a large cistern of water in the courtyard before the synagogue and auxiliary rooms.

Gaza-Yam—The synagogue is in a public area which includes workshops and storage facilities. It appears that the synagogue building replaced part of the public buildings.

Hammath-Tiberias—Here ruins were found next to the synagogue of a multi-room building with no furniture or other equipment. The archaeologist therefore hypothesizes that this building served as a hostel. All the evidence of hostel at the synagogue is from the amoraic period. We will return to this point later.

Ḥorvat Susiya— Near the synagogue hall, in the synagogue complex, there is a *mikveh*; in the courtyard there was a large water cistern; beside the synagogue, a lower milistone for grinding flour.

Khirbet Shema'—A *miqweh* in the synagogue; auxiliary rooms.

Kefar Bar'am—A large cistern at the synagogue entrance.

Kefar Nahum (Capernaum)—A large courtyard with columns within the synagogue complex east of the prayer hall.

Ma'on—A *miqweh* near the synagogue, and adjoining it, an additional water installation. A collection box was found within the synagogue.

Maon (in Mt. Hebron area)—a *miqweh*.

Meiron—Auxiliary rooms and storage facilities; a water installation within the synagogue.

Meroth—A courtyard with a sitting room (perhaps a *bet midrash*).

Na'aran—The synagogue is incorporated in the network of aqueducts.

In a number of synagogues (Meroth, Ramon, Gush Ḥalav, Caesarea, Beth She'arim, and others) hoards have been found that apparently contained the community funds. Kindler has collected the list of these hoards and discussed the Meroth hoard in depth.[68] This hoard was the richest of all, and included numerous gold coins. The hoards found in other synagogues were also very rich and some included gold coins. Apparently, these were the funds of the community leaderships. This testifies to the connection between the synagogue and the community leadership. It is only natural that the town treasury should have been held in the offices of the community, and the synagogue served as the natural location of both the offices and the treasury.

To summarize, many of the synagogues (almost all of those whose surroundings survived) had auxiliary rooms. Very often the synagogue is connected with or is near public structures such as cisterns, *miqwaot,* bathhouses an oil press or mill. These findings fit our conclusions about the communal function of the synagogue.

---

[68] A. Kindler, "The Coins of the Excavation," in Z. Ilan and A. Damati, *Meroth* (Tel Aviv, 1988), pp. 121-125 (in Hebrew). [Eds.—See also Ilan's article in this volume.]

In many of the villages in the Land of Israel settlement has continued without interruption. During the various historical periods the village was never completely abandoned. In these places it is sometimes possible clearly to discern the continuity of the public area. That is to say, after the synagogue ceased to function, the area continued to be a public one and was used in keeping with the character of the population and its needs.[69] Here are a number of examples:

*Synagogues that were converted to mosques or on part of which a mosque was built, such as at Eshtemoa, Susiya, Qaṣrin (a mosque and a sheikh's tomb), and others.

*Synagogues now situated in a public area:

Eshtemoa—The synagogue is in the center of the village near the new mosque.

Bar'am—The synagogue is in the center of the Arab village with the church nearby on the south and the hostel (*madafa*) on the north.[70]

Sepphoris—The synagogue is beside the Crusader church and the modern monastery.

Gush Ḥalav (Giscala)—The settlement's large synagogue was swallowed up in the church building erected at the start of the century. Previously this was an empty public area. Other examples of this sort can be found which lend further evidence of the synagogue's location in the public area of the village.

The early synagogue served as both a community center and a house of prayer. For our concerns it is of no importance when prayer and divine worship in the synagogue were established, but it is clear that from the Yavneh generation onward, the arrangement of prayer was institutionalized and improved, and it occupied an increasingly important place in social life and consciousness. By virtue of its role as a house of prayer, the synagogue was considered a holy place; it was here that the holy books were kept and here that public religious ceremonies were held. Naturally there was a tension between these two functions. It seems that in the early synagogue, the role of community center was of greater importance; this was major daily function of the building. In contrast, in Babylon, the synagogue was considered as a holy building only, and the community functions were secondary. The Babylonian Talmud presents the synagogue solely as a holy building, as already discussed by Gafni, at the same time as its public functions were

---

[69] This phenomenon is recognized and known in the development of the settlements in the Land and throughout the world and this is not the place to deal with the general aspect of the phenomenon.

[70] In our opinion, the arab village of Bar'am preserves the basic plan of the village of the Roman period. The planned character of the village and the centrality of the early synagogue are characteristic not of the structure of an arab village but rather of an ancient one. We hope to deal with this further elsewhere.

reduced.[71] The synagogue was located outside the city, it did not house the school, rabbis sat and studied in other buildings, and the community leadership did not work out of this building. This is reflected in the prohibition in the Babylonian Talmud—or at least the lack of evidence—of the custom of eating in the synagogue. This stands in sharp contrast to the custom of festive meals in the synagogues in Palestine.[72]

Moreover, the components of the 'holiness' were concealed in the ancient synagogue in Palestine which is the reason that only a few of the rituals of the Temple were transferred to the synagogue. Later, at the end of the amoraic period and later, rituals and the ritual component were added in the synagogue and the institution of prayer grew.[73] After the amoraic period, the Jewish community diminished. However the increasing importance of the 'holy' component evidently stems from other factors, which are beyond the scope of this work.

THE SYNAGOGUE IN THE TANNAITIC PERIOD

The nature of the synagogue in the tannaitic period is one of the mysteries in the study of Palestine. It is mentioned frequently in the literary sources, but to date we have not found even one building that could have been a synagogue between 70 and 200 C.E. This issue is beyond the scope of the present discussion; here we must ask only which functions the synagogue fulfilled during the tannaitic period. In the course of our discussion we have mentioned several functions, all the evidence of which comes from the amoraic period only. It is reasonable to assume, then, that these did not exist during the tannaitic period. In the tannaitic period, the synagogue already served as a community center; we know this not only from its name but also from the activities that took place there. As we have shown, the national assembly was held in the synagogue as was collection for charity, including the 'allocation,' taxation, and tax collection. The court, and apparently the municipal leadership, as well, were housed in and worked out of the synagogue. In contrast, we have no evidence from the tannaitic period of

---

[71] I. Gafni, "Synagogues in Talmudic Babylonia: Tradition and Reality," in Kasher et al., eds., *Synagogues in Antiquity* (Jerusalem: Yad Izhak Ben Zvi, 1987), pp. 155-164.

[72] Above, note 51. As noted, it might be argued that these feasts were held in the additional rooms. On this issue, it is implied in the Bavli that the synagogue served as a hostel and that guests resided there on the Sabbath, and because of them there was need for the *kiddush* at the end of the prayer. However, this argument is only presented in a dialectic discussion in order to explain an existing custom. Moreover, this sentence may refer to the custom in Palestine and not in Babylonia. See B. Pes. 101a.

[73] Z. Safrai, "From Minor Temple to Synagogue," *Proceedings of the Tenth World Congress of Jewish Studies* (Jerusalem, 1990), pp. 23-28.

the operation of a hostel in the synagogue, with the exception of one story, of late character and style, about Rabbi Meir who slept in the synagogue.

The issue of Torah study is more complex. The interpretation is that public Torah study, and of course reading and translation of the Torah took place mainly, or exclusively in the synagogue. However, we have no evidence of rabbis who studied with their groups in this building. Only at the end of the amoraic period did an ideology develop regarding the importance of studying in a building, that is, in a constructed *bet midrash* or synagogue. On the other hand, the Theodotus inscription mentions study of the Torah and the commandments; this may refer only to the interpretation and reading of the Torah during prayer, but it may also refer to regular Torah study, and it may only be by chance that we have other evidence of this from the tannaitic period. The evidence regarding the court that operated in the synagogue should evidently be interpreted as referring to the municipal community court and not to the rabbinical courts.

As to education, it is reasonable to assume that the children sat and studied in the synagogue but there no tannaitic sources indicating this. In our discussion we presented Mishnah Shabbat 1:3, which mentions the *hazzan* who teaches the children, but does not state that this teaching took place in the synagogue, although it is likely that the *hazzan* is the *hazzan* of the synagogue and that he worked in the building that he managed. In the parallel in the Tosefta (Shabbat 1:6) there is mention only of "the babies correcting their interpretations." Even here it is unclear that this refers to regular school activity. It is also possible that the Theodotus inscription which mentions learning the commandments refers to the school, but this is only a hypothesis. The conclusion regarding the character of the synagogue in the tannaitic period requires, as noted, a broader discussion than appropriate here.

SUMMARY

The synagogue was the main public institution in the Jewish city and many of the organized community's activities were implemented in the synagogue. The communal leadership met in the synagogue and part of the communal activities took place therein, such as the study of Torah on all levels, compulsory education, public meetings, and the communal collections of funds, wayfarer hospitality, and communal services. Presumably, city officials also operated from the synagogue and its attached rooms. The synagogue had an independent public administration, apparently not identical with the leadership of the city, even though, as we have seen, some of the synagogue's *parnasim* played roles in the Jewish town's leadership.[74] One can assume that in small communities the connection between the synagogue leadership and the municipal leadership was much greater than in the large communities. Similarly, it is clear that in a community that had a number of synagogues, the connection was even weaker.

The *hazzan is* a perfect example of the synagogue's communal functions. The holder of this post also functioned, as we have seen, as *sofer*, as the one implementing the religious court's decisions, the collector of charity and the municipal taxes. He also carried out other communal functions such as sounding the shofar to signal the end of the work week on the eve of the Sabbath, and the pilgrimages to Jerusalem were also led by the *hazzanim.*[75] In this instance he is called *hazzan ha-kneset*, the *kneset* being the 'congregation,' and the *hazzan*, as it were, an official of the 'congregation' (the community). Similarly, the *hazzan* appears on the list of the "seven who occupy themselves with the needs of the community."[76] The story of the appointment of R. Levi bar Sisi of Simonia (Shimron) is characteristic of this situation.[77] According to the version in Genesis Rabbah, the residents wanted someone "who would teach them Scripture and Mishnah and be our judge." According to the Jerusalem Talmud, they asked for a person who "would be preacher, judge, *hazzan*, *sofer*, teach them Mishnah, and tend to all their needs." If so, it was an undeveloped community, without institutions of communal leadership and the residents were seeking a person who would be *hazzan*, judge, *sofer*, and overall community official.

In light of all that has been said, the synagogue may be defined as the true community center, encompassing nearly the entire constellation of services that existed in the Jewish community. The officials of the synagogue were counted among the *parnasim* of the town and the line between the synagogue and the communal leadership was blurred. Thus, for example, the pilgrimage to Jerusalem which was a general community event appears as an activity of the 'town residents.' That is to say, all of the town's residents go as a single unit. Concomitantly, we hear that the pilgrimage is described

---

74 See Safrai, "Town," pp. 933-837.

75 Tos. Bikkurim 2:8; Tos. Sukkah 4:12-14.

76 Huppat Eliyahu Rabbah, see *Menorat Ha-Maor* 14, of R. Israel ibn al-Nakawa, 4 vols. (New York: Bloch, 1929-1932), p. 487. In the Geonic period the term *hazzan* was replaced by the term *shaliah tzibbur* [emissary of the congregation]. In Pirkei de-Rabbi Eliezer, the *hazzan* appears as the one who blesses the bride at her *huppah* [wedding canopy] and it may be that the *hazzan* in this instance is the *shaliah tzibbur*. And similarly Masekhet Soferim 10:7 and 11:4. See also note 45.

77 Genesis Rabbah 81:2; Y. Yeb., ch. 12, 13a; B. Yeb. 105a and in the Tanhuma (Buber edition) 96:7 and 96:5. What is spoken of is only a person to teach the city folks. And see also a similar story of the Bosra community (already considered to be outside of the Land of Israel), Y. Shebiit, ch. 7, 36d.

by the *tannaim* as it was done within the synagogue framework.[78] And indeed the synagogue and the residents of the city are one and the same.

[78] On the pilgrimage to the Temple in Jerusalem as an activity of the city residents, see M. Bikkurim 3:1; S. Safrai, *The Festival Pilgrimage during the Days of the Second Temple* (Jerusalem, 1965), pp. 106-107 (in Hebrew). On the festival pilgrimage within the synagogue framework, see Tos. Bikkurim 2:8.

SYNAGOGUES AS 'HOUSES OF PRAYER' AND 'HOLY PLACES' IN THE JEWISH COMMUNITIES OF HELLENISTIC AND ROMAN EGYPT

ARYEH KASHER*

Until the first century, all the Jewish synagogues in Hellenistic and Roman Egypt were called 'προσευχή'—a 'place of prayer' or a 'house of prayer'—at least according to inscriptions, papyrus documents, and literary sources.[1] The archaeological, or more precisely, epigraphic finds reveal the existence of synagogues in the second half of the third century B.C.E., that is to say, from the reign of Ptolemy III Euergetes (Benefactor) (246-221 B.C.E.). These synagogues were located in Schedia south of Alexandria, in Arsinoë-Crocodilopolis in the Fayûm, and in a Jewish settlement in Lower Egypt whose name is unknown.[2] According to S. Safrai, the source of the growth of synagogues was not in the Diaspora, as is the prevailing widespread opinion, but rather in the reality of the Land of Israel in the period of the Return to Zion. Their coming into being, he believes, is rooted in the public assemblies held in the days of Ezra and Nehemiah in the Temple courtyards in which the reading of the Torah (the Pentateuch) played a central role, with prayer also involved. These gatherings were at first held for special and specified purposes, but over the years they became fixed gatherings on Sabbaths and festivals and then also on weekdays. The institutionalization of this practice of holding the gatherings and the festive convocations is what, in his opinion, created the infrastructure for the establishment of synagogues.[3] Even if, like Safrai, we deny the accepted opinion that the synagogues were considered substitutes for the Jerusalem Temple, we cannot ignore the fact that it was a likeness of that Temple which was always in the mind's eye of the bearers of the Talmudic tradition. These sages specifically interpreted

* This essay was originally published in A. Kasher, A. Oppenheimer, and U. Rappaport, eds., *Synagogues in Antiquity* (Jerusalem, 1987), pp. 119-132 (in Hebrew). It has been translated with the permission of the author and of Yad Izhak Ben Zvi. It was translated by Dr. Nathan H. Reisner.

[1] For detailed lists of references, see Krauss, pp. 263-265; Schürer, vol. 2, pp. 425-426 (n. 5) and 439-440. See also III Maccabees 7:20; and *CPJ*, I, 129. On the use of this term in Philo, see Mayer.

[2] For Schedia, see *CIJ*, II, 1440 (= *CPJ*, III, 1440) and Kasher, pp. 106-107 (English. ed. pp. 107-110). For the Fayûm, see *CPJ*, III, 1532a; Kasher, pp. 128ff (English. ed. pp. 135ff). For the other settlement, see *CIJ*, II, 1449 (= *CPJ*, III, 1448); Schürer, vol. 2, p. 425(c).

[3] See Safrai, "Synagogue," pp. 46-47.

Ezekiel 11:16 ("Although I have removed them far off among the nations, and although I have scattered them among the countries, yet have been to them as a little sanctuary (*miqdash me'at*) in the countries where they are come") as referring to the synagogues and houses of study in the Diaspora. The same is the case with other biblical verses such as Psalms 90:1 ("Lord, Thou hast been our dwelling-place") and Psalms 26:8 ("Lord, I love the habitation of Thy house") which the sages also interpreted in the same context as meaning synagogues and houses of study. It is probable that this resemblance was created against the background of the fact that, in the Diaspora, the reading of the Torah and prayer were the two clearest and strongest expressions of worshipping God for both the individual and the community.[4] Indeed, in our opinion, synagogues were erected in the Diaspora on this basis. But they also stemmed from the builders' deliberate intention that they should resemble the Jerusalem Temple in their functions, and more precisely, for those functions not involved with the sacrificial worship, as we shall see below. In other words, the aspiration to resemble the Temple, not to replace it, guided those who erected the synagogues in the Dispersion. Such, at least, was the case in Egypt, to which we will devote our consideration here.

The truth is that in this matter, as in others, there is no comparing one dispersion to another. For example, it is clear that the Jews of Egypt, unlike their brethren in Babylonia, did not refrain from sacrificial worship. They were not concerned with the impure status of the land of Egypt (being in the religious category of 'a foreign country') and therefore they were not deterred from erecting two temples there in the course of history: one at Elephantine and the second at Leontopolis. They offered sacrifices at both. The prophecy of Isaiah 19:19, "In that day shall there be an altar to the Lord in the midst of the land of Egypt, and a pillar at the border thereof to the Lord," served as a biblical basis and justification at least for the erection of the temple of Onias,[5] whose structure and altar were built with the intention of imitating

---

[4] See B. Meg. 29a and the Aramaic translation of Ezekiel 11:16: "And I have given them synagogues secondary to My Sanctuary etc." For a representative example of the prevalent opinion on this matter, see J. Wellhausen, *Israelische und jüdische Geschichte* (Berlin, 1901), pp. 149 ff., 196 ff.; Oesterley & Robinson, pp. 243 ff. Later Robinson even argued that the liturgy of the synagogues was established by Ezra but was inspired by what was being done in the Babylonian Exile from which he came. See W. O. E. Oesterley, *A History of Israel* (London, 1932), pp. 137ff., 167. Also consult the opinion of Ephal who sees prayer as an alternate way of worshiping God in the Babylonian Exile. He refrains however from stating definitively whether and to what extent prayer was institutionalized in the life of the community there or even if it is already possible in the sixth-fifth centuries B.C.E. to find the beginning of the synagogue. See Ephal, p. 25, note 37.

[5] *Jewish Antiquities* XIII, 64, 68; *The Jewish War* VII, 431-432. Thus also in the talmudic tradition: Y. Yoma 6, 43c ff.; B. Men. 109b ff. And see Kasher, pp. 124ff (English ed. pp. 132ff.). It is possible, and even logical, to think that the prophecy of Isaiah quoted above also provided the authority and justification for the erection of the Elephantine Temple, see B.

the Temple in Jerusalem.[6] Certainly also the ritual worship itself conducted therein was done as an imitation of the worship service of the Jerusalem Temple.[7] Nevertheless, the offering of sacrifices by the Jews of Egypt was not, as we know, an easy or simple thing to implement. This becomes clear from the enmity and obstructionist activity of the Egyptian priesthood against the worship at the Elephantine Temple and that renewal of worship there be only on condition that there be absolutely no offerings of sheep, goats or, oxen—only frankincense and meal offerings.[8] It seems that the problem of religious hostility on the part of the Egyptian priesthood, in addition to the jealousy and the differences of opinion among the Jews themselves, was also the lot of those erecting the temple of Onias (*Antiquities* XIII, 66).[9] Perhaps primarily for this reason, among the others, the royal permission to erect this temple was given at the outset for a "God-forsaken" site like Leontopolis on the edge of Egypt's eastern desert, and not in a large Jewish center like Alexandria. Almost certainly the original purpose of the temple was to serve only the military settlement of the

---

Porten, "The Jews in Egypt," in *Restoration,* p. 98; S. Talmon, "The Beginning of the Return to Zion," in *Restoration*, pp. 32 ff.

[6] *Jewish Antiquities* XII, 388; XIII, 67, 72; XX, 236; *Jewish War* I, 33. Only the version in *Jewish War* VII, 426-428 points out that the Temple of Onias was not like the Jerusalem Temple, but it specifically states that the altar was built on the basis of an exact replica of the altar in Jerusalem. V. Tcherikover (in his book *Hellenistic Civilization and the Jews* [New York: Atheneum, 1977], p. 499, n. 34) properly noted, "It is in any case clear that Onias built his temple wholly or partly in intentional imitation of the Temple of Jerusalem." It should be noted that this is indeed well verified by the archaeological finds, see F. Petrie, *Hyksos and Israelite Cities* (London, 1906), pp. 19-27; F. Petris, *Egypt and Israel* (London, 1923), pp. 102ff.

[7] Attesting to this is the invitation to Jerusalem of the Jewish *kohanim* from Egypt (in the original, from Alexandria) who were skilled craftsmen in "the making of the shew-bread" and "the making of the incense," in order to overcome the obstacles resulting from the sanctions placed by the *kohanim* of the House of Garmu and the House of Avtinas. If the Jewish priests in Egypt had not preserved the original ritual-worship traditions as they were practiced in Jerusalem, they would not have been turned to at all. It is not improbable, and perhaps even logical, to think that those expert-priests were of the House of Onias, since it is presumable that the 'Alexandria' of the Talmudic traditions about this incident is a Talmudic term borrowed and applied to all of Egypt, as expressed in the Talmudic legends about the establishment of the House of Onias. See Y. Yoma 3, 41c; Tos. Yom ha-Kippurim 2:6 (Zuckermandel edition, p. 184); B. Yoma 38a; B. Sheq. 14a, B. Arak. 10b, Cp. Y. Yoma 6, 43c ff., and B. Men. 109b ff.

[8] See Cowley, No. 33. The research literature on this is rather extensive.

[9] The differences of opinion among the Jews are well intimated in *Jewish War* VII, 431. It states there that "(Onias) had a competitive instinct regarding the Jews of Jerusalem, against whom he held a grudge because of his flight." See Kasher, pp. 124-127 (English ed. pp. 132-135). In this context the significant fact should be noted that the Temple of Onias left no impression whatever on the Jewish literature in Egypt, especially since the Jews of Alexandria in particular preserved their loyalty and evidenced great admiration for the Jerusalem Temple. See A. Kasher, "Jerusalem as a Metropolis in Philo's National Consciousness," *Cathedra* 11 (1979): 45ff.

'land of Onias.' Because of its location far from large centers there was no fear it might rouse the ire of the Egyptian populace by the sacrifice of animals sacred to them, nor would it stir up differences of opinion among the Jews themselves. It should be noted here, and with the utmost of emphasis, that the temple of Onias left no impression whatsoever upon Egyptian Jewry; it is not mentioned even once in the rich local Jewish literature. Not only did Philo fail to mention it, but he expressed his complete admiration for the Jerusalem Temple. This fact reveals the reservations that the Jews of Egypt had about Onias' Temple, even though the Sages of the Land of Israel did not entirely invalidate the worship there (Y. Yoma 6, 43c ff; B. Men. 109b ff). To sum up, there were essential internal and external Jewish reasons as well as pragmatic reasons, given the background of Egyptian reality, which prevented the Jews of Egypt from building other temples in which to perform sacrificial worship. They therefore, in practice, made do with less ostentatious institutions which fulfilled only part of the Temple worship, that is, 'houses of prayer.'[10]

Let us return now to the original and first name by which synagogues in Egypt were designated—προσευχή (a house of prayer)—which can help us understand the background of the establishment of this institution on the basis of its similarity to the Temple. As is known, prayer held an important, and often central, place in the worship of God as early as the First-Temple period; it was crystallized as a self-sufficient religious activity independent of the sacrificial worship.[11] Indeed, it could take place anywhere and not necessarily in the Temple, although its being held there gave it greater importance because it was thought one was closer to God.[12] Not for naught was the Temple considered as the 'house of prayer' *par excellence*, not only for Israel but for all the nations in the prophet Isaiah's vision of the end of days (Is. 56:7). In truth, the image of the Temple as a house of prayer is attributed in the Hebrew Bible to its having been established from the very beginning, a fact which can better explain how it served as a source of inspiration for other houses of prayer both in the Land of Israel and in the

---

[10] On the personal pretentiousness of Onias IV as a main cause for the erection of the Temple, see *Jewish Antiquities* XIII, 63-64; *Jewish War* VII, 432.

[11] See E. E. Urbach, *The Desert and the Chosen Land*, vol. 2 (Tel-Aviv, 1963), pp. 195-196, 240-241 (in Hebrew); Kaufmann, vol. 4, pp. 34-39; vol. 5, p. 501; *The Biblical Encyclopedia*, vol. 8 (1982), pp. 910, 916 (in Hebrew); see further Ephal, pp. 25-26.

[12] See 1 Samuel 1:9 ff, 1 Kings 8:54. See also Kaufmann, pp. 500-501, 542. It should be noted in this context that when Philo of Alexandria made his holiday pilgrimage to Jerusalem, he sought to pray in the Temple and not only to offer sacrifices therein, see *On Providence* 64. It is almost certain that also in Elephantine prayers were held near the altar for the restoration of the local Temple, along the lines of the Biblical examples mentioned above, see Porten, p. 156. And in general, prayer fulfilled an important function in the ritual worship therein, consult the full details in Porten, pp. 144-146.

Diaspora.[13] Indeed, just as prayer and sacrifices were combined in the consciousness of the Israelite prophets as two central components of the worship of God (compare, for example, Isaiah 1:11-16; I Kings 8:27-28), so too were these things perceived in the consciousness of the Jews of Egypt headed by Philo, who even raised prayer to an ethical and philosophical level high above that of the sacrifices. In this way, he expressed the ethical and philosophic uniqueness of the religion of Israel as compared to other faiths.[14] From this perception, the conclusion necessarily follows that the 'house of prayer' could well fulfill the non-sacrificial functions of the Temple, and therefore it was thought of as the place in which Jews could give faithful expression to their beliefs. The Septuagint translates 'house of prayer' (*bet tefillah*)—οἶκος προσευχῆς—which, as has been stated, is one of the designations of the Temple, and from which, apparently, the shortened designation προσευχή is derived which we know from the Jewish synagogues in Egypt.[15]

The term συναγωγή in the Septuagint (and in the parallel Aramaic translations), by contrast, generally indicates a 'gathering' (אספה), a 'community' (עדה) and a 'congregation' (קהל). It is no wonder then, that, in the course of time, this term came to indicate the organized Jewish communities, that is, the *qehillot*.[16] Instructive is the fact that the distinction between these two terms appears in a single context in the Septuagint, in connection with the prophecy of Isaiah 56:6-7. As stated, the Temple was called οἶκος προσευχῆς, whereas the completing verse (8) "Yet I will gather others to him, beside those of him that are gathered" is translated thus, ὅτι συνάξω ἐπ' αὐτὸν συναγωγήν. Its literal meaning is, "Yet will I gather him a gathering" or "Yet I will congregate him a congregation." Of significance for our study are these essentially identical usages based upon the same distinction that occur in an Egyptian Jewish papyrus document from the second half of the first century B.C.E. (*CPJ*, I, 138). The document clearly refers to "an assembly that was held in the house of prayer" (ἐπὶ τῆς γενηθείσης συναγωγῆς ἐν τῇ προσευχῇ) on behalf of some society or association (σύνοδος). In spite of the fact that the document was preserved in a very poor condition, the term σύνοδος is discernible at least another three times,

---

[13] See 1 Kings 8:22ff, 2 Chronicles 6:12ff, 2 Kings 19:14ff, Isaiah 37:14ff, 2 Chronicles 30:27, etc.

[14] See *Aristeas* 234 and Philo, *On Noah's Work as a Planter*, 126. See at length I. Heinemann, *Philons griechische und jüdische Bildung* (Breslau, 1932), pp. 66, 472; Wolfson, *Philo*, vol. 2, pp. 237-252; Hengel, "Proseuche," pp. 157-184, esp. p. 162.

[15] See the Septuagint on Isaiah 56:7, 60:7. Cp. 2 Maccabees 7:37; Mark 11:17; Matthew 21:13; Luke 19:46.

[16] See Schürer, vol. 2, pp. 429-430; Safrai, "Synagogue," pp. 47-48. It should be noted here that the standard opinion is that the συναγωγή designation is due to Land of Israel influence. See Hengel, "Proseuche," pp. 181ff.

indicating that the designation συναγωγή was intended to define in that context the very act itself of convening in the 'house of prayer' and not the body that was convening.[17] To summarize: προσευχή is the official and accepted designation of the synagogues in Egypt in the Ptolemaic and Roman period, and it is self evident in the inscriptions of dedication to the kings. The fact that this designation is repeated again and again—nineteen times—in Philo's historical writings, while the term συναγωγή is not mentioned even once, requires explanation.[18]

There is every basis for thinking that the term προσευχή is also short for the full name ἡ προσευχή θεῷ ὑψίστῳ ("house of prayer to the Supreme God," or "...the Most High God") which appears three times in the Egyptian inscriptions: two inscriptions of the second century B.C.E.—one from Athribis in the eastern delta (*CPJ*, III, 1443 = *CIJ*, II, 1443) and the second from Alexandria itself (*CIJ*, II, 1433 = *CPJ*, III. 1433)—whereas the third is also from Alexandria, but a bit later, from the end of the first century B.C.E. (*CIJ*, II, 1432 = *CPJ*, III, 1432). It has a slight change of text in the way that the expression "to the Great God" (θεῷ μεγάλῳ) replaces the expression "to the Supreme God." These inscriptions have not the slightest connection whatever with the worship of Ζεὺς ὕψιστος which spread mainly through Asia Minor in the Roman period, since the "Supreme God" designation was customary, first of all, in the Jewish world and common enough in the Septuagint and Hellenistic literature in general. Therefore it is no wonder that other synagogues in the Hellenistic-Roman Diaspora, not only in Egypt, also were dedicated to the "Supreme God."[19]

As stated above, the two most prominent non-sacrificial functions performed in the Temple in the presence of the community and which served the synagogues as an example were praying and Torah-reading. It is logical

---

[17] See further with Philo's usages of the verb συνάγω in connection with gatherings in the synagogues: *Gaius* 157, 311, 315; *On Dreams* II, 127. And see further Schürer, vol. 2, p. 440 (and note 46). See also Hengel, "Proseuche," pp. 169-170.

[18] For exact references to προσευχή in Philo, see Mayer, p. 247. The fact that Philo calls the Great Synagogue in Alexandria a 'house of prayer' (*bet tefillah*) disproves Oesterley and Robinson's theory (Oesterley & Robinson, p. 295) that the 'house of prayer' is a small institution in a small settlement and that 'synagogue' is characteristic of a large city.

[19] See the Septuagint on Genesis 18:20; Psalms 7:8, 17:14, 49:14, 67:35; 2 Maccabees 3:31; 3 Maccabees 7:9; Josephus, *Jewish Antiquities* XVI, 163; for references in Philo see Mayer, p. 291. See also in the New Testament: Mark 5:7; Luke 1:76, 6:35, 8:28; Acts 7:48, 16:17; Hebrews 7:1. On the synagogues dedicated to the "Supreme God" in Delos, Phrygia, and Bosphorus, see *CIJ* I, 690, 727, 729, 769. And see also Smallwood, *Philo*, p. 241; A. Pelletier, *Legatio ad Caium, traduction et notes* (Paris, 1972), pp. 181-182; Wolfson, *Philo*, vol. 1, p. 40; A. T. Kraabel, "Ὕψιστος and the Synagogue at Sardis," *Greek, Roman and Byzantine Studies* 10 (1969): 81-93; L. Roth-Gerson, "The Jews in Asia Minor," in *Diaspora*, pp. 84-85, 88, 91-93 (in Hebrew); M. Stern, "Jewry of Greece," in *Diaspora*, pp. 118-119 and note 32; B. Lifshitz, "The History of the Jews in the Kingdom of the Bosphorus," in *Diaspora*, p. 129, 131-133. Further see M. Hengel, *Judaism and Hellenism* (London, 1974), vol. 1, p. 298; vol. 2, pp. 199 (note 261), 200-201 (notes 262, 265).

to assume that these liturgical activities began to crystallize in Egypt after the Torah was translated into Greek mainly after the reign of Ptolemy II Philadelphus (285-246 B.C.E.). It is likely that the story in the Letter of Aristeas (305) about how the translators of the Septuagint prayed every day and busied themselves with the Bible and its translation provided an important paradigm for imitation. This observation probably also holds true for the ceremonial convocation held in honor of the translation's completion—during which the Torah was read with great festivity.[20] Philo provides a description of Sabbath worship, which probably reflects the rites of the Alexandrine Jews (Philo, *Moses* II, 41-42):

> to gather in one place on the Sabbath days and, sitting together in awesome reverence and exemplary order, to listen to the reading of the Torah...and a *kohen* (priest) among those present or one of the Elders (that is, one of the members of the Gerusia [council]) reads before them the sacred laws and explains them one by one, until the later hours of the afternoon approximately.[21]

It seems that lines of similarity exist between the description in the Letter of Aristeas and Philo. It reveals not only the actual existence of a festive convocation for reading the Torah but also the participating in, or more precisely, the conducting of it by a *kohen* or a Gerusia member (see *Aristeas* 310). Even the duration of the convocation "till the late hours of the afternoon approximately" was done in imitation of the duration of the work of the Torah translators (*Aristeas*, 303; *Antiquities* XII, 104). The worship of God in the synagogues of Alexandria thus not only developed from the aspiration to duplicate the non-sacrificial worship of the Temple, but alongside this imitation developed independent patterns based upon the convocation of the Septuagint translation preserved in the local tradition.

Philo's works give full and detailed description of this activity of the synagogues on the Sabbaths and Festivals, as it took place in Alexandria (see below) and most probably in the provincial towns of Egypt.[22] In his *On the Embassy to Gaius* (156), Philo attests to the ancient custom of the Jews to assemble in their 'houses of prayer' "primarily on the holy Sabbath days, when they publicly study the wisdom of their fathers."[23] In *On the*

---

[20] *Aristeas* 308ff. Josephus adds in his parallel (*Jewish Antiquities* XII, 107-108) that at that same assembly they also interpreted the scriptures for the assembled.

[21] See *Hypothetica* 7:12-13; cp. *Special Laws*, Book II, 62, except that there he does not describe "one of special experience" who reads the Torah as specifically one of the priests or elders.

[22] Verification of this can be found in an inscription from Naucratis in which "a Sabbath gathering" (σύνοδος σαμβατική) is mentioned, see A. Bernard, *Le Delta égyptien d'apres les textes grecs*, vol. 1 (Cairo, 1970), No. 28.

[23] In this context attention should be paid to the fact that the synagogue was sometimes called by the gentiles σαμβατεῖον (=Sabbath house). This is mentioned, for example, in one of the Imperial orders to the Jews of Asia Minor, see Josephus, *Jewish Antiquities* XV 1, 164.

Life of Moses (II, 216), Philo adds that they dedicate their time on that same occasion also to acquire knowledge and delve into the matters of Nature in general, and that the 'houses of prayer' are really only 'houses of study' (διδασκαλεῖα) of good sense, courage, temperance. righteousness, fear of God, holiness, and every virtue by which one's duties toward God and man can be discerned (*Special Laws*, II 62).[24] In spite of the connection of these things to the biblical topics and the explanation of the texts, they are also directed to the realities of Philo's time—witness the analogy to the customs of the Therapeutae with which Philo was closely acquainted (*Contemplative Life* 30-32). It is worth noting that Philo uses similar terminology in his comments about the man who reads the Torah: he is one of the 'Elders,' that is, someone of great stature, such as a scholar and leader.[25] There is good reason to assume that one of the sources of Philo's Jewish knowledge was the Great Synagogue in Alexandria, which was most likely also visited by the sages from the Land of Israel and who brought their teachings, preaching, and wisdom to their brethren in the Diaspora.[26] Josephus also bears witness to the study of Torah and its homiletic exposition in the synagogues on the Sabbaths (*Against Apion* II, 175; *Antiquities* XVI, 43) as do the books of the New Testament (Mark 1:21-22; 6:2; and Luke 4:15 ff. 31; 6:6; 13:10; John 6:59; 18:20 etc.). Elsewhere Philo attests to the gatherings of the communities of worshipers in Egypt on holidays and festivals (in addition to the Sabbaths) in the synagogues. For example, in his work *Flaccus* (116-118) he describes the custom of his brethren to live in *sukkot* ('booths,' or 'tabernacles') for the entire festival. The Jews also come together for festive gatherings that take place in the synagogues—during

[24] In Greek, 'the philosophy of their fathers,' a term used by Philo on other occasions to refer to the Jewish Holy Scriptures. See *Moses* II 216; *On the Creation* I 28; *Special Laws*, Book II 61; *Contemplative Life* 28. It seems that Philo thought this custom to be ancient, to have begun with Moses; see *Hypothetica* 7:12; cp. Eusebius, *Praeparatio Evangelica*, VI 1, 7, 359d-360a. See also Josephus, *Against Apion* II, 10, 175; Acts 15:21; M. Meg. end of ch. 3; Y. Meg. 4, 75a; Targum Pseudo-Jonathan on Exodus 18:20; Yalkut Shimoni, Exodus 408 (Parashat Vayakhel). There is no doubt that the traditions which attributed this practice of gathering in the synagogues on the Sabbath to Moses were intended to make it a force of compelling sanctity, and they in no way relate to the pure historic truth.

[25] In the source: ὁ πρεσβύτερος καὶ τῶν δογμάτων ἐμπειρότατος and likewise *Hypothetica* 7:11 & 13; *Contemplative Life* 67. He was chosen as President of the ceremony (ὁ προέδρος) who would teach those assembled chapters from the Holy Scriptures (τὰ ἱερᾶ γράμματα), repeat the material aloud with them, and interpret the material thoroughly placidly and pleasantly. Finally he would conclude with a ceremonial rendition of psalms of praise and glory to the Creator, in which the congregation also took an active part (ibid., 75ff).

[26] Compare it with the introduction to Ben Sira, see M. H. Segal, *The Complete Ben Sira* (Jerusalem, 1959), p. 1 (in Hebrew). See also. Y. Amir, "Philo's Homilies on Fear and Love and their Relation to Palestinian Midrashim" *Zion* 30 (1962): 47-60 (in Hebrew); Y. Amir, "Philo of Alexandria," in *Diaspora*, p. 240.

which there certainly are ceremonial readings of the Torah.[27] That there was a special festive character during the days of the Festival of Sukkot we also know from the Jewish community at Edfu (Apollinopolis Magna) from a defective papyrus document of the second century C.E. (*CPJ*, III, 452a), where "a *pannychis* of the Feast of Tabernacles" was held. This apparently refers to *simhat bet ha-shoevah* (the Water Drawing Festival).[28] These festivals were also observed in the synagogue of the Jews of Berenice in Cyrenaica along with the New Moon feasts and other festivals.[29] There is no doubt that Sukkot's centrality in the lives of the Diaspora communities in general and in the worship of God in the synagogues in particular stemmed from the importance of this Festival in the Jerusalem Temple from the First-Temple period and especially the Second-Temple after the Covenant ceremony by Ezra and Nehemiah. This was particularly evident, as we have said, in the festive convocations held on the basis of their similarity to the fulfillment of the commandment of *haqhel* ("Assemble Me the people") for the purpose of reading the Torah. Not for nothing did the enemies of Israel in Alexandria choose to attack the Jews and their synagogues in the years 38, 41, and 115 C.E. specifically on the Festival of Sukkot (see below).

The functioning of the Great Jewish Synagogue in Alexandria as a house of prayer in which ceremonial holy Torah-reading convocations were held accompanied by public blessings led by a special *memuneh* ('appointee') and a *hazzan* is well illustrated in the Talmudic tradition (Y. Sukkah 5, 55a; B. Sukkah, 51b). The fact that the congregation praying in the synagogue "did not sit mixed but rather each craft by itself," is indicative not only of the internal structure of the community but also of this organization's view of the status of the Torah reading and the accompanying ceremonial blessings.[30]

The central place of the synagogues in Jewish religious life *ipso facto* also gave them a central place in the social and organizational life of the Jews, with all of the influences and the legislative and judicial consequences resulting therefrom. Not in vain did Tcherikover determine that whenever the existence of a synagogue is mentioned in a place of Jewish settlement, one can also assume that an orderly and recognized communal organization exists there.[31] Such an institution can be erected only where a sizable Jewish

[27] On the plots against the synagogues in Alexandria during the Festival of Tabernacles, see below.

[28] For details on the special importance of the Festival of Tabernacles in the life of the Jewish communities of the Hellenistic-Roman Diaspora, see Stern's explanations of that document. See also Kasher, pp. 153-154 (English ed. pp. 165-167).

[29] See *CIG*, 5361-5362; *REG*, LXII (1949): 283ff., 286ff.

[30] See Kasher, pp. 311-314 (English ed. pp. 349-355).

[31] See *CPJ*, I, pp. 7 ff., and also Kasher, pp. 104-106 (English ed. pp. 106-107).

community required its services, which means that the synagogue was situated at the very heart of the area of settlement, a Jewish residential area such as a town or village, or a neighborhood or quarter of a large city. Any Jewish community with a synagogue must number at least some tens of families, for it would otherwise be difficult to understand how that community could build such a structure and maintain it properly. The erecting and building of a synagogue certainly required considerable sums of money and the existence of communal funds to underwrite its organized activity. Furthermore, one cannot imagine the erection and operation of such an institution without government authorization, especially not in a country with a centralized, absolutist regime such as Egypt in the Ptolemaic and Roman period. In addition, we can also conclude that the synagogue building, including the land on which it was erected, was community property owned by all the Jewish residents of the place. Its erection and regular ongoing operation could not take place without the existence of an organized religious and communal leadership recognized by the authorities and authorized by the Jewish community itself to make decisions and act in its name.[32] All this adds up to the conclusion that the existence of a synagogue clearly points to the existence of an organized, well-established Jewish community.

What is known of most of Egyptian synagogues comes, as stated, from epigraphy. These consist primarily of dedicatory inscriptions placed in the synagogues or upon their gates in honor of the royal family at the time. These inscriptions can, in fact, teach us not only about the right of decision (the '*psephisma*') which the local Jews possessed, but also about their organizational structure. This organization was necessary, for without it they would not have been able to make and implement even the simplest decision, such as dedicating an inscription in honor of the royal house. The terminology adopted in those inscriptions, as far as the communities that erected the synagogue are concerned, is in keeping with the accepted official rules relating to organized local organizations. The formulations such as "The Jews of place such and such" or "The Jews from place so and so" (οἱ ἐν...᾿Ιουδαῖοι, οἱ ἐκ...᾿Ιουδαῖοι, οἱ ἀπο...᾿Ιουδῖοι) attested to a Jewish independent organization separate from the local community organization by whose name the community was called (see note 31 above). The legal basis for such an organization could only be with governmental permission, which recognized the right of the Jews "to live by their ancestral laws," a right which was also given to other ethnic communities in Egypt.[33]

---

[32] The right to make a community decision (ψήφισμα) was a characteristic right granted to bodies organized and recognized by the central authorities; see Kasher, in a number of places.

[33] About this version in antiquity in general, see for example, Arrian, *Anabasis* I, 4:17, 2:18 & VII, 1:20; *Polybius* I, 1:20; *SIG*, I, 4, 390; *BCH* 44 (1920): 73, No. 4 et al. multa. In the usages of the formulation in connection with Diaspora Jewry, see for example, *Jewish*

The permission to erect a synagogue and hold regular activities was, in practice, conditional and obviously dependent upon official recognition by the central authorities of the synagogue's status as a 'holy place,' which enjoyed protection against desecration (the right of asylia).[34] One of the inscriptions from an unidentified community in Lower Egypt (*CIJ*, II, 1449=*CPJ*, III, 1449) confirms the existence of this right in the clearest way "By order of the Queen and King, in place of the previous tablet of the dedication of the house of prayer, let there be written above what had been written below: 'King Ptolemy Euergetes [proclaimed] the house of prayer as a refuge'" (ἄσυλον). At the bottom of the inscription there appear a few words in Latin—"The King and Queen have ordered (this)." Scholars are divided over whether the reference is to Queen Zenobia of Palmyra and her son (270 C.E.) or to the last Ptolemaic Queen, Cleopatra VII and her son Caesarion.[35] In any case, the later inscription relates to the right of asylia already given to the synagogue in the days of Ptolemy III Euergetes I (247-221 B.C.E.). This date thus reveals the antiquity of the local community and the early royal recognition of its sanctity. A papyrus document from Alexandrou-Nesos in the Fayûm of 218 B.C.E. (*CPJ*, I, 129) also verifies, albeit indirectly, the right of asylia which protected the local synagogue in such an early a period. The document is arranged as a petition of an anonymous woman who complained that a local Jew named Dorotheus had stolen her cloak and demanded justice be done. From her charge, it turns out that when she called out for help, Dorotheus fled to the synagogue with the item. With the involvement of a third party, the stolen cloak was deposited with the *nakaros* of the synagogue until the verdict would be decided. The very fact that the item was deposited with the *nakoros* (the one in charge of the services, the maintenance and supervision of sacred property) attests to the right of asylia which the place enjoyed.[36] Another inscription, from Alexandria itself, mentioned the existence of a 'sacred precinct' (ὁ ἱερὸς περίβολος), in which the local 'house of prayer' stood along with the structures or installations appended to it (τὰ συγκύροντα) which we shall discuss later. The very definition of the area as a 'sacred precinct' indicates the power

---

Antiquities XI, 338; XII, 126, 150; XIV, 213, 234, 242, 246, 260, 263, 264; XVI, 28, 60,163, etc.

[34] In this regard the synagogue was no different from other holy places. On the right of asylum in ancient Egypt, see F. V. Woess, *Das Asylwesen Agyptens in der Ptolemäerzeit* (München, 1923); M. I. Rostovtzeff, *Social and Economic History of the Hellenistic World* (Oxford, 1941), pp. 899 ff. See also on this right given to the synagogues, W. Schrage, "συναγωγή," in *Theologisches Wörterbuch zum Neuen Testament*, vol. 7, p. 285, nos. 175-177; Krauss, pp. 226ff.

[35] For details see: *CIJ*, III, p. 144; and likewise Hengel, p. 169, note 2.

[36] For full details on this document, see Kasher, pp. 137-138 (English ed. pp. 146-148).

of the sanctity afforded it and those in need of the religious services which the structures and installations erected therein provided. This picture also finds verification in Philo's writings about the synagogues in Alexandria of his day (*Flaccus* 48, and compare *Gaius* 137) as well as the epigraphic evidence touching upon other synagogues throughout the Hellenistic-Roman Diaspora.[37] The fact of the existence of non-Jewish 'sacred places' in Alexandria that also enjoyed asylia, indicates that the synagogues were comparable to them in status in this regard. They enjoyed protection by virtue of orders and decrees of the central authorities and not of the urban authorities—the sworn enemies of the Jews.[38] Very instructive in this context is the fact that the synagogue in Arsinoë-Crocodilopolis was erected on a plot of land whose official legal definition was 'sacred land' (ἱερὰ γῆ). It was registered in the local land registry at the end of the second century B.C.E. (*CPJ*, I, 134) to indicate that the synagogue was recognized as a 'sacred place' in the eyes of the authorities and placed on par with other sacred sites in the city.

Information about structures and installations connected with synagogue buildings have survived from a number of places in Egypt. In Xenephyris in the northwest Delta, a 'gate-house' (πυλών) was mentioned upon which had a dedicatory inscription in honor of King Ptolemy VIII Physcon Euergetes II (145-116 B.C.E.) affixed to it by the local community (*CIJ*, II, 1440=*CPJ*, III, 1440). Since normally such a structure was erected at the entrance of a compound which surrounds the main building for purposes of protection and supervision, one can conclude that the synagogue at Xenephyris stood on a plot of land surrounded by a wall or a stone fence so that the gate-house allowed supervision of those who came there.[39] It is very logical to posit that the plot was called a 'sacred precinct' or a 'sacred plaza' (ὁ ἱερὸς περίβολος) as in the instance noted above. The mention of buildings or appurtenances (τὰ συγκύροντα) but without details, is expressed in the dedicatory inscription in honor of King Ptolemy VIII in the synagogue at Nitriai, which is surely Natrun on the western desert border of the Egyptian Delta (*CIJ*, II, 1442 = *CPJ*, III, 1442). In Athribis in the eastern Delta, there is mention in a private dedication inscription, apparently to Ptolemy VI

[37] See *CIJ*, II, 738 (Phocaea); *CIJ*, II, 752 (Thyateira). Compare Sukenik's comments on the finds from the synagogues of Miletus, Priene, Stobi and Dura-Europos, see Sukenik, *ASPG*, pp. 40, 42, 49, 79, 83. The same holds for the synagogues in the Land of Israel, such as Capernaum, Chorazin, and Naaran (ibid., p. 8, 22, 28). The right of asylum is indirectly also indicated by the writings of Josephus (*Jewish Antiquities*, XIV, 261; XV, 163-164) in relation to the synagogues in the cities of Asia Minor.

[38] Cp., for example, *Gaius*, 150-151; *Flaccus* 51. For complete details on religious life in Alexandria, including mentions of the temples and the places of ritual-worship, see at length P. M. Fraser, *Ptolemaic Alexandria*, vol.1 (Oxford, 1972), pp. 189 ff.

[39] See M. Maas. 3:6; M. Erub. 8:4; M. Sotah 8:9.

Philometor (180-145 B.C.E.), of an exedra structure contributed by some family or other and appended to the synagogue building (*CIJ*, II, = *CPJ*, III, 1444).[40] In a papyrus document (*CPJ*, III, 432) from Arsinoë-Crocodilopolis of 113 B.C.E., prepared as an official accounting of the income and expenses relating to the city water supply, two local synagogues were mentioned among the largest of the water consumers. The large water bill may indicate that they had a few water installations such as *miqwaot* for ritual-purity immersions, water basins for ritual washing of the hands and for drinking, and perhaps even installations for the household needs of the Jews living nearby.[41] It is very plausible that in the protected 'sacred precinct' of the synagogue there also was a community archive in which Jews deposited for safekeeping 'papers' and documents of importance (wills, contracts, deeds and the like).[42] It was also customary to preserve in the archives the genealogical lists of the members of the community and especially of those eligible to marry into the priesthood.[43] The monies for sacred causes and the contributions of the half-shekels collected to be sent to Jerusalem were also deposited there, and also, of course, the community funds for underwriting the life of the community itself.[44] To the extent that in different communities there were permanent religious courts, of the sort we have found in Alexandria, it is logical to assume that they also sat in or near the synagogue.[45] The accepted opinion is that the court in Alexandria was organized along the lines of the Great Sanhedrin, which sat in the Chamber of Hewn Stones in the Jerusalem Temple, and is the basis for the tradition that the Great Synagogue in Alexandria had seventy (or seventy-

40 The exedra was an entrance hall, portico or arcade built as an appendage to the main building, and it is known in the Greek gymnasia as well as in the Jewish communal construction in the Hellenistic-Roman period. For further details see Kasher, pp. 112-113 (English ed. pp. 116-117).

41 For an extensive discussion of this document, see Kasher, pp. 132-133, 135-136 (English ed. pp. 140-141, 143-144).

42 Papyrological evidence of this has survived from Alexandria, see: *CPJ,* II, 143. There is a recollection of another Jewish archives in the Hellenistic-Roman Diaspora from the Phrygian Hierapolis (*CIJ,* II, 775). The fact that in Alexandria there also existed a parallel city archives (*CPJ,* II, p. 9) and likewise in the Phrygian Hierapolis (see *CIJ*, II, 776, 778-779) may be indicative of their parallel legal status as institutions recognized and protected by the force of the law.

43 See, for example, *Against Apion*, 31-36; *Life* 6. And see Kasher, pp. 123, 151, 238, 309 (English ed. pp. 132, 162, 262, 347).

44 See, for example, Philo, *Gaius* 156-157, 216, 291, 312, 316; *Special Laws*, Book I, 77. Cp. further, *Jewish Antiquities* XIV, 110-113, 227; XVI, 27-28, 45, 160, 166-172, etc.; Cicero, *Pro Flacco* 28, 66-67. For further details see Kasher, "Jerusalem as a Metropolis," *Cathedra* 11 (1979): 51, note 26.

45 See Tos. Peah 4:6 (Zuckermandel edition, p. 23); Tos. Ket. 3:1 (ibid., p. 263); B. Ket. 25a. And see also S. Lieberman, *Tosefta ki-Feshutah, Moed (Sukkah)* (New York, 1962), pp. 889-890; ibid., *Peah*, p. 182.; and *Jewish Antiquities* XIV, 235, 260.

one) seats of gold.[46] Even if we have our reservations about that detail, arguing that the similarity is only based upon the sanctified Biblical model mentioned in Numbers 11:16,[47] we cannot ignore the actual existence of a similarity. After all, the Talmudic traditions about the Great Sanhedrin in Jerusalem also aver that its composition was on the basis of that very Biblical model itself.[48] Be that as it may, the functioning of the Great Synagogue in Alexandria as the seat of the community religious court, according to the Talmudic tradition, can strengthen our argument above concerning the similarity of synagogues and the Temple in Jerusalem.[49]

As stated above, Philo tells of the synagogue's use each and every Sabbath also as a 'house of study' (διδασκαλεῖα) for learning good sense, humaneness, temperance and righteousness, fear of God, holiness, and every virtue by which one's duties toward God and man can be discerned (*Moses*, II, 216). In his work *On the Embassy to Gaius* (115), he praises and glories in the tutors and instructors that have always existed in all the Jewish communities, enjoined to instruct in the Written Torah and the Oral Torah, to teach one both about the educational and scholarly ceremonial-festive activities and also about the ongoing daily activities that took place within the synagogue or the nearby structures.

The protection of the public using the synagogues and their installations could in no way be adequate if based only upon the right of asylia granted the place and its precinct. The right to assemble itself had to be legally valid, properly formulated, and publicly known. Indeed, Philo a few times stressed that the gatherings of the Jews in their synagogues were permitted by law, and that the known prohibitions of assembly that had been instituted since the days of Julius Caesar and Augustus did not apply to them.[50]

---

[46] Y. Sukkah 55a; Tos. Sukkah 4:6 (Zuckermandel edition, p. 198); B. Sukkah 51b. And see, for example, Schürer, vol. 2, p. 211; S. Hoenig, *The Great Sanhedrin, The History and Activities of the Great Beth-Din in the Days of the Second Temple* (Jerusalem, 1961), pp. 87-88 ff. (in Hebrew); See Kasher, p. 310ff (English ed. pp. 349 ff.).

[47] See Y. Efron, *Studies of the Hasmonean Period* (Tel Aviv, 1980), pp. 268, 287 and note 155 (in Hebrew).

[48] See, for example, Mishnah Sanhedrin 1:5-6, 2:4; and Schürer, vol. 2, p. 210, note 34.

[49] The similarity motif was emphasized even in relation to the glory of the synagogue in a similar linguistic style. "Whoever did not see the double colonnade of Alexandria never in his life saw the the glory of Israel" (Y. Sukkah 55a;) as was said of the Temple of Jerusalem: "Whoever did not see the glory of the Temple structure never in his life saw a magnificent structure" (B. Sukkah 51b) and "Whoever did not see Herod's structure never in his life saw a beautiful structure" (B. Baba Batra 4a).

[50] On *Lex Julia Caesaris de Colegiis*, see Suetonius, *Julius* 42:3; ibid., *Augustus* 1:32. And see the comprehensive survey of Z. Yavetz, *Julius Caesar and His Public Image* (London, 1983), pp. 85-96. As for what Philo wrote on this, see *Flaccus* 5, 135-136; *Gaius* 156, 311-312, 316; cp. Josephus, *Jewish Antiquities* XIV, 213-216, and see also: E. Schürer, *Geschichte des jüdischen Volkes im Zeitalter Jesu Christi* (Leipzig, 1909), pp. 64ff; Smallwood, *Philo*, pp. 205-206, 236-237; J. H. Levi, *Studies in Jewish Hellenism* (Jerusalem, 1960), pp. 102 ff., 198 (in Hebrew).

Therefore he condemned the desecration of the synagogues as a "revolutionary innovation and an abomination that has never been done" (*Flaccus* 41). His emphasis on "the revolutionary innovation" which was strongly expressed in a number of his attestations, was intended to protest against the desecration of Jewish *sancta* or to denounce and condemn the damage to their laws in general.[51] Not for naught did Philo raise the alarm at the danger of the Alexandrine precedent for the Jewish communities in the Roman Empire (*Flaccus* 45-47, 152; *Gaius* 346).[52] The desecration of the synagogues in Alexandria was expressed in practice in many ways; synagogues were seized and plundered (*Flaccus* 52, 123), which is obvious from the information about the banishment of the Jews from four of the city's neighborhoods to a single, small neighborhood in the eastern section of the city (*Flaccus* 55 ff. & 171; *Gaius* 121 ff.). The seizure of the synagogues in the four neighborhoods was also accompanied by their destruction and razing to the very foundations, including the burning of the structures made of wood (*Gaius* 132-133). This was made possible by virtue of the fact that cooperative non-Jews also lived in those neighborhoods. On the other hand, the attack on the synagogues in the residential area with a dense Jewish population was not accompanied by such acts of destruction and arson (because of the absence of cooperating enemies living there), but it was expressed by the removal of the dedicatory plaques, the various shields and steles in honor of the emperors (*Flaccus* 53; *Gaius* 133) and especially by the erection of images of Emperor Caligula, and in the Great Synagogue—a large bronze statue (*Flaccus* 41, 43, 51; *Gaius* 134ff.). It should be pointed out that the disturbances in Alexandria continued through the entire month of September (38 B.C.E.) and reached their climax during the Feast of Tabernacles (*Flaccus* 116ff.). That is to say, they continued through the entire Jewish holiday period, when Jewish communal life was especially lively. In 41 B.C.E., the disturbances were renewed twice: first at the beginning of the year with Jewish instigation which began immediately after the death of Caligula, and second, in the months of September-October with Greek instigation.[53] It is reasonable to posit that, as in 38 B.C.E., the Greeks directed their attack upon the Jewish community specifically during the holiday period in order to do damage to their *sancta* and their religious sensitivities in the most painful and malicious way. It could not have been

---

[51] See, for example, *Flaccus* 47; *Gaius* 152, 157, 165, 208, 292, 300, 333. The "innovation" matter is emphasized linguistically by means of the verb νεωτερίζω.

[52] Also, the restoration of their rights to the Jews of Alexandria, and foremost among them the defense of the things sacred to them and the laws of their forefathers, was considered a paradigm and a legal, immutable norm throughout the Empire. Not incidentally did Emperor Claudius also publish, alongside his Alexandrian Edict (*Jewish Antiquities*, Book XIX, 280-285), his Ecumenical Edict (ibid., 286-291, 292).

[53] For complete details on this, see Kasher, pp. 247-249 (English ed. pp. 272-274).

accidental that the period of the "battle of the Romans against the Jews" in the 'War of Quietus' also took place during the holiday period, and most likely was done with the cooperation and inspiration of the hostile Greek population in Alexandria.[54]

In sum, the Jewish synagogues in ancient Egypt were erected on the basis of similarity to the Temple in Jerusalem as a place of prayer and gathering together in festive convocations on Sabbaths and festivals. Since all the communal institutions clustered around them, and since they enjoyed the right of asylum, they stood at the center of the daily Jewish communal life. It is no wonder, then, that in days of calamity the synagogues were the first and primary targets for the attack and malevolence of Israel's enemies.

---

[54] The date of the publication of the Edict by the governor, Lupus—the 13th of October, 115 C.E.,—may allude to this, since it is the *terminus ante quem* for the outbreak of the disturbances. See *CPJ,* II, 435; E. Fuchs, "The Revolt of the Jews in Egypt, 115-117 C.E. in Light of the Papyri," in D. Rokeah, ed., *Jewish Rebellions in the Time of Trajan, 115-117 C.E.* (Jerusalem: Zalman Shazar Center, The Historical Society of Israel, 1978), pp. 124ff (in Hebrew).

SYNAGOGUES IN BABYLONIA IN THE TALMUDIC PERIOD

ISAIAH GAFNI*

The Babylonian Talmud records the following statement, which, while somewhat enigmatic, nevertheless suggests a unique status for the synagogues of Babylonia, in comparison to their counterparts in the Land of Israel: "Rav Assi said: Synagogues in Babylonia are built 'with a stipulation' (על תנאי) and nevertheless they may not be treated disrespectfully" (B Megillah 28b). The 'stipulation' here, following Rashi's commentary, is that upon their establishment it was understood that they may be used for certain non-sacral purposes, as opposed to synagogues in Palestine, where the following *baraita* lists precisely what is permitted and forbidden within the synagogue:

> Our Rabbis taught: "Synagogues[1] must not be treated disrespectfully: One cannot eat in them, drink in them, dress up in them, stroll about in them nor enter them in hot weather to get out of the sun or in rainy weather to escape the rain, nor eulogize in them a private eulogy; it is, however, permissible to read [i.e., Torah] in them and study (שונים) in them and speak a public eulogy in them." R. Judah said: "When [are these laws applicable]?—when they [i.e. the synagogues] are in use, but in their destroyed state you leave them and allow the grass to grow in them, and the grass is not plucked so as to cause anguish."[2]

Rav Assi's statement regarding the uniqueness of Babylonian synagogues is thus intended as a qualification of the above prescription that regulates synagogue behavior, although the various medieval talmudic commentators disagree as to what he precisely meant. It is unclear whether the special 'stipulation' regarding Babylonian synagogues indicates they may be used for non-sacral purposes only once they have been destroyed (unlike Palestinian synagogues), or that even when they are functioning synagogues

---

* This essay was originally published in A. Kasher, A. Oppenheimer, and U. Rappaport, eds., *Synagogues in Antiquity* (Jerusalem, 1987), pp. 155-162 (in Hebrew). It has been translated by the author and with the permission of Yad Izhak Ben Zvi.

[1] Ms. Munich reads: בתי כנסיות ובתי מדרשות (synagogues and houses of study), as do other manuscripts and medieval commentators; cf. *Diqduqe Soferim* ad loc., p. 145; the addition of '*batei midrashot*' also appears in the parallel in Y Megillah 3:4, 74a.

[2] B Megillah 28a-b; cf. Tosefta Megillah 2:18 (ed. Lieberman, p. 353) and Y Megillah 3:4 74a; for a discussion of the *baraita* cf. Lieberman, *Tosefta ki-Fshutah*, Moed (New York, 1962), pp. 1162-1164.

the structures may be utilized for certain non-sacral purposes.[3] Whatever the original intention in Rav Assi's statement, one thing is apparent: someone, at some time, considered the formal status of synagogues in Babylonia to be different from that of their Palestinian counterparts. While we might never successfully uncover any explicitly cited 'stipulation' regarding the intentions behind the very building of synagogues in Babylonia, the question nevertheless may be raised, did synagogues in Sasanian Babylonia perform a different social function or operate in a communal context that would suggest a social setting at variance from that of other synagogues, whether in Palestine or the Greco-Roman diaspora? It is this question that serves as the focus of the following study. It requires, at the outset, certain methodological observations and words of caution, which relate to the broader question of any historian's attempt to recover Babylonian Jewish social history.

Research on the social life and communal structure of Palestinian Jews under Roman and Byzantine rule has a varied corpus of source material from which a fairly convincing picture can be drawn. Although the problems relating to the use of rabbinic literature for historical purposes have been recognized and enunciated by scholars of various disciplines, this literature does not present itself to the historian of Judaism in Late Antiquity in a vacuum.[4] For many questions, it serves neither as the single source of information nor even as the primary one. The history of synagogues in Palestine and the Greco-Roman diaspora in late antiquity is a case in point. Alongside the numerous rabbinic literary allusions to synagogues and their functions, we have a wealth of parallel, non-Jewish, literary sources—contemporaneous with rabbinic sources but nevertheless from a different vantage point or for decidedly tendentious reasons—that describe what others saw as happening in the synagogues. These sources include, of course, the numerous Christian references to synagogue activity—from the New Testament to the writings of Church fathers—even the vehement anti-synagogue polemics evinced, for example, in the writings of John Chrysostom.[5] To these we can add the numerous legal issues relating to the synagogue and its

[3] For a list of both opinions among various medieval commentators cf. *Talmudic Encyclopedia*, vol. 3 (Jerusalem, 1981), p. 195 and notes 193-197 (in Hebrew).

[4] See, for example: J. Neusner, "History and the Study of Talmudic Literature," *The Allan Bronfman Lecture*, Shaar Shamayim Synagogue, Montreal 1978; W. S. Green, "What's in a Name"?—The Problematic of Rabbinic Biography," in *Approaches to Ancient Judaism: Theory and Practice*, vol. 1, ed. W. S. Green, (Missoula, MT: Scholars Press, 1978), pp. 77-96; D. M. Goodblatt, "Towards the Rehabilitation of Talmudic History," in B. M. Bokser, *History of Judaism—The Next Ten Years* (Chico, CA: Scholars Press, 1981), pp. 31-44; L. I. Levine, *The Rabbinic Class of Roman Palestine in Late Antiquity* (Jerusalem-New York, 1989), pp. 16-20; J. Fraenkel, "Research on the Aggadic Story: A Look to the Future" *Jewish Studies* 30 (1990): 21-30 (in Hebrew).

[5] Much of the material has been collected and examined in Cohen, "Evidence."

leadership, taken up in the Roman Imperial legislation of the time.[6] Yet a third literary component of the non-Jewish sources on synagogues are the references to the Jewish institution found in the Greek and Latin writings of pagan authors.[7] Most of these sources were available to our predecessors involved in the study of the ancient synagogue, whereas our own generation has been enriched by the mass of archaeological evidence concerning synagogues. These discoveries are indispensable not only for examining the development of the synagogue in all its physical manifestations, but also as a control for appraising rabbinic or non-rabbinic influences that are apparent in the structure. Furthermore, the archaeological evidence enables scholars to establish the general position of the rabbis within Palestinian Jewish society. Much of this holds true, albeit to a lesser degree, when discussing diaspora Judaism. While we have archaeological evidence of synagogues in the diaspora, this amounts to much less than what has been unearthed in Israel. But luckily, archaeological evidence is not our sole source of information about diaspora synagogues. Roman legal decrees relate to diaspora synagogues no less than to Palestinian ones, and clearly some Christian or pagan authors have the image of a non-Palestinian synagogue before them.

All this changes radically when focusing on the role of the synagogue in the largest of all Jewish diaspora communities of late antiquity, the Jews of Babylonia. Here our information derives from one source alone, the Babylonian Talmud. Indeed, physical evidence of these structures is non-existent, and few Christian authors writing east of the Euphrates—not even those in contact with the Jews there (e.g., Aphrahat)—supply us with anything remotely like the amount of material available for the synagogues of the western world. Needless to say, therefore, our ability to derive hard reality from this unique literary source is greatly diminished. The nature of our sole source requires not only a careful preliminary textual, philological and literary analysis, but we must constantly distinguish between two types of synagogue discussions in the Bavli. Inasmuch as the Bavli follows and elaborates on all mishnaic and other early Palestinian sources on synagogues, we must realize that many of these discussions are only academic and hypothetical analyses of earlier, Palestinian statements. These have the aim of establishing halakhic principles and guidelines—regardless of whether these guidelines accurately reflect the historical *sitz-im-leben* of synagogue reality in Sasanian Babylonia. For our purposes, the stories of Babylonian sages about *their* synagogues are far more important. Although

[6] See Linder, and listings under 'Synagogue' in the subject index, p. 429.

[7] See M. Stern, *Greek and Latin Authors on Jews and Judaism*, vols. 1-3 (Jerusalem, 1974-1984), and listings under 'Synagogue,' '*Archisynagogus*,' and '*Proseuche*' in the index of subjects in vol. 3.

it is certain that these stories contain a legendary component that may render the vast majority of *events* described totally unhistorical, it is no less probable that a certain perception of the synagogue—one which relates to what the storytellers assumed was the obvious activity taking place in the synagogue—clearly presents us with solid information concerning the nature of synagogue life in Babylonia. Moreover, to the extent that Babylonian and Palestinian sources preserve parallel accounts or commentaries on earlier sources relating to synagogues, a comparison of the contents of these versions may often reflect the different settings and realia familiar to each of the transmitters. This comparison may enable us to identify Babylonian reality, unknown to and therefore lacking in the parallel Palestinian version. Indeed, it is precisely through such a process of comparison, and with all the above-stated reservations notwithstanding, that a particular picture of Babylonian synagogues emerges from the Babylonian talmudic stories concerning synagogue life and activity. Moreover, these stories may shed light not only on the nature of Babylonian synagogue activity, but also on the organization and authority structure of the Babylonian Jewish community as a whole.

Much has been written about synagogues serving not only as centers of worship (that is, prayer) in their earliest Palestinian settings, but also about their role as the nucleus of local communal life,[8] providing the population with "a wide range of activities."[9] Synagogues can serve as the location for courts of law, the collection of local charity funds, a hostel, a banquet hall, a place of refuge and a local primary-level schoolhouse.[10] To the extent that some formal form of worship played a part in synagogues of the Second-Temple period, this frequently focused on the reading of the Torah and instruction of the Law, either by means of a translation and elaboration of the text or in the form of a public sermon. Indeed, the question of how early we can identify fixed and obligatory prayer as a function of the synagogue has repeatedly been raised, most recently and forcefully in a major study by E. Fleischer. He not only raises doubts regarding the very establishment of a fixed prayer system in Second-Temple Palestine,[11] but categorically states

[8] See S. Zeitlin, "The Tefillah, The Shemoneh Esreh: An Historical Study of the First Canonization of the Hebrew Liturgy," *JQR* 54 (1963-1964): 228-238; Baron, p. 280ff.; S. Safrai, "The Synagogue," in S. Safrai and M. Stern, eds., *The Jewish People in the First Century*, vol. 2 (Philadelphia, 1976), pp. 942-944.

[9] Levine, *SLA*, p. 14

[10] See Z. Safrai, "Communal Functions of the Synagogue in Eretz Israel during the Mishnaic and Talmudic Periods" in S. Schmidt, ed., *Memorial Volume for Mordechai Wizer*, (Jerusalem: Yavneh, 1981), pp. 230-248 (in Hebrew) (=Z. Safrai, ed., *The Ancient Synagogue, Collected Articles* [Jerusalem, 1986], pp. 105-124) [It is also translated in this volume—Eds.]; cf. Baron, p. 286: "In a word, the synagogue focalized in itself the whole communal life of Jewry, and thus became the culminating expression of Jewish autonomy."

[11] E. Fleischer, "On the Beginnings of Obligatory Jewish Prayer," *Tarbiz* 59 (1989-1990): 397-441 (in Hebrew).

that "the early synagogue, in all the authentic sources, was not a place of prayer but a forum for public gatherings and for reading and studying the Law and the Prophets."[12]

Be that as it may, the picture reflected in the Bavli is dramatically different from the varied communal roles commonly ascribed to the synagogues of Palestine and the Greco-Roman diaspora. A systematic review of all synagogue stories in the Bavli shows that the dominant—almost exclusive—activity described as taking place within the confines of the synagogue is prayer, and sometimes the reading of the Torah. Moreover, the Bavli frequently alludes *en passant* to the synagogue as a place of prayer, while linking most other manifestations of communal activity listed above to other frameworks or authority structures within Jewish Babylonia. The following are a few examples of this one-dimensional representation of the synagogue in the Bavli:

1. B Berakhot 7b: "Rav Isaac said to Rav Nahman: Why does the Master (=you) not come to the synagogue to pray? He replied: I cannot [come]."
2. B Rosh Hashanah 24b: "There was a synagogue at *Shaf ve-yateb* in Nehardea that had a statue (*andarta*; Rashi: a statue of the king), and Rav, Samuel, Samuel's father and Levi would enter and pray there, and were not afraid of arousing suspicion [of idolatry]."
3. B Baba Batra 3b: "Rav Hisda said: One should not tear down a synagogue until another synagogue has been built. Some say this is out of fear of negligence (i.e., not fulfilling the plan to build another synagogue), and some say because of prayer (i.e., that prayer will be discontinued until a new synagogue is built)." This tradition, in passing, fears that the absence of a synagogue will disrupt prayers, but makes no mention of any other public functions that are likely to be neglected.
4. B Berakhot 8b: "Rava told his sons: '...and do not walk in back of a synagogue while the congregation is praying.'"
5. B Berakhot 30b: "Although there were thirteen synagogues in Tiberias—R. Ami and R. Assi did not pray except among the columns, the place where they would study." (This is one of numerous examples purporting to describe a Palestinian setting, but possibly also reflecting the Babylonian reality with which the transmitters of the source were familiar).
6. B Megillah 29a: "Abaye said: At first I would study at home and pray in the synagogue, but when I heard what David (i.e. King David, author of Psalms) said: 'O Lord I love the habitation [*me'on*] of Your house' (Ps. 26:8) I would study in the synagogue." In the parallel to this source, in B Berakhot 8a: "When I heard what R. Hiyya b. Ami said in the name of Ulla—'From the day the Temple was destroyed God has in His world only the four cubits of halakah'—I pray only where I study."

This last source is interesting for a number of reasons. If we noted the element of learning or teaching as one of the major functions of the Palestinian

[12] ibid., Eng. Summary p. IV.

synagogue, with prayer possibly establishing itself only later, in Babylonia the process may have been reversed. The synagogue serves primarily as a place of prayer, with other functions—such as learning—entering only later, and with some difficulty. This process is apparent in yet another tradition, which describes two sages—Ravina and Rav Adda b. Matna—standing near a synagogue and discussing a question of halakah with Rava. "It began to rain heavily and they entered the synagogue, saying, We entered the synagogue not because of the rain but because the halakic discourse requires a clear mind like a day of the north-wind" [that is, a clear day]; (B Megillah 28b). While the question here was obviously the permissibility of entering a synagogue to get out of the rain, it is nevertheless noteworthy that the rabbis make excuses for entering the synagogue for the purpose of studying.

Moreover, the highlighting of prayer in the Babylonian synagogues points to what is lacking in those same traditions, namely, the projection of the synagogue as the central institution of Jewish communal life and the seat of its authoritative officers. Thus, for instance, much has been written on the "*archisynagogus*" found in sources relating to Palestine and the Greco-Roman diaspora.[13] While some see this as referring to a particular position of leadership within the synagogue, others consider the phrase to be synonymous with 'head of the community.' This last use apparently is supported by the references to the office in the Theodosian Code, but the term may have taken on different meanings in different localities.[14] In Babylonia, nowhere do we encounter any such link between officers connected to the synagogue and any role of communal authority. In fact, the Bavli hardly even refers to such officers connected to the synagogue.[15]

In general, the reality and activities connected with synagogue life are stressed far more in Palestinian sources than in the Bavli, even when the particular case at hand does not relate directly to aspects of the synagogue. A good illustration of this may be found in the two traditions surrounding the attempt of Hananiah, the nephew of R. Joshua, to intercalate the calendar in Babylonia, only to be forced by the Palestinian authorities to back down.[16] The context of the clash between Hananiah and the Palestinian messengers is strikingly different in the two versions. In the Bavli's version, the messengers literally pick a fight with him in the following manner: "They told

[13] See Juster, pp. 450-453; Krauss, pp. 114-121; and Schürer, vol. 2, pp. 434-436.

[14] Codex Theodosianus 16:8:4 (Linder, n. 6, p. 135); 16:8:13 (Linder, p. 202); 16:8:14 (Linder, p. 216); cf. Linder, p. 137, n. 10.

[15] The Bavli refers a few times to the *hazan* in Babylonia: B Eruvin 74b, Berakhot 53a, Arakhin 6b ('*hazanei de-Pumbeditha*' are missing in Arakhin 6b in Mss. Munich and Vatican 119); cf. M. D. Yudelowitz, *Jewish Life in Talmudic Times: Sefer Nehardea* (Vilna, 1905; repr. Jerusalem 1971), p. 26 and n. 6 (in Hebrew), who suggests that these references may be later additions to the original Bavli text, possibly by the Saboraim.

[16] B Berakhot 63a-b; Y Sanhedrin 1:2, 19a.

him: We have come to study Torah...He began to proclaim 'unclean' and they decreed: 'clean,' he proclaimed 'forbidden,' and they—'permissible'. ...He said to them: Why do you declare clean when I declare unclean?...They said: Because you intercalate years and fix New Moons outside the Land of Israel." The framework for this episode is obviously the '*bet midrash*,' and in fact after the clash erupts, Hananiah is warned that if he does not accede to the demands of the messengers, he will be 'excommunicated' (יהא בנידוי). This phrase, in the Bavli, almost always alludes to a banishment from the *bet midrash*, and is the logical conclusion in the context presented in the Bavli.[17] Not so in the Palestinian Talmud, where tradition places the clash in a totally different context: "R. Yizhak arose and read in the Torah: These are the festivals of Hananiah, nephew of R. Joshua....R. Nathan arose and completed (the *haftarah*): For out of Babylonia shall come Torah, and the word of God from Nehar Pekod"! For the Palestinian storyteller the public clash would naturally take place in a synagogue setting, where Torah and the Prophets are read publicly, and it is highly probable that the two versions in fact reflect the differences in communal life between the two Jewish centers. The probability that synagogues in Babylonia did not assume the same communal position they occupied in Palestine and the Greco-Roman diaspora may also be adduced from the fact that, although persecutions were not unknown to the Jews of Parthia and Sasanian Babylonia, these attacks never focused on the local synagogues to the degree that is apparent in the western communities. Synagogues were singled out for attacks both in Second-Temple Palestine as well as in the Egyptian diaspora,[18] and it goes without saying that the synagogue became a primary target during the Byzantine period.[19] Not so in Babylonia, where attacks against Jews—although less frequent than in the Roman west—took place, but rarely depict local synagogues as a major target. During the middle of the first century C.E. the two major diaspora communities—the Jews of Alexandria in Egypt, and those residing in and around Seleucia in Parthia—felt the wrath of their neighbors vented upon them. While reports of the events in Egypt single out the synagogues of Alexandria as a major target of the local mob,[20] the sources that describe the slaughter of fifty thousand Jews at Seleucia make no mention of synagogues.[21] The same holds true for the

[17] D. Goodblatt, "The Story of the Plot against R. Simeon b. Gamaliel II," *Zion* 49 (1984): 358-361 (in Hebrew).

[18] In Judaea, see the case of the synagogue at Caesarea, Josephus, *Jewish War* 2:285ff; for the events in Roman Egypt in the days of Gaius Caligula see Philo, *Gaius* 134.

[19] Even to the extent that the Christian-Roman legislator felt compelled to intervene, and thereby prevent the destruction of synagogues in the name of Christianity; cf. Codex Theodosianus 16:8:9 and see Linder, pp. 189-191.

[20] Cf. Smallwood pp. 235-242.

[21] Josephus, *Antiquities* 18:310-379.

latter part of the period under discussion, the fifth and sixth centuries C.E. While the harassment and even destruction of synagogues in the Byzantine world has been documented and frequently discussed,[22] the role of synagogues as targets of the Persian clergy in the Sasanian empire is far more subdued.[23] Sherira Gaon notes only one case of synagogues in Babylonia being closed down,[24] with the major targets of the persecutions there being the rabbis and Exilarch, accompanied by the destruction of *batei midrash*, religious decrees outlawing Sabbath, and in certain cases the forced conversion of children at the hands of Zoroastrian clergy.[25]

In a legal and formal sense as well, the synagogue in Palestine was identified with the community at large far more than in Babylonia. Palestinian sources refer *en passant* to the synagogue as public property, belonging equally to all residents of the community. Consequently, if a man has taken an oath to derive no benefit from another, he is forbidden not only to derive any advantage from that other person's private possessions, but also from those things that belong to the particular town: "And what are the things that belong to the town? The public square, the bath-house, the synagogue, the Ark [of the Law] and the Books [of Scripture]" (M. Nedarim 5:5). Although Palestinian sources also mention a "private synagogue," these cases are not the norm.[26] Responsibility for building and maintaining the synagogue is almost always assumed to have fallen on the entire local community. In contradistinction, the Bavli frequently refers to single personalities and sages as having complete control over their synagogues, and therefore having the authority to either tear it down or build another one. Examples of such authority include: Maremar and Mar Zutra rebuilt a summer synagogue during the winter and a winter synagogue during the summer

[22] The incident of a synagogue at Callinicum being burnt in 388 is only one example of a wider phenomenon, cf. J. Parkes, *The Conflict of the Church and the Synagogue* (London, 1934), pp. 166-168.

[23] For general overviews of these events, see G. Widengren, "The Status of the Jews in the Sassanian Empire," *Iranica Antiqua* 1 (1961): 142ff.; J. Neusner, *A History of the Jews in Babylonia,* vol. 5 (Leiden: Brill, 1970), pp. 60-69; it should be noted, however, that the persecution of Jews or Judaism in Sasanian Babylonia was not a standing and ongoing policy of the Zoroastrian church, but rather a sporadic phenomenon. By and large a spirit of coexistence seems to have prevailed between Persians and Jews in the talmudic era; see R. Brody, "Judaism in the Sasanian Empire: A Case Study in Religious Coexistence," *Irano-Judaica* 2 (1990): 52-62.

[24] Iggeret R. Scherira Gaon, ed. B. M. Lewin, (Haifa, 1921) p. 97.

[25] Ibid., pp. 94-97; *Seder Tanna'im ve-Amoraim*, ed. K. Kahan, (Frankfurt, 1935) p. 6 (no mention is made here of the destruction of synagogues); cf also *Sefer Ha-Qabbalah*, ed. G. D. Cohen, (Philadelphia, 1967), p. 31, which only refers to forced conversion. The Bavli refers only once to the destruction of synagogues (Yoma 10a), but as will be noted below, this reference indeed points to the role and status attributed by the Babylonian rabbis to the synagogue.

[26] Mishnah Megillah 3:2; Y Megillah 3:4, 74a.

(B Baba Batra 3b); Rav Ashi, who saw cracks in a synagogue at Mata Mehasya and tore the building down (ibid.); Rami b. Abba, who built a synagogue and attempted to tear down another one to use the bricks and beams (B Megillah 26b); and one source records a gentile contributing to "the synagogue of Rav Judah" (B Arakin 6b).

Is there an underlying reason for the different projections of the synagogue in the Palestinian and Babylonia sources? Quite possibly the answer may be found in the patterns of communal development among the Jews of Babylonia, which appear to be strikingly different than those known to us from Jewish communities in the Roman world. The autonomous lifestyle granted the Jews of Babylonia at least as far back as the Parthians, seems to have led to the creation of uniquely Babylonian patterns of communal life and authority structures. The very same functions that were assumed by officials attached to the local community and synagogue in Palestine, as well as in much of the Roman Empire, seem to have been taken over in Babylonia by the centralized Jewish governing bodies—in particular the Exilarchate, and later the heads of the rabbinic institutions. Thus, for instance, I have elsewhere attempted to show that at least a major component of the judiciary functioned—and was physically situated—either alongside the rabbinic academies[27] or was attached to the court of the Exilarch.[28] In a similar manner, charity was neither collected in Babylonia by anonymous *gabbaim*, nor linked at times to public appeals made in the synagogue. What we find more frequently in the Bavli is that one or more of the well-known Talmudic sages is responsible for the local system of charity collection and disbursement; indeed, the Bavli is not the least bit hesitant to declare a rabbi's overriding responsibility for these activities.[29]

If, indeed, the practical role of synagogues in Babylonia was limited in comparison to that of their Palestinian counterparts, why the great stress in the Bavli regarding the antiquity of these synagogues? The phenomenon itself has been documented by A. Oppenheimer (see his article in this collection), and the results of that study dovetail quite nicely with what we have seen here. The references to the antiquity of the synagogue of *Shaf ve-yateb* in Nehardea, or of the synagogue at Hutsal where God's presence is to be found (B Megillah 29a), and likewise Daniel's synagogue (B Erubin 21a)—do not stress any major role for those synagogues in contemporary

[27] Cf. I. Gafni, "Court Cases in the Babylonian Talmud: Literary Forms and Historical Implications," *PAAJR* 49 (1982): 23-40; see also D. M. Goodblatt, *Rabbinic Instruction in Sasanian Babylonia* (Leiden, 1975), p. 272, who describes the rabbinic disciples in Babylonia as 'apprentice lawyers' who sit before their mentors as the latter serve as judges.

[28] See Beer, pp. 57-93.

[29] B Megillah 27b; B Baba Batra 8b; B Baba Qamma 119a; B Ketubot 67b; B Baba Qamma 93a. See also I. Gafni, *The Jews of Babylonia in the Talmudic Era: A Social and Cultural History* (Jerusalem, 1990), pp. 105-106 (in Hebrew).

Babylonian life. What they do stress, rather, is part of the all-embracing Babylonian Jewish preoccupation with the continuity of their communal existence, stretching as far back as the end of the First-Temple period. The rubble of the destroyed Temple was removed to Babylonia where it served as the building material for local synagogues, and this too serves as ammunition in the ongoing debate between Babylonia and Palestine over issues of supremacy and legitimacy.[30] These sources on the antecedents of the Babylonian synagogues go hand-in-hand with the Babylonian claim to the longevity of the office of Exilarch, who was considered none other than a descendent of Jehoiakin, King of Judah.[31] Through these claims, the Babylonians transferred to their own community the two social and religious underpinnings of ancient Palestinian Judaism, namely, Temple and Monarchy. This will explain the frequency with which the Bavli identifies synagogues with the Temple: "'And I was to them as a minor *sanctuary*' (מקדש מעט; Ezek. 11:16)—These are the synagogues and houses of study in Babylonia" (B Megillah 29a). Wherever Israel was exiled, the *shekinah* accompanied them "...and where is it in Babylonia? Abbaye said: In the synagogue of Hutsal and the synagogue of *Shaf ve-yateb* in Nehardea" (ibid.). This would also explain an interesting association between the two institutions found in the Bavli, namely, the laws of synagogues are frequently discussed in conjunction with the laws of the Temple. A lengthy discussion in B Baba Batra 3b raises the question of tearing down a synagogue before a new one is built. Since the decision there prohibits such an act, the Bavli immediately asks: How could Baba ben Buta advise Herod to tear down the Temple before a new one was erected (B Baba Batra 3b-4a)?

Yet another example of the Babylonian perception of a linkage between synagogue and Temple is found in an interesting exercise in what might be termed 'future history' carried out by the Bavli. The question is raised, Will Rome fall to the Persians, or Persia to Rome? The solution offered follows the typical talmudic logic of *a minori* (*kal va-homer*):

> If the First Temple [was] built by the descendants of Shem (i.e., the Israelites) and destroyed by the Babylonians, [and] the Babylonians fell to the Persians; the Second temple, built by the Persians and destroyed by the Romans—is it not fitting that the Romans fall to the Persians? Rav said: Persia will fall to Rome! Rav Kahana and Rav Assi asked Rav: The builders in the hands of the destroyers? Yes, he told them, it is the decree of the

---

[30] Cf. S. Spiegel, "On the Controversy of Pirqoi b. Baboi," in *H. A. Wolfson Jubilee Volume*, Hebrew Section (Jerusalem, 1965), pp. 266ff (in Hebrew).

[31] A. Neubauer, "Seder Olam Zuta," *Medieval Jewish Chronicles*, II, (Oxford, 1895), p. 74; see also Seder Tannaim ve-Amoraim (above n. 25) p. 4 ("and the city of Nehardea was settled from the days of Yehoiakhin until the death of Samuel"); see Beer, pp. 11ff.

> King (=God); some say he told them: They (the Persians) also *destroy synagogues* (B Yoma 10a).[32]

Again, the stress here is not on the synagogue as the center of communal life, but rather as the equivalent of the Temple destroyed by the Romans.

When a Palestinian sage was asked how one knows that God's presence may be found in the synagogue, he answered: "The Lord is in the *Community of God*" (עדת אל; Ps. 82:1).[33] When, on the other hand, the Babylonian Abbaye explains why he transferred his studies to the synagogue, his choice of scripture is: "O Lord I love the habitation of *Your house*" (מעון ביתך; Ps. 26:8).[34] Might it be that the two perceptions of the essence of the synagogue are reflected in the different choice of Scriptures? For the Babylonian it is the house of the Lord, as was the Temple in its day; whereas for the Palestinian sage, the synagogue is indeed a sanctuary, but the source of its sanctity derives from the fact that God resides within His community, and the synagogue is, in the final analysis, the focal point of His community.

---

[32] This anonymous elaboration of Rav's statement may have been added in the latter part of the third century, following the persecution of religious minorities by Kartir; cf. E.S. Rosenthal, "For the Talmudic Dictionary" in S. Shaked, ed., *Irano-Judaica* 1 (Jerusalem 1982), p. 63-64 and notes on p. 131 (in Hebrew).

[33] B Berakhot 6a.

[34] B Megillah 29a.

THE HOUSE OF ASSEMBLY AND THE HOUSE OF STUDY ARE THEY ONE AND THE SAME?

DAN URMAN*

In a colloquium, F. Hüttenmeister raised the question of the connection between the 'house of assembly' (*bet ha-knesset*) and the 'house of study' (*bet ha-midrash*) in the Land of Israel during the rabbinic period,[1] and his main conclusion is that "in general, one building served for prayer and instruction and was called both '*bet knesset*' and '*bet midrash*,' according to its function in that particular context."[2] In his opinion, this also explains why no remains of buildings dedicated to function as houses of study have thus far been uncovered.[3]

A. Oppenheimer and S. Safrai have not accepted this conclusion,[4] stressing that from the corpus of sources of that period "it is clear that what is being spoken of are two different institutions located in separate buildings."[5] There was also no unanimity of opinion among the colloquium participants on the question of "the absence of any archaeological find related to 'houses of study' as against the abundance of such concerning every aspect of 'houses of assembly,'" even though one can occasionally discern points of contact among their various conclusions.[6]

According to Hüttenmeister, "the sources that specifically speak of two separate buildings may refer to large cities in which it was not possible to conduct both activities in the same building; rather, the 'house of study' existed in a nearby building that was part of the 'house of assembly' building complex."[7]

In Safrai's opinion, the house of study was not "necessarily a small room attached to a 'house of assembly,' for at times the 'house of assembly'

---

* This essay originally appeared in the *Journal of Jewish Studies* (1994). It is reprinted by the permission of the Editor, *Journal of Jewish Studies*. It was translated by Dr. Nathan H. Reisner.

[1] Hüttenmeister, "Connection," pp. 38-44.

[2] Hüttenmeister, "Connection," pp. 43-44.

[3] Hüttenmeister, "Connection," p. 44.

[4] Oppenheimer, "Study," pp. 45-48; Safrai, "Halakah," p. 49.

[5] Thus Oppenheimer, "Study," p. 46. And Safrai, "Halakah," p. 49 noted, "In my opinion, two specifically separate buildings are spoken of in many of the sources."

[6] The formulation is Oppenheimer's, see Oppenheimer, "Study," p. 48.

[7] Hüttenmeister, "Connection," p. 44.

itself was small...."[8] On the other hand, he argues, that "one need not necessarily find a separate structure for the 'house of study,' since few used it."[9] A similar claim emerges from Oppenheimer's conclusions: "It is clear that the 'houses of assembly' very greatly outnumbered the 'houses of study.' Whereas in each and every settlement there was one or even more 'houses of assembly,' only central settlements or locations of important Sages possessed a 'house of study.' Third, while 'houses of assembly' were constructed in known characteristic forms that are uniquely theirs and allow for their identification, we have no knowledge of a special construction method customarily used for the 'houses of study.'"[10]

Oppenheimer goes on to say: "Not only is it logical to assume that the 'house of study' was not in a special building, which naturally contributes to the difficulty of identification which may be insurmountable, but it turns out that it sometimes was not even in a separate building of its own..., i.e., there sometimes is not even the possibility that there be anything material to survive; and more than indicating this building or another, the 'house of study' concept appears in the sense of a 'school.'"[11] These last statements of Oppenheimer's were later carried further by Z. Safrai to the conclusion that in most "of the instances in which the sources mention 'the house of study,' they refer not to an architectural structure but to the fact of people's gathering to study together."[12]

We are witness here to a series of conclusions, some of which swallow up the institution of the house of study in the house of assembly complex (Hüttenmeister and Z. Safrai),[13] while the rest transform it from an important, central institution in the landscape of Jewish society in the Land of Israel in the rabbinic period into the abstract concept of a 'school,' or "the fact of people's gathering to study together." These surprising conclusions warrant reexamination, using all of the mentions of the house of assembly and house of study in the historical sources touching upon the Land of Israel in the mishnaic and talmudic periods.

It seems that the source of the weaknesses in the above mentioned conclusions stems largely from a misreading of the place and functions of the house of assembly in the life of the Jewish community in the Land of Israel at that time. Was the house of assembly there really a house of prayer throughout the entire period of the Mishnah and the Talmud, as

[8] Safrai, "Halakah," p. 49.

[9] Safrai, "Halakah," p. 49.

[10] Oppenheimer, "Study," p. 48.

[11] Oppenheimer, "Study," p. 48.

[12] See Z. Safrai, "Notes on the Essence of the 'House of Study' in the Land of Israel," *Cathedra* 24 (1982): 185 (in Hebrew).

[13] Ibid.

Hüttenmeister[14] and many other scholars maintain?[15] A systematic study of the literary sources of the period leads to different conclusions.

THE HOUSE OF ASSEMBLY

For a hundred years now, so much has been written about the house of assembly as an institution in the life of the Jewish people in the Land of Israel and in the Diaspora during the days of the Second Temple and the Mishnaic-Talmudic period that it would seem that everything about it in those times, about its place and functions in the life of the Jewish society, is already known.[16] However, one who attentively reads the instructive chapter that S. Safrai devoted to the house of assembly will discover how many are the questions for which modern scholarship has not yet found satisfactory answers, questions related to the beginnings of this institution, its developmental fluctuations over the different generations, its contents, its procedures, its prayers, its conduct, and the like.[17] For all that, no one today challenges the conclusion that after the destruction of the Second Temple the house of assembly became the central institution in the religious and social life of the Jewish community in the Land of Israel.

If, during the days of the Second Temple, the houses of assembly in general served the communities as such,[18] and for the reading of the Torah, and the *derashah* (the sermon) in particular,[19] nevertheless, it was the Temple that mostly served as the focus of religious life in the Land of Israel. It was after its destruction that the religion of all the communities in

---

[14] Hüttenmeister, "Connection," p. 38, writes: "The House of Assembly according to the Talmud [the Babylonian!—D.U.] is 'a place wherein they raise up prayer'...in other words, the house of assembly is a house of prayer, a place of worship."

[15] Among the scholars of the earlier generations, see, for example, Elbogen, *Jewish Prayer*, pp. 331-368. (Note the chapter heading on p. 331: "Batei ha-Tefilah"). Of contemporary scholars, see E. Meyers, "The Early Houses of Assembly in the Galilee," E. Schiller, ed., *Sefer Zev Vilnay*, (Jerusalem, 1984), pp. 259-262 (in Hebrew); Tsafrir, pp. 165-189, 285-299 (in Hebrew). See especially what he wrote on p. 165, "It is logical to assume that in every Jewish community in the Land of Israel (and in the Diaspora) there was a 'house of prayer'; if not an elaborate synagogue, at least a modest prayer room such as the one in the Leontis House at Beth-Shean (designated by the scholars as 'the small synagogue')."

[16] Among the pioneering studies of this subject, especially noteworthy is Elbogen, *Jewish Prayer*, and the important work of S. Krauss, found in Krauss. For an extensive bibliography on the subject, up-dated to 1977, see Ruth Goldschmidt-Lehmann, "Ancient Synagogues in the Land of Israel," *Cathedra* 4 (1977): 205-222 (in Hebrew). For the recent years, see the notes in Tsafrir.

[17] Safrai, *Second Temple*, pp. 143-170 (in Hebrew).

[18] See, for example, Josephus, *Life* 277: "The next day there was a general assembly in the Prayer-house, a huge building capable of accommodating a large crowd."

[19] Cf. Luke 4:16-22; Acts of the Apostles 13:15.

the Land of Israel became centered on the houses of assembly and fixed public prayers gradually constituted their central liturgical component.[20]

S. Safrai has already emphasized the fact that when the tannaitic sources mention the house of assembly and its functions, they first and foremost point out the reading of the Torah, and prayer is frequently not mentioned at all.[21] The outstanding example of this is found in the *baraita*:

> Houses of assembly, one does not conduct oneself frivolously in them, nor enter them to escape the heat of the sun, nor to escape the cold, nor to take shelter from the rain, and one does not eat in them, nor drink in them, nor sleep in them, nor stroll in them, nor enjoy oneself in them, but one reads [Scriptures] and studies [Mishnah] and teaches [delivers homilies] in them. A public eulogy is delivered in them.[22]

It is interesting to note that even in the passage from *Avot de-Rabbi Nathan*, upon which Hüttenmeister sees fit to base his point of view, which says that "the house of assembly is a house of prayer,"[23] prayer is the last item mentioned in the order of things the Jew does upon entering the house of assembly in the evening after his day's work:

> And what is the limit that the Sages placed upon their words? That the Sages recite *qeriat shema* in the evening till midnight, and Rabban Gamaliel recites it till dawn. How [does this apply]? Let not a man who comes from his [day's] work in the evening say "I shall go home, eat a bit, drink a bit, sleep a bit, and then I shall recite the *qeriat shema* and pray [the Eighteen Benedictions]." For sleep will overcome him and he will find himself without *qeriat shema* and without prayer. However, when one comes from work, he should go to the house of assembly; if it was his practice to read [Scriptures], let him read; to study [the Mishnah], let him study; and then he reads the *qeriat shema* and prays, and goes home, eats his bread, and sleeps. And whoever transgresses the words of the Sages is deserving of death.[24]

Only in the amoraic sources does prayer gradually begin to occupy an honored place in the houses of assembly in the Land of Israel. Thus, for example, in the Jerusalem Talmud:

> Rabbi Abba and Rabbi Hiyya in the name of Rabbi Yohanan: "A person should pray in a place that is set aside for prayer. And what of 'in every place where I cause My name to be mentioned' (Ex. 20:21)? 'Where you cause My name to be mentioned' is not written, but 'in every place where I cause My name to be mentioned.'" Said Rabbi Tanhum bar Hanina: "A per-

---

[20] Cf. Safrai, *Second Temple*, pp. 150-153.

[21] Safrai, *Second Temple*, p. 145.

[22] Tos Meg. 2 (Erfurt ms. 3), 18, (Lieberman edition p. 353). And also see Y Meg. 3:4, (74a); B Meg. 28a-b. In all translations in this essay, any words I have added to help make the English understandable have been inserted inside brackets.

[23] See above, n. 14.

[24] ARN, Addendum B to Version A, (Schechter edition, p. 154). Cf. B Ber. 4b.

> son should set aside for himself in the house of assembly a place for prayer. And what of 'When David reached the top' (2 Sam. 15:32)? 'Where he prostrated himself to God' is not written here but rather 'Where people would prostrate themselves to God' (2 Sam. 15:32)."[25]

And further on in that same tractate we read:

> Huna said: "One who prays behind the house of assembly is called wicked, for it is stated, 'On every side the wicked roam' (Ps. 12:9)." Rav Huna said: "Whoever does not enter the house of assembly in this world will not enter the house of assembly in the world to come." What of "On every side the wicked roam"? Said Rabbi Yohanan: "One who prays in his house is as if surrounded by an iron wall." R. Yohanan's statement must be reversed. There said Rabbi Abba, said Rabbi Hiyya in the name of Rabbi Yohanan: "A person should pray in a place that is set aside for prayer." And here he said thus? One instance speaks of an individual; one of the public. Rabbi Phineas in the name of Rabbi Hoshaiah: "One who prays in the house of assembly is considered as if bringing a pure offering." What is the reason? "Just as the Israelites bring an offering in a pure vessel to the House of the Lord" (Is. 66:20).[26]

It would seem, then, that seeing the house of assembly institution in the Land of Israel throughout the entire period of the Mishnah and Talmud only from the viewpoint (and conception) that the house of assembly is a house of prayer is both narrow and misleading.

Many researchers have already shown that in addition to the house of assembly being a place for the reading of the Torah and its "teaching,"[27] it also served as a platform for the *derashah*[28] which was a frequent and central event in the religious and social life of the Jewish communities in the Land of Israel in the rabbinic period.[29] It seems that the public *derashah* had become institutionalized in the Land of Israel long before prayer. About this last fact one can learn from the *baraita* quoted in full above: "The houses of assembly...one reads the Torah, studies Mishnah, and delivers homilies in

[25] Y Ber. 4:4, 8b. See also L. Ginzberg concerning this passage in his work *Commentaries and Innovations for the Yerushalmi*, vol. 3 (New York, 1941), pp. 360-366 (in Hebrew).

[26] Y Ber. 5:1, 8d.

[27] This refers to the teaching of the *mitzvot*. Cf. this with the version appearinq in the Theodotus inscription found in Jerusalem: ...ὠκοδόμησε τὴν σύναγωγ[ὴ]ν εἰς ἀνα̣[γ]ν̣ωσ[ιν] νόμου καὶ εις [δ]ιδαχὴν ἐντολῶν' ("...built the house of assembly for the reading of the Torah and the teaching of the religious commandments"); see Schwabe, p. 362.

[28] About the discourses in the house of assembly, see I. Heinemann, *Public Discourses in the Talmudic Period* (Jerusalem, 1971), pp. 7-29 (in Hebrew), and the bibliography there.

[29] We find clear evidence of this in Y Sotah 1:4 (16d): "R. Meir used to preach in the house of assembly of Hamath every Sabbath eve...." See also Leviticus Rabbah 9:9 (Soncino Press, English edition, p. 117; the Hebrew edition of Margulies, p. 191 also indicates the other parallels to this).

them..."[30] and likewise from other mentions of this in the sources of the period.[31]

In addition to the reading of the Torah, the study of *mitzvot*, and the public *derashah*, the house of assembly also served as the locus for a wide variety of institutions and activities in the religious and social life of the community with which S. Krauss has already dealt extensively.[32] Recently, Z. Safrai has reexamined this variety that flourished in the period under discussion,[33] and he suggests, among other things, that the house of assembly also "served as the office for the administration of the community and its various *parnasim* [i.e., communal leaders]."[34] It seems that this suggestion brings us closer to a more accurate view of it in the time of the Mishnah and the Talmud.

In our opinion, the house of assembly in the period under discussion should be seen, first and foremost, as a community center, *bet ha-qehillah* the community house.[35] In the words of S. Safrai: "The term 'house of assembly' need not be interpreted specifically as a house in which people gather, but rather as a people's house, as the public house, the home of the community."[36] They assembled in the 'community house' (the συναγωγή in Greek, the *bei kenissta* in Aramaic, the *bet ha-knesset* in Hebrew) for the reading of the Torah, the study of the *mitzvot* and the *derashah*.[37] But in addition to these clearly religious and religious-educational activities, religious-social activities took place there, such as *se'udot mitzvah*—namely, meals in conjunction with a particular religious event[38]—as well as social-organizational occasions such as charity collections,[39] announcements of

30 Tos Meg. 2:18.

31 See above, n. 19. And also see Y Taa. 1:2 (64a); Leviticus Rabbah 35:12 (Soncino edition, p. 453); Lamentations Rabbah 1:3 (Soncino edition, p. 99); Ecclesiastes Rabbah 6:2 (Soncino edition, p. 158); Pesikta De-Rab Kahana 18:5 (Jewish Publication Society, Braude-Kapstein edition in English, p. 319); and others.

32 Krauss, pp. 182-198.

33 Z. Safrai, "The Communal Functions of the 'House of Assembly' in the Land of Israel in the Period of the Mishnah and Talmud," S. Schmidt, ed., *Mordecai Weiser Memorial Volume* (Jerusalem, 1981), pp. 230-248 (in Hebrew). [It is translated in this volume—Eds.]

34 Ibid., p. 240. [In this volume, the quote appears on p. 196—Eds.]

35 *Domus ecclesiae*. Cf. Y. Tsafrir, "On the Architectural Origins of the Ancient Galilean Synagogues—A Reconsideration," *Cathedra* 20 (1981): 38-39 (in Hebrew). But we must note that he has assumed that house of assembly= house of prayer. See above, n. 15.

36 Safrai, *Second Temple*, p. 143.

37 See above, notes 19, 22, 27-31.

38 See Y Ber. 2:5 (5d); Taa. 4:5 (68b); MQ 2:3 (81b) = Sanh. 15:2 (26b); and others.

39 See Matthew 6:2; Tos Shabbat 16 (in print and London ms.: 17):22 (Lieberman edition, p. 79); Tos Ter. 1:10 (Zuckermandel edition, p. 26) = BB 8:14 (p. 409); Y Demai 3:1 (23b); and others.

lost items,[40] sessions of the courts,[41] etc. Occasionally, alongside the house of assembly there were schools[42] and hostels.[43]

As has been said, it was only in the generations of the *amoraim* that prayer became a central liturgical component in the *bet ha-knesset* in the Land of Israel.[44] But, in contrast to Christianity, where the liturgy in the nave of the church was already in this period seen as "the true and legitimate heir" to Temple worship,[45] no clear proofs can be found in our sources indicating that 'the prayer hall' (the προσευχή) of the *bet ha-qehillah* (the συναγωγή) in the Land of Israel was perceived in this way.[46] It would therefore be an error to define the Jewish *bet ha-knesset* in the Land of Israel, throughout the period of the Mishnah and Talmud, as a *bet tefillah* (a 'house of prayer').

THE HOUSE OF STUDY

If we see the *bet ha-knesset* of the Land of Israel in the rabbinic period as a *bet qehillah* (a 'community house') we can understand how, alongside the appearance of synagogue buildings, separate buildings to serve specifically as *batei midrash* ('houses of study') were developed and institutionalized therein. Furthermore, we shall also be able to explain why many of the Palestinian Sages preferred the *batei midrash* to the *batei knesset*, a fact with which we shall deal below.

The sources of the period clearly indicate that after the destruction of the Second Temple, under the leadership of the Sages, the goal of limiting controversy and eliminating the sects current in Jewish society in the Land of Israel in the days of the Temple became stronger within Palestinian Jewry.[47] Yet, while the Sages heading the Yavneh generation (and later on, those at the head of the Usha generation and those that followed) were very actively

[40] See, for example, Leviticus Rabbah 6:2 (Soncino edition, pp. 78-79). And cf. B BM 28b.

[41] See M. Mak. 3:12 and parallels; Matthew 10:17; Acts of the Apostles 22:19. And see further in Krauss, pp. 186-188.

[42] See M. Shab. 1:3; Y Meg. 3:1 (73d); ibid., 3:4 (74a); Genesis Rabbah 52:4 (Soncino edition, p. 452); and others.

[43] Such a lodging is mentioned in the Theodotus inscription, see Schwabe, p. 362. And see further in Krauss, pp. 195-196.

[44] See above, n. 20.

[45] For an example, see the discourse of praise for the building of churches delivered by Eusebius to Paulinus, Bishop of Tyre—Eusebius, *Hist. Eccl.* X, IV 2-71.

[46] Cf. Hengel, "Proseuche," pp. 157-184.

[47] See Tos Ed. 1:1 (Zuckermandel edition, p. 454); Y Ber. 1:7 (3b); B Eruvin 13b. And also see S. Safrai, "The Period of the Mishnah and the Talmud (70-640)," in H. H. Ben-Sasson (ed.), *History of the Jewish People*, vol. 1, (Tel-Aviv, 1969), pp. 313-315 (in Hebrew).

attempting to remove the barriers between the nation's different classes out of a strong desire to create a normative Judaism which would make national life possible without a Temple; they themselves, as national leaders, became an 'elite' social stratum which revealed, as is natural to the human species, clear tendencies to separatism and segregation.[48]

One of the clearest manifestations of this can be seen in the creation of a class called *bnei hakamim* ('sons of the sages'),[49] who gained that status by dint of *zekut avot* ('the merit of their fathers').[50] From the abundance of the Sages' statements derogating the *'am ha-aretz* ('the common man')—which became more and more caustic between the destruction of the Temple and the time of Rabbi Judah the Prince[51]—one can learn much about the separationist tendencies of many of the Sages of that period.[52] Two such statements are of especial importance for our issue. In Mishnah Avot 3:10 we read: "R. Dosa ben Harkinas said: 'Morning sleep and midday wine and children's talk and sitting in the meeting-houses of the *'ammei ha-aretz*, put a man out of the world.'"[53] And in the Babylonian Talmud Shabbat 32a: "It has been taught in a *baraita*, R. Ishmael ben Eleazar said: 'For sinning in two matters the common folk perish: for calling the Holy Ark "the chest," and for calling the *bet ha-knesset* "*bet 'am*" [i.e.,'the people's house'].'"[54] These two statements clearly reflect the daily reality of Jewish society in the Land of Israel in the period of the Mishnah. Many Sages of that time, as a social and religious 'elite,' absented themselves from the *batei ha-knesset* in which *'ammei ha-aretz la-Torah* ('the common folk as to the Torah,' i.e., those ignorant of the Torah) congregated.[55] In the light of this, it was but natural that these Sages and the circles of their students set up *batei midrash* for themselves as institutions that served their different needs, namely, for

[48] Cf. Oppenheimer, *'Am Ha-Aretz*, p. 182.

[49] About this class, see G. Alon, "Sons of the Sages," in *Researches in Jewish History*, vol. 2, (Tel-Aviv, 1970), pp. 58-73 (in Hebrew).

[50] See for example: Y Ber. 4:1 (7d); B Ber. 27b, and cf. Oppenheimer, *'Am Ha-Aretz*, pp. 182-183.

[51] A. Oppenheimer has already discussed this at length in Oppenheimer, *'Am Ha-Aretz*, and especially see pp. 172-195 there.

[52] Ibid.

[53] In the Kaufmann and Parma mss. and in a Genizah fragment from the Antonine collection [see I. J. Katz, *Ginzei Mishnah* (Mishnah Genizah Fragments), (Hebrew), Jersualem 1970, p. 111)], the text reads "...sitting in the meetings of the *'ammei ha aretz*...."

[54] In the mss. and in the earlier rabbinic authorities (Rishonim) these are cited in the name of the fifth generation *tanna*, R. Simeon ben Elazar; see *Dikdukei Soferim* for tractate Shabbat. And it seems that it should be this way, cf. Oppenheimer, *'Am Ha-Aretz*, p. 174, n. 13.

[55] On *'ammei ha-aretz la-torah*, see Oppenheimer, *'Am Ha-Aretz*, pp. 97-114 and the additional bibliography there.

study and instruction,[56] for preaching,[57] and for various religious and social gatherings.[58]

We see further evidence of this Palestinian reality in the tradition preserved in the Babylonian Talmud: "R. Ammi and R. Assi, though they had thirteen synagogues in Tiberias, prayed only between the pillars where they used to study."[59] From this tradition it appears that even in the generation of the *amoraim*, when the *batei knesset* gradually came more and more to serve as *batei tefillah* ('houses of prayer') and there had even been a softening of the attitude of the Sages to the *'ammei ha-aretz*,[60] there were outstanding Sages of the time who preferred not to pray in the *batei knesset* but rather where they studied, namely, in the *bet ha-midrash*.[61]

---

[56] Dozens of texts testify to the *bet ha-midrash* as a place of instruction and learning, e.g.: "And the boys grew" (Gen. 25:27).—R. Phinehas said in R. Levi's name: "They were like a myrtle and a wild rose-bush growing side by side; when they attained to maturity, one yielded its fragrance and the other its thorns. So for thirteen years both went to school and came home from school. After this age, one goes to houses of study (*batei midrashot*) and the other to idolatrous shrines." (Genesis Rabbah 63:10) [Theodor-Albeck edition, pp. 692-693 (in Hebrew), and see the parallels references there]. "I will divide them in Jacob..." (Gen. 49:7)—which means that from Simeon there would be scribes in the synagogues, and students and teachers of Mishnah from the tribe of Levi engaged in the study of the Torah in the houses of study. (NV Genesis Rabbah 97) [Theodor-Albeck edition, p. 1207].

[57] See, for example, Tos Sotah 7:9 (Lieberman edition, pp. 193-194): R. Yohanan ben Beroka and R. Eleazar Ḥisma had come from Yavneh to Lydda and paid their respects to R. Joshua at Peki'in. Said he to them, "What was new for you today at the house of study?" They replied, "We are your pupils and it is of your waters that we drink." Said he to them, "A house of study with nothing new is impossible. Whose Sabbath was it [i.e., whose turn was it to deliver the Sabbath discourse] ?" "It was that of R. Eleazar ben Azariah." "And on what did he discourse?" "'Gather the people—men, women, children...' (Gen. 31:12)—The men come to learn, and the women come to hear, but why do the children come? To gain reward for those who bring them!" Cf. Y Sotah 3:4 (18d-19a); Y Hag. 1:1 (75d); B Hag. 3a; Mekhilta of R. Ishmael, *Ba*, 16 (Horowitz-Rabin edition (Hebrew) pp. 58-59); ARN, Version A, ch. 18 (Schechter edition, p. 67).

[58] The Babylonian Talmud contains a few statements in the name of Palestinian *amoraim* which indicate that in the period of the Mishnah and the Talmud various gatherings were held both in the houses of study and the houses of assembly "to supervise public affairs." For examples, see B Shab. 103a=Ket. 5a; Ket. 63b; BM 28b. But we cannot verify this from Palestinian sources. On the other hand, the Jerusalem Talmud indicates in a number of passages that *se'udot mitzvah* were held in the houses of study in the Land of Israel. On that, see below.

[59] B Ber. 8a and 30b.

[60] On the sages' change in attitude toward the *'ammei ha-aretz* in the generations of the *amoraim*, see Oppenheimer, *'Am Ha-Aretz*, pp. 188-195.

[61] Rather than agreeing with Oppenheimer, who sees the tradition preserved in B Ber. 8a as an indication that the house of study "was not located in a separate building," i.e., that R. Ammi and R. Assi pursued their studies between pillars in some sort of open space (see Oppenheimer, "Study," p. 48), we follow Bacher, who concluded that these sages "used to pray...'between the pillars' in the house of study where they were studying." See Bacher, *Agadah*, vol. 2, part 1, p. 137 of the 1927 Tel-Aviv edition. It seems that the pillars mentioned in this tradition were those of some kind of *exedra* (open hall) of the house of study in which they studied and taught.

It also seems that in the tradition cited in the Palestinian Talmud, Taanit 1:2, 64a, according to which "R. Aha preached in the *bet ha-midrash*, R. Jeremiah preached in the council *bet ha-knesset*,"[62] there are intimations of the prevailing 'separation' between *batei ha-midrash* and *batei ha-knesset* in the Land of Israel in the rabbinic period.[63] It was the practice of Rabbi Aha, apparently one of those Sages who kept away from the popular *batei knesset*,[64] to deliver his sermons in the *bet ha-midrash*; while Rabbi Jeremiah, who from the sources of the period seems to have been an exceptional personality among the scholarly circles of his generation,[65] preached in the *bet knesset* designated in the sources as the 'council synagogue,' and he may have done that when he was removed from the *bet ha-midrash*.[66]

We shall now discuss a few of the mentions of *batei midrash* in our sources which indicate beyond a doubt the existence of separate structures for houses of study in the Land of Israel in the latter stages of the Second Temple times and in the Mishnaic-Talmudic period. An examination of these will also provide many details of the contents and procedures of the various houses of study in the Land of Israel at that time.

A number of traditions indicate the existence, even during the Second Temple period, of study-house structures in Jerusalem. The first of these which we shall cite appears in Tosefta Sanhedrin 7:1:[67]

---

[62] Bacher and Klein interpreted the *kenishta deboulei* as a house of assembly located near the building of the council (βουλή) in Tiberias. See Bacher, *Agadah*, vol. 3, part 1, p. 94, n. 6 of the (1930) edition. See also Klein, *Land*, p. 99.

[63] It should be noted that Hüttenmeister sees this tradition in particular as "a connection...between the house of assembly and house of study...in the reality of daily life, for one building served the two" (Hüttenmeister, "Connection," p. 43).

[64] For the existence of such houses of assembly, see the words of R. Dosa ben Harkinas in M. Avot 3:10: "R. Dosa ben Harkinas said: 'Morning sleep and midday wine and children's talk and sitting in the meeting-houses of the *'ammei ha-aretz*, put a man out of the world.'" It may be that the *kenishta deboulei* was counted among these houses of assembly, see Y Sheq. 7:4 (50c).

[65] See Bacher, *Agada*, pp. 90-100; Heiman, *History*, pp. 803-811; Albeck, *Introduction*, pp. 340-342, 622-625.

[66] See B BB 23b: "Because of that they removed R. Jeremiah from the house of study"; and B BB 165b: "Because of that they returned R. Jeremiah to the house of study." About R. Jeremiah's ouster from the house of study, see the discussions in Bacher, *Agada*, p. 90, n. 5 (and the references there to earlier investigators); Heiman, *History*, pp. 808-810 (and the references to the earlier scholars); Albeck, *Introduction*, p. 342, pp. 624-625; A. Steinsaltz, "Why Was R. Jeremiah Removed from the House of Study?" *Sinai* 54 (1964): 339-341 (in Hebrew).

[67] It should be noted that chronologically, the earliest mention of the house of study in our sources is in Ben-Sira 51:47 (Segal edition, p. 358): "Draw near unto me, ye unlearned, and dwell in my house of study." If Ben-Sira was in fact a Jerusalemite (see M. Z. Segal, *The Complete Book of Ben-Sira*, 2nd ed. [Jerusalem, 1972], p. 6 [in Hebrew]), then his mention of *bet ha-midrash* here can be seen as the first evidence of the existence of houses of study in Jerusalem already in the 2nd century B.C.E. About Ben-Sira's house of study, also see Segal, p. 7.

> Said Rabbi Jose: "At first there were no dissensions within Israel except in the Court of Seventy in the Chamber of *Gazith* [i.e., the Temple compartment in which the Great Sanhedrin sat]....Although the Court in the Chamber of *Gazith* consists of seventy-one, there are [to be] no less than twenty-three. Should one have need to leave, he checks: if there are twenty-three, he leaves; if not, he may not go until there are twenty-three. They sat there from the [time of the bringing of] the morning daily burnt-offering until the afternoon daily burnt-offering. On Sabbaths and festivals they would only enter the *bet ha-midrash* upon the Temple Mount. When a question [of law] was asked, if they had the answer, they gave it; if not, it was put to a vote—if those holding that it was impure were in the majority, they ruled 'impure'; if those holding that it was pure were in the majority, they ruled 'pure.' From there the halakah went forth and prevailed in Israel."[68]

This tradition indicates that on the Temple Mount some sort of structure existed called *bet ha-midrash* in which the Sages of the Sanhedrin used to gather on Sabbaths and festivals to study Torah and issue rulings of halakah.[69] It is difficult to determine if it is to that "*bet ha-midrash* on the Temple Mount" or to other houses of study that the words of R. Eleazar b. R. Zadok and R. Joshua b. Hananiah refer when they recall the practices in Jerusalem during the Festival of Tabernacles:

> Said R. Eleazar b. R. Zadok, "Thus were the men of Jerusalem accustomed to do: he enters the *bet ha-knesset* with his palm branch in his hand; he rises to translate and act as reader of the prayers, with his palm branch in his hand; to read from the Torah and raises his hands to pronounce the priestly benediction, he places it on the ground; he leaves the *bet ha-knesset*, with his palm branch in his hand; he enters to comfort mourners with his palm branch in his hand; he enters to visit the sick, his palm branch is in his hand; when he enters the *bet ha-midrash*, he gives it to his servant or his emissary who returns it to the house."[70] Said R. Joshua b. Hananiah, "All the days of the *simḥat bet ha-shoevah* [i.e., the festival of the place of the drawing of the water] we saw no sleep. We rose early for the daily morning burnt-offering, from there to the *bet ha-knesset*...from there to eat and drink and from there to the *bet ha-midrash*, from there to the daily afternoon burnt-offering, thence to the *simḥat bet ha-shoevah*."[71]

However, as A. Oppenheimer has already pointed out, there is enough evidence here to show "that from its outset the *bet ha-midrash* was an institution separate from that of the *bet ha-knesset*."[72]

---

[68] This is according to the Erfurt ms. version (Zuckermandel edition, p. 425). Also see Y Sanh. 1:2, 19c; Tos Hag. 2:9 (Lieberman edition, p. 383).

[69] Cf. Lieberman, *Tosefta ki-fshutah*, vo. 5, p. 1298.

[70] Tos Suk. 2:10 (Zuckermandel edition, p. 195; Lieberman edition, p. 265). Also see B Suk. 4lb.

[71] Tos Suk. 4:5 (Lieberman edition, p. 273). Also see B Suk. 53a.

[72] Oppenheimer, "Study," pp. 46-47.

It is also possible that R. Eleazar b. R. Zadok and R. Joshua b. Hananiah, who were considered part of the circle of Rabban Yohanan b. Zakkai's disciples,[73] were referring to the particular building of Rabban Yohanan b. Zakkai's house of study. The Jerusalem Talmud discusses this structure when it deals with the question of whether it is permitted to "sell a *bet knesset* and purchase a *bet midrash*," a matter to which we shall return later:

> May one sell a *bet knesset* to acquire a *bet midrash*? R. Joshua b. Levi said "It is permitted." For R. Joshua b. Levi said, "'And he burnt the house of the Lord' (2 Kings 25:9), i.e., the Temple; 'and the king's house,' i.e. Zedekiah's palace; 'and all the houses of Jerusalem.'" There were four hundred and eighty synagogues in Jerusalem. For Rabbi Phinehas said in the name of R. Hoshaiah: "There were four hundred and eighty synagogues in Jerusalem, and in each was an elementary school (*bet sefer*) and an advanced school (*bet talmud*), an elementary school for Scripture and an advanced school for Mishnah." And Vespasian went up and destroyed all of them. "Even every great man's house burnt he with fire," i.e., the academy (*bet midrash*) of Rabban Yohanan ben Zakkai, where they studied the greatness of the Holy One, blessed be He, as in "Tell me all the great things that Elisha has done" (2 Kings 8:4).[74]

If indeed Rabban Yohanan had his own academy building in Jersualem, then we have evidence that already in the days of the Second Temple there were private *batei midrash* in the country, "of the individual,"[75] alongside communal houses of study, "of the public." It may be to such a reality that the tradition preserved in the Babylonian Talmud alludes:[76]

> It was said of Hillel the Elder that he busied himself to earn half a *denar*,[77] half of which he would give to the doorman of the house of study, keeping the other half for his own and his family's livelihood. Once he could not earn anything and the doorman would not allow him in. He went up [on the roof], dangled over the edge, sitting near the *arubah* [i.e., the roof aperture looking towards the ground floor] in order to hear the words of the Living God uttered by Shemaiah and Abtalyon.

---

[73] See, for example, ARN, Version A, chap. 4 (Schechter edition, p. 23); Lamentations Rabbah 1 (Buber edition, p. 67); B Git. 56a.

[74] Y Meg. 3:1, 73d. Also see Lamentations Rabbah, Proem 12 (Buber edition, p. 12); Pesikta De-Rav Kahana 4:10 (Mandelbaum edition, p. 76); *Pitron Torah*, Pareshat Zot Hukat Ha-Torah (Urbach edition, p. 181).

[75] "Of the individual"—in the style of "house of assembly of the individual" mentioned in Y Meg 3:1, 73d: "Rabbi Samuel b. Nahman in the name of R. Jonathan: What you are saying refers to the house of assembly of the individual, whereas in the house of assembly of the public it is forbidden"; and in other places.

[76] B Yoma 35b.

[77] *Tarpik*=half a *denar*; See Jastrow, p. 557; D. Sperber, *Roman Palestine 200-400: Money and Prices*, (Ramat-Gan, 1974), p. 101.

Whether this tradition is authentic or anachronistic,[78] containing Palestinian or Babylonian motifs,[79] it can be taken as evidence of the fact that buildings were specifically set aside as houses of study in the Land of Israel during the rabbinic period. For this tradition, which mentions the *arubah* of the house of study, can be included among the references to the house of study in the Palestinian sources in which items and parts of the *bet ha-midrash* are mentioned incidentally. Thus, for example, it is reported that R. Judah b. Pazi went up to "the upper chamber of the house of study" and saw two people in close embrace.[80] And it is told of R. Berekiah, that he would station his *amora* at "the middle gate of the house of study."[81] Likewise, it is related that one Sabbath they forgot the "keys of the great house of study" and came to ask R. Jeremiah, who apparently was serving at that time as head of this *bet midrash*,[82] what they should do.[83]

In the Babylonian Talmud traditions are preserved which mention items and parts of the house of study. And even though these traditions sometimes have no parallels in the Palestinian sources, it would seem that their authenticity should not be questioned.[84] Thus for example, like the story of the "keys of the great house of study" in the days of R. Jeremiah, we have in the Babylonian Talmud a report that R. Isaac b. Bisna lost "the keys of the house of study" in the public domain on the Sabbath and came to R. Pedat to ask what to do.[85] It is likewise reported that R. Abba, son of R. Hiyya bar Abba, and R. Zeira were standing in the market-place of Caesarea near "the entrance to the house of study" when R. Ammi came out and found them there.[86]

From the tradition about Hillel the Elder's great diligence one can also learn of a door-keeper to a house of study who collected the students' tuition

---

[78] See J. Neusner, *The Rabbinic Traditions About the Pharisees before 70*, (Leiden, 1971), vol. 1, pp. 258-259; S. J. D. Cohen, "Patriarchs and Scholarchs," *PAAJR* 48 (1981): 78, n. 51.

[79] Cf. S. Safrai, *The Land of Israel and Its Sages in the Period of the Mishnah and the Talmud*, (Jerusalem, 1984), pp. 170-172 (in Hebrew); D. Goodblatt, "On the Story of the 'Conspiracy' Against Rabban Simeon ben Gamaliel II," *Zion* 49 (1984): 361 (in Hebrew). But on the other hand, see what he wrote in his article "New Developments in the Study of the Babylonian Yeshivot," *Zion* 46 (1981): 35 (in Hebrew): "The term *bet midrash* is Palestinian in origin. A comparison of the use of its parallel Aramaic term *bei midrasha/midrasha* in the Babylonian Talmud with the use of the term *bei rav* (lit. place of the teacher) indicates a clear intent to use the first term in Palestinian matters (i.e., in statements of or stories about Palestinian figures) and the second, in matters Babylonian."

[80] Y Sanh. 13:6, 23c.

[81] Y Ber. 7:6, 11c.

[82] Cf. Bacher, *Agada*, p. 94.

[83] Y Shab. 19, 16d.

[84] See Goodblatt's statement quoted above in n. 79; and likewise in his book: D. M. Goodblatt, *Rabbinic Instruction in Sassanian Babylonia*, (Leiden: Brill, 1975), passim.

[85] B Yeb. 113b.

[86] B Hul. 86b.

fees before allowing them in.[87] There is also an allusion to the existence of functionaries who looked after the houses of study in Jerusalem during the Second Temple days in the tradition respecting the start of R. Eliezer b. Hyrcanus' study with Rabban Yohanan b. Zakkai:

> They said that that very day Rabban Yohanan b. Zakkai was sitting and teaching in Jerusalem with all the great men of Israel before him. He heard about (R. Eliezer's father), and set up bodyguards with instructions that if he came, he should not be admitted. He came and they did not admit him.[88]

In the Babylonian Talmud it is related that on the very day that the Sages revolted against Nasi Rabban Gamaliel of Yavneh, "they removed the door-keeper [of the house of study] and gave the students permission to enter."[89] And indeed, since the Yavneh generation there is no mention whatever in our sources of the presence of guards at the entrances to the houses of study in the Land of Israel.

While there has been some questioning of the veracity of the sources in relation to the presence of guards at the entrances to the academies and their ability to reflect the Palestinian reality,[90] there seems to be no doubt concerning the existence of another functionary at the academy, the *meturgeman* or *turgeman* ('interpreter'), who occasionally appears in the sources as an '*amora*.'[91] Of his existence in the Palestinian academies already in the Yavneh generation, we learn from the Jerusalem Talmud:

> Once a student came and asked R. Joshua: "What is the formal evening prayer"?...He responded: "Tomorrow, when I come into the *bet ha-va'ad* [i.e., the house of study],[92] stand and ask for the law on this"....And Rabban Gamaliel was sitting and teaching and R. Joshua was standing on his feet, until the whole audience began to murmur against him. Said they to R. Huzpit the Interpreter [*turgeman*]: "Dismiss the people." Said they to R. Zinon, the *hazzan* [beadle]: "Say 'Commence [the debate]!'" They said [as they were instructed]: "Commence the debate!" and all the people stood on their feet.[93]

There also were interpreters (*meturgemanin*) in the Palestinian academies in the generation of Usha and those of the *amoraim*. Thus, for example, we read in the Babylonian Talmud: "It happened that the son of R. Judah b. Ilai

[87] B Yoma 35b.

[88] ARN, Version A, chap. 6 (Schechter edition, p. 31).

[89] B Ber. 28a.

[90] See above, n. 79.

[91] See Y Meg. 4:10 (75c); B Sanh. 7b; B MQ 21a; B Qidd. 31b. Cf. A. S. Amir, *Institutions and Titles in Talmudic Literature* (Jerusalem, 1977), pp. 79, 86-87, 91 (in Hebrew), and other places.

[92] *bet ha-va'ad=bet ha-midrash.* Cf. J. N. Epstein, *Introduction to the Text of the Mishnah*, 2nd ed. (Tel-Aviv, 1964), p. 489 (in Hebrew).

[93] Y Taa. 4:1, 67d. Also see Y Ber. 4:1, 7c-d; B Ber. 27b; B Bek. 36a.

died and he went into the house of study. R. Hananiah b. Akavia entered and sat down beside him. He whispered to R. Hananiah b. Akavia who whispered to the interpreter, and the interpreter repeated it aloud publicly."[94] And in the Jerusalem Talmud: "R. Berakiah placed his interpreter at the middle gate of the house of study and he recited the grace after meals for those on either side."[95]

The law in the Tosefta tells us of the limitations accepted by the interpreter when he served the Sage in the house of study: "An interpreter standing before a Sage in the house of study may not [redeem],[96] nor subtract, nor add, nor alter, unless he is his father or his teacher."[97] It should be noted that in the discussion of this law in the Jerusalem Talmud,[98] two names of Sages who served as interpreters are mentioned: R. Pedat who was R. Yose's interpreter, and Bar Yashita who served R. Abbahu.[99]

It is difficult to determine whether the *amoraim* or *meturgemanin* were in the Palestinian public houses of study only. From the Jerusalem Talmud, Berakot 7:5, 11c, ("R. Berakhiah placed his interpreter..."), it would seem that an *amora* was possibly also present in a private house, but we cannot be sure that this was R. Berakiah's own house or whether it was a public building, in which he served.

The inscription uncovered at Dabura in the Golan, "This is the house of study of Rabbi Eliezer Ha-Qappar," attests in a most tangible way to the existence of private houses of study in the Land of Israel in the rabbinic period.[100] But other private houses of study are mentioned in the sources of the period. We have already mentioned the house of study of Rabban Yohanan b. Zakkai, the existence of which in Jersualem is established by the homily preserved in the Jerusalem Talmud, Meg. 3:1, 73d and elsewhere.[101] In the second generation of *tannaim*, we know of the houses of study of R. Eliezer b. Hyrcanus and R. Tarfon that existed in Lod.[102] Of the

---

[94] B MQ 21a.

[95] Y Ber. 7:6, 11c.

[96] Thus according to the Lieberman edition; and see his comments on this in Lieberman, *Tosefta ki-fshutah*, vol. 5, p. 1223.

[97] Tos Meg. 4 (3):41. This version is according to the Zuckermandel edition, p. 229. Also see the Lieberman edition, p. 364.

[98] Y Meg. 4:10 (75c).

[99] For additional names of *amoraim* and *meturgemanim*, see Amir (above, n. 91), p. 84ff.

[100] See D. Urman, "Jewish Inscriptions from the Village of Dabbura in the Golan," *Tarbiz* 40 (1971): 406-408 (in Hebrew); idem, "On the Location of the House of Study of Bar Qappara and Rabbi Hoshaiah Rabbah," M. Stern, ed., *A Nation and its History*, vol. 1, (Jerusalem, 1983), pp. 164-170 (in Hebrew).

[101] See above, n. 74.

[102] The following tradition about the house of study of R. Eliezer ben Hyrcanus was preserved in Song of Songs Rabbah 1:3:

> Once R. Aqiba came late to the house of study, so he sat outside. A question arose, "Is such-and-such the halakah?" They said, "The halakah is outside." Again a question

fourth generation of *tannaim*, the house of study of R. Jose b. Halafta in Sepphoris,[103] and that of R. Meir,[104] apparently located in Tiberias,[105] are mentioned. In the fifth generation of *tannaim*, we hear of the house of study of R. Hiyya,[106] apparently also in Tiberias.[107] Of the first generation of *amoraim*, the houses of study of R. Benaiah and R. Hanina in Sepphoris[108]

---

arose, and they said, "The Torah is outside." Again a question arose, and they said, "Aqiba is outside." They made way for him. He came and sat at the feet of R. Eliezer. The house of study of R. Eliezer was shaped like an arena, and there was in it a stone which was reserved for him to sit on. Once R. Joshua came in and began kissing the stone and said, "This stone is like Mt. Sinai, and he who sat on it is like the Ark of the Covenant."

Cf. Aboth De Rabbi Nathan, Version A, chap. 25 (Schechter edition, p. 80): "When R. Eliezer became ill, they said that it was on the eve of the Sabbath (Friday) and R. Aqiba and his colleagues came to visit him. He was asleep in his room, seated upon his curtained couch, and they sat in his reception room." Rabbi Tarfon's house of study is mentioned in Y Erubin 4:4 (22a): "They said, Was not R. Tarfon's house of study within the two thousand cubits?"

[103] B Ned. 81a: "Isi b. Judah did not come to R. Yose's academy for three days. Vardimus b. R. Jose found him and said to him: 'Why has my master not come to my father's academy for these past three days?'" For new discussions of this segment, see: I. Gafni, "*Yeshiva* and *Metivta*," *Zion* 43 (1978), pp. 35-37 (in Hebrew); D. Goodblatt, "New Developments in the Investigation of the Academies of Babylonia," *Zion* 46 (1981): 25ff (in Hebrew).

[104] B Sanhedrin 11a: "A woman came to R(abbi) M(eir)'s house of study. She said to him, My Master, one of you has sanctified me in marriage by means of intercourse. R. Meir rose, wrote her a writ of divorce, and handed it to her."

[105] We find allusions to this in Y Sotah 1:4, 16d (=Leviticus Rabbah 9:9 [Margulies edition (Hebrew) p. 191, and see the references there to further parallels]): "R. Meir used to preach in the *knishta* of Hammath every Sabbath night"; and in Y Ber. 2 (4b): "R. Yohanan was leaning on R. Jacob bar Idi and R. Eleazar saw him and hid from him.... As they were walking, he saw a house of study; said he to him: this is where R. Meir sat and preached." The last account is undoubtedly taken from the milieu of Tiberias—cf. S. Klein (ed.), *Sefer Ha-Yishuv*, vol. I, (Jersualem, 1939), p. 51 (in Hebrew).

[106] Sifré Numbers, *Shelah*, 115 (Horowitz edition, p. 129): "Said she to him: 'I swear I shall not release you until you write me your name and the name of your city and the name of your [house] of study where you study Torah'; and he wrote her his name and that of his city and the name of his Master and the name of his [house] of study wherein he studies Torah; she then proceeded to squander her money: a third to the government, a third to the poor, and a third she took with her and stood in the house of study of R. Hiyya." Also see B Men. 44a.

[107] Cf. Heiman, *History*, p. 434; Albeck, *Introduction*, p. 144.

[108] A mention of R. Benaiah's house of study in Sepphoris has been preserved in the sources of the period thanks to the discourses delivered there by R. Yohanan, the greatest of the Palestinian *amoraim*. Thus, for example, in Y BM 2:13, 8d=Y Hor. 3:8, 48b, we read, "R. Hiyya bar Va(Abba) (was) in Sepphoris (and) saw everyone running. Said he to him: 'Why is everyone running?' He answered, 'R. Yohanan is sitting and preaching in R. Banaiah's house of study and everyone is hurrying to hear him.'" And in the Y Shab. 12:3, 13c=Y Hor. 3:9, 48c, "R. Simeon b. Lakish asked R. Yohanan [a legal question]. R. Yohanan went and delivered (the answer) in R. Benaiah's house of study: 'even [in a situation of] a bastard scholar and an ignorant High Priest, the bastard scholar has priority over the ignorant High Priest.'" By contrast, B Ket. 23a tells of the house of study of R. Hanina, "Mar Samuel's daughters were taken captive and were brought to the Land of Israel. They let their captors stand outside and entered R. Hanina's house of study."

and, in the second generation, of R. Yohanan in Tiberias,[109] are mentioned. Also located in Tiberias were the houses of study of Bar 'Itiyyan and Bar Ulla, in the fourth generation of *amoraim*.[110]

It should be recalled here that the mention of Bar Ulla's house of study in the Jerusalem Talmud, Shabbat 4:2, 7a is one of the two sources from which we can learn with certainty of the feasts—meals taken in a group associated with a religious occasion—customary in a number of the Palestinian houses of study on Sabbaths and New Moons.[111] Thus we read there:

> R. Yonah and R. Yose visited the house of study of Bar Ulla where there was a feast, and there were beams there. They came and asked him whether they were permitted to move them [on the Sabbath]. He replied: "If you had it in mind yesterday, you may move them; but if not, you may not."

The second source is in the Jerusalem Talmud, Sabbath 20:1, 17c:

> In the days of R. Judah b. Pazi there was a feast in the house of study, and they would spread the curtains a day before to the length of four cubits, and the next day they would spread them all. They thought it was in accordance with the words of R. Judah b. Pazi. They investigated and found that it was not.

Admittedly, in the Jerusalem Talmud, Meg. 3:4, 64a it says:

> It has been taught: In houses of assembly and houses of study, one does not behave frivolously, one does not eat or drink in them, nor stroll in them, nor sleep in them, nor take cover in them from the sun when it is sunny, nor from the rain when it is rainy, but one studies (Mishnah) and lectures in them.

---

[109] B Sotah 22a: "There was a widow who had a synagogue in her vicinity. Each day she would come and pray in R. Yohanan's house of study. Said he to her: 'My daughter, is there no synagogue in your neighborhood?'"

[110] We learn of the existence of Bar 'Itiyyan's house of study from the Y BB 6:2, 15c: "R. (I)lla in the name of R. Leazar, R. Yassa in the name of rabbis who came and attended the house of study of R. 'Itiyyan." And as for the house of study of Bar Ulla, we read in Y Betzah 1:6, 60c: "R. Yonah ordered his colleagues: 'Do not sit on the outer benches of Bar Ulla's house of study because they are cold.'" Concerning Bar Ulla's house of study, also see in Y Shab. 4:2, 7a cited above.

[111] About group meals and meals associated with religious occasions in the traditions and customs of the Jews of the Land of Israel in the period of the Mishnah and the Talmud, see what A. Oppenheimer's "*Havurot* that Were in Jerusalem," in A. Oppenheimer, A. Rappaport, and M. Stern (editors), *Essays in the History of Jerusalem During the Second Temple: In Memory of Abraham Shalit* (Jerusalem, 1981), pp. 178-190 (in Hebrew) (and especially pp. 185-189, with references there to earlier research). About the 'feasts,' also see what was written by J. N. Epstein, "On the Remains of the Jerusalem Talmud," *Tarbiz* 3 (1932): 243 (in Hebrew); S. Lieberman, "Jerusalem Talmud Fragments," *Tarbiz* 6 (1935): 234 (in Hebrew); J. N. Epstein, "On the Jerusalem Talmud Fragments," ibid., pp. 236-237 (in Hebrew); S. Lieberman, *The Literal Jerusalem Talmud* (Jerusalem, 1935), p. 213 (in Hebrew).

But in the Jerusalem Talmud, Pes. 1:1, 27b, we read:

> R. Jeremiah inquired: What of houses of assembly and houses of study regarding checking for leaven? It is required because (leaven) is brought in on Sabbaths and New Moons.

We have suggested that the portion of the inscription uncovered in the excavations of the complex of public Jewish buildings at Qaṣrin in the Golan, "...Uzi made this accommodation...," should be seen as evidence of the existence of special rooms or halls near the houses of assembly and houses of study in which the 'feasts' were arranged.[112] J. Maitlis sees in this inscription "almost certain evidence that there was a house of study in Qaṣrin."[113] In our opinion it is still too soon to decide whether the Qaṣrin site served as a house of study or a house of assembly.[114] In any case, we do clearly have an inscription dedicated to a benefactor who contributed to the building of an "accommodation," that is, a hall for *se'udot mitzvah* (i.e., meals associated with a religious event), and its finding leads us to theorize that it was a public one (*shel rabbim*).[115]

Not a little evidence preserved in the sources of the period attests to the existence of public houses of study. For example, in the Jerusalem Talmud, Hag. 2:1, 77b, we read:[116]

> R. Meir was sitting and teaching in the house of study of Tiberias. Elisha his teacher passed, riding on a horse on the Sabbath. They came and told him [R. Meir]: "Behold, your teacher is outside." He interrupted his lesson and went out to him.

"The house of study of Tiberias" is also known in the sources as "the great house of study of Tiberias"[117] and as "the great house of study."[118] A close look at its many mentions indicates that it was in existence for at least two hundred and twenty years, from the time of Rabbi Meir until and including the fifth generation of *amoraim*.

In relation to this house of study, the Jerusalem Talmud, Sheq. 5:7, 49b relates:

---

[112] See D. Urman, "Jewish Inscriptions of the Mishnah and Talmud Period from Qaṣrin in the Golan," *Tarbiz* 53 (1984): 533-534 (in Hebrew).

[113] J. Maitlis, "On the Significance of the 'Revu'ah' in Qaṣrin," *Tarbiz* 53 (1984): 466 (in Hebrew).

[114] Cf. Urman, "Hellenistic," p. 462.

[115] See above, n. 75.

[116] Also see Ecclesiastes Rabbah 7:8; Ruth Rabbah 6:4.

[117] Cf., for example, "It happened once that R. Hiyya (bar Abba) was collecting charity" in Deuteronomy Rabbah 4:8 with the parallels in Y Hor. 3:7 (48a) and in Leviticus Rabbah 5:4 (Margulies edition, p. 113).

[118] The Aramaic expression *sidrah rabbah* used here for "the great house of study" of Tiberias appears a number of times in the Palestinian Talmud. For example, see Y Shab. 6:2 (8a) = Sanhedrin 17:1 (28a).

> R. Abun contributed to the making of these gates of the great house of study. R. Mana came to him. Said (R. Abun) to him: "Look at what I have done." Replied he: "'Israel has ignored his Maker and built temples' (Hosea 8:14). Were there no people to occupy themselves with [the study of] Torah?"[119]

Here, then, is evidence of a Sage's contribution to the making of the gates of the public house of study of Tiberias in the fourth century C.E. From R. Mana's words of criticism to R. Abun, identical to those of R. Hoshaiah to R. Hama bar Hanina when they were both strolling among the houses of assembly of Lod, it is clear that R. Abun's gates were monumental.[120] From another mention of that same house of study we learn that it was customary to take up collections in the houses of study:

> It happened once that R. Hiyya [bar Abba] took up a collection in the great house of study in Tiberias and someone promised one pound of gold.[121] R. Hiyya thereupon took him and seated him next to himself and applied to him the verse: "A man's gift makes room for him" (Proverbs 18:16).[122]

Other evidence of the existence of public houses of study in the Land of Israel in the period under discussion is found in the Tosefta:

> R. Eleazar [b. R. Zadok] said: It once happened that the 14th [of Nisan] fell on the Sabbath and we were seated before Rabban Gamaliel in the house of study at Lod when Zinon, his officer, came and said: "The time has come to remove the leaven," and I and father went to the home of Rabban Gamaliel and removed the leaven.[123]

Elsewhere we read:

> Said R. Simeon b. Eleazar: We were once seated before R. Meir in the house of study in 'Ardascis and someone said, "I prepared the *Erub* with onions," and R. Meir seated him within his four ells.[124]

We conclude with the public house of study at Sepphoris, mentioned in the Jerusalem Talmud:

> R. Hananiah was a seller of bees honey but also had date honey. A few days later some people passed. Said he to them: "Lest I mislead you, know that the honey I sold you was of dates." Said they to him: "That is what we

---

[119] Cf. D. Urman, "Jewish Inscriptions from the Village of Dabbura in the Golan," *Tarbiz* 40 (1971): 400-401, and n. 6 there (in Hebrew).

[120] Y Peah 8:9 (21b) = Sheq 5:7 (49b): "R. Hama bar Hanina and R. Hoshaiah were strolling among the houses of assembly of Lod. Said R. Hama bar Hanina to R. Hoshaiah: 'How much money my fathers invested here!' Replied the latter: 'How many souls did your fathers invest here? Were there no people to occupy themselves with Torah?'"

[121] According to the parallels in Y Hor. 3:7 (48a) and Leviticus Rabbah 5:4 (Margulies edition, p. 113).

[122] Deuteronomy Rabbah 4:8.

[123] Tos Pesahim 2(3):11 (Zuckermandel edition, p. 159; Lieberman edition, p. 154).

[124] Tos Eruvin 9(6) (Zuckermandel edition, p. 148; Lieberman edition, p. 119).

> want, for it is good for our work." And R. Hananiah set aside the money received for it and built a house to serve as a house of study in Sepphoris.[125]

It is true that this text is somewhat truncated, but there is no doubt about the meaning of its last part: R. Hananiah contributed to the building of a house of study in Sepphoris.

THE ARCHAEOLOGICAL FIND

It is clear from what emerges above that the houses of study in the Land of Israel in the last days of the Second Temple and the rabbinic period were actual structures. Some were undoubtedly monumental edifices, as is attested by the remains of the *bet midrash* of R. Eliezer Ha-Qappar discovered at Dabura,[126] as well as by the mention of "the upper chamber of the house of study,"[127] "the middle gate of the house of study,"[128] and the magnificent gates which R. Abun "made" for the great house of study of Tiberias,[129] and more. The question, then, must be asked: "Why is it that in the Land of Israel there is clear archaeological evidence of many synagogues and only one evidence of a house of study?" as Hüttenmeister writes.[130] It seems that the answer to this question is to be found in the words of one of the fathers of Israeli archaeology, S. Yeivin, of blessed memory, who about twenty years ago published an article titled "Non-Existent Temples."[131] This, it is true, deals with a matter different from ours yet very similar, both in the shared investigative background and in the methodological conclusions that necessarily follow from the investigation.

In his introduction headed "The Atmosphere of the Archaeology of the Land of Israel" he wrote:

> The beginning of the scientific activity in the research of the Land of Israel in the middle of the past century was in fact but a direct, unintermediated continuation of the interest in the Holy Land evinced by its inhabitants and, later on, by pilgrims and ordinary tourists, from the days of the Mishnah and Talmud to our own day. It is no wonder, then, that from the outset, most of those involved with this research emerged first and foremost from the circles of Jewish students of Torah, and from men of the clergy and theologians of the various Christian sects. Therefore one can also understand the tendency to see in every to a greater or lesser degree un-

125 Y Peah 7:4, 20b.

126 Urman, "Hellenistic," pp. 462-464. Also see Z. Ilan, "The Village of Dabbura, Its Artifacts and Its Identification," *Shenaton Muzeion Ha-Aretz* 13 (1971): 39-46 (in Hebrew).

127 Y Sanh. 13:6, 23c—see above, n. 80.

128 Y Ber. 7:6, 11c—see above, n. 81.

129 Y Sheq. 5:7, 49b—see above, n. 119.

130 Hüttenmeister, "Connection," p. 40.

131 See Yeivin, "Temples," pp. 163-175.

> usual find, something related to ritual worship and sacred sites, whether these were remains of structures, or whether they were utensils or utensil fragments....Without expanding the discussion about this problem in general here, one can immediately make a sufficiently long list of discoveries that, when uncovered, were thought to be remains of temples and "pillars," that later turned out not to be so and were as if they had never been.[132]

Under the heading, "Continuation of the 'Tradition,'" Yeivin adds:

> It is known that there is nothing as conservative and persistent as 'traditions,' be their courses 'correct' or 'aberrant.' But, behold today, even though most of those busy with investigating the Land of Israel have no connection with theology nor any occupation with religion, the roots of the tradition spoken of above [in the chapter "The Atmosphere of the Archaeology of the Land of Israel"] have sunk deeply even into them, so that the research of the past two-three generations has been blessed with structures that have been called temples or worship-sites on the basis of most doubtful proofs.[133]

In that "Atmosphere of the Archaeology of the Land of Israel" so sharply but most accurately described by Yeivin, there has in our opinion also developed a 'tradition' to identify every structural relic bearing Jewish ornamentation or symbols as a *bet knesset*, a house of assembly, and generally out of the assumption that "a 'house of assembly' is a 'house of prayer.'" As a result, "there is in the Land of Israel clear archaeological evidence of...only...one 'house of study.'"[134]

It must be remembered that the first of those to identify 'house of assembly' remains in the Land of Israel in the modern age was the American theologian, E. Robinson, considered to be the "father of the study of the Land of Israel."[135] He discovered the "synagogue" structures in Galilee on his second visit to the Land of Israel in 1852, and describes frankly the thinking that led him to class them as such:

> As these remains were the first of the kind that we had yet seen; and were of a style of architecture utterly unknown to us; we were at a loss for some time what to make of them. They were evidently neither Greek nor Roman. The inscription, if authentic, obviously marks both structures as of Jewish origin; and as such, they could *only* have been Synagogues.[136]

In keeping with his approach, Robinson did in fact succeed in recognizing a number of monumental structures in Galilee as Jewish public structures, and

---

132 Yeivin, "Temples," p. 163.

133 Yeivin, "Temples," p. 164.

134 See above, n. 130.

135 Cf. J. Ben-Arieh, *The Land of Israel in the 19th Century—Its Rediscovery* (Jerusalem, 1971), p. 69ff (in Hebrew).

136 E. Robinson, *Biblical Researches in Palestine and the Adjacent Regions: Journal of Travels in the Years 1838 & 1852*, 3rd ed, vol. 3 (London, 1867), p. 71.

was even wise enough to date them more or less accurately—to the first centuries of the Common Era. However, among these "synagogues" he also counted remnants of a large structure preserved in eastern Tel Kedesh,[137] known today to be a pagan temple.[138]

Researchers in the second half of the nineteenth century all followed in Robinson's footsteps, as did the surveyors and excavators of the first half of the twentieth century. Almost all of them, on the assumption that "a 'house of assembly' is a 'house of prayer,'" identified practically every Jewish structural remain from the period of the Mishnah and Talmud as a "synagogue."

The development of this 'tradition' of identification has often led to absurd definitions and identifications. Thus, for example, a wine-press[139] uncovered at Hulda in 1953 was at first thought by M. Avi-Yonah to belong to "a special type of [Jewish] place of prayer which was perhaps combined with a ritual bath."[140] Later, Avi-Yonah retracted this[141] but the remains are nevertheless still marked as "a synagogue site" even in new publications.[142] Yeivin was certainly right in observing that "...there is nothing more conservative and persistent than 'traditions,' be their courses 'correct' or 'aberrant.'"[143]

Hüttenmeister, whose article serves as a springboard for the present article, faithfully represents the continuity of this identification 'tradition.' A synagogue, he writes,

> is identifiable only by these clear and specific characteristics: if, according to its size or plan, it is a public building; or if symbols clearly connected with the ritual worship, such as a menorah, a *lulav*, a *shofar*, an *ethrog*, are found; or if an inscription is found identifying the structure as an *atra kadisha* [i.e., a holy site].[144]

It would seem that the remains of the wine-press uncovered at Hulda possess all the peculiarities listed by Hüttenmeister except one: a "holy site" inscription. But can such an indication really serve as "a clear and specific" synagogue sign? It is obvious from our sources that at least some of the Sages saw the houses of study as holy sites no less than the synagogues, and some even attributed to them a higher degree of holiness.

---

137 Robinson (see note 136), pp. 71 and 367-368.

138 See A. Ovadiah et al., "The Roman Temple at Kedesh in the Upper Galilee," *Qadmoniot* 15 (1983): 121-125 (in Hebrew).

139 Cf. Kloner, "Synagogues," p. 17.

140 M. Avi-Yonah, "Ten Years of Archaeology in Israel," *IEJ* 8 (1958), p. 62.

141 See M. Avi-Yonah, "Synagogues," in *EAEHL*, vol. 1, pp. 106 (in Hebrew).

142 See the map on p. 2 of Levine, *ASR*.

143 Yeivin, "Temples," p. 164.

144 Hüttenmeister, "Connection," p. 42.

We have already cited from the Jerusalem Talmud the segment dealing with whether a synagogue may be sold to purchase a house of study.[145] The Palestinian *gemara* responds there in the name of one of the greatest of the Palestinian *amoraim*: "The word of R. Joshua b. Levi is—'it is permitted.'"[146] Also, elsewhere in the Jerusalem Talmud we read: "R. Yonah in the name of R. Hiyya bar Ashi: '*Haverim* will in the future tire themselves out from the synagogues to the houses of study. What is the reason? [For it is written,] "They go from strength to strength, appearing before God in Zion" (Ps. 84:8).'"[147]

SUMMARY

Whether or not buildings were especially set aside for use as houses of study in the Land of Israel in the period of the Mishnah and Talmud has been the focal point of this paper. For an investigation of how Jewish society and its institutions in the Land of Israel looked at that time, the importance of a clear answer to this question is well known.

It seems that until about one hundred years ago, no scholar would have doubted the existence of specific houses of study, but in recent years, some have had them disappear within the synagogue, and some have transformed the house of study from a structure and central institution in the life of a respected segment of Jewish society in the Land of Israel into an abstract concept of a 'school,' or "the act of gathering together for common study."

In our opinion, two factors have merged to contribute to these conclusions. The first is the prevalence of an erroneous conception that sees the function of the house of assembly in the Land of Israel during this whole period as a house of prayer. The second is the development of a tradition that identifies almost all structural remains with inscriptions of Jews, or Jewish ornamentation, dating to that time as a synagogue.

The house of assembly in the days of the Second Temple and in the generations of the *Tannaim* was first and foremost a *bet ha-qehillah*, namely, a community house. Only during the era of the *amoraim*, with prayer becoming established as a central liturgical component in the house of assembly, and perhaps also under the influence of the Christian houses of prayer

[145] Y Meg. 3:1, 73d. Also see n. 74 above.

[146] It is of interest to note that the Babylonian Talmud in this case also prefers the house of study over the house of assemply (i.e., synagogue). And in B Meg. 26b-27a we read as follows: "R. Papi said in the name of Raba: 'To turn a synagogue into a college (lit. 'house of Rabbis') is permitted; to turn a college into a synagogue is forbidden.' R. Papa, however, also reporting Raba, states the opposite. R. Aha said: 'The statement of R. Papi is the more probable, since R. Joshua ben Levi said: It is permissible to make a synagogue into a house of study.'" This seems conclusive.

[147] Y Shebi. 4:10, 35c. And also see: B Ber. 64a and B MQ 29a.

in the East, did the Jewish house of assembly increasingly become a house of prayer.[148] The natural tendency to segregate on the part of the Sages, as a social and religious elite, let to the erection of separate structures to serve as houses of study.

The inescapable conclusion of our discussion is that a good part of the structures uncovered thus far and identified as houses of assembly were, in fact, houses of study. To deal with the question of criteria whereby it is possible to identify and differentiate between a house of assembly and a house of study in the period of the Mishnah and Talmud is beyond our purview here. Let us point out, however, that the most certain criterion is the finding of an inscription that mentions the functions of the structure, as that of Theodotus son of Vettenos, or the inscription from the house of study of R. Eliezer Ha-Qappar, who had already expressed the hope that "the synagogues and houses of study in Babylonia will in time to come be established in the Land of Israel."[149]

---

[148] The reciprocal influences of the Christian churches in the East and the Jewish synagogues in the Land of Israel warrant a systematic, detailed investigation which has not as yet been done.

[149] B Meg. 29a.

THE SYNAGOGUE AND STUDY HOUSE AT MEROTH

ZVI ILAN*

Research into the communal center of the Jewish settlement at Meroth, which began only a few years ago, sheds light on the history of the Jews in Northern Galilee from the time of the Second Temple up to the Middle Ages. It also brings forth new material concerning synagogues and study houses of antiquity. The site is located at Ḥorvat Maros, north of the road between Tel Hazor and 'Alma (coordinates 1998-2707), about seven kilometers northeast of Safed. I identified it as Meroth, a settlement that marked the northern boundary of Galilee facing the border of Tyre, which was fortified during the rebellion of 66-72 C.E.[1] The first suggestion of the identification of the site appeared in a document from the Cairo Genizah mentioning Kefar Meroth, which I read in 1977.

I first explored the site in 1981, and upon discovering the synagogue there, continued to conduct field excavations in subsequent years. Excavations at the site continued until October 1986, and what follows here is, therefore, a summary of ten years of research.[2] [For a table of the synagogue's stages, please refer to the back of the article—Eds.]

STAGE A.1—FOUNDATION OF THE SYNAGOGUE

The synagogue is built on "the heights of the town" in the area from which, looking eastward, the houses of the settlement are built on terraces, facing

---

* This essay was originally published in A. Kasher, A. Oppenheimer, and U. Rappaport, eds., *Synagogues in Antiquity* (Jerusalem, 1987), pp. 231-266 (in Hebrew). It has been translated with the permission of Mrs. Zvi Ilan and of Yad Izhak Ben Zvi. It was translated by Dr. Nathaniel Stampfer.

[1] Regarding the discovery and identification, see Z. Ilan, "The Location of Meroth—A Fortified Settlement on the Border of Galilee," *Qadmoniot* 16, nos. 62-63 (1984): 83-85 (in Hebrew); Ilan, "Fortified Settlement," pp. 141-146; Z. Ilan and E. Damati, "Excavation of the Synagogue at Meroth," *Qadmoniot* 18, nos. 69-70 (1985): 44-50 (in Hebrew); Z. Ilan, "Hidden Treasures in the Galilee. Meroth—An Ancient Jewish Settlement," *Teva va-Aretz* 28 (1986): 12-15 (in Hebrew); *HA* 88 (1986): 2-3 (in Hebrew). Entrance to the area requires permission of the Israel Defense Forces.

[2] The excavation was conducted under the auspices of the Israel Antiquities Authority. Beginning with the second full season of excavation, Emanuel Damati joined me in its directorship, and the summary is essentially the result of our joint deliberation. Assisting us

the Huleh Valley. The orientation of the structure is north-south, i.e., toward Jerusalem. It is built of large hewn chalk stones, some of which are decorated with relief work, common in Galilean synagogues. The structure is in basilica form, having two rows of columns which divide the prayer hall into a central area (5.5 meters wide) and aisles on two sides. The width of the east aisle is 2.5 meters and the western is 2.25 meters. This is similar to the synagogue at Beth Alpha, where likewise the aisles are of unequal width. The interior measurements of the hall are 17.75 x 11.5 meters. At the front of the building on the south there is an entrance porch with a columned front (a portico) built along the width of the structure. Its width is 3.75 meters. The overall length of the building was, accordingly, 22.5 meters. On the west side of the building, a store-room was attached, having a vaulted ceiling, four meters in length. The width of the building including the store-room is 15 meters. In front of the south facade was a courtyard whose south wall was built seven meters from the south end of the portico. The courtyard had a wing which extended along the entire east side of the building, and was connected to the prayer hall by an opening pierced in the east wall of the hall. The width of the courtyard was accordingly 20 meters, and this was also the width of the entire synagogue, while the overall length reached 30 meters. Apparently, the courtyard wing east of the hall was intended to permit access and entry into the hall for latecomers to prayers and for those desiring to leave during the service. As is well known, the main entrances to Galilean synagogues were situated at the south end of the structures. South was also the direction the worshippers faced. This fact affected entry and exit of the worshippers, as will be evident below, and this was what necessitated the opening of a side door which exists in many synagogues. In the center of the synagogue's courtyard, there was a well. A courtyard (atrium) with a well was quite typical in churches, and evidently the builders of our synagogues were influenced by the designs of contemporaneous churches. This was the first courtyard excavated in a Galilean synagogue. Courtyards at the front of synagogues which contain wells are also known at Beth Alpha, Beth She'arim, Ḥorvat Sumaqa, Na'aran, Ḥorvat Susiya, Eshtemoa, and others.

At the southern facade wall of the structure there were three openings that were found closed up (reasons for this, see below in the description of Stage C). The length of the opening is 252 cm, and the length of the engraved

---

were T. Amit, Z. Nitzan, D. Reizel, L. Marcuson, G. Sinah, Y. Bar Yehuda, N. Pesah, A. Shub, Y. Sahar, and A. Bar Or. Surveyors—M. Feist, Y. Vatkin, A. Okonew. I received ideas and suggestions for interpreting this and other discoveries from the scholars N. Avigad, Sh. Applebaum, M. Bayer, M. Bar Asher, A. Berman, M. Gihon, R. Hachlili, R. Talgam, B. Mazar, J. Naveh, Z. Ma'oz, A. Ovadia, G. Foerster and A. Kindler. My thanks to them. Nevertheless, they should not be held responsible for any detail stated here, which is my responsibility alone.

lintel is 280 cm. The lintel rests on two heavy, monolithic door posts, also engraved. In the vicinity of this opening there were discovered five stones of the arch that had originally been over the opening. On the narrow edge of each of these stones there was a relief carving of a frame decorated with a plant motif. Inside the frame were depictions, all of which had been destroyed. This defacing is dated to the period following the edict of Yazid II on this subject (721 C.E.).[3] This dating conforms to our knowledge about the history of the synagogue at Meroth where in both the synagogue and the adjoining study house we found evidence of iconoclasm. From that destruction there survives, on one of the corner stones, the relief of a pomegranate, and in the portion beneath it, parts of the figure of a fish. On another stone is the figure of a pitcher (resembling a basket) from which, it may be surmised, a stream of water is pouring. If this is so, then we have here the zodiac sign of Pisces on one stone and the sign of Aquarius on another. This suggests that there were originally twelve stones in the arch and on each of them was one of the twelve monthly zodiacal signs. Although in synagogues the months and their signs were usually depicted on mosaics graphically (at En-Gedi in the form of a list), we cannot exclude the possibility that they were also depicted on stone. Furthermore, it has been suggested that in an embellished tablet from Kefar Bar'am there was a calendar with the signs of the zodiac.[4] It is also possible to identify other depictions on stone in [ancient] synagogues as zodiacal signs, as at Kh. er-Rafid and at Dabura in the Golan Heights.[5] At the Beth She'arim synagogue were found engraved on marble slabs fish, a lion, a ram and a pitcher—all of which the excavators assumed to be zodiacal signs.[6] It should be pointed out that on the lintel over the entrance of the Church of the Redeemer in Jerusalem, which dates to the Crusades, are depicted the twelve zodiac signs, apparently based on an earlier tradition.

Inside the synagogue hall at Meroth, at the two sides of the main entrance, the remains of two platforms were discovered. The measurements of the easterly of the two are 90 x 176 cm; of it only one course of stones had been preserved. The measurements of the second of these platforms at this stage are not entirely clear, because another platform was built upon it at the second stage of the synagogue (see below). Apparently, the western platform served as the pedestal for a wooden cabinet in which the Torah scrolls were kept. The easterly platform was evidently used during the

---

[3] Tsafrir, p. 432.

[4] R. Amiran, "A Fragment of an Ornamental Relief from Kefar Bar'am," *Eretz Israel* 3 (1953): 178-180 (in Hebrew).

[5] For Kh. er-Rafid, see Sukenik, *el-Ḥammeh*, p. 91. For Dabûra, see Ma'oz, *Golan*, p. 28.

[6] B. Meisler, "The Fourth Excavation Season at Beth She'arim," *Yediot* 9 (1944): 12 (in Hebrew).

reading of the Torah. The placement of the platforms between the entrance and the rows of pillars, where the platforms stood in Galilean synagogues, is the only possible place for them given the fact that the entrances face southward. This placement made them visible from every other position in the building during the time, at least, when the location of the Torah Ark was fixed and the scrolls were regularly placed in it.

Benches were placed along the length of the walls, apparently two benches on each side, one above the other. It appears that in order to increase the capacity of worshippers a gallery was added. The possibility of this being the case even at the first stage stems from the fact that more architectural items were found than are required for a single story. It should be mentioned that the German scholars, Kohl and Watzinger, reconstructed synagogue structures as two-storied. Furthermore, there is a discrepancy between the size and elegance of the synagogue structures and the number of seats provided by the main-floor benches alone. Even if we assume that on Sabbaths and festivals the people sat on mats and rugs, it still would have been difficult to provide for comfortable worship in the larger settlements. We estimate that there were 1000 to 1200 inhabitants in the village of Meroth, and so in order to enable all of them to pray together, they added a gallery. In any case, we have clear evidence of the existence of a gallery in stage C (see below).

The synagogue was built in an area in which there were stone quarries and various installations, including a series of six underground rooms dug beneath the southeast portion of the building. It is not clear why this particular location was chosen since the pits beneath might well weaken the structure. Several of the openings at the top of the pits were sealed up and over them the floor of the synagogue was placed. It is conceivable, therefore, that some of the hollow spaces are where the stone was quarried for building the structure and afterwards these spaces were utilized for storage rooms. In these rooms have been found pottery sherds of the second to the fifth centuries, and several coins of the same period (e.g., of the emperors Hadrian, Antoninus Pius, Diocletian and Constantine the Great). One of the pits contained a well, and a second a *miqweh*, which had an entrance along the south wall of the portico. Conceivably, the well water was intended for the *miqweh* which was adjacent to it. The original entrance to the *miqweh* has not been found. Judging by its size, the *miqweh* was used by the officiants of the synagogue only, rather than by the public at large.[7] Between the rooms, short passages were dug which connected them. These

[7] Regarding water installations in synagogues, the inscription of Theodotus son of Vettenos is informative, see *CIJ*, vol. 2, pp. 332-335. Concerning *miqwaot*, see Dothan, "Hammath-Tiberias," p. 123, and Y. Shenberger, *Miqwaot*, (Jerusalem, 1974), pp. 25-27 (in Hebrew). [See also R. Reich's article in this volume—Eds.]

are similar to the well-known hiding caves known primarily from the Judean Plain.[8] At the bottom of one of these rooms a small bell-shaped cistern was dug. Since a system of this kind has never been discovered in synagogues to date, it is difficult to assess its nature.[9] In the settlement itself several hide-away systems were found, as well as portions of a defense wall, a tower, a huge ditch, a catapult stone, and a number of iron arrow-heads. According to Josephus, he fortified several towns during the rebellion against the Romans, including Meroth and Gamala. In connection with the latter, Josephus states that he added a wall and tunnels (*Jewish War*, 4, 1, 2). If this was Josephus' usual procedure, it cannot be ruled out that at Meroth as well systems for hiding were dug as early as the first rebellion. Later, with the erection of the synagogue building, perhaps a connection was dug between the tunnel system beneath it (via the bell-shaped hole) and the settlement's tunnels. If it should become clear that the system of Meroth was dug during the first rebellion, this would be a contribution to the research on the hiding systems in general.

The synagogue structure was paved with plaster, and signs of repair were visible. The walls and the pillars, too, had evidently been plastered and on them decorations had been painted in red. From the hundreds of pieces of plaster found with remnants of red decorations, it would appear that these were simple geometric designs. At least, it may be said, no evidence remains of any writing, plant designs, human figures, or animals. The roof was covered with tiles, apparently in all three stages of the building's existence. Many broken tiles were discovered of various forms and methods of firing.

We date the foundation of the synagogue building to the end of the fourth century or the beginning of the fifth C.E. As is known, research accepts the view that synagogues of the Galilean type were established in the third century (and some also in the second century).[10] Yet, discoveries of the last several years show that synagogues in the north, of the Galilean type or similar to it, were rebuilt or newly built in the fifth-sixth centuries, as at Capernaum,[11] Nabratein (Kefar Neburaya),[12] and in the Golan.[13] After the

[8] A. Kloner, "Hideout Complexes from the Period of Bar Kokhba in the Judean Plain," A. Oppenheimer and U. Rapaport, eds., *The Revolt of Bar Kokhba—A New Approach* (Jerusalem, 1984), pp. 153-171 (in Hebrew).

[9] Beneath the synagogue courtyard at Susiya there was discovered "a system of caves which were perhaps originally dug as stone quarries and in later times became store rooms." See S. Gutman, "Excavation of the Synagogue at Ḥorvat Susiya," *Qadmoniot* 5, no. 18 (1972): 48 (in Hebrew).

[10] Foerster, "Synagogues," pp. 241, 243; Tsafrir, "Israel," pp. 165-189.

[11] Loffreda, "Capernaum"; Foerster, "Notes"; Avi-Yonah, "Comments."

[12] E. Meyers, "The Torah Ark of Nabratein," *Qadmoniot* 16, nos. 58-59 (1982): 78 (in Hebrew); Naveh, *Mosaic*, p. 32.

[13] Ma'oz, *Golan*, p. 30.

excavation at Meroth, we are able to reinforce the view that the term 'Galilean Synagogue' has a geographic rather than a chronological significance.[14] Thus, synagogues of this plan were built for a long period of time between the third and the sixth century. The building tradition of this type extended for hundreds of years and was not restricted to the third and fourth centuries alone. From the historical viewpoint this fact is important, since it adds to earlier knowledge about the establishment of synagogues and about their construction during the Byzantine period, including the period when the law prohibited their being built. Similarly, it testified to the viability of these communities, and, from the discoveries at Meroth, it is clear that this viability continued for even a longer time.

STAGE A.2—THE MOSAIC FLOOR

Two or three generations after the building's construction, in the second third of the fifth century, a mosaic floor was laid on top of the plaster floor. This mosaic was the first to be discovered in a synagogue in the Upper Galilee. Previously, stone pavements had been considered characteristic of Galilean synagogues.[15]

Other Galilean synagogues have since been found to have had mosaics.[16] The presence of the mosaic and courtyard in Meroth can be understood in context of the late date of the building. Once we saw that the Galilean synagogue type could not be associated with the third century alone, it became clear that synagogues of this later type include both elements of early synagogues of the same group, and contemporaneous elements such as mosaics and courtyards, which are found in Byzantine churches and synagogues of the time. The stage appears to end at the close of the fifth century—perhaps as a result of fire, as evidenced by the burned spot on the mosaic. We do not know if this fire represents a hostile act or an accident, and we can suggest no suitable historical event during which it might have occurred.

A fragment of the mosaic 1.70 x 2.15 meters in size was found in the northern part of the eastern aisle. The mosaic was discovered thanks to the

---

[14] See Kloner, "Synagogues," p. 18. Although there are also some in Galilee exceptional in form, and the intent is regarding the transverse synagogue at Khirbet Shema', and see E. M. Meyers, "The Synagogue at Khirbet Shema'" in Levine, *ASR*, pp. 70-74. See the basic questions raised on this matter in light of discovery of Byzantine period synagogues in the Galilee in L. I. Levine, "Ancient Synagogues—Historical Introduction," in Levine, *ASR*, pp. 9-10.

[15] Foerster, "Synagogues," p. 237.

[16] For a detailed listing of locations of synagogues with mosaic floors, see Ilan, *Ancient Synagogues*, p. 2; Z. Ilan, "A Survey of Synagogues in the Upper Galilee," *Eretz Israel* 19 (1987): 170-198 (in Hebrew).

fact that a portion of the stone pavement which covered it (see below) was removed in a later period. Another small fragment was found in the northern part of the western aisle. On it may be distinguished a design that seems to represent a cluster of grapes. No remains of the mosaic were found in the rest of the building. Two coins were discovered under the base of the mosaic. One of the coins was ascribed to Valentinian III (425-455 C.E.). The floor would thus appear to have been constructed in the second quarter of the fifth century. This estimation agrees with the character of the floor.

The colors of the mosaic are white, red, yellow, pink and black, and its stones are 8 x 8 centimeters in size. A dovetail pattern in the borders of the floor creates a frame around the subject of the picture: the figure of a seated man surrounded by articles of war. No parallel to this picture has yet been found either in synagogues in Israel or the Diaspora, nor in any mosaic associated with non-Jews. The figure is of a young man in a short, white tunic with long sleeves. A red cloak (*sagum*) covers his left shoulder and is fastened above his right shoulder with a pin (*fibola*). The upper part of the body, the surviving portion of which measures 28 x 67 centimeters, leans slightly to the left. The face is inclined in the direction of the vestibule. The eyes, apart from a portion of the left eye, have been gouged out, perhaps purposely. On the garment, over the right arm and the right thigh, are flower-like decorations (there was a similar symbol on the left thigh, as appears from the outline left in the foundation of the floor after that part of the mosaic was destroyed [see below]). The head is outlined in two colors: the front in black, with upward projections, and the center and back in red. The two colors may have been chosen for reasons of composition alone, but there could have been a desire to show the color of the man's hair (red), and to portray in the foreground a kind of crown or diadem. The hands of the figure are extended and only parts of a few fingers have survived. Most of the right hand has been preserved. The left hand is preserved up to the wrist, and its outline, up to beyond the thumb. Near the right palm, where the sleeve ends, there survived a cuff (*manchette*) in black. It is unclear what the man held in his hands. It may be some object mentioned in the biblical account (see below), or perhaps a rod or palm branch as conquerors in ancient depictions occasionally hold (suggestion of B. Bayer).

The man is leaning on a large, elliptical shield, with a projection (*umbo*) at the center. Such an image of a soldier leaning on a shield exists in Roman art. Near the shoulder and head appears a full helmet, designed to cover the face and neck. It has a projection on the top.[17] The helmet is made with yellow stones meant to represent copper or bronze. In the late Roman period, such a helmet was usually designed for a cavalry soldier or a

[17] For a similar helmet, see S. James, "Evidence from Dura-Europos for the Origins of Late Roman Helmets," *Syria* 63 (1986): 130, fig. 21.

gladiator. There may be some lack of proportion between the size of the helmet and sword, on the one hand, and that of the figure on the other (see below).

Above and to the left of the head appears a particularly long sword (*spatha*), apparently of a cavalry soldier. It has a strap for hanging on one side, and a straight object with protrusions, apparently a leather strap used to secure the sword to the belt, on the other. There is a burned spot on the mosaic in the area of the sword. The fact that the man is not carrying the arms indicates that they do not belong to him. The mosaic is destroyed below the figure's knee, but we may assume that the legs were extended diagonally or were crossed, and that the soles rested on the western line of the frame.

In front of the lower portion of the figure are remains of an elliptical design formed by a black band, encircled from both sides by a line of white stones, of which a fragment some 20 centimeters in length is preserved near the figure, and smaller fragments on the opposite end. A small red and black fragment was preserved within the ellipse. The width of the elliptical black band is 4 centimeters. In the fragment near the figure a rectangular form, 3.7 x 4.5 centimeters in size and made of black stones lined by white, protrudes from the band. At a distance of 13 centimeters to the west (left) of this design, the broken beginning of a similar design has been preserved. At one point we weighed the possibility that the design should be interpreted as a wall with towers, which would have surrounded a city before most of the picture was destroyed. This interpretation rested on depictions of cities with surrounding walls, such as Jerusalem, and particularly Neapolis, on the Madaba map.[18] These show both gate towers and ordinary towers joined to an elliptical wall. However, the depiction on our floor is not identical. We now incline more to the belief that what lies before us is some piece of military equipment analogous to the weapons found on the other side of the figure. We also considered the possibilities of a chariot or perhaps a hippodrome (of the sort shown on the mosaic floor in Carthage), but because of the state of preservation of the fragment we reached no conclusion in the matter.

About a meter south of the figure, near the remains of the elliptic band mentioned above, a straight fragment of black stones, apparently the border of the picture, was preserved. Beyond the frame, to the west, a circular design resembling a chessboard was uncovered. On the surface between the circle and the frame appears an 'Amazon's Shield' (*peltate*) pattern which, as far as we know, is the first to be discovered in a synagogue mosaic.

---

[18] M. Avi-Yonah, "The Map of Madaba—a Translation and Commentary," *Eretz Israel* 2 (1952): 135, 146 (in Hebrew).

The Mosaic Inscription

In the space between the northern frame line of this mosaic and the helmet and shield, a two-line Aramaic inscription was inserted.[19]

Text	Transliteration
יודן בר שמעון	Yudan bar Shimon
מני	mny

The names Yudan and Shimon are common among Jews of the talmudic period, and there is even a sage with the name Yudan bar Shimon.[20] We have not found in any source a historical personage who may be identified with Yudan bar Shimon from Meroth. The word MNY is more difficult. It is recognized as a given name, a shortened form of Menachem, known to be the name of sages; but here it occurs at the end of the inscription, and may in our case be interpreted in various ways: (1) As the name of the grandfather, though the lack of the term of affiliation "bar" before MNY makes it difficult to accept this interpretation. (2) As a family name, such as Kimber or Katushion from En-Gedi or Goliath from Jericho, at the end of the Second-Temple period and afterward.[21] (3) As a name or title of a functionary, perhaps derived from the word *memani* (appointed functionary) in Aramaic. The phenomenon of dropping the first *mem* when two *mems* fall at the beginning of a word is well known, and it may be that this has occurred here as well—especially as, if another *mem* were added to the inscription, little empty space would be left between the helmet and the shield. The functionary may have belonged to the imperial government, for example as 'appointee of the emperor,' or, as seems more likely, to the internal Jewish administration.[22] We learn of the existence of such a position in the period of the *geonim* when appointments in the local communities (*qehillot*) were made by the Gaon, the head of the Palestinian Academy. The local leader was appointed by the Academy and was known as '*meqadem*.'[23] We learn of such local administrators from a synagogue inscription from Nabratein, near Meroth, which mentions the fact that the

[19] This is the first inscription, of course, in synagogue mosaics north of an imaginary line drawn from Sepphoris through Ḥorvat 'Ammudim to Hammath-Tiberias. See Naveh, *Mosaic*, p. 6.

[20] M. Margaliyot, *Encyclopedia of the Talmudic Sages and the Geonim* vol. 1, (Jerusalem, 1959), p. 431 (in Hebrew).

[21] See R. Hachlili, "Names and Nicknames of Jews in the Second Temple Period," *Eretz Israel* 17 (1984): 196, 203 (in Hebrew); Y. Yadin, *Searching for Bar Kokhba*, (Jerusalem, 1971), pp. 233-234 (in Hebrew).

[22] Tanna Debei Eliyahu, Chapter 14 (13), M. Ish Shalom, ed., p. 66.

[23] Gill, *Palestine*, vol. 1, pp. 468-470, and vol. 2, letter no. 25, a letter from Tiberias from circa 1020, on the subject of communal appointments in northern Palestine or Syria. See also vol. 1, pp. 475-479, (paragraph 799).

building was erected during the rule of Tanina and Luliana.[24] (4) As the size of a contribution to the floor's construction, a *maneh* of silver, which according to this interpretation, was spelled here with a final *yod*. (5) The word is *mini*, that is, *mimeni* ('*from me*') referring to the donor. However, it has been pointed out in connection with this suggestion that we would expect the word *mini*—if indeed grounds exist for this interpretation—to come at the beginning of the inscription.

Here, then, are several interpretations that have been suggested for this word, the difficulty of which arises from its uniqueness among ancient inscriptions. The last two suggestions are based on the assumption that we are dealing with the dedication inscription of the man who donated the money for the floor's construction. If this is indeed the case, the text is missing the usual components of a dedication inscription, such as "remembered for good," "who donated," "he made," "may he be strengthened," and so on. But even an inscription that lacks the aforementioned verbs may occasionally be expected.[25]

The central question is, is the name that of the figure depicted in the mosaic or that of the mosaic's maker? In this regard, can special significance be attached to the fact that the inscription was placed at the side of the figure and not above it?[26] If indeed the inscription refers to the figure, it could well have fit in the space above it, as is usual in mosaics.

Of all the possibilities that suggest themselves, it seems most likely that the name refers to the donor or to the artist, and not to the man depicted in the mosaic. Most synagogue inscriptions are of the names of donors. The writing of the artist's name on mosaic floors is known from a limited number of sites: the synagogues in Beth Alpha and Beth-Shean (Marianus and Hanina his son), and churches in Kissufim and in Mahayyat (Mt. Nebo).[27] The artist in our case could, if this indeed be his signature, have placed it in the wide borders of the mosaic and not inside the picture. However, the artist may have chosen to put his signature further inside the mosaic because worshippers sitting on benches around the mosaic would put their feet in the borders. The writing of an artist's name within the floor itself is known from other sites, among them the last two mentioned above.

---

[24] Naveh, *Mosaic*, p. 32.

[25] As, for example, "Ana Yehuda Ḥazaana" (lit. "I, Judah the sexton") in the inscription at Aphek in the Golan. See Naveh, *Mosaic*, p. 50. See also inscriptions at Bar'am, Gaza and 'En Nashuṭ.

[26] Occasionally, we find vertically written inscriptions in mosaics, including mosaics of gladiatorial combat, and on tombstones. See Mazer, *Beth Shearim*, p. 135. See also H. J. W. Drijvers, *The Religion of Palmyra*, (Leiden: Brill, 1976), pl. XXXIV; A. F. Blanco, *Mosaicos Romanos de Italica*, vol. 1, (Madrid, 1978), pl. 55. Descriptions are known of individuals who died. At their burial their weapons are described, see, e.g., C. I. Makaronas et al., "The Tomb of Lyson and Kallikles," *Archaeology* 27 (1974): 249-259.

[27] Naveh, *Mosaic*, pp. 72, 78 (No. 47); and Tzori, p. 159.

Significance of the Depiction

The symbols on the figure's arm excite special interest. They appear in mosaics and representations from the Byzantine period frequently, on the clothes of simple people, soldiers and dignitaries. In our case, they may be symbols of a military unit or of membership in an organization or class, rather than purely for decoration. A symbol similar in form is that of the unit known as *Victores*, a mobile unit that served in the eastern empire and perhaps also in the Land of Israel. It also appears in the early fifth-century list '*Notitia Dignitatum.*'[28] In the list, a cross also appears on the symbol, but the creator of the mosaic may have left the cross out. It should be noted that government and administrative functionaries in the provinces wore uniforms. These facts suggest that the commissioners of the mosaic wished to portray a man who distinguished himself in battle, perhaps a hero, soldier or other personage from ancient times, but clothed in the military dress of the time the mosaic was made.

If in fact the mosaic portrays a figure unknown from the sources, it is unlike any synagogue mosaic discovered to date, in which biblical or mythological scenes alone have been found (as in Gerasa, Beth Alpha, Na'aran, Hammath-Tiberias, Japhia and Susiya). The late Professor Yadin therefore believed, in keeping with earlier finds, that the Meroth figure represents David son of Jesse, surrounded by the weapons he took from Goliath (1 Samuel 17:4-7, 38-58). We had raised the suggestion that the figure is David even earlier, at the time of its discovery, along with other possibilities.[29]

This suggestion banishes most of the difficulties involved in understanding the depiction: it is a biblical scene, known from other synagogues. It explains the unusually large size of the helmet and the sword; and clothing David in the dress of the *Victores* unit makes sense for this particular scene. The theory is supported by the fact that the depiction on the floor recalls details of scenes showing David/Orpheus playing the lyre to a group of animals. There is similarity between the form of the seated figure from Meroth and that of many Orpheus representations: the placement of the hands (which usually hold a lyre) and the tunic (in Meroth and in several other depictions).[30] Our interpretation also explains why the figure wears a crown.

---

[28] O. Seeck, *Notitia Dignitatum* (Frankfurt, 1962), p. 12, no. 22. This unit is listed before the three Theodosian units. The Theodosian unit served, as known, in Nessana in the Negev. See C. J. Kraemer, *Excavations at Nessana*, vol. 3 (Princeton, 1958), pp. 20-21. It is interesting to note that the troops were born in Palestine.

[29] See Z. Ilan, "Discoveries at Meroth," *Devar Hashavu'a* 22 (June 1, 1984), p. 20 (in Hebrew).

[30] M. Barasch, "The David Mosaic of Gaza," *Assaph* 1 (1980): 1-41; A. Ovadiah and S. Mucznik, "Orpheus Mosaics in Roman and Early Byzantine Periods," *Assaph* 1 (1980): 43-

There remains the question of why David's name was not written above the figure, as was done on the Gaza Maritima floor, and for biblical figures on other mosaic floors.[31] It may be that in Meroth, the name was placed off to the side, on the destroyed part of the mosaic. We had hoped to find additional fragments of the mosaic, on the assumption that if they too contained biblical figures, it would strengthen the hypothesis that the figure represents David. To this end we removed the stone pavement that had been laid above the mosaic in several places. However, we found no mosaic fragments, apart from the fragment with the cluster of grapes mentioned above. If ever the entire floor is removed and a contiguous fragment of the picture is found, it will help to resolve the question of whether we are dealing with a biblical scene, and whether it represents David.[32]

STAGE B—THE STONE PAVEMENT

At the end of the fifth and beginning of the sixth centuries, the building underwent a general renovation, and several changes worthy of mention were made though the basic structure of the building of the previous stage was preserved. Most of the stones in the walls were replaced by stones of a hard limestone, as opposed to the chalkstone (*qirton*) from which the walls of the first stage were built. The pedestals of the large columns in the prayer hall (which also had to bear the weight of the balcony) were not laid on the same foundation stones as in Stage A, but on new foundation stones. These were set to the south of the old ones. Upon the mosaic floor was laid a pavement of large, polished stones (one of the paving stones was 40 x 60 centimeters in size and 30 centimeters thick). The raising of the floor required the installation of new benches, to conform to the new height, and these were placed above the benches from the previous stage. The new benches were apparently built in two rows, out of a series of bench stones of a type common in synagogues (e.g., in Capernaum), in which the part that was sat on was wide at the top and narrow at the bottom, so as to leave room for the feet. Only two pieces of the bench stones have been preserved. The *bemot* (at least the western one) were extended to the interior of the building and were constructed in part on the stone pavement. The dimensions of the western *bemah*, which is well preserved, are 144 x 182 centimeters. Its

---

56. At a certain level we weighed the possibility of detecting in the depiction a use by the ancient artist of an Orphic scene, in which he utilized weapons instead of living things around it. No other example is known of this type of use of a basically Orphic scene.

[31] A. Ovadiah, "The Synagogue at Gaza," *Qadmoniot* 1, no. 4 (1969): 124 (in Hebrew).

[32] Z. Ilan and E. Damati, "The Mosaic from the Synagogue at Ancient Meroth," *The Israel Museum Journal* 4 (1985): 51-56.

height at the front is 113 centimeters. The front corners of the *bemah* were decorated with two stepped pilasters. Similar pilasters appear in the picture of the Torah Ark in the synagogue mosaic of Beth-Shean. The stones of the eastern *bemah* have been pillaged to the height of the paving stones. In the vicinity of the *bemot* were found fragments of decorated stones which apparently belonged to them. They include double half-colonette incised with a spiral design on one of which was a fragment of a rounded branch from a menorah. These details fit in with the relief depiction of the Torah Ark in Peki'in and the pictures of the ark in the floor from Susiya. Other finds included pieces of a small base and miniature columns, a basalt stone incised with a gable design, and a stone with an *aedicula* engraving.[33]

With the increase in the height of the synagogue floor, the floor of the vestibule also had to be raised. A pavement of a soft stone was laid on the earlier floor which had been constructed of a hard stone. A new, higher threshold was laid above the threshold at the entrance in the eastern wall of the prayer hall.

Outside and adjacent to the western wall was discovered the top of a stairway, whose foundation was constructed in part from sections of columns from the building's previous stage. On two of the sections were engraved the letter *aleph* and perhaps other letters as well. The stairway led to the gallery which had probably already existed in the first stage of the building. The arched roof of the synagogue storeroom served as part of the foundation. The use of arches in synagogues is quite rare, and it would appear the storeroom was originally constructed with an arched roof in order to bear the weight of the stairway. In places where the stone pavement had been raised, were found many coins from the late Roman and Byzantine periods, of which the latest date to the end of the fifth century. The coins were apparently scattered as a sign of blessing, a custom known as well from Capernaum. The discovery of the coins indicated that the floor was laid at the end of the fifth and beginning of the sixth centuries C.E. The end of this stage came after about a century, perhaps as a result of an earthquake characteristic of this area near the Jordan rift.

STAGE C—REVERSAL OF THE SYNAGOGUE'S ORIENTATION

In this stage, the building underwent significant changes, with implications for the study of the history of early synagogues in general. In the first quarter of the seventh century, before the Arab conquest, the need for a renovation of the building arose, and the community decided upon an

---

[33] Concerning the problem of the *bemah* and its placement, see Kloner, "Synagogues," p. 12.

important alteration in the building's form. The southern wall, which had been the front wall of the building, was rebuilt, and its three entrances were sealed. Meanwhile, the orientation of the building was reversed, and the three entrances were thereafter in the northern wall. The change also entailed moving the northern wall some 130 centimeters inward. As a result, it became necessary to build the wall on top of the stone pavement, and to install steps—apparently made of wood— leading down from the entrances, which were 130 centimeters higher than the floor. This arrangement was required because the area to the north of the synagogue was some 130 centimeters higher than the foundations of the wall. It may be that the presence of a nearby structure to the north of the synagogue led to the length of the building being shortened, in order to permit approach to the entrances of the synagogue and to a small plaza in front of them. We found portions of the three entrances which were built opposite their original locations in the south. In the eastern entrance we found several stones from the door posts and the threshold *in situ*.

In the area between the western entrance and the synagogue floor were found nails and metal door parts, which must have belonged both to the doors and to the steps.

What motivated the builders to make such a significant change in the orientation of the building? Apparently, they acted in accordance with the practice, familiar from later synagogues, of having the doors open in the direction opposite that of Jerusalem (cf. the synagogues in Beth Alpha, Na'aran, Jericho). The change in orientation, which ran counter to the usual practice in Galilean synagogues, was designed to correct the basic defect of these early synagogues—the fact that the worshippers entered the synagogue with their backs to Jerusalem and the Torah Ark. With the front of the building to the north, an entering worshipper would be facing the prayer service. In Meroth the change was made in the same, earlier building during a renovation, in accordance with the custom prevalent at the time. Thus, we may now see the two systems at work in a single structure.[34]

During the construction of this stage, use was made of architectural items from earlier levels. Inserted into the north part of the eastern wall were two large pedestals, apparently taken from the portico in the south, which had ceased to function as such (see below). The sections of a column were placed in the foundation of the eastern part of the portico, so as to permit the creation of the classroom (see below). The builders of this stage, mindful perhaps of the lesson learned from an earlier demolition or collapse

[34] Concerning the change in orientation of the synagogue, tied to the closing of the main entrance of the front and the setting of a niche in its place, apparently for architectural rather than religious reasons, see Mazer, *Beth She'arim*, p. 25. Concerning a change for ritual reasons, from south to north, see Dothan, "Hammath-Tiberias," p. 120.

of the walls, seem to have constructed a protective framing wall around the building, some 1.5-2.0 meters from the outer wall. The builders paid little heed to the quality of their work on the framing walls. They filled the area between them and the synagogue walls with material from the remains of the earlier synagogues. The fill, yellowish in color, contained packed earth, stones, pieces of pottery and tiles, pieces of glass vessels,-and even several coins. The framing wall, designed to strengthen the walls of the building, has been excavated along the length of the northern wall of the building and southwest of the eastern wall of the courtyard.

The Amulet

In order to remove the mosaic floor (which was to be transferred to the Israel Museum in Jerusalem), we were forced to dismantle part of the northern wall of the building, where the eastern entrance stood in Stage C. Below the threshold of the entrance was found a bronze amulet 4.8 x 13.8 centimeters in size. The amulet contains 26 lines in Hebrew and Aramaic. It dates to the foundation of Stage C, that is, the beginning of the seventh century, as it was placed in the wall during construction. It presents the supplication of one Yosi ben Zenobia, who asks God that the villagers be utterly subjected to His rule.

The text and translation of the amulet are as follows. The translation is based on the modern Hebrew rendering of Joseph Naveh:[35]

1. For your mercy and faithfulness	1: על חסדך ועל אמיתך
2. in the name of YHWH will we act and succeed!	2: בשם יהוה נעשה ונצליח
3. God strong and mighty praised be your name	3: אל חזק וגיבור ברוך שמך
4. and blessed your kingdom! As you subdue	4: וברוכה מלכותך היך דכבשת
5. the sea with your horses and stamp the earth	5: ימה בסוסיך ורקעת ארעה
6. beneath your feet and as you subdue	6: במסנך והיך מה דאת מכבש
7. the trees in winter and the grasses	7: אילנייה ביום סיתבה ועסבה
8. of earth in summer so may be [subdued]	8: דארעה ביום קייטה כדין ית[כבשון]

[35] The opening of the amulet was done by the Israel Museum staff. See its publication, J. Naveh, "A Good Conquest, One of a Kind," *Tarbiz* 54 (1984): 367-382. The reading and [Hebrew] translation of the amulet is by Joseph Naveh, the reconstruction of line 9 is the reading of the author. [Editors' note: the English translation is original, but done in consultation of Naveh's modern Hebrew rendering.]

9. [the inhabitants of this (*[qr]tha*) [vill]age	9: [ ]תה
10. before Yosi ben Zenobia. I pray you, may	10: קודם יוסי ברה דזינביה יהווי
11. my word and authority be (imposed) over them just as	11: מימרי ומשמעי עליהון הך מה
12. the heavens are subdued before God,	12: דשמיה כבישין קודם אלהא
13. and the land is subdued before	13: וארעה כבישה קודם בני
14. mankind, and mankind is	14: אנשה ובני אנשה [כבישין]
15. subdued before death,	15: כבישין קודם מותה
16. and death is subdued before	16: ומותה כביש קודם
17. God. So may the people	17: אלהא כדין יהוון עמה
18. of this village be subdued,	18: דהדה קרתה כבישין
19. routed, and fallen	19: ות[ב]ירין ונפילין
20. before Yosi son of Zenobia.	20: קודם יוסי ברה דזינביה
21. In the name of Hatuaa the angel	21: בשם חטועע מלאכה
22. who was sent before Israel	22: דאשתלח קודם ישראל
23. I make the sign צלח ('success')	23: אנה עבד סימן צלח
24. צלח *amen*	24: צלח אמן
25. *amen selah*	25: אמן סלה
26. *halleluyah*	26: הללויה

Unlike other oriental amulets, which deal purely with personal matters, this amulet, though personal in content, has implications for the whole, and provides additional evidence for the vitality of the community here. It contains a hint of a power struggle, and we may reasonably assume that such a struggle would occur in a flourishing community, not one in a process of decay. The owner of the amulet would appear to have been a village head who wished to remove constraints on his rule, perhaps because others sought his power, or because of opposition to his rule by slandering individuals. He appears to have been involved in the building of the synagogue, and thus had the opportunity to hide the amulet in the wall during construction. It is likely that he placed it under the threshold on purpose, perhaps so that his supplication would rise heavenward through the bodies of those who passed through the entrance and stepped on the sill.

The name Zenobia is uncommon, and this may be the first discovery of it in a Hebrew inscription as a person's given name. It is known as the name of two women, probably from Tadmor, who were buried in Beth She'arim. One other woman with the name is known in Moab, and several men are known to bear the name Zenubius, but nearly all of these are gentiles and their names are written in Greek.[36] The name comes from Zenobia, a third century queen of Tadmor, and it is likely that the name in Meroth originated with someone from Tadmor.

In the conclusion of Naveh's article on the amulet, he raises the possibility that it is of later date than amulets previously discovered in the Land of Israel (which are primarily from the Byzantine period—Z. I.). This takes into consideration the archaeological context, the similarity in content, and the fact that several formulas are known only from the Geniza. He notes that it is becoming increasingly clear that the magic literature of the Geniza continues an earlier tradition from the Land of Israel. These conclusions have important implications for the late existence of the synagogue and the community in Meroth.

The Synagogue Treasury

One of the important and unanticipated discoveries made by the excavators on the site was the synagogue treasury under the floor of the storeroom west of the prayer hall. In this room, both in the level part of the floor (most of whose stones had been pillaged), and beneath it, were found whole and broken pottery lamps and glass lamps which doubtless served for illuminating the hall. The stones of the floor which remained attached to the walls and difficult to remove survived at the edges, especially in the northeast corner of the room. There, found in place was a stone, only half of which survives, with a hole pierced in it. This stone rested above a hollow, carved in the rock, the western half of which was clogged. In the eastern half, under the hole, there was uncovered a sort of sloping path hewn in the rock which led to a niche dug at the edge of the large hollow. The dimensions of the niche, actually the treasury, are 35 x 37 centimeters. In this niche 485 coins were found, mingled with dirt, 245 of them gold and the rest bronze. The distance between the edge of the hole and the top of the niche is 95 centimeters. That is to say, they had to use a ladle-like tool in order to remove money from it. It is noted that at the top level of the edge of the large hollow were found a number of gold coins scattered outside the treasury as well as small bronze scales. This indicates that the treasury was well hidden, that it was difficult to remove money from it; and, it is reasonable to assume that over the hole in the floor, in which there had obviously been a stopper, they had placed a mat or carpet in order to cover it. These are the coins discovered: one coin of Alexander Jannaeus (minted between 80-76 B.C.E.), six coins from the fourth century C.E., of Caesars from the reigns of Constantine up to Theodosius I. In the find there appears

[36] M. Schwabe and B. Lifshitz, *Beth She'arim*, vol. 2, (Jerusalem, 1974), p. 18, no. 24; pp. 157-158, no. 183.

a gap of about 100 years, ending with coins from the time of Anastasius I (491-518), and from that time there is a continuous sequence up to 608-609, the time of Heraclius as regent, namely coins of Justinus I, Justinianus I, Justinus II, Tiberius II, Mauricius Flavius Tiberius (Maurice), and Phocas. Similarly, in the treasury was found a golden 'Abbasid dinar of the Caliph Muhammed al-Mahdi al-Hujjah from the year 783; the latest coin found was Ayyubid, from 1193. This coin marks the end of the era of the usage of the treasury and of the synagogue. This dating conforms to our conclusions based on results of the excavation and other considerations (see below). It appears the place was abandoned in sudden and extreme haste, apparently as the result of an attack by a hostile force. It also appears that during their flight they attempted to remove the moneys from the treasury and thus several coins fell at the edge of the hollow depression; as there was not sufficient time to gather them up, they fled, leaving behind most of the treasury or at least a substantial part of it.

It seems that the Jannaeus coin does not shed light on the early days of the treasury; it was probably placed in it for reasons of sentiment at the time the synagogue was erected. It should be noted that in excavating the synagogue, there were found another Jannaean coin as well as coins from the first and second centuries B.C.E., just as coins were found from each of the early centuries C.E. The coins were discovered in an indeterminate stratum belonging to an earlier period of Meroth. They may have been brought to this place along with filler and paving materials, or were somehow swept into the area from the settlement. It appears, too, that the individual coins from the fourth century do not date from the time of the treasury's functioning. They may have been included in it only for safekeeping and were not money that circulated during the synagogue's existence. One may note here the repetition of a phenomenon—that of finding coins from over a span of hundreds of years in ancient synagogues. The gap in time between the end of the Byzantine coins and the start of the Muslim coins at Meroth attests to a discontinuation in the use of the treasury in the days of Heraclius, perhaps related to the Persian invasion by Chosroes II in 614, as known from other sites. It is possible that construction of Stage C occurred between 610-635. On the other hand, it is possible to explain the absence of coins from the period of the last usage by virtue of their use for ongoing maintenance needs of the synagogue, and for the reason that whoever attempted to remove the coins in haste succeeded in removing only the last-added coins placed in the treasury. Since they were at the top of the pile, only two of the coins remained from the latest period of the synagogue's use. It is clear that those who knew about the treasury and its contents were unable to return to empty it, either because they were killed or exiled to a distant land.

In the past, collections of coins were discovered in synagogues, generally found scattered in small caches in a wall or in the vicinity of the synagogue. In a few such places where a treasury was found, it was either empty or it contained a few bronze coins of little value. The treasury discovered at Meroth contains the greatest number of coins ever discovered in a synagogue treasury in their original location, and their value is also the largest. This observation applies to coins found in synagogue treasuries as well as those discovered in underground treasure troves.[37] This attests to the level of wealth of the community and to the readiness of its members to contribute to the public fund. The money in the treasury was worth, by cautious estimate, about 2,235 days of work. The real value of the money in the treasury is 17,874 *polis*. The calculation was done by A. Kindler on the basis of 6-10 *polis* for a day's work (see Genesis Rabbah 70, 14). If so, we speak of a large sum that could be used not only for on-going maintenance of the synagogue, but also for its basic repairs and even for the general needs of the community.

It should be noted that in the synagogue were finds attesting to its existence in the Muslim period that should be identified with the third and final stage of the building's history. They include pottery vessels of the type from Khirbet el-Mafjar from the Umayyad era, Arab and Crusader coins (in addition to the coins in the treasury) from each of the centuries from the seventh to the thirteenth. Also found was a bronze band of a dagger with the Arabic phrase "power and long life" on it. It is dated to the thirteenth century.[38]

The Classroom

As mentioned above, the entire built-up area south of the prayer hall was cleared with the change of orientation northward. This area included the portico and the courtyard. We discovered that their space was utilized for erecting two institutions of learning: a classroom for young children and a building for a study house (*bet midrash*). In the eastern half of the portico, a number of preparatory measures were taken toward the use of the area for

---

[37] These are some of the treasuries discovered in synagogues and their contents: Beth Alpha—Sukenik, *Beth Alpha*, p. 12. (36 copper coins); Hammath-Tiberias—Dothan, "Hammath-Tiberias," pp. 122-123; and Dothan, *Hammath-Tiberias*, p. 31 (several coins and broken lamps). For the numbers of discovered coins: Caesarea—*EAEI*, vol. 2, p. 504; En-Gedi—Dan Barag and Y. Porath, "The Synagogue at En-Gedi," *Qadmoniot* 3, no. 11 (1970): 97 (in Hebrew); Ḥorvat Netur—Ilan, *Ancient Synagogues*, p. 34; 'En Nashuṭ—Ma'oz, *Golan*, p. 24. These are several of the places in which troves have been discovered in synagogues or nearby them: Beth She'arim, Gush Ḥalav, Rehob, and Ma'oz Ḥayyim. See Levine, *ASR*, pp. 75, 88, 90; and for Rimmon, see A. Kloner, "The Synagogue of Ḥorvat Rimmon," Qadmoniot 16, no. 62-63 (1984): 68-69 (in Hebrew).

[38] Thanks are due to Na'ama Brosh of the Israel Museum and to Ḥazi Brosh for assistance in translating the inscription and establishing its dating.

purposes other than previous uses. We found that the foundation of the portico was widened by 60 centimeters by laying down eight split column halves on the rock. On three of these sections a Greek letter was carved. The widening was intended to make possible the connection with the eastern part of the courtyard, cleared in order to form a single expanse, measuring 7.5 x 4 meters.

Along the north and east walls stone benches were set. In the eastern section of the south wall there was set in place, as part of the bench, a stone lintel on which was an 'eared frame' (*tabula ansata*) measuring 50 x 160 centimeters. Apparently, a classroom was set up here, being one of the institutions associated with synagogues, as evident from the sources.[39] Several classrooms were discovered in excavations at Gamala,[40] and, apparently, in other places.[41]

THE STUDY HOUSE

The building occupying most of the courtyard area, that is, the entire width of the area south of the synagogue, was the study house (*bet midrash*). The structure was erected in the western half of the courtyard, while the eastern half became the courtyard for the house of study. It is possible to trace two distinct stages of use: early (having a plaster floor) and a later (having a mosaic floor).

In the construction of the study house, the existing south and west walls of the courtyard were utilized. Its north wall was set on the western section of the portico's stylobate while the east wall was of new construction, with an entrance into the hall of the study house. The entrance was placed in the north portion of the wall because the builders had to reckon with the location of the well which had been, originally, in the center of the courtyard but now was situated alongside the middle of the east wall of the study house.

---

39 In the name of Rabbi Hoshayah it is stated that in every synagogue in Jerusalem there was a *bet sefer* and a *bet talmud* (Jerusalem Talmud, Megilla 3, 73d). About the teaching of precepts in the synagogue we learn from the inscription of Theodotus son of Vettenos. See Safrai, "Functions," pp. 106-108. It is appropriate to quote S. Safrai in this connection. The main equipment of the school were "the seats for the teachers of the young" (*At the End of the Second Temple and in the Mishnaic Period*, [Jerusalem, 1983], p. 176, [in Hebrew]).

40 S. Gutman, *Gamala*, p. 121, and the sketch attached to the inside cover.

41 These places were often thought to be houses of study. See Dothan, *Hammath-Tiberias*, p. 123 (by virtue of a portion of a seat at the side of the wall of the area adjoining the west side of the building). At Chorazin, a single bench was discovered in the side of the wall of the area adjoining the synagogue on the west. In Khirbet Susiya, a room was uncovered, adjoining the prayer hall on the west, having benches along three of its walls. See Gutman, Yeivin & Netzer, p. 47 (sketch), p. 48. In the explanation of the photograph on p. 49 the area is referred to as the 'south foyer.'

The *bet midrash* is a hall, almost square in shape, whose axis is east-west. Internal dimensions are 6 x 7.05 meters (outside dimensions are 7.65 x 7.97 meters). The thickness of the walls is about 70 centimeters and, in certain sections, the walls have survived to a height of two meters. A portion of the wall stones had been previously used. In the ruins two architectural stones were also found. It appears that the source of these stones is from the earlier stages of the synagogue, whose stones were now utilized in its third stage. The roof of the study hall was supported by arches. Two foundation stones for the pedestals of the arches were found. In the thick ruin layer which covered the floor of the hall, many broken tiles were discovered. Generally, roofs which are supported by arches are not covered with tiles. If, indeed, these tiles did not cover the roof, it is possible that they were brought here, after the study house was destroyed, for paving and other purposes. Nails of various sizes found here evidently belong to the roof structure and to the doors of the building. Along the four walls were benches of stone. The walls and the benches had been attractively plastered, some small sections of which survived on the east wall and bench. Many pieces of plaster were found, on some of which there was ornamentation of red color. It was impossible to identify any specific subject matter other than lines and curved brush strokes in red color.

The bench stones on the west wall are larger than those on the other walls (30 x 80 centimeters are the measurements of one of these stones and its height from the floor 30 centimeters). This bench is directly opposite the entrance, and the main frame of the mosaic faces it (see below). It appears to have been the seat of the chief dignitary of the study house, possibly the eldest of the scholars. At approximately the middle of this seat, which also marks the middle of the hall, there is a space in the bench and a fault, at the bottom of which a piece of the foundation juts out about 5 centimeters from the seat toward the floor. North of the fault, recessed into the length of the bench, is an engraved architectural stone, having a triangular shape. Another such triangular stone was found, but not in its place. Conceivably, in the space in question there had been an elevated stone seat or a chair of stone or wood, taken from its place, of which only the remnant of the base survives. The triangular stones served perhaps as the back support for the person sitting on it, presumably the leading scholar of the academy. The early rabbis highly regarded the seat or the bench occupied by the chief scholar of the study house. Regarding the academy of Rabbi Eliezer it is said, "One stone was there reserved for him to sit upon. One time, Rabbi Joshua entered and kissed that stone, saying 'this stone may be compared to Mt. Sinai, and he who sat on it is compared to the Ark of the Covenant'" (Song of Songs Rabbah 1:3). Elsewhere, we find this statement, "Upon this bench did Rabbi Aqiba sit" (Babylonian Talmud, Yebamoth 98a). Also in the southwest corner of the hall, at the juncture of two benches, we found in place a vertical stone, higher than the level portion of the bench, whose upper part was smoothed. Possibly it too was intended to serve as a support at the side of those sitting at the end of the benches. In the excavations were found parts of chains and other small items of bronze, as well as broken glass lamps, among them such as those intended for insertion in a '*kelilah*' (a round iron chandelier with holes for lights) for illuminating the hall.

In the first stage of the hall there had been plaster flooring, and the benches had been erected in keeping with its height. This floor had been laid on a layer of stones and earth originally used to pave this space. In this layer we found a coin of Arcadius (395-408 C.E.), which indicates that the plaster floor was laid after this date, apparently at the beginning of the seventh century. After a short time, use of the plaster floor was discontinued, a layer of earth ten centimeters thick was placed on it and on this layer the foundation for the base of the mosaic (see below). It should be mentioned that a similar phenomenon, of the use of a plaster floor for a short period of time, we discovered in the synagogue itself. It seems that the maintenance of a plaster floor was not convenient because it wore out so quickly. In order to adjust the level of the benches to the new flooring created with the laying of the mosaic, the benches were raised by laying stone slabs, 15 centimeters thick, on the original benches.

The Entrance and the Inscription on the Lintel

During the excavation, most parts of the entrance were discovered, namely, the threshold, one of the doorposts and the lintel. The measurements of the threshold are 2.68 x 0.72 meters. Its south portion is made of what was previously a paved section of an oil press (a part of that surface was also utilized as the threshold of the east entrance to the study hall courtyard). The aperture for the wooden doors is 140 centimeters. The left doorpost, found fallen near the threshold, is a large monolith measuring 78 x 155 centimeters, and its thickness 65 centimeters. The lintel was found fallen face down and broken in two about a meter and a half from the threshold. Its measurements are 203 x 80 centimeters, its thickness 66 centimeters. On it is a relief depicting birds and a Hebrew inscription. Covering most of the lintel there is a relief of two eagles on two sides of a wreath, in high relief, in the lower portion of which is a Hercules knot which ends in an ivy leaf at each end. The depiction of eagles is among the most widespread of synagogue reliefs.[42] On the wreath were added several circles colored red, and inside the letters of the inscription red color was also inserted in order to

42 The lintel of the study house of Rabbi Eliezer ha-Qappar depicts harrier-eagles holding snakes in their beaks. See Urman, "Dabûra Inscriptions—2," p. 133, Ma'oz, *Golan*, p. 5. [See also D. Urman's discussion of the site in this volume—Eds.]

make them stand out. The eagles' heads and parts of their bodies were found smashed, in all likelihood by icon breakers. If so, this was done in the days of Yazid II in 721 C.E. (see above), and this is evidence that the lintel was still in place at that time.

Underneath the depiction of the eagles and the wreath was an inscription in Hebrew whose length is 160 centimeters (the average size of the letters is 5 x 5 centimeters), which is none other than a verse from Scriptures: "Blessed are you in your coming in and blessed are you in your going out" (Deuteronomy 28:6). Although the spelling of בבאך ("in your coming in") in the biblical Masoretic text is without the *waw*, here it is spelled with the *waw*, בבואך. This 'full' spelling is typical of later, post-biblical inscriptions. It appears that the inscription was added to the lintel after its original use elsewhere, possibly in the synagogue. The supposition that the inscription was added is based on the fact that the text is not properly centered with respect to the depiction above it. Its engraving was not planned in accord with the face of the lintel. The inscription begins a considerable distance from the right end of the lintel and ends very close to its left end. After the initial word *baruk* ('blessed') there follows a considerable space, then the remaining five words are carved with no space between them whatever. The inscription begins close to the lower right corner of the lintel, and slants upward till the end where it is at a considerable distance from the lower end of the lintel. Notwithstanding this, it is possible that the relief carving and the inscription were made for the study house originally, but by different artisans.

Hebrew inscriptions from Scripture are extremely rare in ancient synagogues.[43] Two inscriptions consisting of two words each, describing depictions of the sacrifice of Isaac, are found in the mosaic floor of the Beth Alpha synagogue. Inscriptions of Daniel and his depictions are found in the synagogue at Na'aran and, apparently, at Susiya, where there remain only the letters '---el.'[44] A depiction of Daniel, apparently, was found on a lintel at 'Ein Semsem in the Golan biblical depiction is found in the floor mosaic of the synagogue at Gerasa in Transjordan. A biblical inscription in Greek is in a synagogue at Caesarea and also at Tadmor.[45] A biblical inscription in stone has not been found heretofore in a synagogue. Also, an inscription of

---

[43] The comparison is to synagogues, inasmuch as Hebrew inscriptions from study houses are unknown, and see the inscription from Dabûra in note 42.

[44] Naveh, *Mosaic*, pp. 75,97. At Susiya, the archaeologists presumed that the reference was to Daniel in the lions' den. See Gutman, Yeivin & Netzer, p. 50.

[45] On the doorpost of the entrance at Tadmor were found inscriptions containing verses from Deuteronomy, from the same chapter [i.e., Deut. 28], see *CIJ*, vol. 2, pp. 68-71, nos. 821-822. In Caesarea, a Greek inscription containing a biblical quotation was discovered. See M. Schwabe, "The Synagogue at Caesarea and its Inscriptions," *Alexander Marx Jubilee Volume*, Hebrew section (New York, 1950), pp. 433-449 (in Hebrew).

this type which neither accompanies a biblical depiction nor is a dedicatory inscription so widely seen in synagogues, is discovered here for the first time. In this inscription there is a direct address to the individual entering or leaving the study house, which carries the profound implication of the blessings reserved for those who abide by the sacred tenets. Conceivably, the engravers were influenced by inscriptions of a similar type found mostly in Christian structures of the Byzantine period. Thus, it appears there was a connection between the fact that this building had been a place of Torah study and that in this small place were discovered two biblical inscriptions of special content (regarding the second inscription, see below).

The Mosaic Floor and its Inscription

Of the colorful floor mosaic in the study hall, about half has survived, mainly the part at the south portion of the hall. The range of color is not great but the workmanship is of a high order, and an effort was made to produce shading by means of graduated hueing of colors, in order to give plasticity to the depiction. The colors are soft and delicate (there are shades of red, pink, light and dark browns, black, grey and white). The main depictions are not known to us from elsewhere and, indeed, we have not succeeded at this stage of the research to identify the workshop or the school where artisans produced mosaics of this type.

A technical detail worthy of mention is the method used by the makers of this mosaic. They first sketched the entire picture with red paint on the plaster base, and then laid the mosaic on top of it. This method is also known from other mosaics. During the time when the mosaic was treated at laboratories of the Israel Museum, Hani Kestenbaum discovered that the inscription itself on the back of the mosaic floor was in mirror-image in red color. Much to our surprise, this inscription is larger in size than that in the mosaic! The word TLH ('lamb') is altogether removed from the location of the inscription in the mosaic, and also larger than the word in the mosaic. In addition to the unusual state of preservation of the paint to the point of legibility, it is possible to deduce from this discovery that the artisans apparently intended to allocate a larger area for the inscription than that done in fact, and in the course of the work reduced it in the mosaic.

The floor was framed by a border 22 centimeters wide containing pictures of flowers resembling lilies. Borders of this type were discovered at the synagogue in Ma'on (Nirim) and in various Christian structures (the church at eṭ-Tabgha, the octagonal structure at Capernaum, the Orpheus floor in Jerusalem, the villa at Beth Guvrin and others). The surviving portion contains three panels, which presumably had three opposing panels on the missing northern side. The westernmost is composed of a geometric pattern resembling fish scales; segments of this same type of design are found in the floor at the En-Gedi Synagogue, in a church floor at Shavei Zion, in the floor of Ḥorvat Massah (Kefar Tabor), and elsewhere. In the center of the floor there was a frame containing a picture in it oriented westward, the focal picture. At the east side of the floor there is a picture oriented southward. Parts of the mosaic, along the length of the benches, especially along the extent of the westernmost bench, are worn down in a strip measuring about 30 centimeters in width. Conceivably, the wear was created here because it was here that the worshippers placed their feet.

The center frame includes a portion of a scriptural verse and its pictorial illustration. This frame apparently occupied the entire south half of the mosaic, from the main base stone of the arches all the way to the floor's edge on the south. The surviving segment measures 82 x 116 centimeters. In the upper part of the segment there is a Hebrew inscription, "The wolf and the lamb shall graze together." Beneath it and on both sides there are remnants of the depiction of a lamb (on the right) and of a wolf (on the left) and between them a large object, by all appearances an amphora. The size of the inscription is 12 x 33 centimeters (the size of the aleph in the inscription is 4 x 5.2 centimeters). The verse was taken from the beginning of Isaiah 65:25, which concludes a chapter of comfort and hope for the peace and serenity of the Latter Days. As noted, scriptural passages in synagogues are extremely rare, particularly passages from the prophetic books. No biblical inscriptions have been discovered expressing abstract notions relating to the future that are not biblical narratives set in the past and speaking of the "biblical future." We do not know why here they used this particular verse as an expression about the Latter Days and not the more widely-known verse, at least in our own day, from Isaiah 11:6—"and the wolf shall dwell with the lamb."

In the inscription, following the letter *aleph* in זאב ('wolf'), the artist inserted the letter *yod*, thus, זאיב. This spelling is not found in the Masoretic version. This is a vowel letter, testifying to the manner of pronunciation of that word at the time of laying down this mosaic. This form—that is, the use of the letter *yod* to indicate the pronunciation—is known from other inscriptions, especially from those in the synagogue at En-Gedi.[46]

The artisan who arranged the animals set the lamb on the right side and the wolf on the left, although the wolf is the first mentioned in the verse. The lamb's head is set out in different colors and in rounded lines in order to impart to it a soft and composed image. Of the right leg of the lamb only a line of black stones remains. Of the wolf's head only the tip of his sharp nose and his erect ears survive, and of its body there remain its tail, a hind leg the end of one foreleg and some other small fragments. The original size

[46] Naveh, *Mosaic*, p. 107 (see spelling forms קישת: אילול: טבית [with 'full' spelling, i.e., using *yod*]).

of the wolf was 70 x 80 centimeters. According to the remnants of the animal depictions, it appears they were portrayed in exceptionally fine, realistic fashion.

Between the animals appears a vessel, similar to an amphora standing on two legs, in the form of a triangle. The portrayal of amphoras between animals is known from many mosaic floors. As a rule, these amphora pictures are of uniform color, depicting deer, rams or peacocks. Sometimes a vine emerges from the amphora. Here, however, while there are creatures on both sides of the vessel, the two animals are mentioned in the inscription. Apparently, the intent was to depict a vessel filled with clear water for the quiescent animals, creatures at peace with each other in Latter Days.

As mentioned, large portions of the pictured animals are missing; the question is whether they were destroyed on purpose or whether damaged by wear. The possibility of intentional destruction is supported by this evidence: the inscription above them survives in its entirety and the amphora between them almost entirely, as does most of the scale pattern above the frame. In the same structure, the birds pictured on the lintel of the hall entrance were also destroyed, so it is conceivable both mosaics were destroyed by an iconoclast. The following facts support the possibility of wear: The entire section under the animals and the amphora is missing due to wear. If the destruction was due to intention, we would expect the heads of the animals to be destroyed first and foremost (as at Na'aran). It is logical to suppose that wear occurred here; but if intentional defacement took place by governmental decree, then it was only partially carried out. The essential part of the symbolic depiction—that which had significance for those who fashioned it—was left.

THE SHOFAR SECTION

In the southeast corner of the hall there survives a section of another mosaic panel, measuring 139 x 149 centimeters bearing an unusual picture whose composition has not been discovered elsewhere before now. The panel is oriented southward. This is a depiction that is divided by means of lines that form geometric patterns into squares resting on one corner, and in each of which is pictured a design. In the upper row there survives the design of a heart-shaped leaf. In the row below this there are designs of pomegranates, well executed. In the row beneath this, there remains only one square, in which the design is partially missing: a rectangular form, whose wide flanges are in color, and leaning on its side. At its upper end there is a kind of pointed projection. This is possibly the depiction of a Torah Ark (of which only the sloped top survives (18 centimeters in length) and a part of the picture, on the eastern side. The possibility that what is before us is a

Torah Ark is supported by the fact that in the row beneath it, on two sides, is the depiction of two shofars, one at each side, turned outward, similar to the traditional portrayal of shofars at the sides of the seven-branched menorah (the length of each shofar is 17 centimeters, their thickness varies between 2 and 6 centimeters). In their present form they create a sort of frame whose object is the Ark. If this is indeed a Torah Ark, then what we have before us is a depiction unknown from any other place. Generally, synagogues contain depictions of larger arks, most often with *menorot* or lions on both sides. Depiction of free-standing ram's horns, not accompanying candelabra, are similarly unknown from any other site. In the squares below the ram's horns there were revealed depictions of date clusters of which one survives complete. Depictions of date palms, sometimes bearing date clusters, are known from several other places as, for example, on the lintel of the synagogue at Capernaum. A picture of a date cluster in a floor mosaic is not known from any other place. Since the frame here is oriented southward toward Jerusalem, it is conceivable that this was the part of the hall for worship. The sources reveal the fact that prayers were held in houses of study.

The general style of the floor is Byzantine, similar to many other mosaic floors of the sixth century. But several mosaic floors from the Muslim period are known in the Land of Israel which are built in the best Byzantine tradition.[47] On the foundation in which the mosaic panel is set, next to the base stone for the arch at the center of the hall, a coin of the Umayyad dynasty was found dating from the first half of the eighth century (700-730 C.E.). It is possible to assert with certainty that the coin testifies to the date of use of this hall. The time period of erection of the study house was in the first half of the seventh century. The question may therefore be asked whether there is any real implication at all to the choice of a scriptural verse or whether it was determined by chance in the course of choosing from a book of sample mosaics. It is also possible to assume that the choice was more intentional, and that suggests the optimism, hopes, aspirations and beliefs of those who placed the mosaic.[48] If we are right that the mosaic was indeed laid during the seventh century, possibly after the second Byzantine conquest in 629 C.E., or several years after the Arab conquest (no Arab influence is evident in the structure whatever), then it must have been after a period in which the country passed between the Byzantine and the Arabic empires several times. Conceivably, the inhabitants of the land, including

[47] M. Piccirillo, "The Umayyad Churches of Jordan," *ADAJ* 27 (1984): 333-341—a synagogue floor from the Umayyad period at Tiberias, discovered by Ariel Berman.

[48] Practical-historical implications have been suggested as well regarding the Jerusalem inscription containing a quotation from the Bible, See B. Mazer, *The Archaeological Excavations Near the Temple Mount* (Jerusalem, 1970), pp. 20-21 (in Hebrew).

the Jews, longed for peace and aspired for the good and tranquil 'Latter Days,' and this was the background for the selection of this particular scriptural verse. In any case, it appears to us that there is significance to the fact that in a study house we find two scriptural verses while no customary dedicatory inscriptions are found. Apparently it is due to the fact that the place is a place of Torah study rather than a synagogue.

Following the destruction of the building (on the mosaic floor, at one place evidence of fire is discernible), the destroyed layer, a half-meter thick, was leveled, containing stones that had fallen from the walls and the roof, plaster from walls and roof, broken tiles and pottery, shards of glass lamps, iron nails and other items. The destruction occurred, apparently, toward the end of the twelfth century, and included the synagogue structure as well (see below). Over the destruction layer, there is a layer of greyish black earth, related perhaps to some installation or other that was nearby at a later period.

We should mention the existence of the open courtyard to the east of the study hall. At its southeast edge were found the remains of a wall or of paving that suggests perhaps the existence of roofing similar to the roofing over the courtyards on the eastern sides of the synagogues at Capernaum and Susiya. This area and additional ones in the courtyard where, possibly, trees grew, could have served as a place of study when weather permitted. Study under the open sky is known from the sources, with the individual seated on a stone under a tree, etc. The courtyard also made possible the gathering of a larger assemblage for public study on special occasions.

Characteristics of the Structure as a Study House

Many references in the talmud tell of the existence of the study house as an independent institution. It is also mentioned that it was, at least in some instances, close by the synagogue (Babylonian Talmud, Berakot 64a). After 1968, there was discovered a lintel at Dabûra, on the Golan Heights, mentioning the House of Study of Rabbi Eliezer ha-Qappar. This was the first and only time that a house of study is mentioned in an ancient inscription, although the structure of the study house itself has not been excavated yet at Dabûra.[49] Although a number of scholars have assumed that side rooms adjoining excavated synagogues served as houses of study, other scholars have assumed that in actuality the synagogue and the study house were one and the same institution.[50] The scholars who have disputed this

[49] See Urman, "Dabûra Inscriptions—2," p. 133. [See also D. Urman's discussion of the site in this volume—Eds.]

[50] F. Hüttenmeister, "The Synagogue and the House of Study and Their Connection," *Cathedra* 18 (1981): 38-44 (in Hebrew). Among those sites where it has been suggested that a study house can be seen (p. 40) it is possible to include Khirbet Shema'. There, the

latter view, emphasizing that the study house was an independent institution, attributed the failure to discover any study houses until now to the supposition that study houses were generally in large cities and not in villages. At the same time, of course, they expressed the hope that the discovery of study houses would come in time.[51] Regarding this, it should be said that the inscription at Dabûra testifies to the existence of a study house in a village, and it is also thought that there was a study house in nearby Qîsrîn.[52] We also know from the early sources about the existence of another village study house—at Akbarah.[53] That is to say, one may anticipate the discovery of a study house in a village and not only in a large city.

The characteristics which characterize the structure at Meroth as a house of study are:

A) It is a place of assembly.

B) It is a small structure, the nature of its construction being different from that of a synagogue, accommodating a limited number of people.

C) Its orientation, different from the great majority of Galilean synagogues, both in the axis of its architecture and in the positioning of its mosaics.

D) It is an independent structure, serving parallel to the synagogue, and it would be inconceivable to suppose that a synagogue would have been built alongside of a synagogue. At least we know of no such phenomenon from the sources.

E) The nature of its inscriptions.

We have not found in the sources any details about the decor or specifications of the interior architecture of the house of study. It is not surprising that the building at Meroth was suitably adorned. There was in the area a population of some means which contributed a great deal to the needs of its community, as evidenced by the large sums discovered in its treasury. A hint to the fact that study houses were embellished by attractive architectural details is had from the lintel at Dabûra decorated with harrier-eagles designs. In this regard there is double significance in the excavation

---

excavators hypothesized that a room near the northern part of the synagogue, along whose west wall benches had been hewn, served as the house of study. See *HA* 44 (1972): 6 (in Hebrew); *Khirbet Shema'*, p. 83; Z. Safrai, "Notes on the Essence of the '*Bet Midrash*' in the Land of Israel," *Cathedra* 24 (1982): 185 (in Hebrew); Safrai, "Functions," p. 106; Levine, *Sages*, p. 13, note 16.

51 A. Oppenheimer, "The Uniqueness of the *Bet Midrash*," *Cathedra* 18 (1981): 45-48 (in Hebrew); Safrai, "Halakah," p. 49.

52 Urman, "Bar Qappara—2," pp. 163-172.

53 A. Oppenheimer, "Those of the School of Rabbi Yannai," *Studies in the History of the People and the Land of Israel*, vol. 4 (Haifa, 1978), pp. 137-145 (in Hebrew).

at Meroth, because it is thanks to it we have any idea at all about the appearance of an ancient study house. The classrooms discovered adjoining synagogues, including the one at Meroth, as indicated above, were quite simple and functional, whereas in study houses much attention and substantial means were devoted to the structure's decorations.

The research on site informs us of the existence of a village communal center at Meroth which included a synagogue, a class room and a house of study. It also reveals something of the character of the settlement, whose inhabitants were occupied not only in farming and in day-to-day labors but Meroth. In a Cairo Genizah document which we uncovered in 1977— and which served as a starting point for research of the site—there is a reference to a rabbi—a tzaddik, 'holy man'—who was buried in the area. Regrettably, the paper is torn just at the location of the name, which is possibly 'Hana.' Conceivably, his name was preserved as an oral tradition until the fourteenth century, the dating of the document.[54] It is logical to assume that students from other villages in the surrounding area also gathered at this house of study. We found in the Genizah documents of the eleventh century that there were copyists in two of the villages in the region—Dalton and Gush Ḥalav.[55] It appears that reference is to the copying of Torah scrolls. From this and from synthesis with other information about Meroth, a picture emerges of rural settlements having the capability of maintaining an active religious-spiritual life.

THE LATER COMMUNAL CENTER AND CIRCUMSTANCE OF ITS DEMISE

Within the framework of evidence from the sources and investigations dealing with the issue of continuity of Jewish settlement in northern Galilee after the Islamic conquest, the archaeological evidence of the existence of a prosperous Jewish settlement until the end of the twelfth century is an important discovery. As known, it is stated in a ninth-century source, Pirkoi ben Baboi, that, in contrast to the Byzantine rulers, "...the Ishmaelites came and permitted them to engage in Torah [study] and to recite the Shema and to worship."[56] That is to say, Jews were permitted to study Torah and to worship during the rule of Islam.

From Cairo Genizah documents and from travelers' impressions, we know about the existence of Jewish settlements in northern Galilee beginning with the eleventh century. Braslavski stated the opinion in his

---

[54] Ilan, "Fortified Settlement," p. 142.

[55] Gil, *Palestine*, vol. 1, p. 175.

[56] L. Ginzburg, *Ginzei Schechter*, vol. 2 (New York, 1928), p. 552 (in Hebrew).

day that these settlements existed continuously since ancient times.[57] Gil deduced from the continuous existence of ancient settlements the existence of others as well, whose traces have not been preserved.[58] Prawer, in light of Braslavski's opinion (although with the expressed hope of finding further evidence thereof), theorized the Crusaders' need for a stable local population for providing a food supply.[59] From earlier excavations we know about the founding of a synagogue at Hammath-Tiberias during the Umayyad period and of its destruction in the middle of the eighth century.[60] The date of destruction of the synagogue excavated near 'En Hanatziv has been suggested as the middle of the eighth century.[61] These structures, which existed at the beginning of the Islamic period belong to the period of the knowledge gap concerning the Jewish settlement from the end of the Byzantine era until the period covered by Cairo Genizah collection.

It appears to us that Meroth provides the missing link, from an archaeological perspective, between the settlements of the talmudic period and those settlements which continued to exist during the Middle Ages, when the historical documentation resumes. Meroth is not mentioned in the early Genizah documents, except in the document mentioned above, and in the Arabic form of the name—'Maros.' This reference has significance, too, when we examine the possibility of the existence of any Jewish settlement at all in the Galilee during the Middle Ages. We have discovered that in every settlement in which there were Jewish communities, including Meroth, and apparently only in those, there was also the grave of a holy man.[62] In each of these places there was found, too, an ancient synagogue or at least a community of Jews during the rabbinic period.

As to the circumstances of cessation of the settlement at Meroth—the last coin in the treasury, as mentioned, is from 1193, that is, the site was abandoned at approximately this date. On the other hand, among the settlements mentioned by Rabbi Shmuel bar Shimshon in 1211 Meroth is not mentioned, even though he visited settlements in which were Jewish

---

[57] Y. Braslavsky, "The Jewish Agricultural Settlement in Eretz Israel in the 16th Century and the Question of Its Antiquity," *L'ḥeqer Artzenu* (Tel Aviv, 1954), p. 169 (in Hebrew).

[58] Gil, *Palestine*, p. 178. Gil theorized that these settlements were gradually destroyed during the wars waged in Palestine by the Fatimids, and that the final blow was delivered by the Turkomans who invaded the land and by the Crusaders who followed.

[59] Y. Prawer, *The Crusaders—Portrait of a Colonial Society* (Jerusalem, 1985), p. 282 (in Hebrew).

[60] Dothan, "Hammath-Tiberias," p. 123.

[61] Y. Sussman, "A Halakic Inscription from the Beth-Shean Valley," *Tarbiz* 43 (1974): 68 (in Hebrew). On p. 69, Sussman expresses hope for further archaeological discoveries which will shed light on the times that followed the amoraic generations until the end of the *geonim*. It seems that the Meroth excavations shed little light on this little-known period, about which many hope to gain more information.

[62] Z. Ilan. "The Land of the Jews in Upper Galilee" *Etmol* 59 (1984): 3-5 (in Hebrew).

communities in the vicinity of Meroth—'Amoqa, Nabratein, Dalton and others. Concerning synagogues in the settlements in the area, he said, "Some of them are in ruins and others are standing."[63] One might surmise that the Meroth community was not mentioned because it was somewhat removed from the main route of his journey, but it appears the reason is otherwise. Apparently, he visited all the Jewish communities in the region, but the Meroth community is not mentioned because it did not exist at the time of his visit.

The question is, what occurred between the years 1193 and 1211. It should be mentioned that several years before this the battle of the Horns of Hittin occurred in which the Crusaders were defeated and their capital, Jerusalem, captured. A new boundary line was created between the Crusaders and the Ayyubids, not far from Meroth.[64] Conceivably, in the process of the military activities and of the resulting rearrangements a destructive attack was made on Meroth and its stricken populace fled in terror, leaving behind the entire contents of the substantial treasury. The synagogue and the study house were abandoned and later destroyed. During the Mameluke period, the structure served other purposes.

Evidently, during the Ottoman period a new village was established on the site, several hundred meters southward. The inhabitants used stones from the synagogue for erecting fences, dwellings and the like. This was the situation at the start of our expedition's investigation and documentation.

---

[63] A. Yaari, *Letters of the Land of Israel* (Tel Aviv, 1943), pp. 80-82; Y. Prawer, "Hebrew Travel Descriptions in Palestine During the Crusader Period," *Cathedra* 41 (1987): 65-69 (in Hebrew).

[64] See the map in S. Shein, *The Rule of the Muslims and the Crusaders—History of Eretz-Israel*, vol. 6 (Jerusalem, 1981), p. 201 (in Hebrew).

STAGES OF THE SYNAGOGUE AT MEROTH

Stage	Date	Paving	Characteristics	Remarks
X	Roman period	—	Subterranean rooms	Before establishment of the synagogue.
Al	400-450	Plaster	Facade on the south	Construction of soft chalk stone. Colored decoration on plaster wall.
A2	450-500	Mosaic	Facade on the south	
B	500-620	Stone	Facade on the south	Courtyard south of structure.
C	620-1200	Stone	Facade on the north	Construction of hard chalk stone. Half of the portico transformed into a classroom. Area of courtyard south of building transformed into the house of study, whose main hall is in west portion of earlier courtyard, and whose [own] courtyard—in the east portion of previous courtyard.
Dl	1250-1400	Stone	Dwellings	Division of structure into open spaces during Mameluke period.
D2	1400-1600	Stone	Dwellings	New structures, utilizing stone from the destroyed synagogue.

THE SYNAGOGUE AND THE *MIQWEH* IN ERETZ-ISRAEL IN THE SECOND-TEMPLE, MISHNAIC, AND TALMUDIC PERIODS

RONNY REICH*

The literary and the archaeological evidence make it clear that the synagogue and the *miqweh* (ritual bath) emerged as buildings constructed for the service of the Jewish community in the Second-Temple period. Although the date of the earliest synagogues (regardless of their precise original function) remains unclear, it seems that the building excavated in Gamala is the earliest in Palestine.[1] Archaeologists think its construction occurred in the second half of the first century B.C.E. The date of the earliest water installations which may be defined as *miqwaot* (plural for *miqweh*) is clearer; they stem from the second part of the second century B.C.E. These include installations found in Jerusalem, Jericho, Gezer, and elsewhere.[2] From the moment both these institutions were created, they continued to be used, uninterrupted, in one way or another, down to present time, since they are, in essence, inseparable components of the Jewish faith, culture and everyday life.

The synagogue comprises one of the most exhaustively studied subjects in Judaism. Although the *miqweh* characterizes Jewish life no less than the synagogue, its study has been largely ignored by archaeological research. The aim of this essay is to use archaeology to examine whether there was a relationship between the synagogue and the *miqweh* in the Second-Temple, Mishnaic, and Talmudic Periods (from approximately the late second century B.C.E. to the seventh century C.E.). Did the Jews of these periods view the two institutions as related and therefore build complexes which contained both, or did they view them as unrelated and therefore not attempt to place them together?

---

* This essay was originally published in A. Kasher, A. Oppenheimer, and U. Rappaport, eds., *Synagogues in Antiquity* (Jerusalem, 1987) pp. 205-212 (in Hebrew). It has been translated by the author and with the permission of Yad Izhak Ben Zvi.

[1] Gutman, *Gamla*, pp. 58-60; Ma'oz, "Gamla."

[2] E. Netzer, "*Miqwaot* of the Second Temple Period at Jericho," *Qadmoniot* 11 (1978): 54-59 (in Hebrew); E. Netzer, "Recent Discoveries in the Winter Palaces of Second Temple Time at Jericho," *Qadmoniot* 15 (1982): 22-28 (in Hebrew). N. Avigad, *Discovering Jerusalem* (Nashville-Jerusalem, 1983), p. 74. R. Reich, "Archaeological Evidence of the Jewish Population at Hasmonaean Gezer," *IEJ* 31 (1981): 48-52.

THE SECOND TEMPLE PERIOD

Scholars generally recognize three buildings from this period as synagogues. These are located at Gamala, Masada and Herodium. To these, the synagogue of Theodotus should be added. It is known to have existed in Jerusalem from an inscription found in the City of David. A water installation appears in relation to each of these buildings, an installation which probably served as a *miqweh*.

Gamala: In the building to the south and adjacent to the synagogue, a stepped water installation was found which the excavator identified as a *miqweh*.[3] The installation was filled by rain waters drained from the synagogue's roof and conducted by a channel starting near the synagogue's facade. It seems that this channel was originally connected with a second that crossed the rear part of the synagogue, near the town wall. This second channel stretched back to the spring near the town. There is evidence that this channel was added and brought through the premises of the synagogue at a later part of the Second Temple period. It is probably a creation of the Zealots.[4]

Masada: At a distance of about 15 m to the north of the synagogue, a water installation was excavated (locus 1301). It measured 2.6 x 3.4 m, was 2.0 m deep, and was built with a side staircase.[5] E. Netzer has defined this installation as a 'pool,' and related it to the Zealot's occupation period. Although this installation differs from the other Zealot's *miqwaot* on Masada, it bears some resemblance to *miqwaot* from earlier times in Jerusalem and Jericho, and still could have been used as such. In addition, it should be noted that scholars have already suggested that the *miqweh* which was built by the zealots in Building VII, which is about 60 m away from the synagogue to the east, is in fact the *miqweh* which served those who frequented the synagogue.[6] In Building IX, located to the south-east of the synagogue, two additional *miqwaot* were found.[7] One of these is located at a distance of 75 m from the synagogue, and may have been serving the synagogue in the same manner.

---

[3] Gutman, *Gamla*; Ma'oz, "Gamla."

[4] Z. Ma'oz, "Archaeological Excavations in the Golan—Summary of the activities in 1983," *Eretz Hagolan, the journal of the Golan settlements* (1983): 13 (in Hebrew).

[5] *Masada III*, p. 398, Plan 34, Ill. 625.

[6] G. Foerster, "The Synagogues at Masada and Herodion," *Journal of Jewish Art* 3-4 (1977): 6-11; G. Foerster, "The Synagogues at Masada and Herodium," in Levine, *ASR*, pp. 24-29; *Masada III*, pp. 13-16.

[7] *Masada III*, pp. 221-2, Locus 298; pp. 227-8, Locus 368.

The reason for the installment of the *miqwaot* of the Zealot occupation at the northern side of Masada near or in the larger Herodian buildings, and not closer to the synagogue, is quite clear: the possibilities for concentrating rain water at Masada are very limited. The builders could not just construct *miqwaot* anywhere they wished on the upper plateau. A relatively large drainage basin exists only at the southern part of Masada, and indeed, several *miqwaot* are located there.[8] At the northern part of Masada, these installations had to be incorporated within the large Herodian buildings, or adjacent to them, where rain water could be gathered from their roofs and courtyards. It seems that the builders of the *miqweh* did not think that the synagogue's roof and the adjoining roofs of the casemate wall could gather enough rainwater to supply the *miqweh*'s needs. Buildings VII and IX seemed more appropriate and so the *miqwaot* were constructed there. It can thus be said that at Masada as well there are *miqwaot* close to the local synagogue.

Herodium: In the large peristyle courtyard located inside the mountain-palace of Herodium, two *miqwaot* were excavated. The Zealots had cut both directly into the Herodian building remains, in a rather crude manner. The first appears in a bathing room built against the outer wall of the Herodian triclinium, which the Zealots turned into a synagogue. This bathing room contained a small bathtub and a stepped water installation which served, most probably, as a *miqweh*.[9] A second stepped water installation was found nearby, cut into the floor of the large peristyle courtyard.[10] Both installations were filled by rain water gathered from the courtyard and the roofs of the adjacent buildings.

Jerusalem: The inscription which mentions the existence of the synagogue of Theodotus son of Vettenos, was found by R. Weill in a cistern, together with building stones (from the destroyed or dismantled synagogue?) all meticulously laid in the cistern.[11] The inscription points to the existence of a synagogue and an adjacent hospice which included water installations. Several meters to the northeast of the cistern, Weill exposed two stepped water installations of the type frequently found in contemporary private houses and in public areas near the Temple Mount.[12] One installation is

---

[8] *Masada III*, pp. 505-10, Locus 1197; pp. 513-4, Locus 1162.

[9] Corbo, "L'Herodion—quarta campagna," Figs. 7, 18, Pianta No. II, Nos. 24-25; V. Corbo, *Herodion*, I (Jerusalem, 1989), Pls. DF110:c, Tav. III, near No. 24.

[10] For a photo of this installation see: E. Netzer, *Herodion* (Jerusalem: Ariel Publishing House, 1980), p. 16 (upper photo).

[11] Weill, "David," pp. 30-34; Lifshitz, No. 79.

[12] Weill, "David," Pls. III, XVII, XX:b, XXIV:a, in which the installations P-1 through P-4 are marked.

quite large. It measures 6.2 m long and its width varies between 5.5 m and 8.2 m, measurements which place it among the largest of its kind in Jerusalem.[13] The staircase of this installation was originally divided by a low partition which created two parallel lanes. (This style suggests that this installation constitutes a particular type of *miqwaot*—those with a double entrance. I have discussed these elsewhere.)[14] Unfortunately, we do not know whether the location in which the inscription was found was in fact the site where the synagogue once stood. If we assume that this was the case, the close presence of the water installation is of interest. As I said above, water installations are mentioned in the inscription referring to the synagogue (χρησ{τ}ήρια τῶν ὑδάτων), but their precise nature is not apparent from the description. These installations were connected to the hospice described as near the synagogue, and therefore may have been cisterns, bathing rooms, or even *miqwaot*.[15]

THE PERIOD OF THE MISHNAH AND THE TALMUD

A number of synagogues dating to the period of the Mishnah and the Talmud (second to seventh centuries C.E.) have been excavated in Israel. Only in a few cases, stepped water installations were found next to them. Some of these installations have been identified by scholars as *miqwaot*. In my opinion only a few of these identifications are accurate. The following paragraphs examine the details of each of these installations.

Sasa: Several meters from the corner of the ancient synagogue, excavations revealed the remains of a room containing a small water installation (1.1 x 1.65 m; 1.42 m deep).[16] The measurements are quite small but suffice to identify this installation as a *miqweh*.

---

[13] This installation is similar in size to the larger stepped installation (Pool B), adjacent to the "Tombs of the Kings" to the north of the Old City of Jerusalem, which served as a *miqweh* as well, see M. Kon, *The Tombs of the Kings* (Tel Aviv, 1947), pp. 36-38, Pls. III, IVa (in Hebrew); It is also like the installation discovered near the monumental building at Lower Herodium, see E. Netzer, "Herodion—1982/1983," *EASI* 2 (1983): 47.

[14] R. Reich, "Mishnah, Sheqalim 8:2 and the archaeological evidence," in Oppenheimer, Rappaport and Stern, pp. 225-256 (in Hebrew, with English summary on p. XIV).

[15] In this case the Greek term KRHNH seems plausible. It usually refers to "Fountain House" from the type common in Greece and Asia Minor in the Hellenistic period, see: F. Glazer, *Antike Brunnenbauten (KRHNAI) in Griechenland*, Oesterreichische Akademie der Wissenschaften, philosiphisch-historische Klasse, denkschriften, Band 161 (Wien, 1983). This term is mentioned in an inscription from the synagogue at Side, Asia Minor, and there it refers probably to a *miqweh*. See also Lifschitz, no. 37. I would like to thank L. Roth-Gerson for drawing my attention to this find.

[16] E. Braun, "Sasa," *Ḥadashot Arkeologiyot* 63-64 (1978): 12 (in Hebrew).

Khirbet Shema': Two water installations, which were defined by the excavators as *miqwaot* were found at this site. One large installation most probably served as a *miqweh*.[17] Since this installation is located at the border of the site, however, about 120 m from the synagogue, it is not near enough to be relevant to our purpose of examining synagogues and *miqwaot* constructed together.

The second installation is located under the foundation of the synagogue, indicating it existed before the building of the synagogue was constructed.[18] Moreover, the installation is cut into the bedrock and the access to it is difficult. The width of its entrance is 0.7 m, and its height 1.2 m. The installation could be filled with water only to the height of 1-1.2 m, in order to leave ample space for holding the head above water after immersion. The descent into the installation had to be performed by bending or squatting, in order to avoid hitting the head against the ceiling. The suggestion that this installation served as a *miqweh* cannot be accepted.[19]

Chorazin: In Building C, located to the north of the synagogue, a large stepped water installation was excavated, which seems to have been used as a *miqweh*.[20] A large cistern appears nearby, but the *miqweh* apparently was filled by rainwater draining from the plastered courtyard further to the north.

The *miqweh* lies about 40 m from the rear part of the synagogue, and the walking distance is even greater. Although there is no doubt that this installation served as a *miqweh*, it is unlikely that it belonged to the synagogue complex or served it directly.

Beth She'arim: In Building E, which abuts the synagogue on the north, below the stone pavement of Room 4, a staircase of four steps led into a narrow corridor (0.60 m wide) and further into a small rock-cut and plastered cellar (about 1.2 x 1.3 m). It is possible that a water channel, crossing below the *bemah* of the synagogue, diverted rainwater into this installation. It is unlikely, however, that this installation was used as a *miqweh* due to its small size and the inconvenience involved in its use.

---

[17] Meyers, *Khirbet Shema'*, pp. 113-117, figs. 4.8, 4.9, Pls. 4.8-4.12.

[18] Meyers, *Khirbet Shema'*, pp. 39-41, figs. 3.4, 3.5.

[19] Z. Yeivin, "Excavations at Chorazin," *EI* 11 (1973): 144-157 (in Hebrew, with English summary on p. 27*); Z. Yeivin, "A *miqweh* at Chorazin," *Qadmoniot* 17 (1984): 79-81 (in Hebrew).

[20] B. Maisler, "The Fourth Campaign at Beth-Shearim, 1940," *BJPES* 9, no. 1 (1941): 5-20 (in Hebrew), fig. 2, pp. 7, 15; B. Mazar (Maisler), *Beth She'arim, Report on the excavations during 1936-40, I, Catacombs 1-4* (Jerusalem, 1973), fig.3.

Hulda: A building excavated here was defined by Yeivin and Avi-Yonah as a *miqweh*.[21] At its southern part two basins, paved with mosaic, were uncovered. One basin has a circular shape, 2.5 m in diameter, and 1.34 m deep, with three semicircular steps leading into it. This installation is connected by a leaden pipe to a square basin measuring 1.2 x 1.2 m, and 0.79 m deep. On the bottom of both installations are concave depressions. Two Greek inscriptions and Jewish symbols (menorah, shofar, *lulab* and *ethrog*) led to the conclusion that the entire building is a synagogue, containing a *miqweh* on its premises.

Two major factors prevent us from defining this installation as a *miqweh*: first, the architectural characteristics are typical of an industrial installation such as a wine press or even a bath house.[22] Second, the use of mosaic for paving a *miqweh* is unusual. A tessellated floor often cracks in an installation designed to hold water for a long period. A cracked floor presents a severe problem for *miqwaot*. Besides of the loss of water, a *miqweh* whose waters are "creeping" (זוחלין)—that is, leaking—is prohibited by the halakic regulations.[23] In plastered *miqwaot*, the problem of cracks in the plaster was solved by applying a new coat of plaster, an action which is impractical in tessellated floors.[24]

It is possible that the existence of the interconnecting pipe between the basins led to the conclusion that the installation in question is a *miqweh*, as the pipe was identified as the "tube of a water-skin" (שפופרת הנאד).[25] This feature is rare in *miqwaot* in the periods under discussion, however, and when it exists, it usually is located at the rim of the installations. In the Hulda installation, by contrast, it is placed about 45 cm above the bottom

---

[21] Yeivin, *Decade*, p. 42. M. Avi-Yonah, "Various Synagogal Remains—Hulda," *Rabinowitz Bulletin*, vol. 3, pp. 57-60.

[22] See, for example, the confusion which occurred in identifying the installation excavated at Qalandiya, first as a bath house and later as a wine press: D. Baramki, "A Byzantine Bath at Qalandiya," *QDAP* 2 (1933): 105-109, Pls. XXXVIII-XLI; Y. Hirschfeld, "Ancient Wine Presses in the Area of the Ayalon Park," *EI* 15 (1981): 383-390, and especially p. 387 (in Hebrew); A. Kloner, "The Structure at Hulda and its use as a Wine Press," in A. Kasher, A. Oppenheimer and U. Rappaport (eds.), *Man and Land in Eretz-Israel in Antiquity* (Jerusalem, 1986), pp. 197-203 (in Hebrew, with summary on pp. XIX-XX). For baths, see V. Tzaferis, "A Roman Bath at Rama," *Atiqot* (English Series) 14 (1980), Fig. 1:E, F; Pl. XII:1.

[23] Cf. Mishnah Miqwaot 5:3-5; Sifra Shemini 11, 3. On the problem of a *miqweh*'s wall which cracked, see Mishnah, Miqwaot 6:9. Here the case is a crack between two adjacent *miqwaot*, while the obvious case of a crack in an outer wall of a *miqweh* is not under discussion as it undoubtedly defiles the *miqweh*.

[24] About 4-6 coats of plaster can be observed, and even more. We can assume that the annual inspection of *miqwaot*, which is referred to in Mishnah Sheqalim 1:1, was meant not only to inspect the minimal required depth and volume of the water in the *miqweh*, but also to check that the installation was not cracked and the waters were creeping out of it.

[25] Mishnah Miqwaot 6:7.

of the circular installation.[26] The installation in Hulda can therefore neither be defined as a *miqweh* nor can the building be identified as a synagogue. The inscriptions and Jewish symbols in the mosaic floor require a different explanation.

Ma'on: A stepped and plastered water installation, a cistern, and a drainage channel were excavated to the east of the synagogue.[27] The excavators suggested the water installation could be a *miqweh*, but did not elaborate further. The measurements of the installation are 2.25 x 2.50 m. Evidence remains of two steps. The bottom of the installation is only 0.5 m lower than the nearby surface. If one assumes that the installation served as a *miqweh*, its minimal depth should have been about 1.4-1.5 m (3 cubits). This implies that the larger part of the installation was above the ground. There is nothing in this observation to disqualify the installation as a *miqweh*, but the use would have been in this case quite unusual; the user would have ascended by some external steps to the rim of the installation and then descended into it. Such a method of construction and use is unknown from other sites.

A second consideration also militates against the identification of this installation as a *miqweh*. It would have been impossible to fill this installation with rain water gathered from the courtyards. Indeed, the only water which could have been used to fill it would have been rain caught on the synagogue's roof. Since the region under discussion—the north-western Negev—is semi-arid, it is unlikely the inhabitants would have restricted the water collection to such a small area. The identification of the installation in Ma'on as a *miqweh* is therefore doubtful.

SUMMARY

From the data presented above, the following conclusions can be drawn. For the Second Temple period, the remains of Gamala, Masada and Herodium point to a link between synagogues and *miqwaot*. Although the evidence of the Theodotus Synagogue in Jerusalem is incomplete, it may also suggest such a link. The archaeological evidence reveals that these particular

---

[26] Only a handful of *miqwaot* which employ this device have been found. Two installations were found in Masada: *Masada III*, pp. 505, 507-510; one in Herodium, in the peristyle (not published); one in the Jewish Quarter in Jerusalem: Avigad, *Jerusalem*, figs. 145, 175; and perhaps one near the Temple Mount, M. Ben-Dov, *The Dig at the Temple Mount* (Jerusalem, 1982), photo on p. 151, bottom left.

[27] S. Levy, "The Ancient Synagogue of Ma'on (Nirim)," *Rabinowitz Bulletin*, vol. 3, pp. 6-11, figs. 2, 3.

miqwaot appear in settlements of the Zealots, during the first revolt against Rome.

A question arises concerning the nature of this linkage; among the different activities which took place in the synagogue of the Second Temple period, what required an immersion in a *miqweh*? One of the activities which took place in the synagogue in this period was the holding of sacred meals which might have required a certain degree of purity from the participants.[28] Assuming that the building and installations described above belonged to communities of Zealots, who kept a certain type of Pharisaic halakah, another possibility is that the handling of the Sacred Scriptures in reading, studying, worship and prayer, required a degree of purity. This purity could have been obtained and maintained with the assistance of the adjacent *miqwaot*.[29] There is no doubt that any additional discovery of a synagogue dating to the Second Temple period would clarify the picture considerably.

The situation differs for the period of the Mishnah and the Talmud. We may point first of all to a drastic decrease in the construction and use of *miqwaot* in general. This is clearly attested by the small number of excavated stepped and plastered water installations which could have been used as *miqwaot*.[30] Indeed, only three to four score are known from the period after the destruction of the Temple.[31] In contrast, close to 300 such installations have been excavated in sites and strata attributed to the Second-Temple period. These stem from Jerusalem and from sites in Judea and Galilee. *Miqwaot* appear relatively rare in the post-Temple period, despite the fact that several domestic dwellings have been excavated (e.g. Meiron, Khirbet

---

[28] A. Oppenheimer, "Benevolent Societies in Jerusalem," in Oppenheimer, Rappaport and Stern, pp. 178-190, and especially p. 186 and notes 33, 34 Safrai, *Second Temple*, p. 162.

[29] Cf. for example: Mishnah, Yadayim 3:5, 4:6; and see Safrai, *Second Temple*, p. 161.

[30] The significant decline in the number of *miqwaot* should be attributed primarily to the destruction of the Temple and the interruption of its sacrificial cult, since it was the impetus for many of the requirements for purificatory immersion. Some circles, however, continued to observe high levels of ritual purity. See the views of G. Alon, "The limits of the purity regulations," in G. Alon, *Studies in Jewish History*, vol. 1 (Tel-Aviv, 1967), especially pp. 149-156 (in Hebrew); and Safrai, *Second Temple*, p. 131.

The decline in the needs brought about the situation that from the existence of at least one *miqweh* per private house in Jerusalem of the Second-Temple period, to the use of one *miqweh* per community in post-Temple times. This minimal use of *miqwaot* in each community passes on to the medieval Jewish communities of Europe, in which the use of one *miqweh* per community is recorded.

[31] It seems that the relatively high number of *miqwaot* which were found in Kedumim, a small village in the Samarian hills which lived on oil production, deserves a special explanation. See R. Reich, "A Note on Samaritan Ritual Baths," in D. Jacoby and Y. Tsafrir, eds., *Jews, Samaritans and Christians in Byzantine Palestine* (Jerusalem, 1988), pp. 242-244 (in Hebrew); I. Magen, "The *miqwaot* in Qedumim and the Purification Standards of the Samaritans," *Cathedra* 34 (1985): 15-26 (in Hebrew).

Shema', Capernaum, Beth She'arim, Chorazin). Only Sepphoris reveals a large number of *miqwaot* in domestic use, as attested by recent excavations.[32]

For the question of the relation between the *miqweh* and the synagogue, the situation is even clearer. Next to each of the synagogues dating to the Second Temple period, archaeologists found a *miqweh*. Most synagogues from the period of the Mishnah and the Talmud had no *miqwaot* connected to them. Our discussion of the few synagogues which had some sort of water installation connected to them revealed that most of the installations were not *miqwaot*. At Hulda and Ma'on, this was clear from the installation's extraordinary construction. At other sites, the water installations were too small and predated the synagogue (Khirbet Shema', Beth She'arim). The only certain *miqweh* was the installation at Sasa. With some difficulties, we could also include the *miqweh* at Chorazin; it was convenient to use but was located at a distance from the synagogue. Since several score of excavated ancient synagogues are known from all over the country, while only a handful of them are related to *miqwaot*, we may conclude that in the period of Mishnah and Talmud there is no apparent linkage between these two institutions.

---

[32] E. M. Meyers, E. Netzer and C. L. Meyers, "Sepphoris:'Ornament of all Galilee,'" *BA* (March 1986): 17.

STUDIA POST-BIBLICA

23. NEUSNER, J. (ed.). *The Modern Study of the Mishna.* 1973. ISBN 90 04 03669 5
24. ASMUSSEN, J.P. *Studies in Judeo-Persian Literature.* [Tr. from the Danish] (Homages et Opera Minora, 12). 1973. ISBN 90 04 03827 2
25. BARZILAY, I. *Yoseph Shlomo Delmedigo (Yashar of Candia).* His Life, Works and Times. 1974. ISBN 90 04 03972 4
27. BERGER, K. *Die griechische Daniel-Exegese.* Eine altkirchliche Apokalypse. Text, Übersetzung und Kommentar. 1976. ISBN 90 04 04756 5
28. LOWY, S. *The Principles of Samaritan Bible Exegesis.* 1977. ISBN 90 04 04925 8
29. DEXINGER, F. *Henochs Zehnwochenapokalypse und offene Probleme der Apokalyptikforschung.* 1977. ISBN 90 04 05428 6
30. COHEN, J.M. *A Samaritan Chronicle.* A Source-Critical Analysis of the Life and Times of the Great Samaritan Reformer, Baba Rabbah. 1981. ISBN 90 04 06215 7
31. BROADIE, A. *A Samaritan Philosophy.* A Study of the Hellenistic Cultural Ethos of the Memar Marqah. 1981. ISBN 90 04 06312 9
32. HEIDE, A. VAN DER. *The Yemenite Tradition of the Targum of Lamentations.* Critical Text and Analysis of the Variant Readings. 1981. ISBN 90 04 06560 1
33. ROKEAH, D. *Jews, Pagans and Christians in Conflict.* 1982. ISBN 90 04 07025 7
35. EISENMAN, R.H. *James the Just in the Habakkuk* Pesher. 1986. ISBN 90 04 07587 9
36. HENTEN, J.W. VAN, H.J. DE JONGE, P.T. VAN ROODEN & J.W. WEESELIUS (eds.). *Tradition and Re-Interpretation in Jewish and Early Christian Literature.* Essays in Honour of Jürgen C.H. Lebram. 1986. ISBN 90 04 07752 9
37. PRITZ, R.A. *Nazarene Jewish Christianity.* From the End of the New Testament Period until its Disappearance in the Fourth Century. 1988. ISBN 90 04 08108 9
38. HENTEN, J.W. VAN, B.A.G.M. DEHANDSCHUTTER & H.W. VAN DER KLAAUW. *Die Entstehung der jüdischen Martyrologie.* 1989. ISBN 90 04 08978 0
39. MASON, S. *Flavius Josephus on the Pharisees.* A Composition-Critical Study. 1991. ISBN 90 04 09181 5
40. OHRENSTEIN, R.A. & B. GORDON. *Economic Analysis in Talmudic Literature.* Rabbinic Thought in the Light of Modern Economics. 1992. ISBN 90 04 09540 3
41. GERA, D. *The Role of Judaea in Eastern Mediterranean International Politics.* In Preparation. ISBN 90 04 09441 5
42. ATTRIDGE, H.W. & G. HATA (eds.). *Eusebius, Christianity, and Judaism.* 1992. ISBN 90 04 09688 4
43. TOAFF, A. *The Jews in Umbria.* Vol. I: 1245-1435. 1993. ISBN 90 04 09695 7
44. TOAFF, A. *The Jews in Umbria.* Vol. II: 1435-1484. 1994. ISBN 90 04 09979 4
45. TOAFF, A. *The Jews in Umbria.* Vol. III: 1484-1736. 1994. ISBN 90 04 10165 9
46. PARENTE, F. & J. SIEVERS (eds.). *Josephus and the History of the Greco-Roman Period.* Essays in Memory of Morton Smith. 1994. ISBN 90 04 10114 4

47,1 URMAN, D. & P.V.M. FLESHER (eds.). *Ancient Synagogues.* Historical Analysis and Archaeological Discovery. Volume One. 1995. ISBN 90 04 10242 6; ISBN *set* 90 04 09904 2